SCIENCE AND STONEHENGE

PROCEEDINGS OF THE BRITISH ACADEMY · 92

# Science and Stonehenge

Edited by
BARRY CUNLIFFE & COLIN RENFREW

*Published for* THE BRITISH ACADEMY
*by* OXFORD UNIVERSITY PRESS

*Oxford University Press, Great Clarendon Street, Oxford* OX2 6DP

*Oxford   New York*

*Athens   Auckland   Bangkok   Bogota   Bombay*
*Buenos Aires   Calcutta   Cape Town   Dar es Salaam*
*Delhi   Florence   Hong Kong   Istanbul   Karachi*
*Kuala Lumpur   Madras   Madrid   Melbourne*
*Mexico City   Nairobi   Paris   Singapore*
*Taipei   Tokyo   Toronto   Warsaw*
*and associated companies in*
*Berlin   Ibadan*

© *The British Academy, 1997*

*First published 1997*
*Reprinted 1999*

*British Library Cataloguing in Publication Data*
*Data available*

*ISBN 0–19–726174–4*
*ISSN 0068–1202*

*Phototypeset by Wyvern 21, Bristol*
*Printed in Great Britain*
*on acid-free paper by*
*Bookcraft (Bath) Ltd*
*Midsomer Norton, North Somerset*

# Contents

vi CONTENTS

# List of Plans and Plates

## Mapping the Stonehenge World Heritage Site
DAVE BATCHELOR

*At back of volume*

## Environment and Land-use;
## The Economic Development of the Communities who Built Stonehenge
## (an Economy to Support the Stones)
MICHAEL J. ALLEN

*Between pp. 128 and 129*

# Notes on Contributors

MICHAEL J. ALLEN

*Wessex Archaeology, Portway House, Old Sarum Park, Salisbury, Wilts. SP4 6EB*
Mike Allen has been the Environmental Manager for Wessex Archaeology since 1988, where he is responsible for all aspects of environmental work. His specialist skills are in the analysis and interpretation of sub-fossil land mollusc assemblages, soils and sediments, especially colluvial deposits.

Dr Allen's research interests are focused on the development of prehistoric landscapes through the study and interpretation of suites of environmental data. He has been responsible for synthesising the large environmental database obtained from the *Stonehenge Environs Project*. He also coordinated the specialist environmental and radiocarbon dating programmes for the *Stonehenge in its Landscape* volume, as well as providing analysis and interpretation of these data for the Stonehenge landscape as a whole.


DAVE BATCHELOR

*English Heritage, Central Archaeology Service, Fort Cumberland, Fort Cumberland Road, Eastney, Portsmouth PO4 9LD*
Dave Batchelor has worked for English Heritage, and its predecessor, for over 20 years in its fieldwork unit. He has been involved in a number of major projects, including the aftermath of the fires at Hampton Court Palace, Uppark House and Windsor Castle. Mr Batchelor has been heavily committed to Stonehenge for the past three years and is currently project manager for the implementation of GIS as well as having archaeological responsibility for the area within Guardianship.


ALEX BAYLISS

*Ancient Monuments Laboratory, English Heritage, 23 Savile Row, London W1X 1AB*
Alex Bayliss studied medieval archaeology at University College, London and continues research there into the medieval bell-founding industry of England. She worked for the Museum of London on many rescue excavations in the City from 1987, supervising those of a Roman temple at Old Bailey. After this she moved into the ceramics department at the Museum pursuing an interest in quantitative methods. In 1990 she began working on the publication of radiocarbon dates for English Heritage, and in 1993 became scientific

dating co-ordinator in the Ancient Monuments Laboratory. She advises archaeologists and building specialists from all over England on the application of scientific dating to their projects, contributing to numerous academic publications. Her current research interests include the routine application of mathematical modelling to dating problems and radiocarbon sampling strategies.

## CHRISTOPHER BRONK RAMSEY

*Oxford Radiocarbon Accelerator Unit, Oxford University, 6 Keble Road, Oxford OX1 3QJ*
Christopher Bronk Ramsey after completing his doctorate in the physics of accelerator mass spectrometry (AMS) at Oxford University in 1987 has worked at the Oxford Radiocarbon Accelerator Unit (ORAU) which is part of the Research Laboratory for Archaeology and the History of Art. He is now the physicist in charge of the AMS side of the radiocarbon measurements undertaken by the unit and has a particular interest in statistical methods for use in dating studies as well as technical developments in dating. In addition to developing 'OxCal' (Bronk Ramsey 1995) he has published many papers mostly in *Radiocarbon* and *Nuclear Instruments and Methods* as well as the regular ORAU date lists in *Archaeometry*.

## TIMOTHY DARVILL

*School of Conservation Sciences, Bournemouth University, Talbot Campus, Fern Barrow, Poole, Dorset BH12 5BB*
Timothy Darvill is Professor of Archaeology and Head of the Archaeology Group in the School of Conservation Sciences, Bournemouth University. His research interests focus on archaeological resource management and the Neolithic period in northern Europe. He is currently Director of the Billown Neolithic Landscape Project in the Isle of Man, and Chairman of the Board of Directors of the Cotswold Archaeological Trust. Publications include: *Ancient Monuments in the Countryside* (English Heritage, 1987), *Prehistoric Britain* (Batsford, 1987), and *Prehistoric Britain from the Air* (Cambridge University Press, 1996).

## A. DAVID

*Ancient Monuments Laboratory, English Heritage, 23 Savile Row, London W1X 1AB*
Andrew David is a prehistorian who has specialised in archaeological geophysics for over twenty years and is now Head of the Archaeometry Branch of the Ancient Monuments Laboratory of English Heritage. He has responsibility for initiating programmes of survey and research and for the development of standards in archaeological geophysics. Neolithic and Bronze Age monument complexes remain a special interest and, with colleagues, he has undertaken geophysical investigations at several sites in the Stonehenge area, at

Durrington Walls, and at Avebury. He is a co-author of a re-evaluation of the documentary and physical evidence at the latter (*Avebury Reconsidered: from the 1660s to the 1990s*: Ucko *et al.* 1990).

### GEORGE EOGAN

*59 Brighton Road, Rathgar, Dublin 6*

Professor Eogan specialises in the Neolithic and Bronze Ages in Ireland and the comparative archaeology of these periods. Primary amongst these studies are his long-term investigations at Brugh na Bóinne—the Bend of the Boyne—in Ireland and in particular at Knowth. He is also involved in the wider issues of this area, especially regarding the establishment of an archaeological park. He has published widely on the subject of megalithic tombs in Ireland and along the Atlantic sea-ways. Professor Eogan is Chairman of the archaeological research institution, The Discovery Programme.

### C. P. GREEN

*Department of Geography, Royal Holloway, University of London, Egham, Surrey TW20 0EX*

Dr Christopher Green is a Senior Lecturer in the Department of Geography, Royal Holloway, University of London. He recently served as President of the Geologists' Association, is Secretary of the Geological Society's Conservation Committee and a co-editor of *Geological and Landscape Conservation* (1994). He was a founder member of the Romney Marsh Research Trust and co-edited *Romney Marsh: Evolution, Occupation, Reclamation* (1988). He has interests in the physical and cultural landscapes of southern Britain, undertaking research on landform, river development and prehistoric archaeology in the Thames Basin, on Dartmoor and on the Wessex Chalk.

### ANDREW J. LAWSON

*Wessex Archaeology, Portway House, Old Sarum Park, Salisbury, Wilts. SP4 6EB*

Andrew Lawson is the Unit Director of the Trust for Wessex Archaeology, the organisation commissioned by English Heritage to compile *Stonehenge in its Landscape. Twentieth-century Excavations* and earlier *The Stonehenge Environs Project*. Mr Lawson was formerly employed by the University of Chicago and the Norfolk Museums Service. He is a Fellow of the Society of Antiquaries and a Member of the Institute of Field Archaeologists. He has published more than fifty articles in archaeological journals and written less technical accounts for a wider readership. He is part of the Ancient Monuments Advisory Committee for English Heritage and regularly participates in the work of committees of the Council for British Archaeology, the Forestry Commission, as well as more local bodies.

F. GERRY McCORMAC

*Radiocarbon Dating Laboratory, School of Geosciences,*
*The Queen's University of Belfast, Belfast BT7 1NN*

Dr F. G. McCormac worked initially as a post-doctoral research fellow in the Space Physics Research Laboratory at the University of Michigan and later as a research scientist at the same institution. His research was concentrated on the dynamics of the Earth's thermosphere and its relationship to the interplanetary magnetic field. In 1989 he moved back to Belfast to work in The Queen's University of Belfast, Radiocarbon Dating Laboratory. He became Director of the laboratory in 1990 and a senior lecturer in Queen's in 1995. His current main research area is inter-hemispheric radiocarbon calibration.

A. PAYNE

*Ancient Monuments Laboratory, English Heritage, 23 Savile Row, London W1X 1AB*

Having graduated with a degree in archaeological sciences from the University of Bradford, Andrew Payne now works as a specialist in archaeological geophysics at the Ancient Monuments Laboratory where he carries out geophysical surveys on behalf of English Heritage. In latter years he has been actively involved in several programmes of geophysical investigation of the Neolithic monument complexes at both Stonehenge and Avebury. He is the author of the account of geophysical survey at Stonehenge that accompanies the recent publication *Stonehenge in its Landscape: Twentieth Century Excavations* (Cleal *et al.* 1995).

COLIN RENFREW

*The McDonald Institute for Archaeological Research, Downing Street,*
*Cambridge CB2 3ER*

Colin Renfrew (Lord Renfrew of Kaimsthorn) is Disney Professor of Archaeology in the University of Cambridge and Director of the McDonald Institute for Archaeological Research. He has directed excavations in Greece and in the Orkney Islands and has published papers on a range of archaeological subjects. His publications include: *The Emergence of Civilisation. The Cyclades and the Aegean in the Third Millennium BC* (1972), *Before Civilisation* (1973), *Archaeology and Language* (1987) and, with Paul Bahn, *Archaeology: Theories, Methods and Practice* (second edition 1996).

JULIAN RICHARDS

*Foyle Hill House, Foyle Hill, Shaftesbury, Dorset SP7 0PT*

Julian Richards is a graduate of Reading University who has worked in Wessex for over 20 years initially as a field archaeologist in Berkshire, later as a project manager with Wessex Archaeology and as an independent consultant with AC archaeology. Primarily a prehistorian, a major project within the Stonehenge Environs in the 1980s led to both academic and 'popular' publications and involvement with both landscape presentation and the media. In 1994 he was the archaeologist on the 'Secrets of Lost Empires' programme for the BBC which experimented with the engineering of Stonehenge. Mr Richards is currently an archaeologist on English Heritage's Monuments Protection Programme, combining this with teaching for the Continuing Education Department at Bristol University.

## CLIVE RUGGLES

*School of Archaeological Studies, University of Leicester, Leicester LE1 7RH*

Clive Ruggles is Senior Lecturer in Archaeological Studies at Leicester University. He edits the *Archaeoastronomy* supplement to *Journal for the History of Astronomy* and has written and edited/co-edited several books involving archaeoastronomy, including *Astronomy and Society in Britain during the Period 4000–1500 BC*, *Records in Stone*, *Archaeoastronomy in the 1990s*, and *Astronomies and Cultures*. His *Astronomy in Prehistoric Britain and Ireland* (Yale UP) is due to appear shortly.

## J. D. SCOURSE

*School of Ocean Sciences, University of Wales (Bangor), Menai Bridge,*
*Anglesey LL59 5EY*

James Scourse has been a Lecturer in Marine Geology in the School of Ocean Sciences at the University of Wales (Bangor) since 1985. He studied at Cambridge where he completed a Ph.D. on the Pleistocene stratigraphy of the Isles of Scilly and adjacent continental shelf in 1985; he was Research Fellow at Girton College, Cambridge between 1984 and 1985. His principal research interests are now the Quaternary marine geology and palaeoceanography of shelf seas and ocean margins, though he maintains an active interest in the Pleistocene glaciation of southern England. He was editor of *Quaternary Newsletter* between 1992 and 1996 and appointed Assistant Editor of the *Journal of Quaternary Science* in 1997. His publications include a number of papers on the Pleistocene period in southern Britain.

## GEOFFREY WAINWRIGHT

*English Heritage, 23 Savile Row, London W1X 1AB*

Geoffrey Wainwright was appointed Professor of Environmental Archaeology at the University of Baroda on graduating from the Institute of Archaeology, University College London in 1961. In 1963, he joined the Inspectorate of Ancient Monuments, then part of the Department of the Environment and conducted a number of excavations throughout England and Wales which were published in a series of books and articles. In particular, he was responsible for the great henge monument excavations at Durrington Walls, Marden and Mount Pleasant—all of which have been published by the Society of Antiquaries of London and which are of direct relevance to the age of Stonehenge. He is currently Chief Archaeologist for English Heritage.

## MARK WHITBY

*Whitby & Bird, 53–54 Newman Street, London W1P 4DA*

Mr Whitby graduated from King's College London with a degree in Civil Engineering. He is now a partner in Whitby & Bird Engineers, whose projects throughout Europe have included the Igus Factory, Cologne; the Olivetti Research Centre, Bari; the British Embassies in Berlin and Dublin; the Merchants Bridge, Manchester; and the Mappa Mundi Museum, Hereford. Mr Whitby is a Member of the Royal Academy of Engineering, and is a Fellow of both the Institution of Civil Engineers and the Institute of Structural Engineers. He participated in the production of 'Bridging the Future' (1993) for Channel 4 and 'Secrets of Lost Empires' (1995) for BBC2, and has published articles in various architectural and engineering journals.

## ALASDAIR WHITTLE

*School of History and Archaeology, University of Wales Cardiff, PO Box 909,*
*Cardiff CF1 3XU*

Alasdair Whittle has written widely on the Neolithic of Britain and Europe. His latest book, *Europe in the Neolithic: the creation of new worlds*, appeared in 1996 (Cambridge University Press). He has carried out fieldwork in recent years at Neolithic sites in the Avebury area; the most recent publication of the project is *Sacred mound, holy rings* (Oxbow, 1997), on Silbury Hill and the West Kennett palisade enclosures. He is currently working on the publication of excavations at the Windmill Hill causewayed enclosure.

# Acknowledgements

THE CONFERENCE *Science and Stonehenge* was planned by a coordinating committee comprising Sir Alan Muir Wood and Professor Mike Tite (Royal Society), Professor Lord Renfrew and Professor Barry Cunliffe (British Academy) and Dr Geoff Wainwright (English Heritage). The committee was greatly helped by the staff of the Royal Society, and in particular Mary Manning and Kaye Pudney who shouldered the daunting task of organizing and running the conference with characteristic unobtrusive efficiency.

The editors of this volume would particularly like to record their thanks to Dr Neil Brodie of the McDonald Institute for Archaeological Research, Cambridge University for commenting on the manuscripts and Lynda Smithson of the Institute of Archaeology, University of Oxford, for her meticulous work in her capacity as editorial assistant.

Publication of the colour plates and plans has been made possible by the generous financial support of English Heritage.

*Proceedings of the British Academy*, **92**, 1–2

# Introduction

## BARRY CUNLIFFE & COLIN RENFREW

THERE CAN BE LITTLE DOUBT that Stonehenge has always been a place of wonder and speculation. Yet for the 3000 years, after the monument took on its familiar form about 2000 BC, there is no record of people's attitudes to it. Indeed it is not until AD 1130 that Stonehenge is specifically named in literature, in the *Historia Anglorum* of Henry of Huntingdon, presented there as one of the four wonders of Britain. Henry displays admirable caution in his description, concluding 'nor can anyone guess by what means so many stones were raised so high, or why they were built there'. Subsequent writers have been less constrained.

In the quest to characterise and to understand Stonehenge there have been many milestones. In about 1620 King James I began the process by instructing the architect Inigo Jones to produce an accurate plan and description of the monument a version of which was published in 1655. Thereafter observation and speculation has continued. Famous antiquarians like Wallis (1730), Stukeley (1740), Douglas (1793), Colt Hoare (1812) and Petrie (1880), all made their contributions. The era of record and speculation ended dramatically on the last evening of the nineteenth century when one of the sarsen uprights fell and with it a lintel.

It was the unstable state of the monument which led, in the opening year of the century, to the first systematic excavation directed by William Gowland. Although Gowland's work was limited in scale the amount of new information gained about construction processes and date was dramatic. Since then there have been two major programmes of excavation first by William Hawley between 1919 and 1926 and later by Richard Atkinson, Stuart Piggott and J.F.S. Stone between 1950 and 1964. Other minor investigations have taken place since then. This century of scientific excavation has culminated, to everyone's satisfaction, with the definitive publication of the various interventions, all brought together in *Stonehenge in its Landscape: Twentieth Century Excavations* by R.M.J. Cleal, K.E. Walker and R. Montague, published by English Heritage in 1995.

The full and detailed publication of a century of archaeological endeavour, at what is surely one of the greatest prehistoric monuments in Europe, has been greeted with a deep sigh of relief from the archaeological world. With the data now freely available for the first time it is possible to move forward to formulate new programmes of research. To mark the occasion, and to stimulate debate, the Royal Society and the British Academy, with the cooperation of English Heritage, organised a conference entitled *Science and Stonehenge* which was held at the Royal Society's premises on 20–21 March, 1996. The aim was to bring together archaeologists, environmentalists, engineers, astronomers and geologists in common endeavour to move forward our understanding of this remarkable monument. The results of that conference are presented here as a contribution to the continuing debate.

*Proceedings of the British Academy,* **92**, 3–14

# Setting the Scene:
# Stonehenge in the Round

## COLIN RENFREW

## Introduction

THE SYMPOSIUM 'Science and Stonehenge', following fast upon the publication of the important volume *Stonehenge in its Landscape* (Cleal, Walker and Montague 1995) offered an unrivalled opportunity for a reassessment of our country's greatest monument. My introductory remarks will deal less with the natural sciences than with the broader field of knowledge and understanding: *scientia*. For the conference, organised jointly by the Royal Society and the British Academy (in conjunction with English Heritage) sought to bridge the gulf which sometimes separates the natural sciences and the humanities, and to take a broader view of Stonehenge, in the round as it were, in its national and international context. It aspired to the view that interpretation and understanding as well as detailed analysis is the proper work for rational scholars. I am asserting therefore that *Wissenschaft* goes beyond *Naturwissenschaft*, and that the historical sciences need not be inimical to the natural sciences.

What I am seeking to assert here is not merely a play upon words: some aspects of contemporary archaeology are, in a number of ways, seeking to diminish the chasm which often seems to yawn between 'The Two Cultures'. For while some segments of the archaeological community seem to reject the world of the hard sciences, in seeking to attain their aim of a more humanistic approach, others today are following a research strategy which deals in a systematic way with human cognition and the use of symbols within an integrated framework, where the sciences and imaginative interpretation are not necessarily set in opposition.

## The uniqueness of Stonehenge

Stonehenge, as my teacher Glyn Daniel used to say, is *sui generis*: it stands in a class of its own. It is Britain's best known ancient monument (if we exclude those symbolic of current government and kingship, such as Westminster Abbey): it is the most celebrated prehistoric monument in the world.

This justified celebrity rests upon a seeming paradox. For it comes as no surprise that the great and ancient civilisations known to history should have created monuments of sophistication—the pyramids of Egypt, or the acropolis of Athens. These are the products of literate communities, of state societies possessed of the competencies and skills of the urban world. Stonehenge stands for something else: it is the symbol of an era when humans did not yet live in cities, when life was simpler, when wisdom and learning did not yet depend upon the written word, when the religions of the book and the bureaucracies of the state had not yet laid their heavy hand upon society. So Stonehenge has become for some the symbol of a lost age, perhaps even a golden age, when we lived closer to nature and without the cares of a money economy or a welfare state. Seen in those terms the sophistication of its technology and the prodigious success of its engineering is astonishing, to some even miraculous.

This means that there is something a little puzzling here, something which demands explanation. How did they do it? Who were they, these precocious and accomplished builders? And why did they do it?

## The changing image of Stonehenge

It was Jacquetta Hawkes, whose death came, sadly, just a couple of days before the Conference, who remarked that: 'Every age has the Stonehenge it deserves—or desires' (Hawkes 1967, 174). And certainly the image of Stonehenge, as it has been seen and interpreted through the ages, is a mirror of those doing the interpreting as much as of the monument itself. An early mention, in *The History of the Kings of Britain* by Geoffrey of Monmouth, had it as the construction of Merlin, official wizard at the Court of King Arthur, who transported it by his magic art from Ireland. The first serious study and the first known plan was undertaken by Inigo Jones (Jones 1655) who studied the monument at the behest of King James the First. He interpreted it, as an enlightened son of the Renaissance, as a classical work, following the Roman order of architecture, and reconstructed a monument of wonderful and polished symmetry, although rusticated now by the passage of the years.

The Romantic movement, inspired by that early and notable protagonist of the Druids William Stukeley, saw it sometimes as a centre of nameless Druidical rites (which have inspired modern sects, who have no links whatever with their supposed prehistoric precursors, to equally strange goings-on). With the emergence of an awareness of the English landscape it was (and has remained) a favourite subject for painters from John Constable to Paul Nash. Our own century has seen it as an astronomical observatory, and in the imaginings of our noted astronomer and cosmologist Sir Fred Hoyle, as an analogue computer. Others, perhaps a little ahead of the science and engineering of our day, have viewed it as a space station for inter-planetary (or should it be inter-stellar?) travel.

Underlying much of this, as I noted earlier, has been the sheer wonderment that such a notable structure should date back to an early time, long ago recognised to go back way before the Romans reached Britain. Much of this thinking has been based upon the view that the local barbarians could scarcely have done such a thing alone. They needed help, some technological aid mission, whether from Rome (as Inigo Jones would have it), or from outer space (a view embraced by the followers of Erik von Daniken) or perhaps from the Bronze Age world of the Aegean.

The Aegean view arose from the diffusionist assumptions of Oscar Montelius and Gordon Childe, and when I was a student it was the standard, I think universal, position. It had been supported by Stuart Piggott (1938), who had drawn attention to similarities between finds from the Early Bronze Age 'Wessex culture', in whose time span the construction of the great sarsen structure at Stonehenge was (and still is) assigned, and objects from the celebrated Shaft Graves at Mycenae, dating from about 1600 BC. Similarities were adduced also between the Stonehenge trilithons and the massive architecture of the fortified citadels of the Mycenaean world. The principal figure in the major excavations at Stonehenge between 1950 and 1964 was Professor Richard Atkinson, and he gave vivid expression to what was then the prevailing view in his book *Stonehenge* (Atkinson 1960, 165–6):

> And yet were these Wessex chieftains *alone* responsible for the design and construction of this last and greatest monument at Stonehenge? For all their evident power and wealth, and for all their widespread commercial contacts, these men were essentially barbarians. As such, can they have encompassed unaided a monument which uniquely transcends all other comparable prehistoric buildings in Britain, and indeed in all Europe north of the Alps, and exhibits so many refinements of conception and technique? I for one do not believe it. It seems to me that to account for these exotic and unparalleled features one *must* assume the existence of influence from the only contemporary European cultures in which *architecture*, as distinct from mere construction, was already a living tradition; that is from the Mycenaean and Minoan civilizations of the central Mediterranean. Admittedly not all the refinements of Stonehenge can be paralleled in detail in Mycenaean or Minoan architecture... But ... the architecture of the central Mediterranean provides the only outside source for the sophisticated approach to the architecture exhibited at Stonehenge. We have seen that through trade the necessary contacts with the Mediterranean had been established. The Stonehenge dagger too may be seen, if one wishes, to point more directly at Mycenae itself ... Is it then any more incredible that the architect of Stonehenge should himself have been a Mycenaean, than that the monument should have been designed and erected, with all its unique and sophisticated detail, by mere barbarians?

The advent of radiocarbon dating (itself using samples deriving from the meticulous excavations of Piggott and Atkinson) allowed much of this to be doubted, and in 1968 I published an article, 'Wessex without Mycenae' (Renfrew 1968) which called these links and that diffusionist view into question, and suggested that Stonehenge was in fact far earlier than its supposed prototypes, and entirely independent of Aegean (or other outside) influence.

The dates now assigned to Stonehenge, as we shall see documented in this meeting, are:

| | |
|---|---|
| Phase 1 (Bank and ditch enclosure) | *c.*2950 BC |
| Phase 2 (Wooden structures within) | *c.*2900 to 2400 BC |
| Phase 3 (Bluestone circles, then main sarsen structure, realignment of bluestones, construction of Avenue) | *c.*2500 to 1600 BC |

So we may see that the stone structures at Stonehenge had been in use for more than a millennium before the great fortifications at the citadel at Mycenae were constructed. And we do indeed regard them today as the work of 'mere barbarians'.

## Stonehenge in its landscape

In speaking of Stonehenge, we must recognise that one of the great strengths of British archaeology has always been the field approach: landscape archaeology. Already, more than two hundred years ago, William Stukeley was making important field observations and meticulous plans (even if these were embellished by his Druidical speculations). He was the first to record the important linear monument to the north of Stonehenge (which he termed the 'cursus'), and the first also to give detailed record of the Stonehenge Avenue. Sir Richard Colt Hoare himself, in his *Ancient Wiltshire* produced detailed field surveys of many of the monuments, including the Bronze Age barrows, surrounding Stonehenge. And in our own century that great pioneer of field archaeology and of aerial photography O.G.S. Crawford placed modern field archaeology on a sure footing: he was of course the first Archaeological Officer of the Ordnance Survey which, for so many years, made important contributions to archaeological survey.

The principal national agency charged with this responsibility is, however, the Royal Commission on Historical Monuments for England, and their *Stonehenge and its Environs*, published in 1979 (RCHME 1979) is an indispensable source.

The Wessex Archaeological Unit initiated a detailed field-walking survey of the area around Stonehenge (Richards 1990), and this provided a thorough and systematic basis for the understanding of the site in its immediate local context. These resources will prove indispensable to any interpretation of Stonehenge in its landscape, an approach which is currently gaining momentum in archaeology under the influence of currents of thought in contemporary geography, where the subjective, hermeneutic approach has been advocated for some years (e.g. Duncan and Ley 1993) with its keen awareness of a 'sense of place'.

## Modern approaches towards interpretation

Stonehenge must first be situated within the long tradition of monumental architecture of great stones ('megaliths') in Britain and north-western Europe. As a monument it may be 'sui generis', but it is nonetheless the inheritor of at least two architectural traditions.

For the first, let us turn to Newgrange in Ireland, built around 3400 BC. It was Sir Richard Colt Hoare, writing in 1806 (Hoare 1807, 257) who gave the clearest expression to the interpretive dilemma then surrounding such prehistoric monuments:

> I shall not unnecessarily trespass upon the time and patience of my readers in endeavouring to ascertain what tribes first peopled this country; nor to what nation the construction of this singular monument may reasonably be attributed for, I fear, both its authors and its original destination will ever remain unknown. Conjecture may wander over its wild and spacious domains but will never bring home with it either truth or conviction. Alike will the histories of those stupendous temples at AVEBURY and STONEHENGE which grace my native county, remain involved in obscurity and oblivion.

But archaeological advances, so well reviewed in the major new English Heritage publication on Stonehenge (Cleal et al. 1995), have given a factual response to many of the implied questions. We now know, with good reliability, when Stonehenge was built and for how long it was used. And we can situate it within the trajectories of change in British prehistory, and to some extent within a social context in a developing landscape.

The first architectural tradition, then, of which Stonehenge is an inheritor, involves the use of large stones for major monuments, initially funerary monuments, which are found widely in the Neolithic of north-western Europe, and of which Newgrange is a splendid example. One feature of this tradition is a preoccupation with the movements of the sun and moon, as documented monumentally at Stonehenge itself, where the principal axis of the sarsen structure is aligned upon the midsummer solstitial sunrise. Already a millennium earlier the great passage grave at Newgrange was given an analogous alignment, this time upon the midwinter sunrise, and there are numerous other megalithic constructions which show the persistence of these concerns.

The second tradition in monumental architecture is that of circular structures, indeed structures with circular symmetry. They are seen first in Britain in the so-called 'causewayed camps' of the earlier Neolithic. Robin Hood's Ball is one such site, in the vicinity of Stonehenge. Their successors in chronological terms are certainly the 'henge' monuments, among which Stonehenge I can perhaps be situated. But it is still far from clear that the henges are the successors of the causewayed camps in any continuous or genetic sense: there are arguments for setting their origin much further north, perhaps even in Orkney, and beyond the spatial distribution of the causewayed camps.

A component of both traditions, less obvious today in the archaeological record, is in what Glyn Daniel termed 'megaxylic' architecture: the construction of great monuments in wood. It is now known that some of the earliest burial monuments in England, the 'unchambered long barrows', often housed mortuary chambers constructed of wood.

And with the discovery through aerial photography of the site near Durrington Walls, subsequently termed 'Woodhenge', it was realised that the uprights and lintels which are so conspicuous at Stonehenge are in fact part of a tradition of carpentry. This was underlined, again at Durrington Walls, by the subsequent excavations of Geoffrey Wainwright, which revealed complex and large-scale timber structures. It is not the form of the Stonehenge lintels which is exceptional but the specific circumstance that they have been accomplished in stone.

## Trajectories of change, and narratives in history: the social dimension

What we may see today in the archaeological record are patterns or trends, which we may term 'trajectories' of change. But we should not forget that the underlying experienced reality was one of individual experience and collective history. The story, the narrative, is in part lost, but that was how the actors at the time experienced these things.

We can situate the first phase at Stonehenge, a simple circular structure around 2900 BC, in the Neolithic landscape, where burial mounds (long barrows) were the local centres for scattered communities, for which the so-called 'causewayed camps' were the regional centres for meeting and for rituals associated with burial.

Stonehenge II, with its indications of wooden pillars or structures is contemporary with some of the great 'henge' monuments such as Durrington Walls, in the mid third millennium BC. These represented a prodigious investment of labour, and we can situate them in the Late Neolithic landscape, eclipsing in scale the earlier local centres.

Stonehenge III, with bluestones and then the great sarsen structure, from around 2500 BC, was an order of magnitude larger, representing millions of work-hours. Along with the other great monument of its time, Silbury Hill, it was of a scale dwarfing even the large henges, like Avebury or Durrington.

Both the spatial patterning, and the labour investment, allow us to put Stonehenge (and Silbury) at the top of a spatial and constructional hierarchy (Renfrew 1973).

I would venture to say that we have not yet explored fully the implications of all this in terms of power and of identity. In spatial terms—horizontal power, if you like—when we consider neighbouring groups and communities, competing and perhaps even dominating: Stonehenge emerged, with its local group of people around 2500 BC as something special. We can glimpse here the scale of neighbouring groups or 'tribes', and the emergence of new collective or social realities. The story that goes with the monument is now lost, but there were great deeds, alliances and perhaps conflicts. Stonehenge must have been the emblem of the population of its enlarged region, and in this sense a symbol of ethnicity or collective identity.

In terms of personal power—vertical power—Stonehenge must also imply some relations of dominance. Its construction was a formidable organisational feat. It does not need to have been achieved by slave labour or conscription: the labour and services may have been willingly offered. But they were offered to some central authority, and that authority will not have emerged without some internal conflicts within society, and without the aggrandisement of some human lineages at the expense of others. Here too there were stories and tales and songs of leadership and achievement which are lost to us.

## Stonehenge as theatre: Chorea Giganteum

The Oxford English Dictionary defines a *monument* as: 'Anything that by its survival commemorates a person, action, period or event'. I do not believe that we have yet learnt to think with sufficient coherence about the nature of monuments. Let us note that commemoration implies the exercise of memory—of the mind in the temporal dimension. Monuments are, amongst other things, mnemonics, aids to memory. And what is remembered is the story: the people, the events, the places whose detail are now lost to us. But if the detail is lost, there may still be implications in the form and structure of the construct for the society which built it and which used it. By experiencing the monument in space and in its physical reality we can, I believe, begin to approach the quality of some of these things, although this is a task upon which archaeologists are only now beginning to embark in a systematic and explicit way.

Let us remember that Stonehenge in its landscape was not only a place where things *had* happened, it was undoubtedly a place where things *did* happen. It had a continuing function, which went beyond its role as adducing a remembrance of things past. It was a meeting place, a locus for ritual and pageantry, a stage set. It was a place where the individual participated, through movement, through word, and probably through song and through dance. Not for nothing was it known in the Middle Ages as *Chorea Giganteum* —the Giants' Dance.

Movement is an important feature of all monuments: the movements of those participating fully in the local rituals of place, but also the movements of those who may be little more than spectators. In approaching the monument in the first place they experience a series of successive vistas. No-one who has visited Stonehenge and has had the experience of standing inside the great sarsen circle, can doubt that the impressions offered by the monument are different on the inside. A significant part of the experience is one's own locomotion and the transition from external spectator to internal participant.

Let me remind you of that linear monument, the cursus, which lies to the north and which was constructed at the same time as the simple circular enclosure of Stonehenge I. Our great contemporary sculptor Richard Long has shown us through much of his life's work (Fuchs 1986; Renfrew 1990) that one of the most significant of human actions is to walk, and to walk sometimes in a deliberate and organised way. His 'Line Made by Walking (1967)' (Fig. 1; Long 1991, 26) is exactly that: the pattern made on the grass by repeatedly walking up and down, recorded photographically. The very simplicity of

**Figure 1.** Monument as recorded movement: Richard Long's 'A Line Made by Walking' (1967).

**Figure 2.** Monument as permanent record: Richard Long's 'A Line in the Himalayas' (1975).

the action (or 'statement') makes it easy to overlook its power. These very simple and direct traces of human activity take a specific form which is, essentially, the simplest mark which a human can make within the landscape: a straight line. There is something which is basic here to many structured activities, not least to ritual.

Richard Long's 'A Line in the Himalayas (1975)' (Fig. 2; Long 1991, 62), like other lines which he has made in the landscape from locally available materials, is one of the most basic of monuments, which 'by its survival commemorates a person, action, period or event'. It commemorates, at the least, that Richard Long was there, and that he set up this line for the sake of remembrance. That is roughly what the cursus likewise is, although we may hypothesise that it is more besides. It is of such a scale that it must have been a significant collective work, and as such it may have been designed for repeated uses, presumably repeated perambulations along its length. Stukeley may not have been so far off in calling it a 'cursus' (i.e. race track), although it is unlikely to have been used for horse or chariot races, since chariots and horse riding were a feature of the later Bronze and Iron Ages respectively.

Long's 'Turf Circles (1988)' (Fig. 3; Long 1991, 161) at Jesus College, Cambridge, or his other and more permanent circular works in the landscape, remind us of that other basic form which along with the straight line (and generating the concept of enclosure) is at the root of all architecture. By their simplicity they remind us of the very considerable power of these elemental ingredients: circularity, enclosure (inside and outside: participation and exclusion), rotation, repetition, endlessness, perfect circular symmetry. All of these are embodied at Stonehenge, not only by the enclosing bank and ditch but by the great circular barrier of the sarsen circle.

**Figure 3.** Fundamental forms: Richard Long's 'Turf Circles' (1988).

*Colin Renfrew*

Stonehenge is above all miraculous for its verticality. It can be argued that the single upright stone is the most effective assertion of life and of deliberate action: its unstable equilibrium defies the entropy of the universe. It holds the potential for commemoration more effectively than anything else. This was something well understood by the Ancient Egyptians, when they erected those great obelisks at Karnak and at other significant temples (Fig. 4). A single vertical stone establishes an axis—whether an *axis mundi* or a mark of virility. Perhaps the only rival for Stonehenge in this sense among the prehistoric monuments of the world is the great series of stone features in the Carnac region of Brittany: the notable alignments, and above all perhaps the remains of the Grand Menhir Brisé at Locqmariaquer. One of the menhirs currently standing is at Kergadiou (Fig. 5). Yet many other cultures and traditions have produced monuments of comparable simplicity. In Tonga, for instance, there is a single trilithon, the Ha'amonga a Maui on the island of Tongatapu (Renfrew 1984, 221) which is a wonder to modern visitors in Tonga just as is Stonehenge to those in Wessex.

**Figure 4.** The power of the vertical: Egyptian obelisks at Karnak *c*.1500 BC.

**Figure 5.** 'We shall remember them': Breton menhir at Kergadiou.

The conference which formed the basis for the present volume offered the opportunity of defining some of these themes more clearly. We want to know where the stones came from and how they were transported—glacial action or human endeavour. That is still one of the great controversies. We want to know whether Stonehenge was used to observe other astronomical events beyond the midsummer and midwinter solstices. But above all we have to order our own thinking so as to perceive more clearly the principles by which the monument was conceived, and hence to grasp more securely the general intentions of its builders.

When we do so we shall see more clearly that the squalour in which we have allowed Stonehenge to be enmired in our own time, and the petty dealings and rivalries between government departments, betray the brilliant originality of our greatest relic of antiquity. We must see to it that by the Millennium, our Millennium, our collective response is a fitting one in the face of the five millennia to which this extraordinary monument can already lay claim.

*Acknowledgements*

The author would like to acknowledge Richard Long for permission to reproduce Figures 1 and 2 and Barbara Bender for permission to reproduce Figure 5. Figure 4 is reproduced by kind permission of Phaidon Press Limited, London, from *Egypt* by K. Lange and M. Hirmer (1961).

# References

ATKINSON, R.J.C. 1960: *Stonehenge* (Harmondsworth).

CHIPPINDALE, C. 1983: *Stonehenge Complete* (London).

CLEAL, R.M.J., WALKER, K.E. and MONTAGUE, R. 1995: *Stonehenge in its Landscape: Twentieth Century Excavations* (London, Engl. Heritage Archaeol. Rep. 10).

DUNCAN, J. and LEY, D. (eds) 1993: *Place/Culture/Representation* (London).

FUCHS, R.H. 1986: *Richard Long* (London).

HAWKES, J. 1967: God in the machine. *Antiquity* 41, 174–80.

HOARE, Sir R. COLT 1807: *Journal of a Tour in Ireland A.D. 1806* (London).

JONES, I. 1655: *The Most Notable Antiquity of Britain, vulgarly called Stone-heng on Salisbury Plain* (London).

LONG, R. 1991: *Walking in Circles* (London).

PIGGOTT, S. 1938: The Early Bronze Age in Wessex. *Proc. Prehist. Soc.* 4, 52–106.

RCHME 1979: Royal Commission on Historical Monuments (England). *Stonehenge and its Environs* (Edinburgh).

RENFREW, C. 1968: Wessex without Mycenae. *Annu. Brit. Sch. Athens* 63, 277–85.

RENFREW, C. 1973: Monuments, mobilisation and social organisation in neolithic Wessex. In Renfrew, C. (ed.), *The Explanation of Culture Change: Models in Prehistory* (London), 539–58.

RENFREW, C. 1984: Islands out of Time. In Renfrew, C., *Approaches to Social Archaeology* (Edinburgh), 200–24.

RENFREW, C. 1990: Languages of art: the work of Richard Long. *Cambridge Review* 111, 110–14.

RICHARDS, J. 1990: *The Stonehenge Environs Project* (London, Hist. Build. Monuments Comm. Archaeol. Rep. 16).

*Proceedings of the British Academy,* **92**, 15–37

# The Structural History of Stonehenge

## ANDREW J. LAWSON

### Introduction

STONEHENGE, ENGLAND'S BEST-KNOWN PREHISTORIC MONUMENT, was first mentioned in the twelfth century and first illustrated in the fourteenth century. It has been the subject of antiquarian study since the seventeenth century but the factual basis with which to underpin deliberation on its date, development and demise results entirely from a series of excavations conducted in the twentieth century. Although it is known that earlier a number of people had dug at Stonehenge (Chippindale 1983, 117), neither records nor finds survive, so their efforts contribute even less to the understanding of this complex and sophisticated structure than the endeavours of Colt Hoare, Cunnington, and the like, contributed to our knowledge of the surrounding monuments.

The recorded excavations of the twentieth century began in 1901 when, at the behest of the site's owner, Lord Antrobus, Professor William Gowland excavated at the base of the tallest stone (No. 56) so that it could be re-erected. Once the monument had been given to the nation (by Cecil Chubb in 1918), the Office of Works sought to make it safe for visitors by securing more stones in concrete foundations. Between 1919 and 1926, Colonel William Hawley excavated nearly half the monument in advance of this restoration and before non-essential work was halted, being (unfairly) thought to be unproductive. The lack of a detailed publication of the results of Hawley's work and a number of unresolved questions concerning the site's structural history prompted a third series of excavations under the supervision of Professor Richard Atkinson, Professor Stuart Piggott and Dr John Stone. Although this campaign, which started in 1950, was initially small in scale, it grew as further questions were asked of the monument, new discoveries were made, and a decision was taken to re-erect the stones which were known to have fallen in recent history. It continued, intermittently, until 1964. Subsequently, further small-scale work near the periphery of the site has added important new evidence, in particular the work of Professor John Evans on the ditch in 1978, and Mike Pitts adjacent to the Heel Stone in 1979–80.

Throughout this period, a number of excavations have taken place on the Avenue, the delineated route between the river Avon and Stonehenge, so that its form and relationship to the circle could be established.

Unfortunately, until recently, detail of the observations and finds made during most of the pre-1978 excavations had not been made accessible to archaeologists, despite the overwhelming importance of this unique monument. Although Atkinson (1956, 1979) had published his own lucid explanation of the monument, the evidence from excavations was not presented to substantiate his ideas. However, in 1987, English Heritage sponsored Wessex Archaeology to create a comprehensive archive of excavation records and, in 1993, commissioned an analysis and the publication of a report based on this evidence.

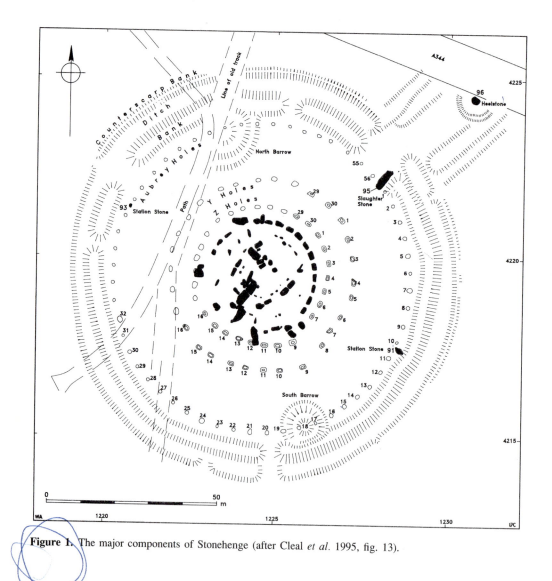

**Figure 1.** The major components of Stonehenge (after Cleal *et al.* 1995, fig. 13).

The results have already been published (Cleal, Walker and Montague 1995), but such is the magnitude of the report that this account can only be a *précis* of it.

Despite the achievements of the report's team, the nature of the surviving records and, indeed, of the monument itself, leave uncertainties in the conclusions: some accounts have been lost, many finds were not retained, certain records cannot be reconciled and in notable instances, no descriptions were made at the time of excavation. Because of the concentric nature of Stonehenge (Fig. 1), stratigraphical sequences built up at the centre cannot be related directly to those at the periphery. Nonetheless, new analysis aided by a large suite of radiocarbon dates (Bayliss, this volume) has enabled a new phasing of the monument to be defined.

Since the pioneering work of Stukeley in the early eighteenth century, archaeologists have appreciated that Stonehenge is merely one component of a wider landscape burgeoning with other prehistoric monuments (Fig. 2). The long history of investigation of these sites has provided a rich source of information, both archaeological and environmental, which enables us to consider how Stonehenge, during its various phases of elaboration, related to its neighbouring monuments.

Excavations on the site of the nearby visitor car park and access underpass, as well as recent geophysical surveys (David and Payne, this volume), illustrate the potential of the area to contain surprising remains of many periods even in close proximity to Stonehenge.

Importantly, the Stonehenge Environs Project commissioned from Wessex Archaeology by English Heritage, and directed by Julian Richards (1990) between 1980 and 1984, has provided a wealth of information, not only from other earthwork structures but from the land between. This research continues and evaluation fieldwork in advance of possible alternative locations for a visitor centre and for roads has provided considerable new evidence. Combining the plethora of data from the surrounding landscape, with the newly available record from Stonehenge, has enabled the authors of the latest Stonehenge volume to consider the monument in a much better-known, wider context.

## Before Stonehenge

The landscape which was later to contain Stonehenge bore witness to both environmental change and monument construction during the millennia before the construction of the stone circle.

The oldest available holocene records suggest that, at that time, the local vegetation probably comprised an open hazel and pine boreal woodland, possibly with denser deciduous cover in the river valleys and a patchwork of natural open areas on the drier upland (Allen, this volume). The evidence for the exploitation of this vegetational 'coarse mosaic' by Mesolithic people is sparse, although a few characteristic flint (and chert) artefacts were recorded by the Stonehenge Environs Project (Richards 1990, 263) or had previously

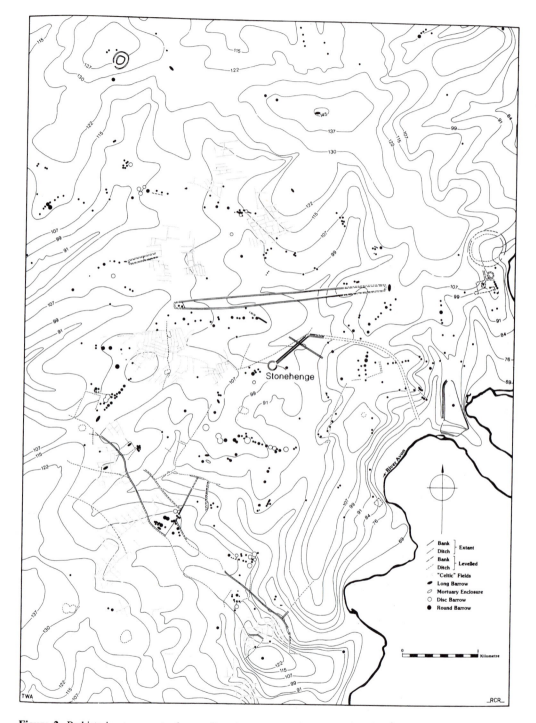

**Figure 2.** Prehistoric monuments close to Stonehenge (after Richards 1990, fig. 3).

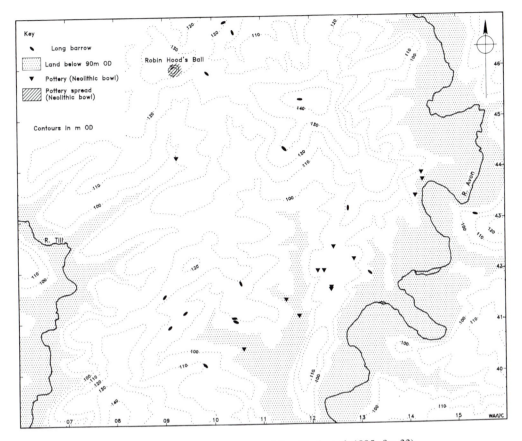

**Figure 3.** Early Neolithic sites in the Stonehenge area (after Cleal *et al.* 1995, fig. 33).

been reported (Wymer 1977, 263). Subsequent re-examination of some of these artefacts suggests that several of them are later in date (J. Gardiner, pers. comm.) and, in consequence, the Mesolithic evidence is even more sporadic than one might hope. Nonetheless, within the area which now forms the visitors' car park, four pits were dug, at least three of which held substantial pine posts (Allen, this volume). Dated to the late ninth or early eighth millennium BC (Bayliss, this volume), such constructional activity is extremely rare in British prehistory and it is difficult to imagine what continuity of tradition, if any, can link the erection of these Early Mesolithic posts with the much later sites close by.

A number of radiocarbon dates relating to sites within proximity of Stonehenge span the fourth millennium BC. Although these sites represent considerable activity prior to the initiation of Stonehenge, a hiatus in the archaeological and environmental record currently exists between the eighth and fourth millennia during which the vegetational cover was dramatically altered. The flint tranchet axes recovered from the area are the sole witness to what must have been a concerted policy, started in the Later Mesolithic to clear woodland, because by the time Stonehenge was started, the surrounding landscape already contained degraded rendzina soils (Richards 1990, 108) supporting a well-established open grassland, probably maintained by grazing animals.

The earliest traces of Neolithic activity, identified most easily from the occurrence of plain pottery, are recognised from isolated individual, or small clusters of pits, but also from collections of lithic artefacts. The meagre evidence suggests that prior to the construction of earthen monuments, domestic activities occurred whose signature in the landscape is difficult to detect, yet is recurrently of a similar nature. As elsewhere in Wiltshire, or, for example, in Dorset (Woodward 1991, 133) pits with no cohesive pattern which might suggest regular structures are found in a variety of locations, some pre-dating Early Neolithic monuments, for example at Robin Hood's Ball (Thomas 1964, 8–10; compare with Windmill Hill (Whittle 1990, 27) or Maiden Castle (Sharples 1991, 49)). Other pits such as the Coneybury 'Anomaly' encapsulate evidence for 'both mobile and more sedentary economies' (Richards 1990, 263) through a wide range of animal bones, botanical remains, and associated artefacts.

Communal monuments including long barrows (e.g. Netheravon Bake), enclosures (Normanton and the Lesser Cursus) and a causewayed camp (Robin Hood's Ball) were created throughout the fourth millennium, possibly in a series of recognised 'habitually used' areas across the downland between the rivers Avon and Till, so that by the end of the fourth millennium, the area already contained a concentration of monuments, and the landscape had been recognisably patterned to serve the varied daily and spiritual purposes of its users (Fig. 3).

# Phase 1

The first monument created at the Stonehenge site comprised the enclosure ditch, visible today as the shallow circular depression some 110 m in diameter, surrounding the later stones (Fig. 4). This ditch was dug as a series of inter-connecting segments, 28 of which can be distinguished in the south-eastern half of the circuit excavated by Hawley (a further three were excavated in the northern part). They were irregular both in plan and form, varying in depth between 1.2 m and 2.3 m below ground level and with a maximum width of 4.3 m. Three intentional breaks, or entrances, into the enclosure can be noted: the widest gap, probably originally about 13 m wide exists in the north-east, while a narrower causeway, originally about 5 m wide between Segments 17 and 18 exists in the south, and a probable third, originally perhaps 4 m wide between Segments 21 and 23, later rendered void by the digging of a 0.9 m wide pit across it (designated Segment 22).

The chalk rubble derived from the ditch was mainly cast *inwards* so as to form a bank between 5 m and 6 m wide. Atkinson (1979, 25) had calculated that although the bank is today much reduced by truncation, erosion, compaction and solution, it was possibly 1.9 m high when first constructed, thus effectively forming a visual barrier

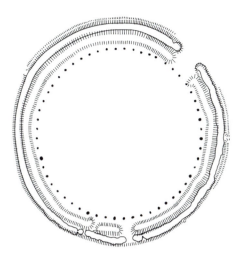

**Figure 4.** Stonehenge Phase 1.

between the inside and outside of the enclosure. Little can be said of the structure of the bank because it has only been examined in three places and on each occasion its remnant was poorly preserved, normally only about 0.5 m of chalk rubble surviving. However, augering suggests that, in the western part of the monument at least, a buried soil survives beneath it, which contains pollen indicative of the grassland within which the monument was built (Allen, this volume).

Outside the ditch, traces of a counterscarp bank can be seen, especially in the north. Thin layers of chalk rubble and flint nodules, the surviving remnant of this feature, have been observed both during augering and in the two places it has been sectioned, but without further evidence it is difficult to place it in the sequence of construction of the earthworks. Although the counterscarp bank may derive from a later modification of the ditch (such as the breaking down of undug chalk 'ridges' between ditch segments, or partial emptying of primary fill), it is probably an early, if not primary feature of the enclosure.

The digging of the ditch is now unequivocally dated by radiocarbon dates to about 3000 BC (Bayliss, this volume). These dates are based on material left on the floor of the ditch, which included antlers and bone, but considerable quantities of flint debitage (little of which was retained after excavation by Hawley) and occasional chalk objects were also left. Concentrations of such finds have been identified at the ditch terminals either side of the entrances. Here the finds include an ox skull and cattle jaws, from which radiocarbon dates, statistically significantly earlier than other dates from the base of the ditch, have been obtained. These dates imply that ancient material occurred in these deposits possibly indicating a special significance of this 'curated' material, or of its location adjacent to the entrances, in some form of 'structured deposition'.

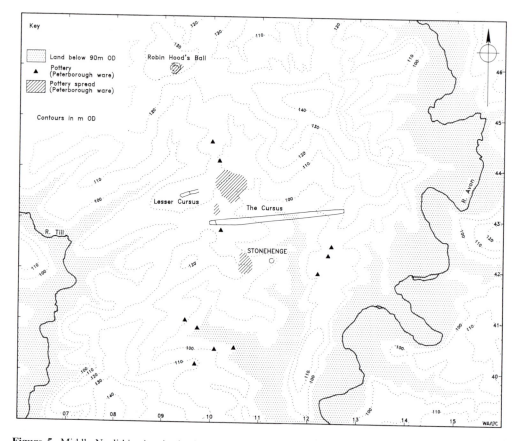

**Figure 5.** Middle Neolithic sites in the Stonehenge area (after Cleal *et al.* 1995, fig. 35).

The earliest soil deposit on the base of the ditch was a thin layer of 'foot-trampled mud' which soon became covered by a primary chalk rubble resulting from the weathering of the ditch sides, and a dark layer, representing a weak soil formation (Evans 1984, 10) and anthropogenic activity, formed once the weathered ditch profile had become more stable.

The internal tail of the bank was marked by a ring of 56 circular pits, each on average 1 m in diameter and 0.9 m deep, set between 4.5 m and 4.8 m centre to centre and describing a circle 87 m in diameter, or nearly 5 m within the median line of the ditch. Thirty-four of these 'Aubrey Holes' have been examined during the twentieth-century excavations.

The recorded fill of the Aubrey Holes is so varied as to make conclusive statements about their original purpose difficult. However, the weight of evidence both from Stonehenge and by analogy with other Neolithic monuments, favours the interpretation that they originally held stout timber posts which were subsequently deliberately removed either by extraction or by burning. The dearth of distinctive artefacts from the primary fill of the Aubrey Holes and lack of direct stratigraphic relationships with other elements of the monument mean that their place in the structural sequence has not been confirmed. Nonetheless, their symmetry which shares the same centre as the enclosure, and the date of their secondary use (below) strongly support the notion of a primary function in the first phase of activity at Stonehenge.

At the start of the third millennium BC the newly-created enclosure was not the only sign of Middle Neolithic activity within the landscape (Fig. 5). The Lesser Cursus had been modified and the enigmatic longer Cursus had probably been created. Discoveries of Peterborough Ware pottery on ridges and elevated areas on most sides of Stonehenge (King Barrow Ridge, Wilsford Down, and Stonehenge Down) are evidence of activity albeit that the exact nature of this activity cannot be ascertained due to the lack of finds and closely-associated structures.

The Stonehenge enclosure itself cannot be classified comfortably as a henge monument, nor as a causewayed enclosure although both in proportion and date it is comparable to late examples of the latter (e.g. Flagstones; Smith *et al.* 1997). It is perhaps best seen simply as an example of the variant forms of circular enclosure current at the time.

## Phase 2

During the first half of the third millennium BC, activities at Stonehenge commenced in a rather destructive fashion. As noted above, the posts set into the Aubrey Holes had been removed and now parts of the bank may have been cast back into the ditch in a number of places. Elsewhere the ditch silted naturally, the distinction between backfill and silt obviously being evident, as Hawley related for Segment 1: 'The rubble layer was still present. . . . but under it, instead of silt, there was clean white chalk. . . .' Clean chalk backfill was not restricted to the segments either side of the entrance, but was clearly present in at least three other segments and clearly deliberate backfilling of the ditch occurred soon after the primary ditch fill had formed. In two places (Segments 7 and 17) the silts contained sherds of Grooved Ware: elsewhere it appears to have been cut into from time to time to place deposits including cremation burials which were also cut into the previously-refilled Aubrey Holes. Eight of these cremation burials were accompanied by bone pins, antler, bone, chalk or ceramic objects. It may also be that many of the other cremation burials found cut into the back of the bank or in the interior also belong with this activity. In all 52 cremations were reported, such a significant number that the site during this phase might be regarded as a cremation cemetery.

Attributed to Phase 2 are a large number of post-holes, forming a rectilinear arrangement at the main entrance, probably a transverse line beyond that entrance, a concentration in the centre, and a 'passageway' in the south (Fig. 6). The majority of these have

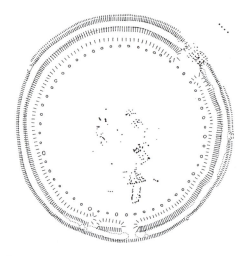

**Figure 6.** Stonehenge Phase 2.

no stratigraphic relationship with other elements of the monument, but where such exist, the post-holes are almost invariably the earliest. Dating is made more problematic by the absence of finds or radiocarbon determinations from their fills, but the very absence of stone chips resulting from the working of structural stones helps to confirm the view that they precede the presence of any of the stones.

It is possible to discern several elements to the array of 55 post-holes at the entrance, namely, at least six transverse rows, at least nine radial rows and a diagonal row of slightly larger posts. The smallest post-hole was 20 cm in diameter and only 10 cm deep while the largest was 63 cm in diameter and 66 cm deep. A few post-holes were juxtaposed but the majority were spaced roughly 1–1.5 m apart. Various interpretations have been offered for these settings, some suggesting a gateway building while others prefer to see them as defining passageways demarcated by free-standing posts.

Some 16 m beyond the outermost row of entrance posts stood another line of posts, four of which were excavated in 1923. These were set at 2 m intervals and varied in diameter from 58 cm to 71 cm and in depth from 46 cm to 83 cm. The full length of this row may not have been defined because its projection lies beyond the limits of excavation.

Between the narrower, southern, entrance and the centre of the enclosure Hawley recorded more than 80 post-holes, some arranged in rough rows, possibly forming a short 'facade' and a 'passageway' of two parallel rows with furrowing of the chalk between. These are not as regular as the rows at the main entrance and the form of structure or superstructure they may once have supported must remain conjectural.

A further 113 post-holes have been recorded within the interior area, but any regular pattern is impossible to reconstruct due to the limits of excavation and the subsequent digging of stone-holes.

To this evidence of timber structures within the enclosure must be added consideration of the palisade discovered in 1967 during the construction of the modern pedestrian underpass beneath the A344 some 75 m north-west of the enclosure earthwork. The palisade appears to have been constructed of contiguous timber posts *c*.0.4 m in diameter set in a V-shaped trench *c*.1.4 m deep and 2 m wide at the surface of the chalk. Unfortunately, no dating evidence was recovered from the excavated length although the upper part of the ditch contained soil layers cut by a crouched inhumation of Iron Age date. The palisade trench can be traced on aerial photographs from Stonehenge Down in the south-west to near the Cursus in the north. It has twice been sectioned in Stonehenge Bottom with inconclusive results. Whatever its precise date, it must have formed a formidable barrier, and if it is of Late Neolithic date, it transforms our view of the setting of Stonehenge, a large barrier separating it from the domain to the north-west.

Phase 2 is perhaps the most difficult in the structural sequence in which to see cohesion. The cremation cemetery lacks radiocarbon dates but is best dated by analogy with sites such as Dorchester-on-Thames (Whittle *et al.* 1992). Similarly the post-holes contain no datable objects, but their arrangements are best compared to timber structures within henge monuments such as Durrington Walls (Gibson 1994), and the palisade beyond the monument to those at West Kennett (Whittle 1991).

Mathematical modelling of the available radiocarbon dates indicates that the secondary fills of the ditch took between 400 and 730 years to develop, the period constrained by the dates of the formation of the dark soil above the primary chalk rubble fill and of a Beaker-style grave of Phase 3 cut into it. These dates suggest placing Phase 2 between 2900 and 2400 BC or within the Late Neolithic when Grooved Ware was the dominant ceramic, and henge monuments are the best known example of communally-constructed monuments.

Locally, the largest monument in the landscape was Durrington Walls, 3 km northeast of Stonehenge. The intervening chalk ridge (King Barrow Ridge) continued to be a focus of activity as not only the discovery of Grooved Ware pottery and other artefacts shows, but also as the construction of the now plough-levelled Coneybury Henge, 1 km east of Stonehenge attests (Fig. 7). One senses, however, that the currently-available archaeological evidence for this phase is restricted and as research continues, spatial gaps will be filled by the traces of complex structures (as at West Kennett; Whittle 1993, fig. 8), smaller structures (as at Coniger Hill, Dorchester; Smith *et al.* 1997), or further nebulous pits.

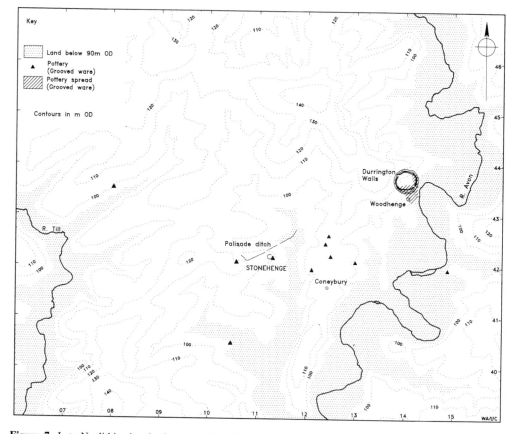

**Figure 7.** Late Neolithic sites in the area (after Cleal *et al.* 1995, fig. 57).

# Phase 3

If Phase 1 sees the construction of the earthwork enclosure and Phase 2 the timber structures, Phase 3 embraces all the stone structures albeit that the central elements (assigned
Sub-Phases 3i-v) are difficult to equate chronologically with stones at the periphery (Sub-
Phases 3a-c) (Fig. 8). Both within the interior and at the periphery (*viz.* around the Heel
Stone) some stratigraphic relationships exist to demonstrate localised sequences but nowhere
can either synchroneity or a full diachronic sequence be demonstrated. Nonetheless, as earlier
authors have attempted, as a result of the re-appraisal of the surviving excavation records
a more or less contiguous succession of modifications can be postulated.

*Sub-Phase 3i*

The earliest stone monument comprises a setting whose form is incompletely known, but
is recognised in the dumbbell-shaped stone-holes (the Q and R Holes) dug to hold pairs

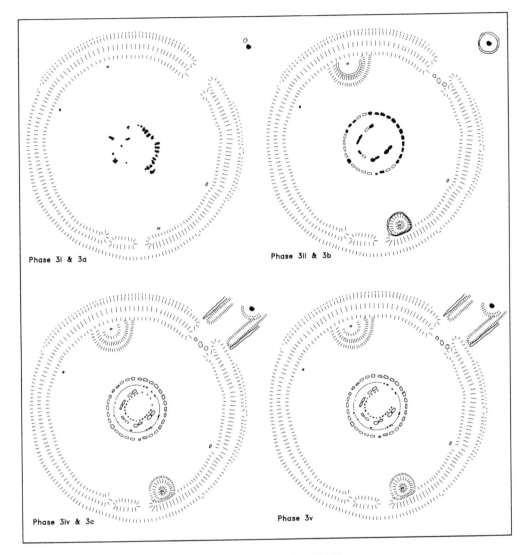

Phase 3i & 3a

Phase 3ii & 3b

Phase 3iv & 3c

Phase 3v

**Figure 8.** Stonehenge Phases 3i-v (after Cleal *et al.* 1995, figs 256–7).

of 'bluestones'. Analysis has demonstrated that the 'bluestones' which remain at Stone-henge are derived from at least ten different sources within the same restricted area of South Wales, at or near Mynydd Preseli (Thorpe *et al.* 1991). In the absence of any convincing evidence for a west to east glaciation beyond the Bristol Channel (Green, this volume), it must be concluded that the stones were transported by people from South Wales to Wiltshire.

This first stone monument appears not to have been circular or symmetrical, but lying just within the north-eastern half of the circuit of the later stone circle is a flattened arc of some 16 chalk-filled features. No similar array of pits was located in the south-western half of the monument, although on stratigraphic grounds five or six further features, including one crescentic in plan, may be attributed to the setting. The size and shape of the Q and R Holes varies but, for example, Q/R Hole 5 is typically *c.*2 m long and slightly more than 0.5 m deep; atypically, it contained two Beaker sherds in its backfill, whereas the others are almost devoid of finds. According to the excavator (Atkinson 1956, 58), stone impressions were visible on the bottom of each pit, some of which retained minute chips of the 'bluestones'. Stratigraphically, the Q-R Holes are earlier than the 'bluestone' and sarsen circles currently standing.

*Sub-Phase 3a*

In the localised stratigraphic sequence outside the main entrance, a large stone-hole (97) 1.75 m across and 1 m deep, excavated by Pitts in 1979 is the earliest in the sequence. The sarsen Heel Stone stands 2 m to the south and may have formed a partner to 97 standing obliquely across the axis of symmetry of the monument. Alternatively, it is possible to suggest that the Heel Stone is the later re-positioned Stone 97 (in Sub-Phase 3b).

Just within the main entrance, the recumbent sarsen Slaughter Stone lies adjacent to two large stone-holes (D and E) and may itself cover a further stone-hole (Long 1876, 56, 85). Hence it appears that there may have been a facade of as many as three stones enhancing the entrance previously constrained by the timber structure.

In the general area between the Heel Stone and the entrance are a number of features including a further possible stone-hole (B). It therefore remains possible that at an early stage some form of stone alignment may have marked the approach to Stonehenge.

Four more sarsen stones known as the Station Stones formerly stood within the enclosure just within the bank and roughly on the line of the earlier Aubrey Holes. They form an approximate rectangle whose long side is at right angles to a line between the centre of the enclosure and the entrance. Only two of these small stones (Nos 91 and 93) survive, although the sockets for the other two (Nos 92 and 94) have been located. No finds have been recovered to help attribute the Station Stones to a precise position in the monument's sequence.

*Sub-Phase 3ii*

Thirty dressed stones set upright to form a Sarsen Circle were linked by horizontal lintels with carefully-worked joints. This Circle surrounded five free-standing sarsen Trilithons, each with two uprights and a lintel, set in a horseshoe plan which lay symmetrically about an axis which passed the Heel Stone. Jointly these spectacular edifices once formed the most sophisticated prehistoric monument in northern Europe. Much of this structure remains as the most dominant feature of Stonehenge today.

The stones of the Sarsen Circle, which had probably been brought from the Marlborough Downs some 30 km to the north were set in chalk-cut pits up to 3 m across and 1.5 m deep, 18 of which have been investigated in some form. Similarly, the Trilithons were set in deep pits: with the exception of one Trilithon (with uprights 51 and 52), the bases of all have been investigated. The depth of the stone-holes was extremely variable, allowance being made for the variable lengths of the stones and the requirement, especially in the case of the Circle, for raising the tops to a level which would enable the lintels to be perfectly horizontal. Hence, at one extreme, that for Stone 58 was cut barely 1 m into the chalk while at the other extreme, that for Stone 56 was more than 2.1 m deep from the current surface. Archaeological finds from these stone-holes are extremely restricted, comprising only worked chalk, stone and antler.

At least eight of the sarsen stones are thought to have prehistoric carvings. Those most clearly visible (on the outer faces of Stones 3 and 4 and the inner face of Stone 53) are representations of unhafted axe blades, probably indigenous flanged bronze axes. At least one carving (on Stone 53) represents a dagger. It seems most likely that these carvings were added after the erection of the stones.

*Sub-Phase 3b*

Outside the entrance the Heel Stone was surrounded by a roughly circular ditch 10 m in diameter, about 1.1 m wide and 1.2 m deep. The fill of the ditch includes 'bluestone' chips and, hence, was probably forming when the internal orthostats were being reworked (for their settings in Sub-Phase 3iii or iv). Two of the Station Stones are also surrounded by circular features: Stone 94 by a ditch probably about 10–12 m in diameter, *c*.1.1 m wide and 0.9 m deep with an external bank, and the former Stone 92, by an irregular V-shaped ditch *c*.11 m in diameter, 0.5 m wide and 0.4 m deep, the quarried material probably having been thrown inwards. These features, the 'North Barrow' and 'South Barrow', respectively, clearly post-date the main enclosure bank and Aubrey Holes and it would not seem unreasonable to suggest contemporaneity in the additions to all three peripheral stones.

The flexed skeleton of a young man apparently killed by arrows and accompanied by Beaker-style grave goods was discovered in the ditch by Evans (1984) in 1978. Within the fill of the grave were fragments of 'bluestone'. This grave is important in providing a point of transition from Phase 2, identified with the clean secondary fill of the ditch, and Phase 3 when the stones were clearly present on the site. The ditch obviously remained to demarcate a central area and was not yet fully silted because the uppermost fills contain broken fragments of 'bluestone'. The fact that similar fragments also occur in the grave fill indicates, like the Heel Stone ditch, that it is contemporary with or later than the scattering of 'bluestone' fragments during the working of the orthostats. Five radiocarbon dates from the skeleton suggest an age of 2400–2140 cal BC.

*Sub-Phase 3iii*

A series of features has been identified in the west sector of the monument which are stratigraphically earlier than the final setting of the 'bluestones' (below). They are devoid of finds and do not appear to form a coherent pattern and, indeed, may not all be precisely contemporary. Nonetheless, they may form part of a setting not obvious elsewhere in the site which included several of the 'bluestones' reworked to form at least two trilithons. It has long been noted that the final 'bluestone' settings re-use two lintels (Stones 36 and 150), three uprights with reduced tenons (Stones 67, 69 and 70), and two stones with a lateral tongue (Stone 66) or groove (Stone 68) but the intended position of these, if, as presumed, was at Stonehenge, has not been resolved. However, it would seem reasonable to suggest that the technically-similar trilithons of sarsen and 'bluestone' stood together.

*Sub-Phases 3iv and 3v*

These sub-phases comprise a reorganisation of the 'bluestones'. It is suggested that contemporaneously they were re-erected as a continuous circle between the Sarsen Circle and the Trilithons (possibly the original number of stones being supplemented by additional stones), and as an oval of 23 'bluestones' within the Trilithon horseshoe. Subsequently (Sub-Phase 3v), at least four of these 'bluestones' were removed so that a horseshoe matching the Trilithon setting was created. Within the oval/horseshoe there may also have been individual or paired stones. One of these, the Altar Stone, currently lies prone beneath the collapsed central Trilithon. This may have had a pair, while a further stone stood at the other end of the oval.

Originally, there may have been more than 70 'bluestones' in the circle. Many stood in individual sockets, but in some areas, there appears to have been economy of effort and a more continuous trench to hold several adjacent stones was dug. Typically, the base of the 'bluestone' was between 1 m and 1.5 m below the current ground level.

*Sub-Phase 3c*

The latest element identifiable stratigraphically at the entrance is the construction of the Avenue, its banks overlying post-holes and the Heel Stone Ditch, the fill of which contained 'bluestone' chips. At its junction with the earlier enclosure, the external ditches are 21.5 m from centre to centre with low banks on their internal edges, but by the time the Avenue reaches the river Avon, some 2.8 km distant, it is 34.5 m across. Only the straight 530 m-long section between Stonehenge and Stonehenge Bottom and a short stretch after its bend in the dry valley are now visible although its course was recorded by Stukeley in the eighteenth century and re-discovered through aerial photography by Crawford in 1921.

There has been a total of twenty investigations of the Avenue between 1919 and 1980.

Seven of these have produced finds including pottery, animal bone and antler, the latter being used to produce six radiocarbon dates which demonstrate broad contemporaneity with Phase 3.

*Sub-Phase 3vi*

Two concentric circles of pits were identified by Hawley outside the stone circle. The inner circle of Z Holes, each 1 m deep and *c*.1.75 m by 1.5 m, lay approximately 3.7 m beyond the Sarsen Circle while the matching ring of 30 Y Holes, each 0.9 m deep and 1.7 m by 1.0 m, lay 11 m from the stones. Seventeen Z Holes and 19 Y Holes have been excavated, at least two of the former being shown to cut stone-holes of the Sarsen Circle.

With the exception of a small stack of antlers in Y Hole 30, there are few finds from the primary fills of these pits, although they appear to have remained open for some considerable time, allowing objects of a wide date range to accumulate in them. It is possible that this final discernible phase of structural activity at Stonehenge was activated with the intention of a further modification to the stone settings, and judging from the scale of the pits, to receive 'bluestones'. However, it appears that this was never realised.

The chronology and duration of the various phases of the stone settings throughout Phase 3 are difficult to resolve because of the small quantities of archaeological finds recovered. In consequence, little suitable material is available for radiocarbon dating. However, 16 new determinations for the monument and two for the Avenue have been obtained (Bayliss, this volume) with the result that certain events can be placed in a sequence on the basis of these dates: *viz.*

| | | |
|---|---|---|
| Sarsen Circle | (sub-phase 3ii) | 2850–2480 cal BC |
| Entrance Stone-hole E | (3a) | 2480–2200 cal BC |
| Burial in the ditch | (3a) | 2400–2140 cal BC |
| Sarsen Trilithons | (3ii) | 2440–2100 cal BC |
| 'bluestone' Circle | (3v) | 2280–2030 cal BC |
| 'bluestone' Horseshoe | (3v) | 2270–1930 cal BC |
| Z Holes | (3vi) | 2030–1750 cal BC |
| Y Holes | (3vi) | 1640–1520 cal BC |

The dates from the Avenue are not precise but confirm that it was constructed during Phase 3.

Nevertheless, practicality would suggest variations to this sequence: for example, that the Sarsen Trilithons were erected at least before the full circuit of the Sarsen Circle was completed.

The duration of Phase 3 appears to have been long, and while Stonehenge may represent continuity of site use despite its modification, contemporary material culture and monumentality changed considerably. The early structures of Phase 3 may have been contemporary with Woodhenge and the end of the Neolithic traditions it represented, but Grooved Ware was replaced by Beakers and round barrows became the dominant funerary

monument. Metalwork was introduced and joined grave goods in some of Britain's most
fancy Early Bronze Age barrow cemeteries.

The results of the Stonehenge Environs Project suggest areas of secular activity to
the west (on Stonehenge Down, near Fargo Plantation and near Winterbourne Stoke
Crossroads), while a discerning review of grave goods from the round barrows which
crowd both near and far horizons demonstrates a gradual encroachment of ritual activity
on the monument (Fig. 9). For example, the Beaker burials towards the western end of
the Cursus Barrows are not as obvious as the mainly Wessex Culture burials of the more
prominent, eastern end, and on Normanton Down, the prominent, skylined cemetery is
also mainly Wessex Culture, with the Beaker barrow, Wilsford G1 not noticeably sited
(Cleal *et al.* 1995, 490).

Wherever buried soils have been examined beneath Early Bronze Age monuments in
the vicinity, they invariably attest short grazed, well-established grassland (Allen, this

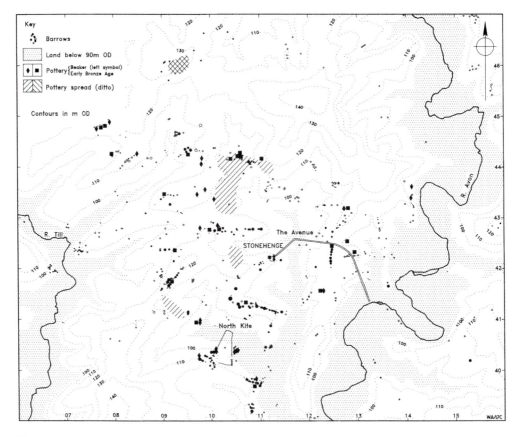

**Figure 9.** Early Bronze Age sites in the Stonehenge area (after Cleal *et al.* 1995, fig. 78).

volume). However, the wider archaeological record implies that arable farming and the production of grain must have been practised, presumably in unenclosed fields, within the vicinity, albeit that this has not been located. Formalised field systems may not yet have been established, but enclosure had commenced as the Wilsford North Kite shows.

The final structural activity at Stonehenge appears to have been the digging of the Y and Z Holes. Thereafter, the monument was undoubtedly visited, but there is little evidence that it played an important role. During the Middle Bronze Age, settlements were established to the west (Fargo Wood) and formalised field systems laid out, covering earlier monuments (the Cursus) and incorporating others (Cursus Barrows) (Fig. 10). The outlook from Stonehenge was irrevocably altered, so that secular activity now fell within the gaze of the sporadic visitors to Stonehenge, although doubtless the monument itself continued to be held in some esteem guaranteeing its survival to the present day (Fig. 11).

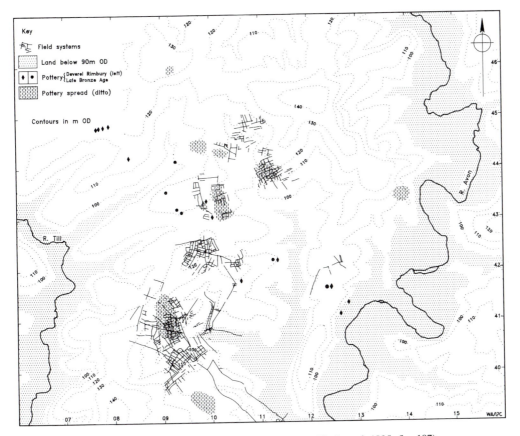

**Figure 10.** Later Bronze Age sites in the Stonehenge area (after Cleal *et al.* 1995, fig. 187).

**Figure 11.** General view of Stonehenge in 1994 from the east (Photo: E.A. Wakefield).

# Retrospect

The outline of the structural history of Stonehenge and its contemporary landscapes given above results from an analysis of the available records from all twentieth-century excavations at the site, a new suite of reliable radiocarbon dates and the results of both excavations and fieldwork in the surrounding area. Our understanding of the subtleties of the complex sequences of prehistoric events within the World Heritage Site continues to develop as each new piece of evidence becomes available. It is, therefore, not surprising that our perception of the evolution of Stonehenge and its setting is somewhat different now than even a decade ago.

The principal differences between the newly-published phasing of the constructional sequence at Stonehenge and that proposed by Atkinson (1979) are:

- the conclusion that (in Phase 1) the Aubrey Holes probably held timber posts

- the recognition that in places the deliberate backfilling of the enclosure ditch occurred very early in the sequence, soon after the primary fill had formed
- a greater emphasis on the importance of the timber structures especially within the centre of the monuments (Phase 2)
- the partial backfilling and secondary fill of the ditch (during Phase 2) precedes the introduction of the 'bluestones' (Phase 3), the chips previously attributed to this fill being recognised as inclusions in an intrusive Beaker-style burial
- the demonstration that the Avenue belongs in its entirety with Phase 3, following the introduction of 'bluestones' and that its construction is largely unrelated to earlier episodes of backfilling at the entrance
- the recognition of three orthostats within the entrance during Phase 3. (Not, as Atkinson suggested, two stones in Phase 1)
- the identification of 'bluestone' settings on the west side of the central area (Phase 3iii) pre-dating the later central 'bluestone' setting
- the rejection of an intermediary 'bluestone' oval (Atkinson's IIIb) which was removed and replaced on the same line by the existing horseshoe (Phase IIIc). Instead, suggesting the interpretation of these stone-holes as part of a central 'bluestone' oval (Phase 3iv) and the subsequent removal of the four widely spaced stones in the north-east to leave a horseshoe (Phase 3v)
- the demonstration that a number of sarsen stones were decorated after they had been erected
- the Y and Z Holes are unrelated to the intermediary 'bluestone' oval (IIIb) and are in places the final, uncompleted modification.

The picture (Fig. 12) is not static, however, and new evidence continues to be gleaned whenever the opportunity presents itself; for example, from the evaluation of potential roadlines or construction sites. Doubtless as investigations continue in pursuit of the research aim of fully understanding human activity within this restricted but significant part of Britain, the complexion of the picture will gradually change.

*Acknowledgements*

This short paper is only a summary and cannot accurately reflect the strenuous and dedicated work undertaken by a team of researchers at Wessex Archaeology. The publication of the major report in 1995 was achieved under the project management of Dr Julie Gardiner, the monitoring of Sue Davies, and the writing skills of Dr Ros Cleal, Karen Walker, Rebecca Montague, Dr Michael Allen, as well as Julie Gardiner herself, supported by Linda Coleman, Elaine Wakefield, Phil Harding, and Jackie McKinley, amongst others. Wessex Archaeology's work could not have been completed without the full financial support of English Heritage and other major contributions, primarily through the Ancient Monuments Laboratory. Every possible assistance was offered by Salisbury and South Wiltshire Museum as well as other holders of archival material. My deepest gratitude

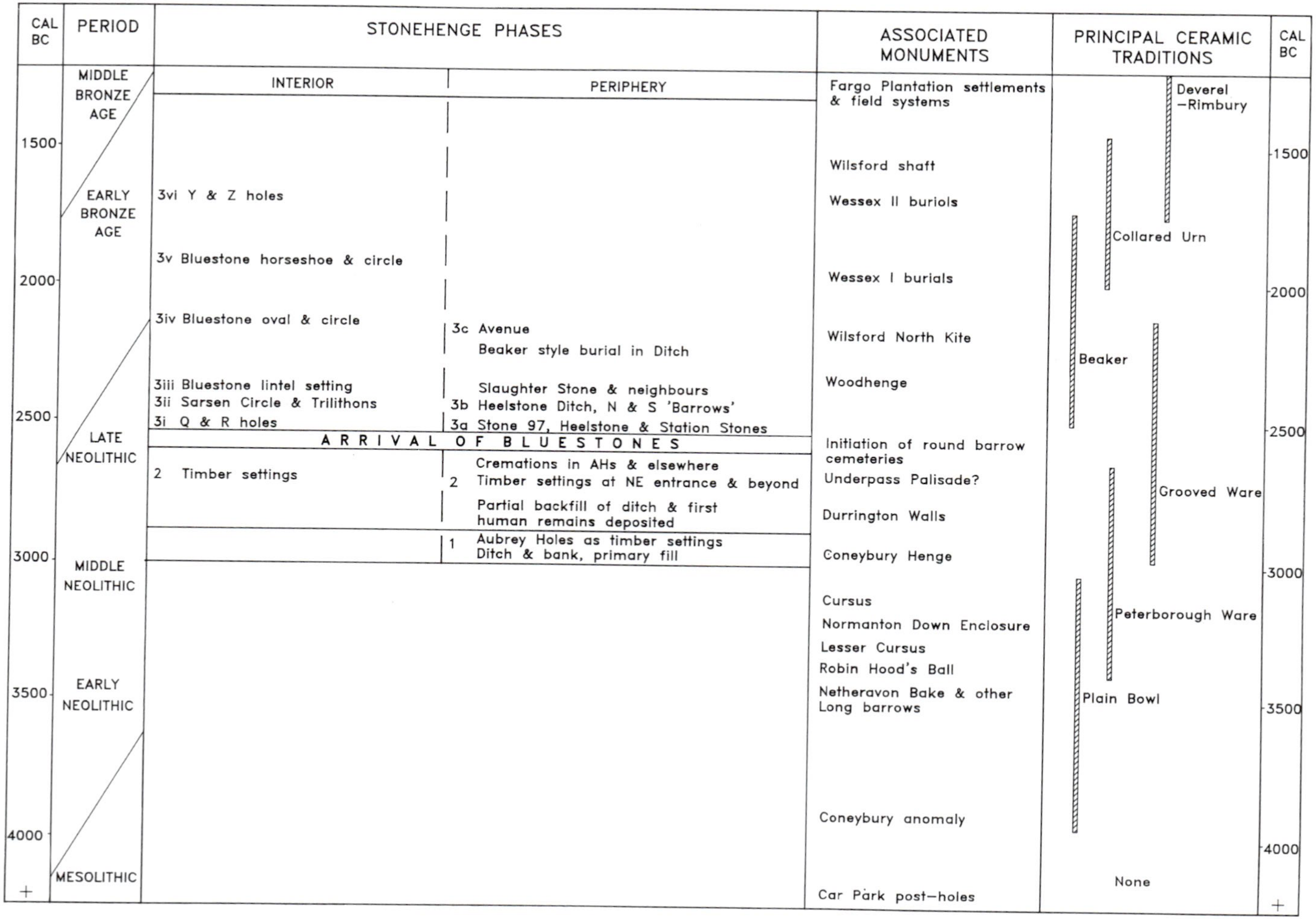

*Andrew J. Lawson*

| CAL BC | PERIOD | STONEHENGE PHASES — INTERIOR | STONEHENGE PHASES — PERIPHERY | ASSOCIATED MONUMENTS | PRINCIPAL CERAMIC TRADITIONS | CAL BC |
|---|---|---|---|---|---|---|
| | MIDDLE BRONZE AGE | | | Fargo Plantation settlements & field systems | Deverel–Rimbury | 1500 |
| 1500 | EARLY BRONZE AGE | 3vi Y & Z holes | | Wilsford shaft | Collared Urn | |
| | | 3v Bluestone horseshoe & circle | | Wessex II burials | | |
| 2000 | | 3iv Bluestone oval & circle | 3c Avenue; Beaker style burial in Ditch | Wessex I burials | Beaker | 2000 |
| | | 3iii Bluestone lintel setting | Slaughter Stone & neighbours, N & S 'Barrows' | Wilsford North Kite | | |
| | | 3ii Sarsen Circle & Trilithons | 3b Heelstone Ditch, N & S 'Barrows' | Woodhenge | | |
| | | 3i Q & R holes | 3a Stone 97, Heelstone & Station Stones | | | 2500 |
| 2500 | LATE NEOLITHIC | ARRIVAL OF BLUESTONES | | Initiation of round barrow cemeteries | Grooved Ware | |
| | | 2 Timber settings | Cremations in AHs & elsewhere; 2 Timber settings at NE entrance & beyond | Underpass Palisade? | | |
| | | | Partial backfill of ditch & first human remains deposited | Durrington Walls | | |
| | | | 1 Aubrey Holes as timber settings; Ditch & bank, primary fill | Coneybury Henge | | 3000 |
| 3000 | MIDDLE NEOLITHIC | | | Cursus | Peterborough Ware | |
| | | | | Normanton Down Enclosure | | |
| | | | | Lesser Cursus | | |
| | | | | Robin Hood's Ball | | 3500 |
| 3500 | EARLY NEOLITHIC | | | Netheravon Bake & other Long barrows | Plain Bowl | |
| | | | | Coneybury anomaly | | |
| 4000 | MESOLITHIC | | | Car Park post-holes | None | 4000 |

**Figure 12.** Correlation of phases of structural activity at the periphery and in the interior of Stonehenge with the generalised date of associated monuments in the landscape and the principal ceramic traditions represented in the archaeological record.

goes to all those involved in the project, not least Professor Geoffrey Wainwright, who made sure it all happened.

Though his health was failing, the late Professor Richard Atkinson never lost interest in Stonehenge. I am grateful to him for sharing some of his thoughts on the subject. Similarly, the late Professor Stuart Piggott's memory of his involvement with Stonehenge has been of the greatest interest.

# References

ATKINSON, R.J.C. 1956: *Stonehenge* (London) (revised ed. 1979, Harmondsworth).

CHIPPINDALE, C. 1983: *Stonehenge Complete* (London).

CLEAL, R.M.J., WALKER, K.E. and MONTAGUE, R. 1995: *Stonehenge in its Landscape: Twentieth Century Excavations* (London, Engl. Heritage Archaeol. Rep. 10).

EVANS, J.G. 1984: Stonehenge – the environment in the late Neolithic and Early Bronze Age and a Beaker-Age burial. *Wiltshire Archaeol. Natur. Hist. Mag.* 78, 7–30.

GIBSON, A. 1994: Excavations at the Sarn-y-bryn-caled cursus complex, Welshpool, and the timber circles of Great Britain and Ireland. *Proc. Prehist. Soc.* 60, 143–223.

LONG, W. 1876: Stonehenge and its barrows. *Wiltshire Archaeol. Natur. Hist. Soc. Mag.* 16, 1–244.

RICHARDS, J. 1990: *The Stonehenge Environs Project* (London, Hist. Build. Monuments Comm. Archaeol. Rep. 16).

SHARPLES, N. 1991: *Maiden Castle: excavations and field survey 1985–6* (London, Hist. Build. Monuments Comm. Archaeol. Rep. 19).

SMITH, R.J.C., HEALY, F., ALLEN, M.J., MORRIS, E.L., BARNES, I. and WOODWARD, P.J. 1997: *Excavations Along the Route of the Dorchester By-Pass, Dorchester, 1986–8* (Salisbury, Wessex Archaeol. Rep. 11).

THOMAS, N. 1964: The Neolithic causewayed camp at Robin Hood's Ball, Shrewton. *Wiltshire Archaeol. Nat. Hist. Soc. Mag.* 59, 127.

THORPE, R.S., WILLIAMS-THORPE, O., JENKINS, D.Q. and WATSON, J.S. 1991: The Geological sources and transport of the 'bluestones' of Stonehenge, Wiltshire, U.K. *Proc. Prehist. Soc.* 57(2), 103–58.

WHITTLE, A. 1990: A pre-enclosure burial at Windmill Hill, Wiltshire. *Oxford J. Archaeol.* 9, No. 1, 25–8.

WHITTLE, A. 1991: A Late Neolithic complex at West Kennet, Wiltshire, England. *Antiquity* 65, 256–62.

WHITTLE, A. 1993: The Neolithic of the Avebury area: sequence, environment, settlement and monuments. *Oxford J. Archaeol.* 12, No. 1, 29–53.

WHITTLE, A., ATKINSON, R.J.C., CHAMBERS, R. and THOMAS, N. 1992: Excavations in the Neolithic and Bronze Age complex at Dorchester-on-Thames, Oxfordshire, 1947–52 and 1981. *Proc. Prehist. Soc.* 60, 143–223.

WOODWARD, P.J. 1991: *The South Dorset Ridgeway: survey and excavations 1977–84* (Dorchester, Dorset Natur. Hist. Archaeol. Soc. Monogr. 8).

WYMER, J.J. (ed.) 1977: *Gazetteer of Mesolithic sites in England and Wales* (London, CBA Res. Rep. 20).

*Proceedings of the British Academy*, **92**, 39–59

# Dating Stonehenge

## A. BAYLISS, C. BRONK RAMSEY, & F.G. McCORMAC

## Introduction

AS PART OF THE RECENT PROJECT to complete the analysis of the twentieth century excavations at Stonehenge (Cleal *et al*. 1995), a series of 46 new radiocarbon determinations was commissioned. The 16 results which had been obtained on material from the monument before 1994 were critically reassessed on the same basis as the new results. Full details of this programme are published elsewhere (Allen and Bayliss 1995; http://www.eng-h.gov.uk/stoneh). The results from two samples measured subsequently, with the consequent slight modifications to the interpretative model, will appear shortly (Bronk Ramsey and Bayliss forthcoming).

This paper attempts to take a wider view and addresses some of the scientific and archaeological problems which have been raised by the Stonehenge dating programme.

## The concept

In 1763 a letter was sent to the Royal Society by the Revd. Thomas Bayes (Bayes 1763) introducing a concept which is fundamental to how we have approached the problem of dating Stonehenge over two centuries later. His ideas are encapsulated in Bayes' theorem (Fig. 1) which provides a coherent and logical framework for revising current beliefs in the light of new information (Buck *et al*. 1991).

Prior beliefs x Standardized likelihood = Posterior beliefs

$$P(\text{parameters}) \times \frac{P(\text{data}|\text{parameters})}{P(\text{data})} = P(\text{parameters}|\text{data})$$

**Figure 1.** Bayes' Theorem.

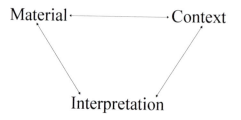

**Figure 2.** The relationships between data and interpretation.

The application of these mathematical techniques in association with Gibbs sampling to the dating of Stonehenge allows the radiocarbon determinations to be interpreted together with the stratigraphic and contextual evidence (Gelfand and Smith 1990; Bronk Ramsey 1995; http://www.rlaha.ox.ac.uk/). This enables us to formalise the links between our archaeological interpretations of the data and the data themselves (Fig. 2), to explore the effects of different interpretations, and so (hopefully) to produce more realistic estimates of the chronological parameters which are of interest to us.

## The mathematical methods employed

The Bayesian analysis described here was performed using the program OxCal (Bronk Ramsey 1995) with a chronological model devised for this site (described below and more fully in Cleal *et al.* 1995 and Bronk Ramsey and Bayliss forthcoming). The exact mathematical methods employed are inevitably fairly complicated but the essential aspects of the method can be explained in terms of a number of simple stages.

The underlying assumption made is that without any of the archaeological information the events under investigation are equally likely to have occurred at any point in time (mathematically this can be expressed as a flat probability distribution extending over all time). Each piece of information at our disposal is then used in turn to modify this 'prior belief' according to Bayes' theorem. With material which has been radiocarbon dated the first stage in this process is to compare the measurement made to those on known age tree rings. This comparison is usually referred to as radiocarbon calibration and generates a new probability distribution.

Radiocarbon and other scientific dating methods rarely give the only information available on the chronology of a site. The Bayesian method allows other information to be treated in a similar way to modify further the probability distribution. We could include very broad-ranging assumptions, such as the site being pre-Roman or post-glacial, but these would not alter the distributions and so there is little point. At Stonehenge, as at many other sites, the most useful information concerns the relative ages of the various phases of the site—information which comes largely from stratigraphic relationships and the archaeological interpretation of these. Most relationships of this sort can be expressed in terms of one object being older than another (or one event occurring before another), but are more elegantly described as phases and sequences. Sometimes we can make more specific assumptions such as events within a phase being uniformly distributed throughout the phase.

It is mathematically possible to include all of this information analytically to produce modified probability distributions, but for anything but the most trivial examples this is impractical from a computational point of view. The program OxCal uses instead a method called Gibbs' Sampling (Buck *et al.* 1991). In this method a very large number of possible scenarios are randomly generated taking into account both the probability distributions from the radiocarbon evidence and the constraints imposed by the chronological relationships. These scenarios are then used to build up new probability distributions which take all of the information into account.

## Phases 1 and 2

The first part of the monument to be constructed was the ditch and bank, with counter-scarp bank (Fig. 3). The ditch gradually silted up, although there was a period of stabilisation during which an organic 'dark' layer formed on top of the primary silt. During the period of secondary silting, some features were cut into the ditch and there were some episodes of backfilling.

Only the ditch sequence provided material which could be dated in the recent campaign. The other structural elements from phases 1 and 2—the Aubrey Holes, the timber settings at the centre of the monument, the north-eastern entrance, and running towards the southern entrance, and the cremation cemetery—remain entirely undated except for a single measurement from Aubrey Hole 32 (C-602; 3798±275BP; 3020–1520 cal BC), which was measured by W.F. Libby in the early 1950s.

*The model*

Altogether there are 24 radiocarbon determinations from phases 1 and 2 which we consider reliable. Twenty-three of these are from the ditch sequence (see Table 1). From the stratigraphic sequence identified during excavation, some of these results can be placed in a relative order (Fig. 4).

When considering the stratigraphic constraints to be included in the model it is essential to consider the relationship between the samples dated and the archaeological parameters which are of interest. For example, in Phase 1 at Stonehenge we are very interested in the date of excavation of the main ditch. However we have actually dated a number of pieces of bone and antler from that ditch. The relationship between the date of the samples and the date of the archaeological event (the ditch digging) is both fundamental and interpretative.

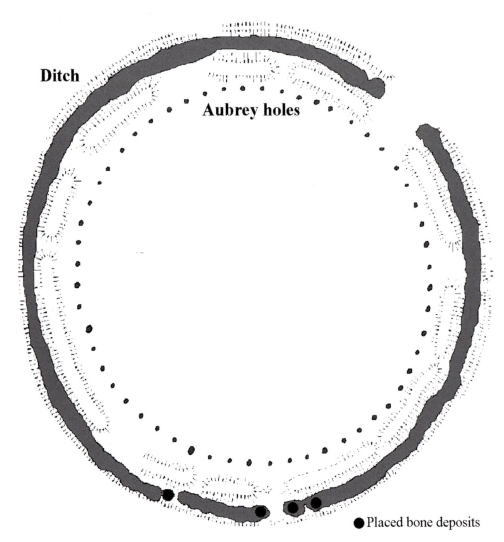

**Figure 3.** Plan of phase 1 at Stonehenge.

*Taphonomy (functionality)*

At the base of the ditch, beneath the primary silting, lay well over 100 antlers, many of which had been converted for use as picks or rakes and showed obvious signs of wear (Cleal *et al.* 1995, 414–26). The discovery of a lump of chalk with the tip of an antler tine embedded within it in Stone-hole 9, supports this functional interpretation (Cleal *et al.* 1994, 426; fig. 98). We interpret these antler tools as those which were used to dig the ditch and were placed on its base almost as soon as it was dug, since primary silt would have started to accumulate almost immediately (Bell *et al.* 1996). We postulate a functional relationship between the material to be dated (the antlers) and its context (the ditch cut).

*Combining the radiocarbon results*

The question then arises as to whether we can treat the date of these antlers as the date of the digging of the ditch, and so be justified in taking a weighted mean of the determinations (as replicate measurements on the same statistical population).

If we assume that all the antler tools are of exactly the same date, we can calculate a weighted mean of the measurements and use a $\chi^2$ test to determine whether all the results are statistically consistent (Ward and Wilson 1978). If all nine determinations are taken together, they are not statistically significantly different at 95% confidence (4375±6BP; T'=15.0; T' for 5%=15.5; ν=8); although the seven high-precision measurements are significantly different at 95% confidence (4374±7BP; T'=14.6; T' for 5%=12.6; ν=6).

However we are not absolutely certain that all the antlers are of the same date; although they must have all been deposited at the same time because of the lack of primary silt beneath them, it is possible that antlers from several different growing seasons are represented. Consequently it is more appropriate to consider the spread of the radiocarbon measurements (Lyons 1991, 31 ff.). In this case the error on the weighted mean of all nine determinations becomes ±10BP, and that on the weighted mean of the seven high-precision measurements ±13BP. These errors, which may be regarded as an experimental measurement of how spread out the results are, are significantly larger than those calculated above, which are the theoretical errors that we expect on the basis of the accuracies of each measurement. This fact suggests that the results are not as consistent as would be expected if the samples were true replicates.

These figures suggest that the results from the antler tools cannot be considered to be from the same statistical population. Alternative explanations may be advanced for this.

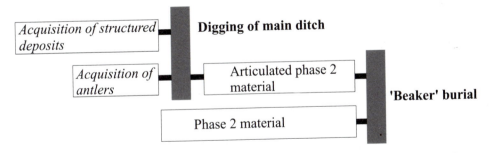

**Figure 4.** Summary of the chronological sequence of the principal phases and events in phases 1 and 2. The solid blocks represent events, the open blocks phases, and the horizontal lines stratigraphic relationships.

**Table 1.** Summary of reliable radiocarbon dates from Stonehenge

| Context | Material | Laboratory Reference | Radiocarbon Age (BP) | Calibrated date range (95% confidence) |
|---|---|---|---|---|
| *Mesolithic* | | | | |
| Post-pit WA9580 | *Pinus* charcoal | OxA-4919 | 8520±80 | 7700–7420 cal BC |
| Post-pit WA9580 | *Pinus* charcoal | OxA-4920 | 8400±100 | 7580–7090 cal BC |
| Post-pit WA9580 | *Pinus* charcoal | GU-5109 | 8880±120 | 8090–7580 cal BC |
| Post-pit A | *Pinus* charcoal | HAR-455 | 9130±180 | 8820–7730 cal BC |
| Post-pit B | *Pinus* charcoal | HAR-456 | 8090±140 | 7480–6590 cal BC |
| *Pre-phase 1* | | | | |
| Sarsen Circle | Animal bone | OxA-4902 | 5350±80 | 4360–3990 cal BC |
| *Phase 1* | | | | |
| Ditch | Antler | UB-3787 | 4375±19 | 3085–2920 cal BC |
| Ditch | Antler | UB-3788 | 4381±18 | 3095–2920 cal BC |
| Ditch | Antler | UB-3789 | 4330±18 | 3030–2910 cal BC |
| Ditch | Antler | UB-3790 | 4367±18 | 3040–2915 cal BC |
| Ditch | Antler | UB-3792 | 4365±18 | 3040–2915 cal BC |
| Ditch | Antler | UB-3793 | 4393±18 | 3095–2920 cal BC |
| Ditch | Antler | UB-3794 | 4432±22 | 3305–2925 cal BC |
| Ditch | Antler | BM-1583 | 4410±60 | 3340–2910 cal BC |
| Ditch | Antler | BM-1617 | 4390±60 | 3330–2910 cal BC |
| Ditch | Animal bone | OxA-4833 | 4550±60 | 3500–3040 cal BC |
| Ditch | Animal bone | OxA-4834 | 4460±45 | 3350–2920 cal BC |
| Ditch | Animal bone | OxA-4835 | 4455±40 | 3340–2920 cal BC |
| Ditch | Animal bone | OxA-4842 | 4520±100 | 3510–2920 cal BC |
| *Phase 1/2* | | | | |
| Aubrey Hole 32 | Charcoal | C-602 | 3798±275 | 3020–1520 cal BC |
| *Phase 2* | | | | |
| Ditch | Animal bone | OxA-4841 | 4295±60 | 3040–2700 cal BC |
| Ditch | Animal bone | OxA-4843 | 4315±60 | 3100–2700 cal BC |
| Ditch | Animal bone | OxA-4880 | 3875±55 | 2560–2140 cal BC |
| Ditch | Animal bone | OxA-4881 | 4300±60 | 3080–2700 cal BC |
| Ditch | Animal bone | OxA-4882 | 4270±65 | 3040–2660 cal BC |
| Ditch | Bone chisel | OxA-4883 | 4300±70 | 3100–2700 cal BC |
| Ditch | Antler | OxA-4904 | 4365±55 | 3300–2900 cal BC |

| | Material | Lab code | BP | cal BC |
|---|---|---|---|---|
| Ditch | Antler | UB-3791 | 4397±18 | 3095–2920 cal BC |
| Ditch | Animal bone (articulated) | OxA-5981 | 4220±35 | 2920–2660 cal BC |
| Ditch | Animal bone (articulated) | OxA-5982 | 4405±30 | 3300–2920 cal BC |
| *Phase 3* | | | | |
| Sarsen Circle | Antler | UB-3821 | 4023±21 | 2655–2485 cal BC |
| Sarsen Trilithon | Antler | OxA-4839 | 3860±40 | 2470–2200 cal BC |
| Sarsen Trilithon | Antler | OxA-4840 | 3985±45 | 2850–2400 cal BC |
| Sarsen Trilithon | Antler | BM-46 | 3670±150 | 2480–1680 cal BC |
| Bluestone Circle | Animal bone | OxA-4878 | 3740±40 | 2290–2030 cal BC |
| Bluestone Circle | Antler | OxA-4900 | 3865±50 | 2480–2140 cal BC |
| Bluestone Horseshoe | Antler | OxA-4877 | 3695±55 | 2280–1940 cal BC |
| Stone-hole E | Antler | OxA-4837 | 3995±60 | 2860–2350 cal BC |
| Stone-hole E | Antler | OxA-4838 | 3885±40 | 2490–2200 cal BC |
| Z Hole 29 | Antler | OxA-4836 | 3540±45 | 2030–1740 cal BC |
| Y Hole 30 | Antler | UB-3822 | 3341±22 | 1735–1530 cal BC |
| Y Hole 30 | Antler | UB-3823 | 3300±19 | 1675–1520 cal BC |
| Y Hole 30 | Antler | UB-3824 | 3449±24 | 1880–1690 cal BC |
| 'Beaker' burial | Human bone | BM-1582 | | |
| 'Beaker' burial | Human bone | OxA-4886 | | |
| 'Beaker' burial | Human bone | OxA-5044 | 3817±27* | 2460–2140 cal BC |
| 'Beaker' burial | Human bone | OxA-5045 | | |
| 'Beaker' burial | Human bone | OxA-5046 | | |
| *Avenue* | | | | |
| Stonehenge terminal | Antler | OxA-4884 | 3935±50 | 2580–2300 cal BC |
| Stonehenge terminal | Antler | BM-1164 | 3678±68 | 2290–1890 cal BC |
| Nr Avon terminal | Animal bone | OxA-4905 | 3865±40 | 2470–2200 cal BC |
| N side of A344 | Antler | HAR-2013 | 3720±70 | 2350–1930 cal BC |
| *Post-monument* | | | | |
| Palisade Ditch | Human bone | UB-3820 | 2468±27 | 775–410 cal BC |
| Sarsen Circle | Bone point | OxA-4885 | 2840±60 | 1260–840 cal BC |

* weighted mean of 3960±60BP, 3785±70BP, 3825±60 BP, 3775±55 BP, and 3715±70 BP.

**1**  the antlers are of different dates;

**2**  the concentration of radiocarbon in the samples is not the same as the concentration of radiocarbon in the atmosphere when the deer died (e.g. following exchange in the burial environment);

**3**  the errors on the radiocarbon measurements have been estimated incorrectly.

The first of these options appears to be the most likely, although, if it is true, it means that a very subtle difference in calendar date has been detected using radiocarbon. The period of collection of the antlers must be quite short because antler tools can only be used for a limited time to dig a ditch in chalk before they wear out, and because antler becomes brittle if curated for many years before use (Cleal *et al.* 1995, 414–25).

The second explanation is also possible. Bone chemistry and diagenesis are not fully understood (e.g. Gillespie 1989; Hedges and Millard 1995; Sobel and Berger 1995). However the samples involved are extremely large—approximately 1000 g of antler producing 15 g of benzene—so the effect of such problems should not be significant, especially as collagen preservation was relatively good. In addition the burial environment of all the material was very similar, and so, even if a difference were to be detectable, we would expect this option to affect the accuracy, rather than the consistency, of the results.

The final option is not considered very likely because of the rigorous and extensive quality assurance programmes routinely undertaken by the laboratories concerned (Otlet *et al.* 1980; International Study Group 1982; Scott *et al.* 1990; Rozanski *et al.* 1992; Scott *et al.* forthcoming), and the specific quality assurance measurements undertaken concurrent with the Stonehenge programme itself (Allen and Bayliss 1995, 516–18; Bronk Ramsey and Bayliss forthcoming, table 2). In particular it should be noted that the high-precision results are inconsistent as replicate measurements on the same population. This is important because the errors on these measurements are estimates of *total* error (including indeterminate error), unlike the previous measurements from the British Museum laboratory where the errors were calculated on the basis of the counting statistics alone (Allen and Bayliss 1995, 519). An error multiplier (Stuiver 1982), which has been determined empirically from the reproducibility of dates on replicate samples of cellulose within the laboratory, is used to account for this indeterminate error. This estimate is normally distributed, although we have no evidence whether the indeterminate error of a particular sample is so distributed. However this concern is, by its very nature, not measurable.

For the reasons given above we have not taken a weighted mean of the measurements from the antlers from the base of the ditch at Stonehenge. In addition we have no positive evidence that they must all have been of exactly the same date. Instead we have chosen to regard the end of the phase of acquisition of all the material which was deposited in the ditch below the primary silt as the most realistic estimate of the date of the ditch digging. This approach is conservative, and provides an estimate for the date of digging the ditch of *3015–2935 cal BC (95% confidence)* (Fig. 5). Because this range is based

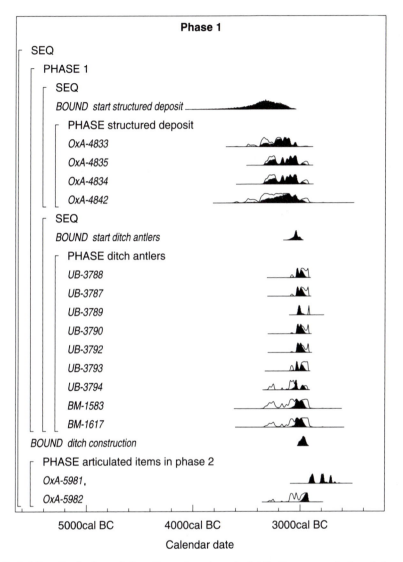

**Figure 5.** Probability distributions of dates from phase 1: each distribution represents the relative probability that an event occurs at some particular time. For each of the radiocarbon dates two distributions have been plotted, one in outline which is the result of simple radiocarbon calibration and a solid one which is based on the chronological model used; the 'event' associated with, for example, the radiocarbon date UB-3788 is the growth of the antler concerned. The other distributions correspond to aspects of the model: we have assumed that the material in the structured deposit started to be accumulated at some point defined as 'start structured deposit' and must have finished by the point at which the ditch was actually dug ('ditch construction'); the acquisition of the antlers also forms a similar sub-phase starting at 'start ditch antlers'; we also use the additional information that the articulated material from phase 2 must post-date the 'ditch construction' event. The large square brackets down the left hand side along with the OxCal keywords define the overall model exactly.

not only on the radiocarbon measurements but also on our chronological model which has changed with new radiocarbon determinations on articulated material found within the ditch fill (see Fig. 5 and Bronk Ramsey and Bayliss forthcoming), it is slightly different from that published in Cleal *et al.* 1995.

*Precision, calibration, and accuracy*

The precision of this estimate, with a range which covers only 80 years at 95% confidence, justifies the major effort which has been made towards quality assurance in the project to demonstrate accuracy of radiocarbon measurements against the relevant calibration data (Pearson *et al.* 1986; McCormac *et al.* 1995). The statistical consistency of the radiocarbon results with each other, and with the stratigraphic sequence, also supports their accuracy. Because the mathematical model of the site's dating includes all the radiocarbon results and archaeological evidence together, the statistical scatter of particular radiocarbon measurements (both from Stonehenge and from the calibration dataset) is counterbalanced by the overall picture, producing a stable and believable estimate of the site's chronology.

*Taphonomy (curation)*

In addition to the antler tools discussed above, there are also a number of large bones which were placed on the base of the ditch beneath the primary fill (Cleal *et al.* 1995, 422–5). These appear to be concentrated in the terminals of the ditch segments (Fig. 3).

A point of note emerged from the analysis of the measurements from these bones and from the antler tools, both of which were found on the base of the ditch. The placed bone deposits are significantly earlier than the digging of the ditch, although obviously they must have been deposited after it was dug. The mathematical model of the chronology of this phase is statistically significantly inconsistent if the structured deposits are constrained to be later than the ditch digging (Bronk Ramsey and Bayliss forthcoming, fig. 5). However the samples date to when the animal of which they were part died, not to their deposition, so this can be explained by the curation of material for some time before it was deposited. Analysis of the information currently available suggests that this was for between *70 and 420 years (95% confidence)*. As well as raising a significant issue in prehistoric archaeology, this emphasises the importance of functionality in the interpretation of the taphonomic relationship between sample and context.

An alternative, more prosaic, interpretation of these results would be that there was some methodological reason for the measurements on these bones being so much earlier. There are essentially two major possibilities which could explain this. Firstly is that, since the measurements on the antler tools and on the placed bone deposits were measured at different laboratories, there is a laboratory offset between the radiocarbon measurements. However the inter-laboratory comparisons (Allen and Bayliss 1995, 516–18) show that this is not the case, certainly not to the extent necessary to explain the scale of the observed difference between the measurements on the placed bones and those on the antler tools. Secondly, it is possible that in either case the pretreatment of the samples may have been in some way insufficient. The close clustering of the large number results on the antler tools suggests that their dating is secure, which leaves us to question the validity of the bone dates.

Given that the measurements give an age which is older than the context, any error would have to be the result of radiocarbon-depleted contamination of some sort. Such an effect could, for example, be due to the incomplete removal of preservatives. There are, however, three internal checks which can be used to test for such an occurrence. First is collagen preservation, since poorly preserved collagen is much more difficult to purify reliably—of the dates in question (OxA-4833, OxA-4835, OxA-4834 and OxA-4842) three had very good collagen preservation (at about 20% of the level found in modern bone) while one (OxA-4842) was a low collagen bone with levels some twenty times lower. Secondly we can use the CN ratio to give us some measure of the purity of the collagen produced—the same three measurements give very similar values of 3.00–3.06 (atomic ratio) which is exactly what one would expect, while the poorly preserved bone (OxA-4842) gave a value of 3.47 indicating that the collagen was not so pure. Finally, the $\delta^{13}$C measurements on the stable carbon isotopes are another indication both of environment and of sample purity—again the three well preserved bones give a consistent set of results in the range −22.4 to −23.1, suggesting a semi-woodland environment, while the poorly preserved bone gives an anomalous value of −23.8. In conclusion we can see that any pretreatment problems would be most likely to show up in sample OxA-4842, although this sample has been given a much larger uncertainty than the others because of this. Nevertheless the radiocarbon measurement still lies within the other three, providing us with an unintentional internal quality control check. It should also be noted that OxA-4842 is not the oldest of the placed bone deposits, OxA-4833, about which there can be little doubt, may well be even older. Although it is never possible to rule out the effect of some methodological offset entirely, this information taken as a whole does imply that the dating is secure and that the archaeological interpretation of the age difference is most likely to be correct.

*Residuality and multiple sampling*

To return to the main ditch, after the primary silt had accumulated, there seems to have been a period when a soil partially developed (Evans 1984, 10). Hawley noted the recurrent appearance of 'wood ash' in this layer, suggesting that burning was a feature of the activity in the ditch at this time. Unfortunately none of this material survives in the archive, so we were unable to date it.

Material from the secondary silts which accumulated above it does survive however. The sampling strategy for these silts was to submit a relatively large number of samples from throughout the profile. Bone samples were chosen in preference to antler because there is relatively little bone known from the primary silts (37 fragments). Therefore the bone fragments found higher up the profile are less likely to be residual from phase 1 than antler samples from the same position, since there are hundreds of antler fragments from the base of the ditch. Items which were uneroded and reasonably large were also selected to minimise the possibility of residuality. Unfortunately the provenance of some of the dated material was shown to be unreliable when additional archival material became available to the project team on the death of Professor Atkinson in October 1994. Four results have been excluded from the analysis for this reason (Allen and Bayliss 1995, 520–1).

The question of residuality is crucial because we know that the secondary silts must have accumulated after the ditch was dug and after the primary silting. If the material can be shown to be contemporary with the silting, then the analysis of the radiocarbon determinations can be constrained by the stratigraphic sequence. In fact if this is done, the model is statistically consistent (Bronk Ramsey and Bayliss forthcoming, fig. 8). Again we have chosen the conservative course however, and have been unwilling to make this assumption because of the lingering doubts over the contextual integrity and taphonomy of the dated material from phase 2 raised by the Atkinson archive.

*Taphonomy (articulation)*

Two further samples were submitted in October 1995, both from partially articulated skeletons within the secondary fill. One sample was from a piglet, and the other from cattle vertebrae. The crucial point is that both must have had tendons at least attached when they were buried, or they would not have been recovered together. This provides a strong argument against residuality or post-depositional disturbance. These two results have been used as an additional constraint for the estimate of the date of the ditch digging, to provide the model illustrated in Figure 5, and the estimated date for the construction of the ditch of *3015–2935 cal BC (95% confidence)*.

*Uniform distributions*

This model treats the material from the base of the ditch in two groups, the animal bone deposits and the antlers. It is assumed that each group of dated material was gathered at a fairly constant rate over the period of collection (uniform phase; cf. Buck *et al.* 1992). In practice this assumption makes little difference to the estimated dates. The date of construction of the ditch is particularly robust, because it is so well constrained by the measurements on the articulated bone from phase 2 and by multiple high-precision measurements. The estimate for the start of the accumulation of the structured bone deposits is less robust, because there are only four measurements in this phase. However using the assumption of a uniform phase allows us to overcome the problem that the natural scatter of radiocarbon results would otherwise tend to give an unrealistically early estimate for this boundary.

## Other distributions

The secondary silting of the ditch at Stonehenge is well constrained. It is preceded by the construction of the ditch which has been discussed above, and succeeded by the burial of an adult human male (Evans 1984) which cuts through the top of the secondary silting. The first dated event in these silts has been calculated using only the dates from the articulated items referred to above, which cannot be residual. The estimate of the last dated event has been calculated using all the reliable results from the secondary fills (Fig. 6). The difference between these distributions can be calculated, suggesting that the infilling of the ditch took between *460 and 740 years (95% confidence)*.

Although this seems to be a reasonable estimate for these archaeological events, there are questions which are still to be answered. It would be particularly useful to be able to estimate the dates when the silting had reached different heights in the ditch. We have not modelled the rate of infill of the ditch, since it can be demonstrated that rates calculated for equivalent chalkland ditches are not uniform (Crabtree 1990; Evans 1990). Recently

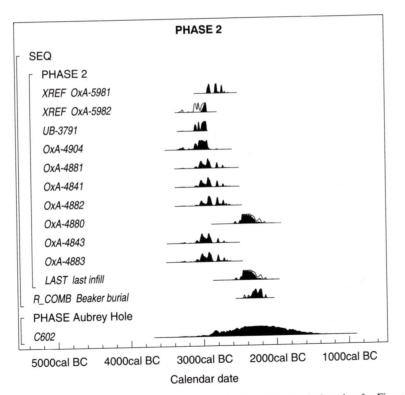

**Figure 6** Probability distributions of dates from phase 2: the format is identical to that for Figure 5. In this phase the model imposed is simply that all of the material in the infill must pre-date the 'Beaker' burial. The two items labelled 'XREF' are also constrained within the model for phase 1 (see Fig. 5). The 'Beaker' burial has the keyword 'R_COMB' because it is based on the combination of several radiocarbon determinations.

work on pollen sequences has used several other possible assumptions about the distribution of dated events (Christian *et al.* 1995), although these have yet to be applied to the silting of ditches. An approach which modelled the rate of infilling using an exponential distribution could provide much better estimates for dating of this process. This would be particularly important on the chalk, where the major source of environmental evidence is from currently undated land snail sequences through the ditches of monuments.

*Our interpretation of the chronology of phases 1 and 2*

To summarise our results so far; the main ditch at Stonehenge was cut in *3015–2935 cal BC (95% confidence)*. A number of bone deposits were placed on the bottom of the ditch immediately after construction, along with the antler tools used in the excavation. At least some of these bone deposits were already old when placed in the ditch, being between *70 and 420 years old (95% confidence)* on deposition. After a short period of between *0 and 75 years (95% confidence)* during which the primary silt and organic 'dark' layer accumulated, the secondary silt started to accumulate. This infilling took between *460 and 740 years (95% confidence)*, and was complete by the time a burial was inserted into the top of the secondary silts in *2400–2140 cal BC (95% confidence)*.

# Phase 3

In this phase the stone settings were constructed (Fig. 7). They seem to echo the timber settings of phase 2 and their pattern developed over many years, with one plan superseding the next. A complex and poorly understood sequence of erection of paired and single stones occurred within the ditched enclosure at this time and the Avenue was constructed.

*The model*

Unfortunately there was very little datable material available from the stone-holes of this phase. In total only 13 new samples could be measured, all from primary silts of stone-holes. A maximum of three items were measured from any stone setting and some settings had no suitable samples at all.

Although the centre of the monument was designed as a concentric setting of stones, allowing little stratigraphic overlap, excavation has nevertheless recovered a partial sequence. This has allowed us to place some of the results from the phase 3 settings into a relative order (Fig. 8).

*Residuality and multiple sampling*

The very small number of samples from each setting raises concerns about the reliability

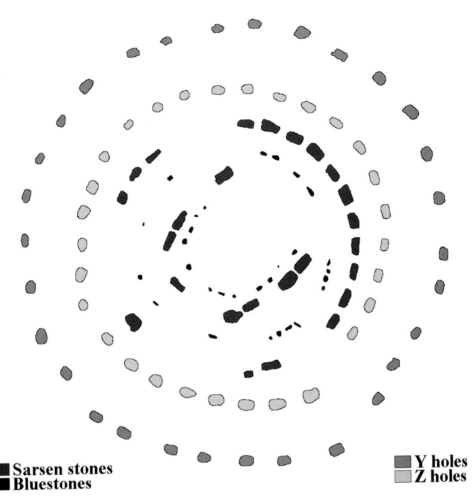

**■ Sarsen stones**
**■ Bluestones**

**■ Y holes**
**□ Z holes**

**Figure 7.** Plan of phase 3 at Stonehenge.

of our estimates. For example, we may be able to say that the results produced from the Bluestone Circle give an estimate of the last dated event of *2280–2030 cal BC (95% confidence)* (Fig. 9). However although we may be fairly confident in this estimate, it is not necessarily very reliable because it is based on only two dated items. If these happen to be residual (and we know that residual material is included in these primary silts, for example OxA-4902 (5350±80BP) from Stone-hole 27 of the Sarsen Circle), then our estimate will not be reliable.

Obviously the more dated items we have from a given setting the more reliable our estimate of the date of interest will be. Because the taphonomic relationship between the samples dated and the archaeological event which is of interest is not clear—there is no articulation or functional relationship demonstrable, then these measurements each provide

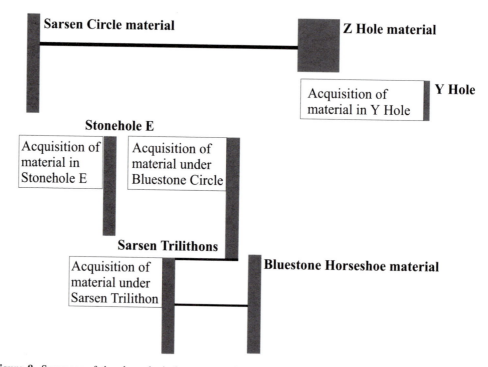

**Figure 8.** Summary of the chronological sequence of the principal phases and events in phase 3. The solid blocks represent events, the open blocks phases, and the horizontal lines stratigraphic relationships.

a *terminus post quem* for the construction of the setting. We hope that by submitting a number of samples from contexts relating to each event, the difference between the actual date of construction and the last *terminus post quem* becomes insignificant. Since this strategy is forced on us by the type of material available, the small number of items which can be dated is a significant problem.

## Reliability vs confidence

Unfortunately the reliability of our estimates cannot be measured quantitatively; it is up to our archaeological judgement to decide how far we wish to trust the reliability of the estimates given the number of items it has been possible to date. In contrast, the level of confidence quoted is an expression of our confidence in the estimate given the data currently available and the model which we have described. This will change (and has already!).

## Taphonomy (more curation)

The curation which has been demonstrated for the items placed on the base of the main ditch is also apparent later in the use of the monument. The pile of antlers which were

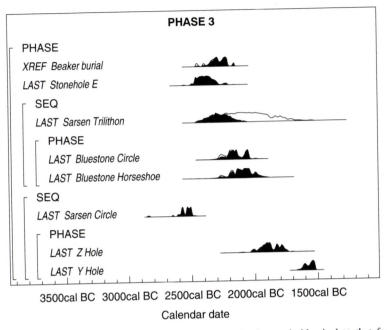

**Figure 9.** Probability distributions of dates from phase 3: the format is identical to that for Figure 5. Here we have made use of the stratigraphic information that the Sarsen Trilithon must pre-date the Bluestone settings and the Sarsen Circle must pre-date the Y and Z holes.

stacked on the base of Y Hole 30 produced radiocarbon determinations which are statistically significantly different (T'=24.1; T for 5%=6.0; v=2; Ward and Wilson 1978). Although this is based on only three measurements—the other two antlers from the base of this Y Hole have been retained in the archive to allow further analyses in the future —the difference is so great in this case that there can be no question that the phenomenon observed is real, and that the antlers grew over a period of between *90 and 255 years (82% confidence) or 260 and 330 years (13% confidence)* before deposition.

It should be noted that these antlers are very different in character from those from the base of the main ditch (Cleal *et al.* 1995, 426) and have not been modified into tools. They also appear to have been gathered and placed in a pile on the bottom of the Y Hole, as 'they were entangled and difficult to remove' (Cleal *et al.* 1995, 260). Although it is not impossible that a residual antler could have been excavated and re-interred, the difference in character between these antlers and the others recovered from the monument, along with the apparently deliberate act of placing them on the base of the pit, makes this unlikely. It seems more probable that the deposition of these antlers was a significant activity.

*LAST dated events*

Where there is more than a single dated item from a stone setting, we have taken the estimate of the last dated event from a setting as the best estimate of its construction. This is
on the principle that a context dates to the latest material within it (see above). The construction of each setting is assumed to be an event, with all the stones erected as a unitary
whole. However this method of analysis may in fact suggest that the erection date is later
than it actually was because of the inevitable statistical scatter of radiocarbon measurements. The small number of measurements available from any one setting probably coun-
teracts the problem in this case, however, and so it is unlikely to be significant. We have
not chosen to use the assumption of a uniform distribution for the dates of the items within
the stone-holes because, as for the ditch filling, this is almost certainly not the case.

*Distributions*

In the future it may be better to attempt to model the distribution of the dates of residual
material in a context, and so to provide an estimate for the end of the phase rather than
of the last dated event. Again a uniform distribution may not be the most appropriate
model, there being a much larger chance that material is residual by a few years than by
many millennia. This is another area where more research is required, although again
an exponential distribution may be a more appropriate way of modelling the process of
the accumulation of material within a context.

*Our interpretation of the chronology of phase 3*

With all of this caution in mind, we estimate that it took between *850 and 1090 years
(95% confidence)* for the stone monument at Stonehenge to reach its final form. The
earliest stone settings, the Q and R holes, remain undated as do the earlier phases of
the bluestone settings. However the Sarsen Circle was in place by *2620–2480 cal BC
(92% confidence)*, and the Sarsen Trilithons by *2440–2100 cal BC (95% confidence)*. The
remodelling of the bluestones into the circle and horseshoe occurred by *2280–2030 cal
BC (95% confidence)* and *2270–1930 cal BC (95% confidence)* respectively. The last
major modifications were completed by *1640–1520 cal BC (95% confidence)* when the
Y holes, and possibly also the Z holes, were excavated.

# Summary of issues raised by Stonehenge
# dating programme

The recent dating programme from Stonehenge has substantially enhanced our knowledge
of the chronology of the monument. It has clearly demonstrated the potential of inte-

grating archaeological and scientific information in a rigorous manner to produce precise and robust estimates of dates of archaeological interest.

The importance of the archaeological interpretation of the relationship between the items to be dated and the archaeological date which is to be estimated is crucial and cannot be overstated. At Stonehenge we have proposed very close links between samples and the events of interest, where articulated bone samples were recovered by excavation and where a functional relationship between sample and context can be determined. However residuality and the deposition of material which was already old when placed in the ground has also been demonstrated. Multiple sampling has been proposed as a method to address these problems, but this raises the question of how many items need to be dated before an estimate can be regarded as archaeologically reliable.

Although exhaustive efforts have been made to ensure that the radiocarbon measurements produced as part of the dating programme are accurate, their interpretation is still limited by problems which are not fully understood. These are areas of ongoing research, and we can do little more than recognise that they exist and attempt to err on the side of caution when interpreting the data.

Undoubtedly future research will also refine the mathematical model which has been proposed for the chronology of the site. In addition to methodological developments, such as the use of exponential distributions, future excavation may well recover more stratigraphic information and more material which can be dated. However, above all, the implementation of the ideas communicated to the Royal Society by the Revd. Thomas Bayes in the eighteenth century has allowed us to propose a model for the dating of Stonehenge which is analytical and interpretative. Other researchers may choose to take our data and reinterpret them against different hypotheses and within different conceptual frameworks, but Bayes' legacy has come to fruition.

## Note on the calibration and citation of radiocarbon dates

Dates in Table 1 are cited in accordance with Mook (1986) and calibrated using the maximum intercept method of Stuiver and Reimer (1986). The date ranges cited *in italics* in the text, and the probability distributions shown in Figs 5, 6, and 9, have been calculated as part of the mathematical analysis presented in Allen and Bayliss (1995) and Bronk Ramsey and Bayliss (forthcoming). All calibrations use data from Stuiver and Pearson (1986), Pearson and Stuiver (1986), Pearson *et al.* (1986), and Kromer and Becker (1993). Further details of the methods of citation and calibration can be found in Cleal *et al.* (1995, 6).

# References

ALLEN, M.J. and BAYLISS, A. 1995: Appendix 2: The radiocarbon dating programme. In Cleal, R.M.J., Walker, K.E. and Montague, R. 1995, 511–35.

BAYES, T.R. 1763: An essay towards solving a problem in the doctrine of chances. *Phil. Trans. Roy. Soc.* 53, 370–418.

BELL, M.G., FOWLER, P.J. and HILLSON, S. 1996: *The experimental earthwork project 1960–1992* (CBA Res. Rep. 100).

BRONK RAMSEY, C. 1995: Radiocarbon calibration and analysis of stratigraphy. *Radiocarbon* 37, 425–30.

BRONK RAMSEY, C. and BAYLISS, A. forthcoming: Dating Stonehenge. In Lockyer, K. and Mihăilescu-Bîrliba, V. (eds), Computer applications and quantitative methods in archaeology (BAR Int. Ser.).

BUCK, C.E., KENWORTHY, J.B., LITTON, C.D. and SMITH, A.F.M. 1991: Combining archaeological and radiocarbon information: a Bayesian approach to calibration. *Antiquity* 65, 808–21.

BUCK, C.E., LITTON, C.D. and SMITH, A.F.M. 1992: Calibration of radiocarbon results pertaining to related archaeological events. *J. Archaeol. Sci.* 19, 497–512.

CHRISTEN, J.A., CLYMO, R.S. and LITTON, C.D. 1995: A Bayesian approach to the use of $^{14}C$ dates in the estimation of the age of peat. *Radiocarbon* 37, 431–42.

CLEAL, R.M.J., WALKER, K.E. and MONTAGUE, R. 1995: *Stonehenge in its Landscape: Twentieth Century Excavations* (London, Engl. Heritage Archaeol. Rep. 10)..

CRABTREE, K. 1990: Experimental earthworks in the United Kingdom. In Robinson, D.E. (ed.), *Experimentation and reconstruction in environmental archaeology*, 225–35.

EVANS, J.G. 1984: Stonehenge – the environment in the late Neolithic and early Bronze Age and a Beaker-age burial. *Wiltshire Archaeol. Natur. Hist. Soc. Mag.* 78, 7–30.

EVANS, J.G. 1990: Notes on some late Neolithic and Bronze Age events in long barrow ditches in southern and eastern England. *Proc. Prehist. Soc.* 56, 111–16.

GELFAND, A.E. and SMITH, A.F.M. 1990: Sampling based approaches to calculating marginal densities. *J. Amer. Stat. Assoc.* 85, 398–409.

GILLESPIE, R. 1989: Fundamentals of bone degradation chemistry: collagen is not "the way". *Radiocarbon* 31, 239–46.

HEDGES, R.E.M. and MILLARD, A.R. 1995: Bones and groundwater: towards the modelling of diagenetic processes. *J. Arch. Sci.* 22, 155–64.

INTERNATIONAL STUDY GROUP 1982: An inter-laboratory comparison of radiocarbon measurements in tree rings. *Nature* 298, 619–23.

KROMER, B. and BECKER, B. 1993: German oak and pine $^{14}C$ calibration, 7200–9439 BC. *Radiocarbon* 33, 125–35.

LYONS, L. 1991: *A practical guide to data analysis for physical science students* (Cambridge).

McCORMAC, F.G., BAILLIE, M.G.L., PILCHER, J.R. and KALIN, R.M. 1995: Location-dependent differences in the $^{14}C$ content of wood. *Radiocarbon* 37, 395–407.

MOOK, W.G. 1986: Business meeting: Recommendations/Resolutions adopted by the Twelfth International Radiocarbon Conference. *Radiocarbon* 28, 799.

OTLET, R.L., WALKER, A.J., HEWSON, A.D. and BURLEIGH, R. 1980: $^{14}C$ interlaboratory comparison in the UK: experiment design, preparation, and preliminary results. *Radiocarbon* 22, 936–46.

PEARSON, G.W. and STUIVER, M. 1986: High-precision calibration of the radiocarbon time scale, 500–2500 BC. *Radiocarbon* 28, 839–62.

PEARSON, G.W., PILCHER, J.R., BAILLIE, M.G.L., CORBETT, D.M. and QUA, F. 1986: High-precision ¹⁴C measurement of Irish oaks to show the natural ¹⁴C variations from AD 1840–5210 BC. *Radiocarbon* 28, 911–34.

ROZANSKI, K., STICHLER, W., GONFIANTINI, R., SCOTT, E.M., BEUKENS, R.P., KROMER, B. and VAN DER PLICHT, J. 1992: The IAEA ¹⁴C intercomparison exercise 1990. *Radiocarbon* 34, 506–19.

SCOTT, E.M., HARKNESS, D.D., COOK, G.T., MILLER, B.F., BEGG, F.H. and HOLTON, L. forthcoming: The TIRI project: a status report. *Radiocarbon*.

SCOTT, E.M., LONG, A. and KRA, R.S. (eds) 1990: Proceedings of the international workshop on intercomparison of radiocarbon laboratories. *Radiocarbon* 32, 253–397.

SOBEL, H. and BERGER, R. 1995: Studies on selected proteins of bone in archaeology. *Radiocarbon* 37, 331–5.

STUIVER, M. 1982: A high-precision calibration of the AD radiocarbon time scale. *Radiocarbon* 24, 1–26.

STUIVER, M. and PEARSON, G.W. 1986: High-precision calibration of the radiocarbon time scale, AD 1950–500 BC. *Radiocarbon* 28, 805–38.

STUIVER, M. and REIMER, P.J. 1986: A computer program for radiocarbon age calculation. *Radiocarbon* 28, 1022–30.

WARD, G.K. and WILSON, S.R. 1978: Procedures for comparing and combining radiocarbon age determinations: a critique. *Archaeometry* 20, 19–31.

*Proceedings of the British Academy*, **92**, 61–72

# Mapping the Stonehenge World Heritage Site

## DAVE BATCHELOR

## Introduction

STONEHENGE AND SURROUNDING MONUMENTS are situated on the southern side of the undulating chalk plateau of Salisbury Plain (Fig. 1) about 13 km north of Salisbury and close to the small historic town of Amesbury, and the military garrison based at Larkhill. The plateau area is bounded by two river valleys running north-south, the larger of the two, the river Avon, to the east and the river Till to the west (Fig. 2). This central area is dissected by a number of relatively shallow dry river valleys, such as Stonehenge Bottom. There is extensive use of the land for arable production, although some of the area immediately surrounding The Avenue close to the stones has been returned to pasture relatively recently, with several plantations dotted throughout the landscape to provide shelter and screening. The northern part of the study area extends into the military occupied Salisbury Plain Training Area which is currently unimproved grassland. The area being studied is crossed from east to west by a trunk road, the A303, and several other major arterial roads bisect the area from north to south.

Stonehenge was inscripted by UNESCO onto the World Heritage List in November 1986, sharing the same designation, site C373, as Avebury. The Stonehenge World Heritage Site, an area in excess of 2,600 hectares, is presently defined by the river Avon in the east, the road known as the Packway to the north and in the west by the A360 and B3086 roads, and a series of field boundaries to the south. The siting of a visitor centre (currently there are some 700,000 paying visitors per year) has been a problem within this sensitive landscape.

It was the unfortunate dislocation of the focal point of this World Heritage Site, the actual monument itself, from the surrounding landscape, which was in use for 1.5 millennia, and has stood for a further 3.5 millennia, by the relatively recent modern development and the resultant intrusion of the current levels of traffic on the surrounding roads that led to recent, and well documented, debate about an alternative route for the A303.

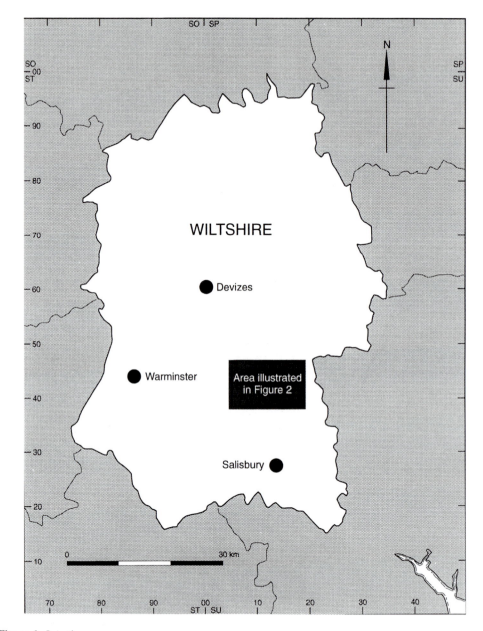

**Figure 1.** Location map.

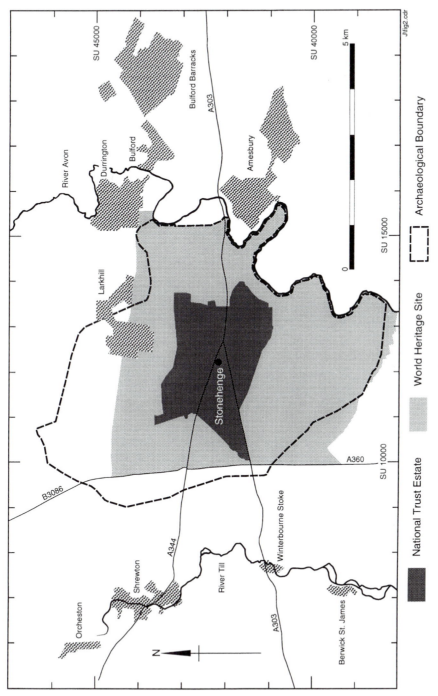

**Figure 2.** World Heritage Site boundary and National Trust Ownership map.

# Background

Whilst preparing this paper the genesis of the project was revisited: a request from Dr Wainwright in early 1994 to undertake an assessment of the impact of a number of alternative road lines for an upgraded A303, to European Highway Standards, that had been put forward by the Highways Agency. This initial request came with the 'generous' timescale of two weeks; we did actually have to take slightly longer, but not that much (Blore *et al.* 1994). While the need to continue the assessment of the impact of the many alternative road schemes put forward has been a major part of the work of the project team, it was always seen that this formed only a component of what were to be the wider aims and objectives of the project as a whole. The core to these objectives has been the collation of a dataset which will be held in a Geographical Information System (GIS) which can then be interrogated, externally by others, to assist in the management, planning and researching of the landscape which surrounds Stonehenge.

English Heritage together with the National Trust, who hold significant amounts of land around the site, are currently jointly formulating new strategies for the future management and interpretation of the landscape. An integral part of this work involves the need to redefine the World Heritage Site boundary to take greater account of the totality of the landscape, and in particular the interrelationship of other monuments both to themselves and to Stonehenge. In fact the staff of the Monuments Protection Programme, when they came to reschedule the monuments in this area, drew a boundary that was determined on archaeological groups and differs from the current World Heritage boundary. As indicated in Figure 2 the area encompassed by the archaeological boundary is marked by the broken line and the current World Heritage Site is shown in the light grey shading with the National Trust land shown in the darker grey shading.

In addition to the longer term aims of producing an integrated management plan for the Stonehenge World Heritage Site was the continuing and pressing need to assess the impact of the Highways Agency's proposals, up to thirteen different options at one time, for a route to upgrade the A303 which currently passes through the World Heritage Site and, as shown, extremely close to the stones themselves. The closure and physical removal of the extant A303 and the smaller A344 is seen as being fundamental to the preservation of the site for the future and to remedy its current inadequate surroundings and presentation. This led to an extension of the study area to include areas to the east and west well beyond the World Heritage Site boundary, or indeed any that may be proposed, to encompass the starting points of various route options that have been tabled. The final area is some 135 sq km of which the World Heritage Site occupies just less than 20%.

## Computing requirements

It is necessary at this point to give some background and explanation of the situation, with regard to the computer hardware and software used, which is currently one of transition and expansion. All of the databases and graphics were initially held on a high specification Pentium-based PC running a variety of commercially available packages to handle separately the text and graphics, including Dbase, AutoCAD and CAD Overlay. Ordnance Survey map data were purchased in the format of 12 scanned Rasta images at 400dpi from 5 × 5 km 1:10,000 scale maps, or 'tiles'. It was necessary to write 'in house' programs to interface the vector data from one source with the OS-sourced Rasta map images. Similarly the programming necessary to apportion values and scores to the surface-collected flint and scored archaeology maps was written specifically for the project. All of the maps were output using an A0 300dpi colour inkjet plotter.

The project team are currently upgrading and converting the datasets such that they will then be run on a full GIS package running the software package ArcInfo on a Sun Sparc 5 computer. This will effect a major change and allow the creation of a dynamic link between the textual data and the mapped outputs. This will incorporate additional data and be able to explore more fully the integration of these data and develop the core of a management system for the whole of the World Heritage Site, which we hope may be developed as a model for other landscape-based World Heritage Sites, such as Hadrian's Wall. It is fair to say that we have yet to explore fully the additional potential that this platform will allow; the efforts to date have been directed at replicating the high quality output of the earlier system.

## Project objectives

Once the initial road impact assessment was successfully completed it was possible to reorientate the project and this led to the larger project based upon the study of 135 sq km centred on the site of Stonehenge.

The objectives of the wider project were
- to compile a database of the known archaeological sites, now known to number 1,490
- to digitise the information to produce a graphical database of the records
- to gather information on: the totals of worked flint recovered from surface collection, all evaluation work undertaken, and areas of grassland that had not been cultivated for the past twenty years
- to devise a method of judging and 'scoring' the recorded archaeological data resulting in a map showing the data zoned into areas of high, medium and low archaeological sensitivity and importance.

All of these objectives were to be met by the examination and use of existing information and no primary data-gathering work was to be undertaken, although this has not been ruled out for the future. It was decided that the basic scale for the mapped output would be 1:10,000, although the data are structured to allow for the use of other scales, most commonly 1:25,000 which fits neatly onto an A1 sheet, whilst remaining a commonly used scale.

## The database

The information that was held on the Wiltshire County Sites and Monuments Record (SMR) was the primary source for achieving the first two objectives. The SMR is held on two separate but related databases held on computer; every text record that is held on one database has a corresponding digitised graphics record on the other. In total some 1,490 SMR entries fell within the study area and as part of the project each one of these was checked and updated where necessary. The entries range from single findspots up to the large ceremonial monuments in the area and the evidence of extensive field systems. The graphics record held by Wiltshire County Council is based on the transcription of aerial photographs, the core of which is the Royal Commission on the Historical Monuments of England's enhanced Aerial Photographic survey. It is seen, at present, as important that the project is utilising publicly available data on commercially available software to ensure maximum transferability to other geographic areas and computer platforms.

This core aerial photographic information has then been enhanced by the addition of data arising out of topographical, geophysical and excavation work, and further interpretation of aerial photographic surveys. All of these data are undergoing translation into the relevant format, point, line or area, for incorporation into the GIS dataset, which is causing a re-evaluation of the terminology used to categorise the individual monuments.

The data for the surface-collected worked flint were primarily sourced from the work undertaken for the Stonehenge Environs Project (Richards 1990). This data source was further enhanced by later field walking, in the main carried out by Wessex Archaeology, arising out of the evaluation of proposed road routes and locations for the siting of a new visitor centre for the monument, as may be inferred from distribution of the areas involved. A database was assembled of all occurrences of evaluation work, including surface collection, geophysical, auger and test pit data, in total some one hundred and seventeen individual occurrences. Excavation data were left out because of the small-scale nature of the majority of the work and the difficulties of presenting these data even at the scale of 1:10,000, although this issue will have to be addressed again during the development of the GIS.

All of this information was then translated into a sequence of four individual maps which show:

- a digitised database of the recorded archaeological sites (Plan 1)—the map shows all of the 1,490 recorded archaeological sites together with an indication of their status, i.e. scheduled or not; this is backed up by the respective entries in the textual database

• the distribution of worked flint recovered from surface collection (Plan 2)—the density of flint recovered is shown by a tripartite division into high (Red), medium (Orange) and low (Yellow) and is expressed by 50 × 50 m quadrats. These ranges translate into above 35 items, 13–35 items and 1–12 items per quadrat respectively

• the range and physical extent of evaluation work that has been carried out (Plan 3)—the colours on the map indicate surface collection in green, geophysical survey in red, test pit evaluation in yellow and auger transects in blue. The differing components are accompanied by an individual database entry and may be expressed by type as this example shows

• areas of uncultivated grassland (Plan 4)—this has been included to give an indication as to why areas appear to be lacking in archaeological information, and could be regarded as a statement of 'archaeological potential'.

The final objective of the project was to represent visually the archaeological 'value' or 'worth' of the landscape by a combination of the different datasets to produce a map on which there was a notional score or value for the known archaeological resource. It is a representation of the known archaeological resource and is in no way predictive. We thought for a considerable period about the reasons for producing such a map, being very aware that it could be perceived in a manner which was not meant; however we felt that in the end the advantages outweighed the disadvantages, a view that has been substantiated since the publication of the map.

To fulfil the final objective it was necessary to combine the two major sources of data available to the project, the first being the recorded archaeology databases and the second being the database arising from the extensive surface collection that has been undertaken over a number of years. The problem with having the two sources was to find a methodology that could combine the differing databases and especially to produce a meaningful graphical representation of the results.

As the basis for the scoring the whole of the study area was divided up into 50 m square quadrats, some 54,000 individual quadrats in total for the study area. Then the tripartite division of high, medium or low was apportioned to the individual quadrat by means of a computer program. The first attempted combination of the data was too simplistic and gave potentially erroneous results when plotted. When analysed the problems lay within the division of the differing datasets into high, medium or low categories and the method by which this score was combined for the individual quadrat.

The basis of the scores for the recorded archaeology dataset was a selection of the criteria to which values had been attributed during the Monuments Protection Programme rescheduling exercise. A re-evaluation of these selected MPP values showed that there was a potential combination of 21 scoring opportunities up to the maximum value of 45, and that these opportunities are not equally spread throughout the range 1–45. Thus the division into high, medium or low scores was adjusted to represent the first seven scored opportunities and then the second seven and finally the third. All Scheduled Ancient Monuments were given a factor whereby they automatically were apportioned a maximum value, a reflection of the importance of such monuments in this landscape. For example there are in excess of 400 individually Scheduled Ancient Monuments in the World Heritage Site which have been grouped into some 90 clusters, mainly Bronze Age barrow groups such as those along the spine of Normanton Down to the south of Stonehenge.

A similar exercise to refine the division of the flint scores across the high, medium and low categories was undertaken; I have already given the values that we finalised upon earlier in the paper.

Discussions were held with colleagues and other organisations working within the landscape around Stonehenge and a more refined method of combining the scores was set upon. The two different values are combined in a computer program by using a matrix of 16 cells (Fig. 3) in which all of the cells were given a high, medium or low value and this was then apportioned to the individual quadrat and represented on the map by the different colours. This method has the benefit that it allows the individual quadrat score to reflect more accurately the 'value' of the known archaeology in question. Within this matrix it will be noted that it expresses a 'prejudice' in favour of the archaeological scores over the flint material, and the author takes responsibility for doing so!

It is in the production of this map (Plan 5) and the visual representation of the archaeological scores that I believe ground-breaking work has been undertaken by the team. This map has had other data, such as proposals for road routes, overlaid on it and when used in this way it has proved to be remarkably effective in communicating to non-

|   | | High | Red | Red | Red | Red |
|---|---|---|---|---|---|---|
| **S** | | **Medium** | Orange | Orange | Red | Red |
| **I** | | | | | | |
| **T** | | | | | | |
| **E** | | **Low** | Yellow | Yellow | Orange | Orange |
| **S** | | | | | | |
| **C** | | | | | | |
| **O** | | **None** | – | Yellow | Yellow | Orange |
| **R** | | | | | | |
| **E** | | | **None** | **Low** | **Medium** | **High** |

FLINT SCORE

**Figure 3.** Scoring matrix.

archaeologists the amount of archaeology in the landscape and therefore the sensitivity of this area (Blore *et al.* 1995, fig. 5).

Up until this point the work of the project had not encompassed elements relating to the 'setting' of the monument or of the wider landscape value as a whole, choosing to concentrate on the individual aspects of direct impact by development schemes. However, once we had come to terms with what monuments are in the landscape and where they are, it was necessary to remedy this by undertaking an analysis of the landscape, with especial reference to the intervisibility between Stonehenge, and surrounding monuments within the study area.

You have only to walk in the landscape to realise that there is a strong visual linking of views, both to and from Stonehenge, and also to and from other monuments, this leading to the description of the topography as the 'Stonehenge Bowl'. It is with this work that the project team came to link and interface directly with Land Use Consultants (Land Use Consultants 1995) who were employed to initiate the development of a basis for a management plan for the World Heritage Site, and this was to encompass the geographical, human and landscape perspectives of defining and then managing the area.

To carry out the computer-based visibility analysis it is first necessary to generate a surface terrain model; initially this was done by a ground modelling program but latterly as one of the functions of the GIS. Using digital contour information supplied by the Ordnance Survey a computer-generated surface terrain model was created of the Stonehenge Study area. Plan 6 uses the model as a background and it is relatively coarse in that the available contour height data are at 5 m vertical height intervals, and in the subtle landscape we are dealing with here it is possible to lose some fairly large and important monuments within that height interval.

The availability of refined contour height data from the detailed photogrammetric plotting of recent aerial photography currently ongoing for the terrain model being developed for the virtual reality project has now demonstrated the degree to which this model could be refined by better contour height data. This Virtual Reality model currently covers only the area immediately around Stonehenge; however it is at a resolution that will allow contour height intervals of less than one metre. These data will be added to and merged with the model in the GIS to allow the generation of more refined analysis in future, and hopefully be able to take into account the actual height of the monuments themselves.

To digress from the visibility aspects for one moment, the topographic model generated can be presented in a number of different ways. Plan 6 has a background with a light source in the north-west casting shadows to the south and east with the resultant model viewed from a position perpendicular to the study area. All of these aspects may be varied in relation to one another. In addition to this any of the aforementioned map data generated by the project may be overlain, such as this example using the recorded archaeology data, to demonstrate other ways of presenting the data. We are investigating scanning of recent aerial photographic coverage of the area and then draping this over the model, or even including high resolution Russian satellite digital images, although these may encounter problems due to the capabilities of the machine being used and the large size of the resultant files.

To return to the visibility analysis, in addition to the site of Stonehenge, twelve surrounding archaeological sites within the study area were chosen, on the basis of their archaeological and landscape significance, to undergo a visibility analysis (Table 1).

The position of the individual grid reference point used was either the centre of the monument, or in the case of the barrow groups was to be the centre of the group. It is also assumed that the view is seen from a height of 2 m, although this can be varied. The areas of ground that are visible from these points are then expressed, by colour, in the same 50 × 50 m quadrats that have been used elsewhere within the project. As you will have noted the model currently does not take into account obstacles such as trees or buildings which would interrupt the view although this may be remedied in future developments of the digital terrain model.

The computer program is able to plot the topographical areas, in GIS terms a 'viewshed' analysis, that would be visible from each archaeological site. It was necessary to check these data by visiting the individual sites as it proved that we could, because of the relatively coarse contour data being used in the computer analysis, apparently lose, for example, the prominent barrows on Kings Barrow Ridge; this obviously necessitated some manual enhancement. This example of a viewshed, from Robin Hood's Ball (Plan 7), gives a representation of the frequently referred to 'Stonehenge Bowl', and also the strong influence that the river valleys of the Till and Avon play on this landscape.

**Table 1.** Locations of sites for intervisibility analysis

| Site Name | OS Grid Reference |
| --- | --- |
| Bush Barrow | 411655, 141300 |
| Coneybury Hill | 413450, 141390 |
| Cursus Barrow Ridge | 411850, 142800 |
| Durrington Barrow Group | 412800, 145198 |
| Lake Barrow Group | 410830, 140200 |
| New Kings Barrow Group | 413433, 142250 |
| Old Kings Barrow Group | 413700, 142950 |
| Robin Hood's Ball | 410200, 145900 |
| Rollestone Camp Tumuli | 409300, 144200 |
| Stonehenge | 412220, 142220 |
| Vespasian's Camp | 414600, 141620 |
| Winterbourne Stoke Group | 410200, 141750 |
| Woodhenge | 415050, 143350 |

Once we had generated the 13 individual viewshed analyses, these data were then combined into a 'composite' plot which represents the visual envelope for the study area. The colour used is an indication of the degrees of visibility and is divided into six class intervals (Plan 8). This scale is arrived at by counting the number of times the usual $50 \times 50$ m quadrat is visible from any of the chosen sites and then combined by grouping as shown. This indicates that the 'Stonehenge Bowl' would appear to be not one single entity but more of a series of nesting bowls set into the chalk plateau which then falls away into the river valleys to the east and west respectively.

This analysis demonstrates not only the very strong visual relationship between these primary archaeological sites with Stonehenge, but perhaps more importantly with each other. This analysis, whilst it undoubtedly reflects the interrelationship of the monuments to one another, is when combined with the recorded archaeological data, indicative of the concentration of the major prehistoric sites on ridge lines, and highlights the focal position of Stonehenge itself within this landscape.

In addition, this analysis allows for the superimposition of the other data generated by the project and therefore, for instance, an assessment to be made of how visible a proposed road route would be within the overall landscape (Plan 9).

It is apparent from this analysis that whilst confirming on-site observation of the prominent siting of barrow groups in particular in the landscape, there are ridge lines that are apparently equally as important visually which have no monuments on them, as those on which the prehistoric sites are concentrated. Comparison of these data with the 'scored archaeology' data gives an indication that visually prominent areas, such as the ridge which continues south of the A303 from New Kings Barrows towards Coneybury Henge, are areas which have a high surface-collected flint score, albeit the available data are far from being comprehensive. This, and it is no more than a personal working hypothesis, may be indicative of the areas within the landscape favoured for settled habitation during the long period within which the monument itself was curated and developed. This is suggested as a research theme which should be investigated in any further research that may be instigated within this landscape. It may actually give an indication where the peoples who built, modified and used Stonehenge and its surrounding monuments lived, a frequent question posed by visitors to the monument, to which at present there is no substantive answer and one which would undoubtedly assist the life of the site custodians.

Further enhancement of this composite visibility analysis will play a major part in the revision of any boundary for the Stonehenge World Heritage Site. This boundary revision which is seen as fundamental to the development of a management plan will have to encompass a number of differing factors or disciplines, including archaeology, that will be acceptable to all of the various parties who hold a stake in this particular landscape.

## Conclusions

To conclude, although emphasis has been put upon the management aspects to which this project contributes, and the topical references to the issues relating to the roads have been kept at a minimum, it must not be forgotten that the creation and dissemination of this resource has a tremendous research potential. Indeed, and it has perhaps been lost in the current politicised climate, that to get this far with the project has in itself been a major research project. This project and the recently published monograph on the Twentieth Century Excavations at Stonehenge (Cleal *et al.* 1995) will, no doubt, combine to rekindle archaeological interest in both the monument itself and perhaps more importantly the surrounding landscape in which it sits. It is my personal wish, and I hope that this is reflected in English Heritage's expressed wish, that archaeological research will form a fundamental element of the management plan for the World Heritage Site and it is more than credible that this project will be a major contributor to this research.

*Acknowledgements*

It is a pleasure to thank the work of the Central Archaeology Service staff who have contributed to the project, especially Frances Blore, Miles Hitchen and Nick Burton who have shouldered most of the work to date. Without the contribution to the project made by Roy Canham and the staff at Wiltshire County Museum and Library Service it would not have developed so far in the timescale it has. The project as a whole has benefited from the advice of an English Heritage working party and the many and varied discussions with fellow professionals who have interests in the landscape of Stonehenge.

## References

BLORE, F.A., HITCHEN, M. and VALLENDER, J. 1994: *Archaeological Assessment of the Stonehenge World Heritage Site and its Surrounding Landscape* (London, Central Archaeology Service, English Heritage) (circulated typescript report).

BLORE, F.A. and HITCHEN, M. 1995: *An Assessment of the Impact of the Alternative Routes of the A303 Amesbury to Bewick Down Improvement on the Recorded Archaeological Resource* (London, Central Archaeology Service, English Heritage) (circulated typescript report).

CLEAL, R.M.J., WALKER, K.E. and MONTAGUE, R. 1995: *Stonehenge in its Landscape: Twentieth Century Excavations* (London, Engl. Heritage Archaeol. Rep. 10).

LAND USE CONSULTANTS 1995: *Stonehenge World Heritage Site, Landscape and Planning Study* (London) (circulated typescript report).

RICHARDS, J. 1990: *The Stonehenge Environs Project* (London, Hist. Build. Monuments Comm. Archaeol. Rep. 16).

*Proceedings of the British Academy*, **92**, 73–113

# Geophysical Surveys within the Stonehenge Landscape: A Review of Past Endeavour and Future Potential

## A. DAVID & A. PAYNE

## Introduction

DESPITE ITS DILAPIDATION, the monumental durability of Stonehenge and its conspicuously planned disposition have perhaps inclined the minds of earlier antiquarians away from the search for less durable traces nearby. Of course the presence of earthen features such as the Avenue and the Great Cursus, and many lesser monuments, did not escape the very acute observations of Aubrey, Stukeley and their successors. However, it is perhaps the remarkable physical persistence of the more obvious monuments that has allowed these to absorb much initial archaeological enquiry, away from a wider and more penetrating search of the surrounding chalkland.

From early in the present century, however, the development of aerial reconnaissance has activated a more holistic appreciation of this landscape in which many subtle and denuded archaeological traces have manifested themselves when viewed from far above. For the future, aerial photography (and now airborne and satellite multi-spectral imagery) will continue to provide a rich source of information about the less tangible physical remains which complement the more upstanding and enduring earthworks so familiar on the ground surface.

From the 1940s it became apparent that there were other methods, aside from observation and excavation alone, which could be used to explore for archaeological features. These geophysical techniques, adapted and scaled down from their geological analogues, were soon shown to be able to locate buried features invisible from the surface. The historic first application of resistivity surveying clearly demonstrated this ability at a monument complex, contemporary with Stonehenge, at Dorchester-on-Thames, Oxfordshire (Clark 1996, 11–14). However, despite such demonstrable promise, these novel and developing methods do not appear to have ever been pursued with much enthusiasm at Britain's most famous prehistoric site. This may be explained, not only by the tentativeness of these first developments in the new technology, but also by the prior existence at Stonehenge of such a relatively well documented landscape of monuments, supplemented by a productive aerial photographic record. Perhaps such methods seemed unnecessary where the surface expressions of so much prehistoric activity already seemed clear enough, and where the thin mantle of soil discouraged belief that much else remained to be found.

R.J.C. Atkinson, excavator at Stonehenge as well as the pioneer of archaeological geophysics at Dorchester, made only very limited use of the latter methodology in his studies at the monument: following the proposal that the Station Stones might be remnants of a stone circle he used resistivity survey to search for settings elsewhere on its presumed circuit, but without success (Atkinson 1979, 79). He also resorted to bosing (thumping the ground and listening for variations in resonance), and probing, the judicious use of the latter being helpful in locating various features such as Aubrey Holes, Z and Y Holes and the stone-hole within the North Barrow (ibid. 32–4).

It was not until the late 1960s that more advanced techniques became available, especially fluxgate magnetometry, and with them the ability to routinely explore larger areas of ground. Such techniques were nevertheless used only sparingly, and not at all at Stonehenge, until 1979–80 when a portion of the Avenue was investigated by the Ancient Monuments Laboratory (Bartlett and David 1982). Then, following emphatic recommendations by the Royal Commission on Historical Monuments (RCHM(E) 1979, xv), several geophysical surveys were conducted in the environs of Stonehenge as part of a wider research and evaluation project (Richards 1990). It was in fact not until 1994–5, following further technical progress, that Stonehenge itself and its immediate vicinity was comprehensively geophysically surveyed (Payne 1994, 1995). This latter project was undertaken specifically to provide detailed geophysical information in support of the preparation of a full account of the twentieth-century excavations at Stonehenge (Cleal et al. 1995).

In fact, after so much apparent neglect in the history of its investigation the Stonehenge area has lately seen an unprecedented amount of geophysical survey activity. This has partly been linked to those research and post-excavation initiatives referred to above, but a very substantial contribution has been made as a direct consequence of development pressures within the World Heritage Site. Both the need to locate a new visitor centre, and to upgrade the existing road network, have necessitated extensive evaluation of the archaeological potential of the areas affected by these plans. Several options for siting the developments have had to be considered, and each assessed by geophysical methods, leading to a vast survey coverage (see Fig. 1). The pattern of this coverage has of course been dictated by many practical considerations, one of which has been a concern to avoid sites of obvious archaeological importance. Whilst the opportunity to undertake such survey is very welcome, and in places coincides with locations of considerable archaeological significance, it must be recognised that it is nonetheless driven by an agenda quite detached from archaeological research.

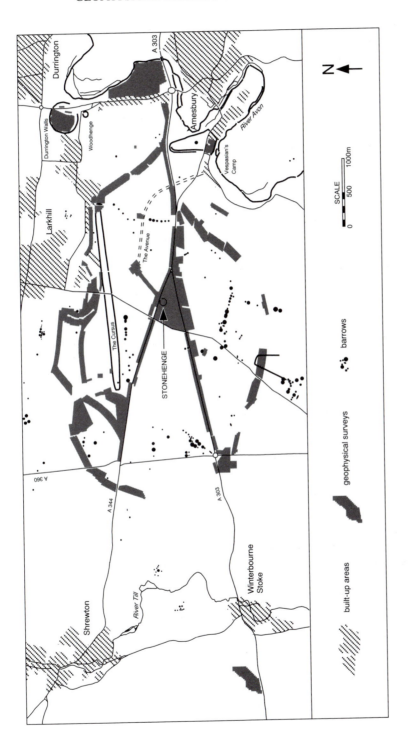

**Figure 1.** The distribution of geophysical survey, almost all of it fluxgate gradiometer survey, in the Stonehenge area.

It is our purpose in the remainder of this paper to review the results of the totality of geophysical survey that has taken place within the World Heritage Site, some 183 hectares, concentrating especially upon the work undertaken since 1990. We will conclude by discussing how the current and developing geophysical technologies might be able to address outstanding archaeological issues at Stonehenge, and will propose specific areas and sites where such endeavours might be most appropriately targeted. Firstly, however, it is necessary briefly to summarise the main techniques of archaeological geophysics that are, and will be, relevant to such a programme.

## Geophysical survey methods

The details of the principles and methodologies of archaeological geophysics are by now very well rehearsed in the literature and need not be repeated here (see for instance, Aitken 1974; Tite 1972; Clark 1996; Scollar *et al.* 1990). The methods which have seen greatest employment at Stonehenge are those which already have an established role in the discipline: resistivity and magnetometry, supplemented occasionally by geochemical survey (phosphate and magnetic susceptibility), probing and augering.

Magnetometry involves the measurement of the local magnetic field strength at close intervals (1.0 m or less) across the ground surface. The magnetometer (usually a fluxgate gradiometer) responds to perturbations in the local magnetic field caused by localised concentrations of soil, magnetically enhanced particularly by burning, that infill buried features such as pits, ditches and the larger post-holes. It also detects the remanent magnetisation of hearths and industrial features such as kilns and furnaces. These remains are revealed as patterns of magnetic anomalies visible in computer-generated plots of the areas surveyed.

Resistivity survey, where an electrical current is introduced into the soil and the (apparent) resistance to its passage is measured, responds to variations in porosity and moisture content—variations which can in turn relate to buried archaeological features. This method is often selected when the presence of building foundations is suspected, but is also well capable of detecting large stones, pits, ditches and other features when the prevailing moisture conditions allow. As with magnetometry, the outcome of resistivity survey is a two-dimensional spatial plot of the area surveyed. The depth of detection is related to probe spacing which is often set at 0.5 m, giving a detection depth of some 0.75 m. Current research is aimed at investigating the potential of multiprobe arrays for the reconstruction of resistivity variation with depth (Aspinall 1992; Szymanski and Tsourlos 1993).

Aside from resistivity and magnetometry, electromagnetic methods (EM) of detection have seen much more limited use at Stonehenge, but are likely to have a continuing role in the future. These methods include the (continuous wave) measurement of soil conductivity, soil magnetic susceptibility (MS) and ground penetrating (impulse) radar (GPR).

Soil conductivity survey provides results which are directly comparable with those of resistivity survey but without the necessity for the repeated insertion of electrodes.

Variation in soil magnetic susceptibility is the key to magnetic detection. Topsoil contains a proportion of magnetic iron oxides inherited from the parent material and when these are subjected to burning, as on a settlement or industrial site, they become magnetically enhanced. If this enhanced material, with a relatively high magnetic susceptibility, becomes concentrated within cut archaeological features, such as pits, it can generate a corresponding and detectable magnetic anomaly.

More subtly, the effect of artificially enhanced magnetic susceptibility can be retained in the topsoil alone, whether or not archaeological features survive beneath it. Thus, measurement of topsoil MS (at intervals of, say, 10 m) over a large area (up to many hectares) can, by isolating zones of higher readings, suggest the former presence of settlement or industrial activity. Such a generalisation is not without its problems, however: the mechanisms of magnetic enhancement, apart from burning, are still only imperfectly understood; nor is it yet possible to counteract fully the effects of natural variations in MS, or the effect of modern influences. Whilst MS survey can thus be used as a prospecting technique in its own right, and can be a valuable approach to preliminary site reconnaissance, its results must be interpreted with caution, and preferably in accompaniment with indications provided by magnetometry and/or other survey methods (English Heritage 1995). MS surveys have been made at several locations in the Stonehenge area as a supplement to magnetometer survey.

Despite much recent publicity, the role of ground penetrating radar in British archaeology is not yet well established. Although the technique is suited to the detection of voids and the structural features of building fabric, it has generally been much less successful in the discrimination of archaeological features from amongst their surroundings. The effectiveness of the technique is hindered by moist and clay-rich soils and, whilst capable of detecting major dielectric interfaces, has not demonstrated that it can unravel the more complex and subtle nature of much archaeological stratigraphy. One of the very first occasions on which it was applied archaeologically was at Woodhenge in 1981 (Clark 1996, fig. 91) and, on the same occasion, at Durrington Walls. Transects across both ditches only partially detected their profiles and revealed no stratigraphic detail. Despite this apparent lack of promise, GPR may have a future role in the Stonehenge area and this is referred to again below.

Thus, despite some very tentative experiments with GPR and other EM methods, much of the geophysical prospecting that has taken place around and within Stonehenge has been undertaken with magnetometry and, to a much lesser extent, resistivity. Although these techniques have now been in use for several decades they remain immensely effective. Recent years have seen the development of sophisticated archaeologically dedicated instruments and these, helped by advances in computing, have allowed great improvements in the speed and presentation of these types of survey.

In the next section we will briefly review the results of previous work in more detail.

This is perhaps best achieved by taking first of all the studies of the major individual monuments, before moving out to surveys undertaken more widely within their surroundings.


# The monuments

*The Stonehenge enclosure and stone circles*

The reasons for an apparent reluctance to embark on a survey of the henge itself have already been referred to at the beginning of this paper. Apart from the success of probing, demonstrated by Atkinson, little or no geophysical investigation appeared to be warranted in subsequent years. A trial magnetometer survey by the Ancient Monuments Laboratory (AML) in 1988, just outside the henge ditch, did nothing to dispel a general impression that this method, at least, would not be very revealing. However, this impression was eventually set aside and in 1994–5 a full magnetic and resistivity survey was undertaken. Whilst magnetometer survey might be of limited value because of excessive magnetic interference resulting from twentieth-century activity at the site, there was some confidence that resistivity might be more productive. Recently, the latter had certainly proved able to locate the positions of former stone settings within the Avebury henge and along the line of the West Kennett Avenue (Ucko *et al.* 1990).

The methodology and results of the AML survey have been described and illustrated in detail by Payne (1994, 1995) and only the most salient points should bear repetition here. Magnetometer readings were taken at 0.25 m intervals along traverses spaced 1.0 m apart. Instrument sensitivity (using a Geoscan FM36 fluxgate gradiometer) was set at 0.1 nanotesla (nT). The resulting magnetometer plot, as predicted, is massively interrupted by extreme responses to ferrous litter and clinker in the soil, underground cabling, metal underpinning, former fence lines and trackways. Of the prehistoric features, the enclosure ditch has been detected throughout its circuit, but without sufficient clarity to determine its detailed morphology. Within the ditch circuit, many of the excavated Aubrey Holes have been detected on account of ferrous material in their twentieth-century backfilling. Similarly the backfillings of stone-holes D and E and the hole for stone 92 (one of the Station Stones) have been detected. Up to 15 unexcavated Aubrey Holes have been located, their weakly defined positive magnetic anomalies corresponding with both localised low resistivity (see below) and the much earlier results of probing. Less clearly, it is possible that the magnetometer has picked up a number of Y Holes (Fig. 2).

Resistivity readings were obtained over the same area using a Geoscan RM15 meter. The Twin Electrode configuration was used with a mobile probe spacing of 0.5 m and a reading interval of 0.5 m. The resulting data are illustrated in Figure 3 in the form of a greytone plot which has been numerically enhanced (using a 3m Gaussian high pass filter) to clarify significant anomalies. Figure 4 illustrates the same plot overlain by the outlines of the excavated portions of the site, and with significant resistivity anomalies indicated by letters.

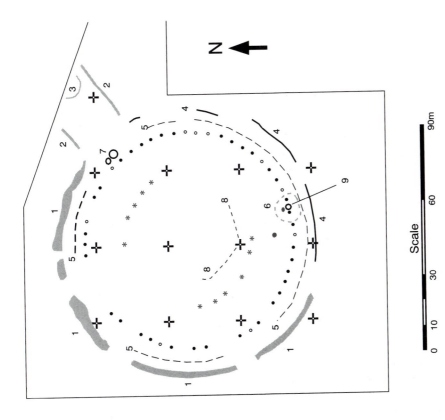

KEY

1. Stonehenge ditch

2. Avenue ditches

3. Heelstone ditch

4. traces of excavated portions of the Stonehenge ditch

5. inner edge of internal bank

6. South Barrow

7. holes D and E

8. excavated X Holes 9 - 16

9. Station Stone hole

        anomalies coinciding with expected positions of Y Holes

        other discrete (possible small pit-like) anomalies

Aubrey Holes :

        noisy response indicating presence of burnt or ferrous material

        weak - normal positive pit-like response

        SURVEY GRID POINTS

Scale

0   10   30   60   90m

**Figure 2.** Features located by magnetometer survey within the Stonehenge enclosure.

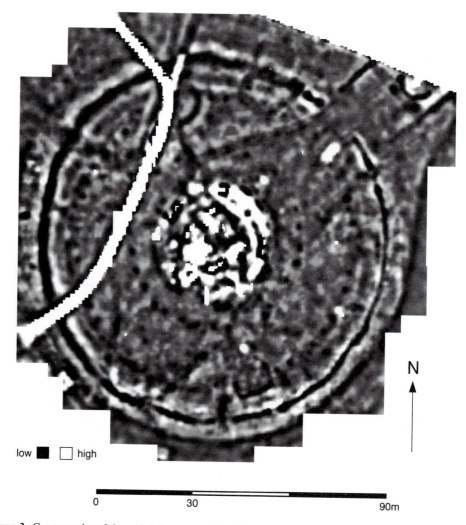

low ■ □ high

0                    30                                    90m

**Figure 3.** Greytone plot of the resistivity survey of the Stonehenge enclosure (3m Gaussian high pass filter).

As with the magnetometer survey, the resistivity results also reflect the recent history of the site—but to a somewhat lesser degree. The low resistance henge ditch is clear, as is the bank within it, defined by a zone of higher readings. More surprisingly, the survey demonstrates that there is also a bank of similar dimensions on the outer side of the ditch. Although a modest counterscarp bank is visible as a slight topographic feature in places, the resistivity data illustrate for the first time that this is the remnant of a once much more substantial and continuous feature. The data suggest that the morphology of the ditch itself, in plan, is a little irregular in places and slightly raised readings here and

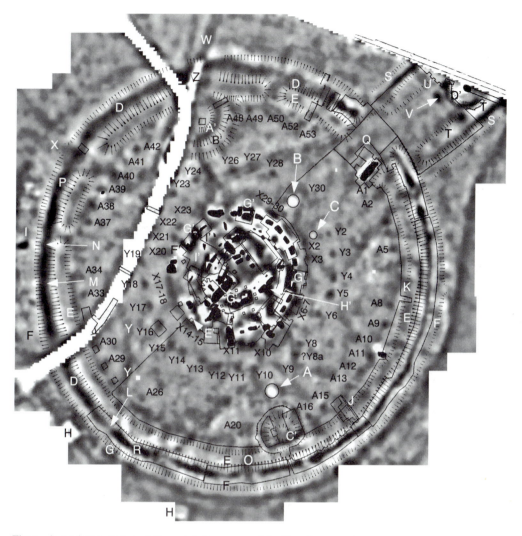

**Figure 4.** An interpretation of the resistivity survey of the Stonehenge enclosure.

there hint at the presence of segmentation. The purported southern entrance causeway has not been clearly detected, due to the influence of Hawley's excavation there, but its existence is confirmed by the faint detection of a corresponding break in the two banks (O on Fig. 4).

Within the henge, up to 28 out of the 56 Aubrey Holes have been detected as very weak anomalies, 13 of them unexcavated. Many would probably not have been recognised were their existence not already known from probing. This rather disappointing result must be accounted for by their small size and the poor moisture contrast offered by their fillings. However, the fillings of the Y and Z Holes are more uniform and fine-textured than those of the Aubrey Holes, and have been detected more emphatically. Some 23 Y Holes and 16 Z Holes, inclusive of both excavated and unexcavated examples, have been found, as have the ditches of the North and South barrows.

Three isolated high resistance anomalies (A, B and C on Fig. 4) have aroused some interest as they could perhaps represent buried stones or stone settings. However, they lie in areas that have apparently been excavated (Cleal *et al.* 1995), and must remain unexplained since no corresponding features have been reported. Amongst the stone circles themselves, the highly complex and interrupted nature of the subsurface has defeated the ability of the survey data to discriminate much useful detail (Payne 1995, fig. 263). The only unexpected result was the location of a previously unidentified excavation trench sited immediately to the south-east of trilithon stone 52. This interpretation seems to be confirmed by the results of augering undertaken by Wessex Archaeology (Allen and Gardiner 1994).

*The Avenue*

Parts of the Avenue have been targeted by geophysical survey on several occasions, and its Stonehenge terminal was included within the resistivity and magnetometer coverage described above. The ditches here were detected by both methods, and resistivity also picked up the bank on the inside of the southern ditch (its counterpart having been eroded by a later cart-track). The Heelstone Ditch was also detected by both methods, and resistivity appears to have picked up the position of the previously excavated stone-hole B.

Survey coverage along the line of the Avenue is now nearly continuous for some 700 m north of its Stonehenge terminal, extending well beyond its angular deflection in Stonehenge Bottom. This coverage is an amalgam of separate surveys, all undertaken by the AML at different times over a period of 11 years (Payne 1995, 506–10). In addition, minor magnetometer surveys have located the Avenue further eastwards along its course at King Barrow Ridge (Bartlett 1990; Richards 1990, 112–13) and just to the north of its intersection with the A303 road (Bartlett 1994).

The earlier surveys, along the straight section of the Avenue north-east of the henge, were motivated by the persistent contention, originated by John Aubrey in 1666 and reasserted by Stukeley and his friend Roger Gale, that there were once twin rows of stones lining the Avenue (Bartlett and David 1982, 90–3). No surface indications now survive, however, and unfortunately neither this nor any subsequent geophysical survey has been able to resolve this problem conclusively. Poorly defined magnetic and resistivity anomalies have been found at a variety of locations in and around the Avenue but no pattern is evident and their significance remains unknown (Payne 1995).[1]

[1] Since this paper was prepared a very detailed caesium magnetometer survey has been undertaken over part of the Avenue north of the A344, in May 1996, in the hope—perhaps—of resolving whether or not former stone settings can be detected here. The survey was undertaken by Dr Jörg Faßbinder in association with the AML and the results are to be compared against a new set of detailed fluxgate magnetometer measurements.

Another contention which has its origins amongst antiquarian observations (e.g. Stukeley 1740, Tab XXVIII) is that there may or may not have been a bifurcation of the Avenue at Stonehenge Bottom, with a now invisible branch leading away northwards towards the Cursus. Whether or not this was the case, the turn in the Avenue presents an obvious locus for investigation should there be any clues there as to why such a deflection was introduced into the overall scheme. Unfortunately, the magnetometer plots (Fig. 5) do not provide any such clues, although they demonstrate conclusively that the Avenue does not divide at this point.

*Other features in the near vicinity of Stonehenge*

As part of the most recent campaign by the AML, the entire triangle of land containing Stonehenge, bounded to the north and south by the A344 and A303, and to the west by the farm track across Stonehenge Down, was surveyed with magnetometers (Fig. 6). This is an area of some 14.4 hectares and represents a substantial part of the core area of the World Heritage Site. The only visible surface remains, excepting Stonehenge itself, are barrows. Apart from the bell barrow (Amesbury 11) adjacent to the A344, there is a scatter of degraded barrows in the western part of the area, on Stonehenge Down, the majority of which are recorded as of simple bowl form (Grinsell 1957).

A glance at Figure 6 graphically illustrates the extent of magnetic interference accumulated from generations of modern activity around the monument, belied by a now comparatively unblemished isolation beneath pasture. This magnetic 'noise' around the stones themselves, along former tracks, fences and roads, and over the sites of former custodians' cottages and airfield buildings, may well mask the response from weaker and more significant magnetic features in some areas. Some of the modern anomalies may not be without interest themselves, however. For instance, the three large and strong (ferrous) anomalies isolated 100 m south of the centre of Stonehenge (Fig. 6) are unexplained. They do not appear to mark the location of huts used by Hawley's field team, nor that of 'Hawley's Graves', which were placed nearer the monument (Cleal *et al*. 1995, 18–19, fig. 11).

If the scatter of ferrous interference in the Stonehenge Triangle is ignored it may be suggested that most of this area is nearly devoid of obvious unsuspected prehistoric features. The survey has certainly located the ditches of each of the barrows and, for those on Stonehenge Down, has greatly clarified their outlines (Fig. 7). The latter are remarkable for their variety and it is notable that the smaller ring ditches (Amesbury 6–9) are incomplete, even 'hengiform' in outline. Most of these barrows were dug into by Colt Hoare in the early nineteenth century. He was unable to locate anything at Amesbury 10a, however, nor is there any magnetic indication that this 'barrow' is a genuine feature. On the other side of Stonehenge, an extremely weak and intermittent curving linear magnetic anomaly, some 60 m long, has been traced to the east of Amesbury 11 and *may* be a ditch. Elsewhere in the Triangle there are isolated instances where discrete anomalies

*A. David & A. Payne*

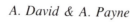

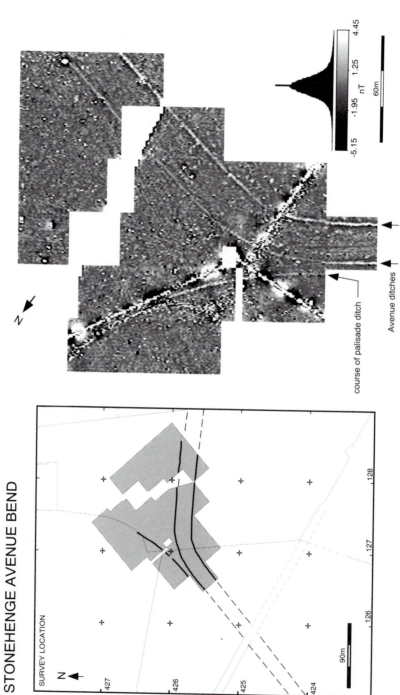

**Figure 5.** Greytone plot of the 1990 magnetometer survey of the bend in the Avenue. Note that, despite magnetic interference from pipes and fences, the course of the Palisade Ditch has been detected clearly.

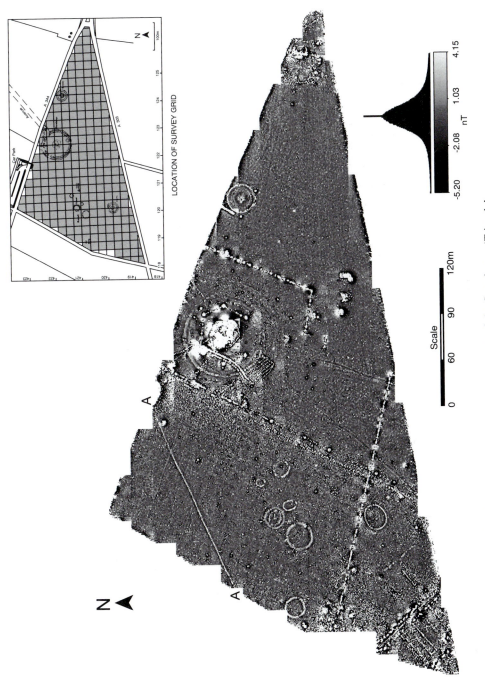

**Figure 6.** Greytone plot (much reduced) of the entire magnetometer survey of the Stonehenge 'Triangle'.

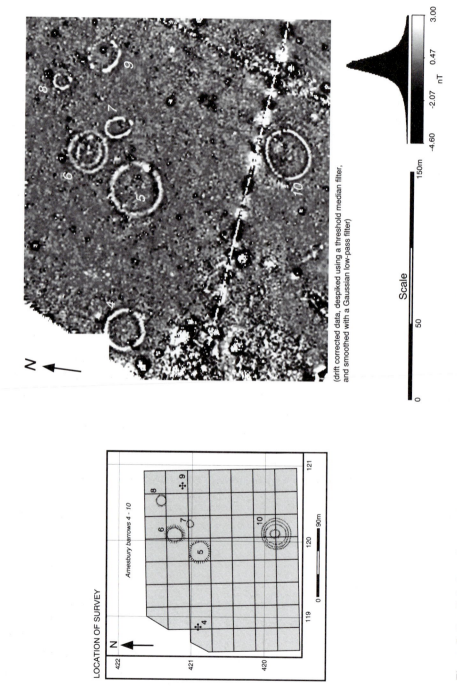

**Figure 7.** Detailed view of part of Figure 6, illustrating the detection of barrow features on Stonehenge Down.

could represent pits (some of which are 2 m or more in diameter), although nowhere are these unequivocal or concentrated in clusters suggestive of any particular focus of activity (Payne 1995, figs 8–11).

## The Palisade Ditch

This ditch, passing to the north-west of Stonehenge and extending in a NE-SW direction for over a kilometre, was formerly thought to have been of Late Bronze Age date. Although still undated it has recently been reinterpreted as an earlier feature, maybe of the Late Neolithic, and perhaps then integral in some way to the use of Stonehenge itself (Phase 2: Cleal *et al.* 1995, 155–61, 482). Being palisaded, parallels have been drawn with similar ditches, forming the perimeters of large enclosures, at Mount Pleasant, Dorset, and at West Kennett, Wiltshire (ibid.). This attribution remains to be decided (see below), but for the meantime we can note that the ditch has a distinct magnetic signature (of some 5nT) and has been traced by the magnetometer very clearly, both in its passage past Stonehenge (A on Fig. 6) and, again, where it passes close to the elbow of the Avenue (Fig. 5). Aerial photography suggests that it extends further in both directions but its association with outlying field systems and artefact scatters is at present entirely conjectural (Richards 1990; Cleal *et al.* 1995).

## The Great Cursus

In 1987 a magnetometer survey was recorded over the eastern terminal of this monument (Gater 1987). The ditch was clearly detectable and could be traced as it turned from the south side of the Cursus northward to form the terminal. The response to the northern ditch was obscured by interference from a modern fence. An internal ditch was located as well, orientated SW-NE, as were a number of anomalies that could be interpreted as pits.

Later, in 1988, a magnetometer survey was undertaken by the AML alongside the eastern flank of the long barrow (Amesbury 42) which marks the eastern terminus of the Cursus. This clearly detected the barrow ditch, and an outlying and probably unrelated ditch, but no other anomalies of significance were found (Payne and White 1988).

## The Lesser Cursus

Magnetometer survey of parts of the Lesser Cursus was undertaken by the AML (Bartlett 1988b) in advance of selective excavation by the Stonehenge Environs Project (Richards 1990, 72–93). Since then the entire monument and its surroundings have been surveyed as part of the archaeological assessment associated with the selection of a new visitor centre site (Bartlett and Clark 1993). The result of this substantial survey is a very striking image (Fig. 8) of the Lesser Cursus which not only refines the precision of the aerial

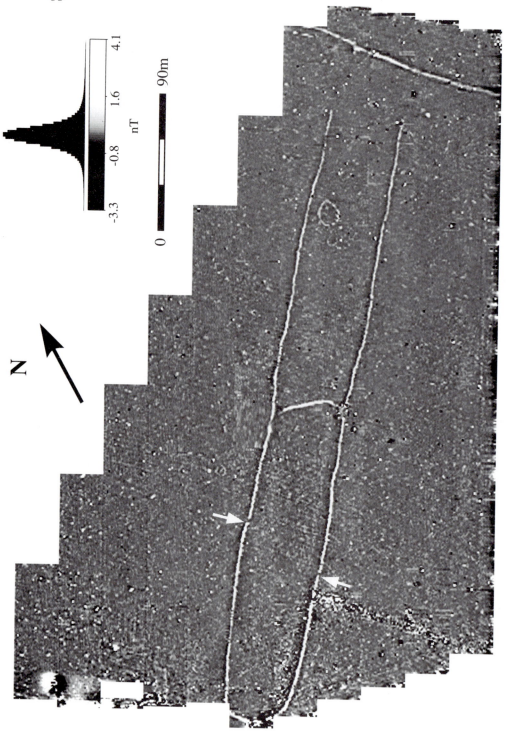

**Figure 8.** Greytone plot of the magnetic data obtained over the Lesser Cursus in 1993 (data courtesy of A. Bartlett).

photographic record but also adds a new feature: an irregular oval enclosure, some 14–15 m across, situated off-centre near the eastern end of the monument. Some pits appear to be associated with this, both inside and outside. Pits also seem to be scattered about sparsely within the cursus and, more profusely, to the north of its western half. There are hints of small ring ditches here and there, too, although both these and many of the pit-type anomalies may arise from naturally caused depressions in the subsurface (ibid.). Of some considerable significance to the interpretation of the use of the cursus must be the narrow gaps (approximately 2 m across) that have been detected in both the northern and (less certainly) the southern ditches of its western half (arrowed on Fig. 8).

*Coneybury henge*

The small henge on Coneybury Hill was surveyed by the AML in 1980 using resistivity and magnetometry prior to sample excavation by the Stonehenge Environs Project (Bartlett 1988a; Richards 1990, 124). Both techniques clearly located the henge ditch and resistivity also traced the completely flattened remnant of the bank. Along with MS measurements they also showed evidence of the plough damage to the site. The magnetometer survey (Fig. 9A) was not able to discriminate anomalies of much significance within the henge (despite the presence of shallow pits around its centre) but did isolate a very distinct anomaly outside it, some 12 m to the north of the henge ditch. On excavation, the cause of this was found, with some surprise, to be the filling of a substantial Early Neolithic pit (Richards 1990, 40–61, fig. 24), extraordinarily rich in lithic, ceramic and faunal remains. So unusual is this feature that it has become known in the literature as the 'Anomaly'. It has provided the earliest Neolithic radiocarbon determination from the Stonehenge area. Altogether, 'a neater summary of the elements traditionally taken to characterise the Neolithic could hardly have been achieved if an archaeologist had been sent out to create a time-capsule representing the period' (Cleal *et al.* 1995, 474). The location of this time-capsule, no mere happenstance, is a vivid demonstration of the potential of geophysical survey.

Also now embedded in the literature are the results from measurement of topsoil MS across the site, made after the initial surveys (Clark 1983a, 1983b, 1986, 1996). The MS values showed a distinct area of enhancement at the centre of the henge that did not correspond with any surviving subsurface features. There was, however, a corresponding increase in density of burnt flint in this area and it has been surmised by Clark (ibid.) that both sets of data combine to indicate a burning event (such as a bonfire) contemporary with the lithic material. Implicit in this interpretation is the inference that a spatially discrete MS signature (if not the result merely of recent localised exposure of ancient soil by ploughing) may be retained in the topsoil for thousands of years. Samples of topsoil from the site were also analysed for their phosphate content but without any obviously significant outcome.

# CONEYBURY HENGE

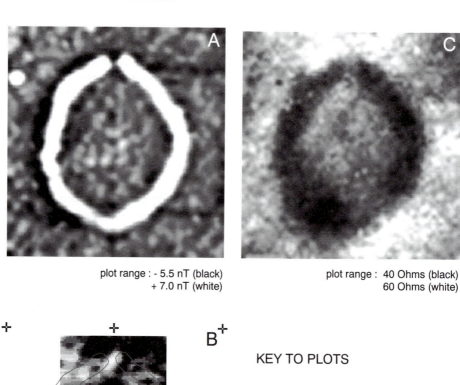

plot range : - 5.5 nT (black)
+ 7.0 nT (white)

plot range :  40 Ohms (black)
60 Ohms (white)

### KEY TO PLOTS

A)  Fluxgate magnetometer survey
(smoothed data)

B)  Field loop magnetic susceptibility survey
(0.7m sample interval, median
filtered data, 1 reading radius)

C)  Twin electrode resistivity survey
(smoothed data)

plot range :  20 x 10$^{-5}$ SI/Kg (black)
40 x 10$^{-5}$ SI/Kg (white)

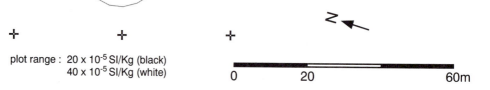

0          20                    60m

**Figure 9.** Greytone plots of (A) magnetometer and (B) MS and (C) resistivity data over the Coneybury henge.

*Durrington Walls*

The 'superhenge' at Durrington has been the target of geophysics on more than one occasion. In the first instance, in conjunction with the rescue excavations of 1966–8 (Wainwright and Longworth 1971), A.J. Clark, then of the AML, undertook a resistivity survey to trace the course of the ditch. This was supplemented by sample coverage of the interior with a proton magnetometer (RCHM(E) 1979). This survey, although only partial (RCHM(E) 1979, fig. 10), successfully confirmed the existence of a small ?Iron Age enclosure abutting the northern perimeter, a double-ditched circular enclosure near the centre of the henge, a number of putative ditches and a scatter of pits—concentrating particularly within an area to the north of the centre of the monument. The identification of several anomalies as pits was confirmed by augering. Because of the incomplete coverage, however, and the coarse survey interval (5 ft) within the sampled areas (50 ft × 50 ft), it was recommended that a complete survey with more modern equipment should be undertaken (RCHM(E) 1979, xv, 18).

This was first attempted by the AML in 1989, but was not fully realised until 1996 when the entire area west of the former line of the A345 was re-surveyed in detail using Geoscan gradiometers and a sampling interval of 1.0 m × 0.25 m. More detailed magnetometer sampling (0.5 m × 0.25 m) and resistivity survey (0.5 m × 0.5 m) was undertaken over selected areas. A full technical report on these results will follow further fieldwork (see below) but we can present a summary here (Figs 10 and 11).

The topography of the henge interior resembles an arena. The uppermost ground, along the western perimeter, encircles a shallow combe that descends south-eastwards across the centre of the monument towards the river Avon. The double ring-ditched feature visible on Crawford's aerial photograph (Crawford 1929), and located by Clark (A on Fig. 11), lies almost in the bottom of this combe in a position commanding a view over much of the eastern half of the henge. The recent survey shows that this feature is the largest (with a diameter of 35 m) of a group of at least four enclosures strung out centrally and very roughly at right angles to the axis of the combe. To the south of the central circle is a much smaller one (B), 12 m in diameter, whilst to the north is an open-ended oval enclosure (C), about 17 m long, with a dense cluster of pit-like anomalies immediately to its east. To the north of this there is a sub-rectangular enclosure (approx. 11 m × 10 m) also apparently with an opening (D). About 100 m to the south of this group is an outlier, a further open-ended oval, approximately 14 m long (E). The openings of the three features where such gaps are detectable in their circuits, all face downslope towards the combe bottom at the centre of the henge. It is noticeable that the survey does not confirm the presence of an inner ring within the larger circle; no coherent pattern of anomalies is visible within it.

As predicted by the proton magnetometer survey, there is a clear concentration of anomalies, many of which must be pits, to the north of the centre of the henge. What is immediately apparent, however, is that (with some significant exceptions) these respect a

*A. David & A. Payne*

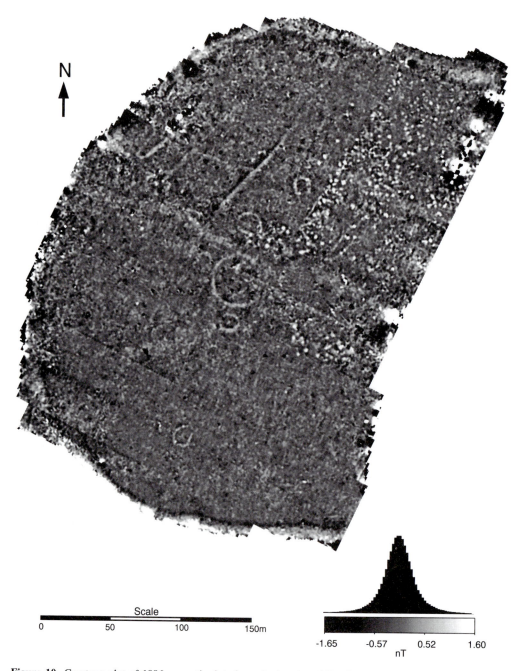

N

Scale

0      50      100      150m

-1.65      -0.57      0.52      1.60
nT

**Figure 10.** Greytone plot of 1996 magnetic data from the interior of Durrington Walls.

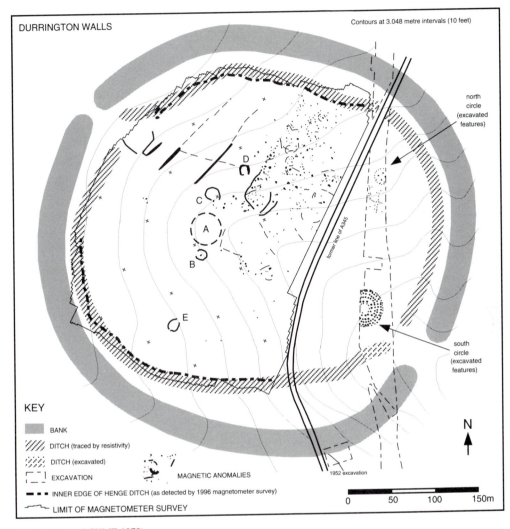

DURRINGTON WALLS

Contours at 3.048 metre intervals (10 feet)

north circle (excavated features)

former line of A345

south circle (excavated features)

KEY

▨ BANK

▨ DITCH (traced by resistivity)

▨ DITCH (excavated)

⌐¬ EXCAVATION

MAGNETIC ANOMALIES

▪▪▪ INNER EDGE OF HENGE DITCH (as detected by 1996 magnetometer survey)

⌒ LIMIT OF MAGNETOMETER SURVEY

1952 excavation

N

0    50    100    150m

(Plan based on RCHME 1979)

**Figure 11.** The main archaeological features detected by the magnetometer survey within Durrington Walls.

largely undetected boundary running NE-SW which separates them from the aforementioned circles and ovals. The alignment of this 'boundary' is approximately parallel with lengths of ditch located further to the north-west and perhaps linked with the Iron Age enclosure there. There are separate clusters of pits in the bottom of the combe. Apart from the one oval ring ditch, archaeological anomalies of any description are noticeably absent from the southern half of the area surveyed.

A full interpretation of these very promising survey results must await a more detailed analysis and further fieldwork (see below). A first generalisation suggests that the circles and 'hengiform' ovals are of Late Neolithic and/or Bronze Age affiliation. As a group they are certainly reminiscent of the barrows on Stonehenge Down (above and Fig. 7). The smaller circle (B) appears to contain a central anomaly which may be a grave pit. At present no clear evidence has yet been obtained for circles of post-holes that could be compared to Woodhenge nearby, or to the Northern and Southern Circles of Durrington, now under the modern road. It remains a strong possibility, though, that such structures are concealed within some of the clusters of 'pit-like' anomalies near the centre of the monument. It is likely, however, that many of the pits and most of the ditch alignments are of Iron Age date, in keeping with other evidence for activity of this date in the imme-diate locality (RCHM(E) 1979; Wainwright and Longworth 1971). With this latter activity in mind it is open to speculation that the northernmost, sub-rectangular, enclosure (D) in the central group may also be of much later date than its neighbours. It appears to be different to the sub-rectangular double-ditched feature recently recognised at Avebury (Bewley *et al.* 1996).

### Woodhenge

Resistivity traverses across the ditches of both Durrington Walls and Woodhenge were undertaken by A.J. Clark as part of his wider study of the effects of seasonality upon the resistivity response (Clark 1975, 1996). The results showed that the massive Durrington ditch remained detectable throughout the year as a low resistance anomaly. More problematically, the response from the much smaller ditch at Woodhenge was more sensi-tive to seasonal variation in moisture balance, being negative for most of the year but changing to a positive anomaly in late summer and autumn. As remarked at the begin-ning of this paper both ditches were also used to test GPR.

### Vespasian's Camp

Very restricted magnetic and resistivity surveys in 1995 within this Iron Age fortified enclosure overlooking the Avon west of Amesbury, south of the Stonehenge Road, revealed little else beyond twentieth-century ferrous disturbance and landscaping. A ring-ditch, perhaps a barrow, was found abutting the southern rampart (Cole 1995).

## The landscape

Now that we have summarised results from geophysical surveys that have taken place over some of the better known monuments in the World Heritage Site, it is necessary to look briefly at those from other surveys in this area.

## The Stonehenge Environs Project

A number of geophysical surveys were undertaken by the AML in advance of test excavation by the Stonehenge Environs Project (Richards 1990; Bartlett 1988b). Reference has already been made above to the surveys of the Coneybury henge, the Lesser Cursus and part of the Avenue, all of which were contributions to the wider Project. The magnetometer survey that detected the northern ditch of the Avenue was situated to cover part of an extensive flint scatter on King Barrow Ridge (Site W59). Over twenty anomalies were located within an area of 0.54 ha and sample excavation of four of these revealed a total of five Neolithic pits of varying ages (Richards 1990, fig. 75). This result is suggestive that at least some of the remainder of the anomalies are probably also pits (rather than natural features, which also occur) and support the excavator's contention that a palimpsest of ?sedentary activity is represented on this part of the ridge.

Small magnetic surveys and MS measurements were also made at Fargo Wood I and II (Sites W32 and W34), and on Wilsford Down (Site W31), all surface artefact scatters, but none of which produced significant geophysical results (but see Entwistle and Richards 1987). It is worth noting that the survey on Wilsford Down located several magnetic anomalies interpreted as possible pits or short lengths of ditch, but which on excavation were shown to be natural features (Richards 1990, 159).

The Stonehenge Environs geophysical surveys were an essentially research-led element of that Project, conducted in the early 1980s. Since then, however, the environs of Stonehenge have seen a much more extensive investment in geophysical survey necessitated by the obligation to make a thorough archaeological assessment prior to the acceptance of planning initiatives (Department of the Environment 1990).

Some of these latter surveys touch upon major field monuments (e.g. the North Kite), but the majority cover swathes of outlying landscape where it has been a major consideration to try and *avoid* overlap with significant remains. In most of these cases, geophysical survey was undertaken as a precautionary measure, to ensure that unsuspected remains were indeed not present. However, if anomalies were located, such survey should be able to contribute to an assessment of their archaeological importance and act as an aid to the targeting of further field evaluation. This 'development-led' survey coverage is very complex in its distribution (Fig. 1) and much of it has not resulted in major new discoveries. For simplicity's sake we will refer only to surveys where positive results were obtained, and categorise the surveys according to the particular development concerned in each case.

## Visitor Centre Sites and approach routes

Surveys related to the various options for re-siting visitor facilities began in 1990 when the AML surveyed parts of an eastern approach to the proposed Larkhill Visitor Centre site (AML archive). This was followed in 1991 by a much more extensive programme of magnetometer and MS survey which covered the proposed Larkhill site itself, the Western Approach to it from the A344, and long narrow strips of ground to either side of the A344 and A303 (Bartlett and Clark 1991). This survey was commissioned from A.D.H. Bartlett and Associates by Debenham, Tewson and Chinnocks and by Timothy Darvill Archaeological Consultants, who were coordinating the project on behalf of English Heritage.

The resulting report (ibid.) notes that the survey responded effectively to a number of known and extant features, particularly round barrow ditches and the western ditch of the Avenue. Ditches corresponding with those sectioned by F. and L. Vatcher close to King Barrow Ridge were located. Elsewhere, findings throughout the survey were in general magnetically weak and scattered anomalies were tentatively interpreted as pits or short linear features, an unknown proportion of which may be natural in origin (ibid.).

In 1993 a further very extensive survey was conducted over other optional routes for a Western Approach to the Larkhill Visitor Centre (Bartlett 1993). This detected a number of archaeologically significant features, including ditches or earthworks associated with the Durrington Down and Fargo field systems known from aerial photography. There appeared to be a relative lack of other features, except occasional pits.

Finally, in 1994, another proposed Visitor Centre Site, at Countess Roundabout, north of Amesbury, was surveyed, as well as its access corridor, extending along the north side of the A303 to King Barrow Ridge. Again, there was a good response to known features but, apart from these, few anomalies of any archaeological significance were found (Bartlett 1994).

*Upgrading the A303: Amesbury to Berwick Down Route Options*

Yet more survey coverage has been undertaken, commissioned by the Highways Agency, as a result of plans to upgrade or re-route the A303 through the World Heritage Site. These surveys, undertaken by Geophysical Surveys of Bradford (GSB) for Wessex Archaeology, took place between 1992 and 1994 (GSB 1992a, 1992b, 1993, 1994). Unfortunately, as elsewhere around Stonehenge, ferrous disturbance prevails in much of these surveys, especially near roads, tracks and over pipes and the sites of military and other installations. However, they have succeeded in confirming the presence of known archaeological features, and have added detail to some of these. Although large areas seem to be mostly devoid of definite archaeological anomalies, a significant number of previously unknown features were located, in widely separate parts of the landscape. Although a detailed review of all these is not possible here, the more important findings can be summarised.

Near Scotland Farm (SU 067 410), over 5 km west of Stonehenge, magnetometer survey mapped in detail a ditched oval enclosure (approximately 175 m × 90 m) the outlines of which were previously visible as cropmarks. The survey revealed, in addition, an abundance of related features, especially pits, as well as evidence for adjacent (but not necessarily contemporary) enclosures (Fig. 12). Some 300 m to the north-east a ring

SCOTLAND FARM, WILTS

N

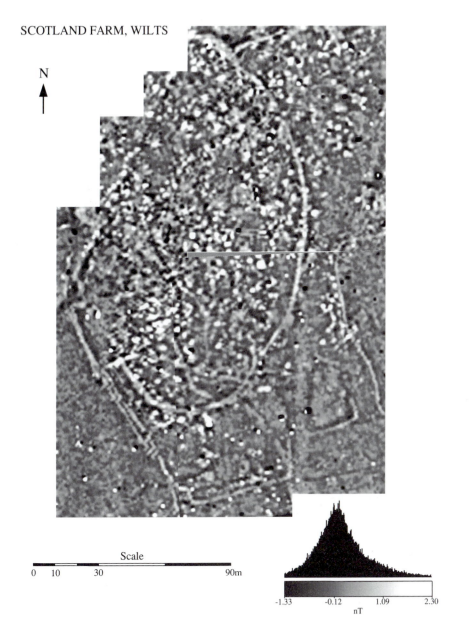

Scale

0    10    30                                90m

-1.33        -0.12        1.09        2.30
nT

**Figure 12.** Greytone plot of the magnetometer survey undertaken by Geophysical Surveys of Bradford near Scotland Farm, Winterbourne Stoke (data supplied by GSB and published by courtesy of the Highways Agency).

ditch about 32 m in diameter was located for the first time and interpreted as a barrow, or perhaps a henge (GSB 1994). Other surveys over the 'Brown Route Options' to the north-west and north-east of Stonehenge yielded occasional linear anomalies and generalised scatters of pit-type anomalies (ibid.).

Nearer Stonehenge, at the Longbarrow Crossroads, another cropmark enclosure (approximately 60 m × 80 m) was located, bisected by the A303, west of the roundabout. It contains a number of magnetic anomalies suggestive of internal features. Just to the north, a ring ditch, about 18 m in diameter and with a weakly defined (perhaps interrupted) ditch circuit was newly identified. To the south of the roundabout various linear ditches and a number of pits were found. Very clearly visible to the magnetometer (Fig. 13), as also from the air (RCHM(E) 1979), is a small segmented ring ditch (Winterbourne Stoke 72) and a larger ring ditch (Winterbourne Stoke 74). The survey clearly demonstrates that this latter circle has a single entrance to the east, indicating that it is probably a henge (GSB 1992b, figs 8.1A-8.4A). Neither circle appears to have detectable internal features.

Of the other survey areas south of the A303, existing aerial photographic evidence was substantiated. Ferrous disturbance and an incomplete coverage have frustrated further definition of the North Kite (GSB 1992b, 1993). Of significance, however, may be the detection of a narrow ditch running parallel to the western side of the Kite, and about 14 m outside it, which could be a counterpart to the one known to run parallel with the eastern limb of the enclosure (Richards 1990, 184). Evidence for features within the Kite is complicated by the presence of scattered ferrous objects.

Another new discovery, but without any known association, is that of a weak magnetic anomaly to the south of Stonehenge Cottages (SU 1347 4195) which clearly defines a ditched square enclosure with sides of about 17.5 m (GSB 1992b, fig. 6.1A). Further to the west, just to the south of the junction of the A344 with the A303, a length of curving ditch, not previously mapped (although perhaps representative of a former road alignment) has been traced for about 150 m, running across Stonehenge Bottom (GSB 1993).

On the south-western flank of Coneybury Hill, traces of the ditches of a field system and other possible enclosures have been located, illustrating again—as elsewhere in this landscape—that magnetic survey is capable of extending the cropmark evidence for so-called 'Celtic field systems'. Evidence for actual settlement, that is the sites of habitation activities, is less obvious—except where enclosure ditches are present and can be seen to be associated with dense concentrations of features, as at Scotland Farm. Where traces of settlement are more diffuse, and/or more poorly preserved, they are very difficult to identify. On Coneybury Hill, for instance, the combined results of topsoil MS surveys, magnetometer survey, and recording of concentrations of surface lithic material were inconclusive (GSB 1993). Like so much of the magnetometer coverage around Stonehenge there are large areas of negligible magnetic activity throughout which are scattered, thinly and seemingly at random, many 'pit-like' anomalies. Whilst a lot of these may be spurious, caused for instance by natural features or more deeply buried ferrous litter, an unknown

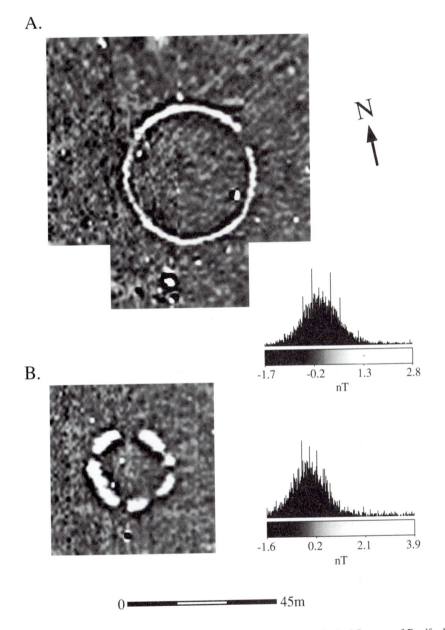

**Figure 13.** Greytone plots of the magnetometer surveys undertaken by Geophysical Surveys of Bradford over Winterbourne Stoke 72 and 74 (data supplied by GSB and published by courtesy of the Highways Agency).

number may yet represent the only indications of genuine 'sites'. The interpreters of geophysical survey plots are loath to omit reference to such anomalies just in case this is so.

# Discussion

It would be useful now to summarise some impressions gained from the foregoing review and then to suggest ways in which geophysics may be able to contribute to archaeological research in the Stonehenge area in the future. That these techniques must have a place in such research should by now, it is hoped, be fully apparent. Before concluding we shall suggest a number of specific targets for future survey.

Of the geophysical methods so far applied in this area the most favoured, by a large margin, is magnetometer survey. This is explained not only by its practical advantage of speed of operation, but by the fact that both the surviving archaeological features themselves, and the contrasting magnetic qualities of the local chalk bedrock and its associated soils, often conspire together to provide a good response. This is illustrated again and again throughout the area, typified for instance by the surveys of the Lesser Cursus and the interior of Durrington Walls and the Coneybury henge. Some important categories of features can easily be missed, however. This is particularly so of the smaller and less magnetic ones such as gullies, post- and stake-holes, and also of some pits and graves which may offer only a poor magnetic contrast between their fillings and the surrounding chalk.

A further constraint on the use of magnetometry, which can limit and, in many extreme cases, entirely nullify its efficacy, is where the landscape is contaminated by recent magnetic debris. This is unfortunately the case, for instance, over the sites of the Stonehenge Aerodrome, the former Horse Isolation Hospital at Fargo and along the margins of most of the roads. Ferrous litter can be widespread elsewhere too, but, if not too dense, its effects can usually be filtered out—as has fortunately been possible at Durrington Walls where rubbish dumping has been a significant problem.

Despite these constraints it has been demonstrated that magnetometry can be extremely effective. As a general rule, it has been shown to respond to the same type of features as those identified by aerial photography. It may thus be used to locate these accurately on the ground and can considerably refine and add to their detail. Examples of this include the enclosure complex at Scotland Farm, the Lesser Cursus, the interior of Durrington Walls, the elbow of the Avenue, the Palisade Ditch, and the Stonehenge Down barrows. Magnetometry has located many new features as well, for example those within Durrington Walls, the Coneybury Anomaly, the ring ditch within the Lesser Cursus, and various pits and ditches from many other locations. Magnetometer survey will also, of course, provide equivalent information to that from aerial photographs over many areas which are for one reason or another not amenable to the recording of crop-marks or soilmarks.

Although there has been much technical improvement over recent years resistivity survey is still much more labour-intensive than magnetometry and responds to a more restricted range of archaeological features. In the Stonehenge area, where ditches and pits predominate, magnetic methods of detection are quicker and more effective. However, if the prevailing moisture conditions are favourable, resistivity is probably better at locating stone settings, and can be sensitive to the presence of severely eroded and flattened earthworks, as has been demonstrated at both Stonehenge itself and at Coneybury. It would be very valuable to see a much wider (and repetitive) coverage by this method of carefully targeted sites.

Other methods of geophysical detection have been attempted only experimentally in this area, for instance at Woodhenge and Durrington, but have not yet played a significant role (but see below). Topsoil magnetic susceptibility survey has been used fairly extensively in support of the interpretation of magnetometer data rather than as a prospecting technique in its own right. 'Pit-like' anomalies in a magnetometer plot may be more securely interpreted as genuine archaeological features when linked with locally elevated topsoil MS values (for example as suggested for the area to the north-west of the Lesser Cursus: Bartlett and Clark 1993). In some instances, such as at the Coneybury henge, MS may be used with other geophysical and excavated data to arrive at specific interpretations of site function. Phosphate measurements, whilst used routinely during the Stonehenge Environs Project, with MS, seem to have only shown modest potential for generalised statements on site and feature function and as yet have little, if any, value for preliminary site location (cf. Entwistle and Richards 1987).

*The future*

There are two linked aspects to the question of future geophysical research at Stonehenge and within its environs. These may be taken in either order, but here we suggest that firstly, it is necessary to define archaeological imperatives and then, secondly, to apply and develop relevant geophysical methodologies to tackle them. Previous experience, summarised above, already allows us a fair appreciation of both the archaeological and technical problems involved.

The archaeological aspect needs to be viewed at several scales. At the largest and most Utopian, one should not shrink from aiming at the total non-destructive examination of the entire World Heritage Site, 6.8% of which has already been magnetically surveyed. This would extend the detailed coverage recently given to Stonehenge itself, and more, to most of the 2666 ha of its surroundings. It would ensure, as far as would be technically feasible at the time, that every buried feature in the area would be mapped. When linked to the surface record (Batchelor, this volume) this would complete the ultimate database for the World Heritage Site.

Aerial remote sensing offers the nearest approach to this ideal. The products of about 90 years of flying have already provided an extensive and detailed record of earthworks, cropmarks and soilmarks, but unsuitable surface conditions preclude total coverage. Airborne and satellite multispectral scanning may in future make up for some of this shortfall but presently lacks the resolution of conventional air photography (Fowler and Curtis 1995; Fowler 1996).

As more land is developed, and as conservation in the World Heritage Site gathers pace, a greater proportion will be taken out of cultivation and will be less amenable to aerial survey. This places a greater onus on ground-based methods. Although total survey may remain unrealistic for the time being, developments in field methodology and in computer capacity and processing power nonetheless allow the prospect of a vastly increased survey coverage. If the whole World Heritage Site cannot be surveyed, then there is at least a reasonable expectation that very large areas within it can be. This could be made possible by the deployment of multiple arrays of magnetometers drawn behind wheeled vehicles and the use of continuous contact resistivity systems also mounted on vehicles. Prototypes of both systems are already in use elsewhere (Clark 1996, 163). EM conductivity instruments could presumably also be applied in this way and, moreover, are theoretically capable of delivering both conductivity and MS data without arduous sampling or the need for ground contact. The open and unobstructed expanses of Salisbury Plain would lend themselves ideally to the detailed coverage of several hectares of open ground per day.

Even without such mechanisation the present methodology has already resulted in an awesome coverage which could and should be extended by whatever means. It makes little sense, for instance, for the survey of the Stonehenge Triangle to be constrained by the geometry of the modern road network when it could be extended widely in every direction. Perhaps a priority in the first instance should be to work northwards so as to embrace the vaster spaces around and within the Avenue and the Cursus. Such large surveys could also be targeted at 'blank' areas, apparently with a dearth of monuments, in the search for the still elusive settlement areas of the Neolithic and Bronze Ages. It has been suggested (Batchelor, this volume) that such a search might profitably be aimed within areas that fall outside those defined by intervisibility between monuments.

At a more reduced scale of enquiry, geophysical methods can be focused down to target particular site complexes, to individual monuments amongst them, or even to components within such sites. There are many quite specific archaeological questions that can be addressed at these levels.

In any consideration of the monuments themselves one has to tackle Stonehenge itself first of all. However, it is our view that, for the time being anyway, there is very little that can be done that will add very significantly to existing knowledge here. The amount of modern infrastructure amongst and around the stones, combined with the irregular honeycomb of intercutting features and backfills, places near insoluble difficulties on geophysical survey interpretation.

It would not do to be too pessimistic, however. It has been suggested (Cleal *et al.* 1995, 492) that detailed geophysical survey of the Ditch and Bank would 'establish the occurrence of further causeways and structures', and this is certainly worth attempting. An even more detailed resistivity sampling interval might be necessary, however, and the survey should be carefully timed to coincide with maximum moisture contrasts. This could be achieved by monitoring resistivity response at selected locations throughout a full year (or more) in order to predict exactly at what time to achieve the best results. It might, in any case, be worth repeating resistivity survey at different times of the year. Such surveys, apart from refining detail of the Bank and Ditch, might also pick up other information, missed by the previous survey, from elsewhere within the monument.

The question of the morphology of the Ditch could also be approached by resistivity profiling, using narrowly spaced multiprobe arrays placed at frequent intervals across the Bank and Ditch. Resistivity profiling, which generates pseudosections or tomographic sections giving an indication of resistivity variation with depth below a linear array of electrodes, is still a relatively undeveloped technique in archaeology (Noel 1992; Szymanski and Tsourlos 1993). Some considerable advances will be required before it will be able to provide the quality of resolution demanded of the Stonehenge enclosure Ditch. There is a possibility that ground-penetrating radar may also offer some prospect of mapping the Ditch in three dimensions, but this technique has not yet matched elsewhere the high expectations generated for it in the 1980s (e.g. Stove and Addyman 1989). The Ditch is very shallow and its fill generally poorly differentiated from its surroundings in terms of clearly detectable dielectric interfaces. Recent experimental work on another shallow chalkland site has been unsuccessful (Meats and Tite 1995).

Both resistivity profiling and GPR could be used in an attempt to target certain areas between the Ditch and the stone circles. Obvious targets of interest, if they cannot be tested by excavation, are the unexplained resistivity anomalies at A and B. Both methods could be used to search for buried megaliths.

Both the Palisade Ditch and the Avenue call for further exploration. If the former is indeed a comparable feature to other Late Neolithic palisades then determining its full extent should be a priority (Cleal *et al.* 1995, 483, 493; Bradley, pers. comm.). The Avenue deserves re-survey of those areas already covered, by both detailed magnetometry and resistivity, and the extension of these surveys along its entire length and, importantly, widely to either side of the alignment. Particular unresolved issues that such surveys could address include the presence or absence of stone placements (see above, and footnote), and the nature of the Avon terminal. Although previous survey has shown that the Avenue does not split into two at the elbow, there remains an enigmatic soilmark that extends the north-eastward alignment of the Avenue well beyond the elbow towards the eastward end of the Cursus (Cleal *et al.* 1995, 313–14, fig. 179). This too deserves to be explained.

Magnetometry has demonstrated how effective it can be at locating pits, and this suggests that further survey to identify these important features would be warranted. There would clearly be advantage to extending the King Barrow Ridge survey, for instance, or to look closely at the area of the Chalk Plaque Pit (Harding 1988), or in the area of Woodhenge. Large pits with a magnetically well enhanced fill are usually easily identifiable as archaeological features (particularly if they are associated with other very suggestive evidence such as ditched enclosures). However, it is worth pointing out that excavation of weaker and less well-defined magnetic anomalies, which are not so asso-ciated, has shown that these may often be non-archaeological. This leads to an unsur-prising diffidence when it comes to interpreting the large numbers of 'pit-like' anomalies that pepper so many of the magnetometer plots from around the outlying areas of Stonehenge. Are they really artificial pits, or not? Are they of ritual, domestic or indus-trial origin? These problems are not easily resolved. Perhaps augering each one would help, but this is not only potentially damaging but also time consuming—as would be any profiling method (even if these could be fully relied upon). Computer modelling of pit morphology (Sheen and Aspinall 1994) could provide clues that might help, for instance, to distinguish a storage pit from a tree-throw hollow but this approach has yet to be tested in earnest on a large scale. MS survey might well give a little weight to one interpretation or another, but would probably not be conclusive. This is therefore an area of interest where more research is needed to develop reliable means of interpreting these anomalies. And it should be added that such research would also benefit, and itself inform, a necessary study of the nature and rates of chalk degradation in the Wessex landscape.

Despite problems such as this it is clear to us that the most valuable geophysical technique in the immediate future will continue to be magnetometry. It is already capable of a high degree of sensitivity, as illustrated by the successful detection of the very weak signals from features such as the central ring ditch within Durrington Walls. Where magnetic contamination is at a minimum, the local chalkland geology can offer a magnet-ically almost inert background against which very subtle signals from significant but slight features may be detectable. There is therefore scope not only for extending the sort of fluxgate gradiometer survey already in use, but also for exploiting even more sensitive magnetometers at even narrower sampling intervals. Commercial portable caesium magne-tometers are now available in the UK but are as yet barely tested on archaeological sites. However, surveys with caesium magnetometers by German archaeogeophysicists have already proved that these instruments have powerful abilities which are at least compa-rable to those of fluxgates, and potentially much more so (Faßbinder 1994; Faßbinder and Irlinger 1994). It should be a priority, then, to experiment with such instruments, and parts of the Stonehenge area would be well suited for this. Although the magnetic cont-amination around Stonehenge itself is discouraging, caesium magnetometry might be a sensible approach to exploring for post- or stone-settings near or beyond the Ditch, for instance on the axis defined by midsummer sunrise and midwinter sunset. The technique would be more effective, however, in the identification of such features in areas where the magnetic background is much more uniform: the sites of 'henge'-type ring ditches such as Winterbourne Stoke 72 and 74 (Fig. 13) would be worth investigating for interior features, as would the newly located sites within Durrington Walls.

If the location of stake-holes is one end of a spectrum of spatial resolutions, then at the other end are the grosser types of feature such as mines and shafts about which so little is known in this area. For instance, three open-cast pits and two shafts 1.5 m deep, interpreted as flint mines, have been excavated near Durrington (Booth and Stone 1952), and their immediate vicinity would be worth investigation for traces of related activity. Magnetometry, resistivity, GPR, and possibly microgravity techniques (Linford forthcoming) would find applications here.

Another opportunity to use GPR has arisen as a consequence of speculation that pond barrows may conceal the sites of shafts such as that found below Wilsford 33a to the south-west of Stonehenge (Ashbee *et al.* 1989). It was suggested that GPR might be one way of testing this hypothesis (ibid. 141) and to this end trial transects were made in 1995 by Mr E.W. Flaxman and Mr John Trust over the Wilsford Shaft itself, as well as over other pond barrows nearby, in the Winterborne Stoke Group (WS 12 and WS 3a) and the Lake Group (WS 78 and WS 77: Flaxman nd). A GSSI SIR2 kit was used and transects were made with both 500MHz and 100MHz antennae. The 500MHz profiles of the Wilsford shaft appear to have clearly detected sides of the upper part of its weathering cone but down only to a depth of approximately 1.2 m (Fig. 14). Unfortunately, however, transects over the other barrows did not produce an equivalent reflection pattern and the radar profiles are difficult to interpret without the support of additional field data. Whilst the profiles over the two pond barrows at Winterbourne Stoke were inconclusive they at least do not discount the possibility that shafts may be present; however, the profiles over the Lake barrows seem to indicate a shallow interface at their centres (Fig. 14) and on this evidence the existence of shafts there seems to be in much more doubt. Magnetic and resistivity surveys of these two latter barrows (including an adjacent smaller barrow) were undertaken by the AML in March 1996. The resistivity data (Fig. 14) clearly identify the higher resistance of the surrounding bank and, as might be expected, the interior is mostly of lower resistance. However, in each barrow there is a central core area of high readings, especially pronounced in the centre of the smallest barrow. Whilst such a pattern appears to be consistent with the GPR data from the two bigger barrows it does not provide a ready explanation, except that there is a drier and probably shallower core area in each barrow. The magnetic data illustrate that there is some ferrous contamination near the centre of WS 78, suggestive of a former excavation, but this does not explain the resistivity phenomena observed. Grinsell (1957) records that all three barrows have been interfered with.

These barrows and some of the examples cited above demonstrate that barrows and ring ditches are particularly amenable to geophysical investigation. Not only is there some hope of establishing information on their internal structure and their state of preservation, there is also the possibility that by careful survey of their surroundings, especially with magnetic methods, it may be possible to identify more ephemeral features (such as the sites of cremation pyres). The interstices *between* barrows deserve more attention.

Whilst individual monuments or groups of monuments thus surely provide considerable incentive for further work, it is clear that the greatest benefit comes from the deployment of a combination of several complementary techniques. To realise their maximum

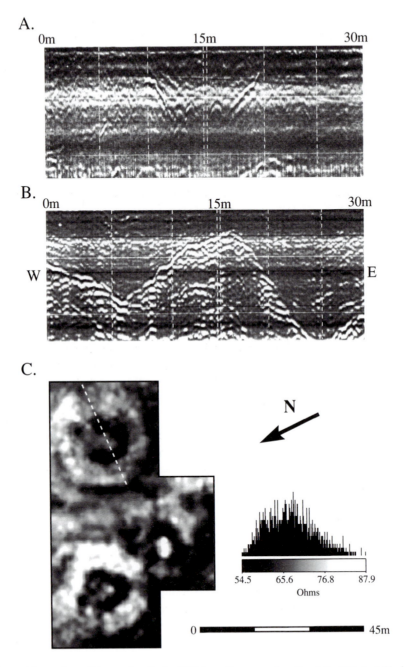

**Figure 14.** A: Ground Penetrating Radar (GPR) profile across the site of the Wilsford Shaft (1995), B: GPR profile across pond barrow at Lake Down (LVG WS78), C: greytone plot of resistivity survey data over pond barrows LVG WS78, LVG WS77 and LVG WS77A. The position of the profile (B) is indicated. (GPR data profiles supplied by courtesy of J. Trust and E. Flaxman.)

effectiveness, however, it will be necessary to accept that these non-destructive methods should preferably be accompanied by some select corroborative test excavation so that 'ground truth' can inform future research.

Geophysical survey can of course also contribute significantly to the study of the Stonehenge area after its *floruit*. Enclosed settlements and field systems seem first to appear in numbers in the landscape in the later Bronze Age and although Stonehenge seems to be maintained and modified in this period, there is evidence that the landscape is changing in character from a mainly funerary emphasis to more domestic use. The evidence for this period of change could be explored further by targeting geophysical survey on areas containing scatters of later Bronze Age and Deverel Rimbury pottery previously located as surface scatters but not investigated further. Such survey could assess these sites for the presence of associated sealed deposits. The potential of evidence for Iron Age, Roman and medieval activity obviously should not be omitted from such studies, either.

*Summary: a possible future programme for geophysical survey at Stonehenge and within the World Heritage Site*

We will now summarise briefly the foregoing suggestions for survey targets and also add a few others for which lack of space does not allow for any further digression. Our assumption is that the entire surveyable area should be covered in as much detail and by as many compatible and relevant techniques as possible. However, it is necessary to be more selective, and the compilation that follows represents some of our own proposals as well as those that have arisen from discussion with colleagues and from within the literature. It must be accepted that this list is of course not comprehensive and that the priorities we have allotted to individual proposals will vary as time and techniques move on.

Having much experience of just how unpredictable the results of geophysical survey may be it is perhaps unwise to prioritise this list. However, it may be helpful to try and we have therefore adopted the following very rough and ready scoring for each proposal, based upon a balance between the practicality of survey and our (more limited) perception of archaeological necessity:

\*\*\*   indicates that the survey is well worth attempting, with a reasonable probability of obtaining clear (positive or negative) results,

\*\*   indicates that a survey is worth attempting, but may result in less clear or more ambiguous results,

\*   indicates that a survey might be worth attempting, but is unlikely to be very informative.

STONEHENGE

1   Detailed resistivity profiling (and perhaps GPR) survey of the Ditch and Bank

(to refine detail of segmentation and possible entrances around the perimeter of the circles). **

   **2**  Detailed resistivity profiling and GPR of resistivity anomalies A, B and C (to investigate the nature of resistivity anomalies here, in parts of the site which have apparently been excavated). **

   **3**  Detailed resistivity and caesium magnetometry of unexcavated western half of the monument (to search this area for more information on unexcavated features). *

   **4**  Detailed resistivity and caesium magnetometry of the area to the SW of the monument, immediately outside the Ditch (to search for undetected features which may lie on the main monument axis). *

THE AVENUE

   **1**  Re-survey the Avenue, with magnetometry and resistivity, at a narrower sampling interval than previously, from its Stonehenge terminal to a position beyond the elbow (to establish the presence and location of any contemporary features such as pits, post- and stone-holes). The survey should take in at least 60 m of ground to either side of the main alignment. **

   **2**  Magnetometer survey of the remainder of the course of the Avenue, also widely to either side (to identify related features). ***

   **3**  Magnetometer and resistivity survey at West Amesbury (to identify the Avon terminal). **

THE PALISADE

   Trace this feature to its full extent (to help establish its overall plan and relationship to neighbouring features). ***

THE CURSUS

   Magnetometer survey of the undisturbed sections of the Cursus, and to either side of it (to determine the detailed outline of the ditches and the nature of any contained or impinging features). **

DURRINGTON

   **1**  Magnetometer survey of the environs of Woodhenge, to its south and west (to clarify and add to the evidence from many cropmarks in this area and to search for further features contemporary with the use of Woodhenge and Durrington Walls). ***

   **2**  Extend this survey to surround the Cuckoo Stone, and survey the latter's previous surroundings with resistivity (to explore for structures that may be related to this isolated stone, e.g. a possible long barrow). **

   **3**  Complete magnetometer coverage of the interior of Durrington Walls, and experiment with high resolution survey over known circles (to extend the results of successful existing survey). **

**4** Magnetometer survey of the area between Durrington Walls and the Packway Enclosure and (where accessible) the immediate environs of the Packway Enclosure (to extend the identification of Iron Age activity in this area and clarify its relationship with the Durrington Walls enclosure). \*\*\*

**5** Magnetometer survey of the eastern approach to Durrington Walls from the river Avon (to seek any features linking the watercourse to the henge). \*

**6** Magnetometer and resistivity survey of any accessible ground near the site of the flint mines located to the north-east of the henge (to locate additional pits and any associated features). \*\*

ROBIN HOOD'S BALL

Magnetometer survey of the causewayed enclosure and its surroundings, inclusive of recently located flint and pottery scatters (to identify details of the enclosure, of outlying activity and of any linkages between them). \*\*\*

KING BARROW RIDGE

Extend magnetometer survey from the area of site W59 (to identify further features linked with the surface lithic scatters here, and to plot their extent). \*\*\*

NORTH KITE

Magnetometer survey of the entire North Kite and any associated features (to clarify the nature of the North Kite and its immediate associations). \*\*

OTHER LOCATIONS

**1** Magnetometer survey of the possible sub-rectangular enclosure (RCHM(E) 1979, 22) located between Stonehenge and Normanton Down barrow group at NGR SU 119 417, a possible Late Bronze Age settlement where fragments of quern have been found (to explore the nature of these traces). \*\*\*

**2** Magnetometer survey of various other possible enclosures of unknown date and function defined by ditches visible as cropmarks in the World Heritage Site, e.g. near Druid's Lodge in Berwick St James at NGR SU 104/388 and SU 097/392 and on Winterbourne Stoke Down (SU 101/422). \*\*\*

**3** Magnetometer survey of the multi-period (Neolithic to Late Bronze Age and Roman) landscape south and south-east of Long Barrow Crossroads. The area contains long barrows, a cluster of small round barrows, linear ditches (possibly dating from the Early Bronze Age), field systems, a possible oval enclosure, and surface scatters of Early and Late Bronze Age, Deverel Rimbury and Roman pottery and fragments of querns. A major linear ditch running from Rox Hill to Winterbourne Stoke Crossroads cuts across the fragmentary field systems in the area. A hut settlement of Thorney Down type recorded by Vatcher and Vatcher near the crossroads in 1967 is probably part of the wider landscape of archaeological features in this area. \*\*\*

**4**  Magnetometer survey of the possible Roman settlement near the summit of Rox Hill plus later Bronze Age activity, linear ditches and 'Celtic' field systems (to complement detail from aerial photography in this area). \*\*\*

**5**  Magnetometer survey in Stonehenge Bottom north of the A303/A344 junction (to locate and follow the curving ditch detected by the 1993 GSB survey just south of this junction). \*\*

**6**  Multi-technique examinations of selected barrows and barrow groups (to determine barrow structure, survival of barrow features and of any features in their vicinity). \*\*\*

## Conclusions

It has not been an easy task to review such an enormous corpus of extant geophysical data and we have had to skim very lightly over much of it. It has not been much easier to propose ways forward either—despite an abundance of archaeological questions to address, at greatly varying spatial scales. We offer here a somewhat conservative view of the place of geophysics in this landscape: that is, that the greatest benefits are still to be obtained, not necessarily from new or emerging techniques, but by the ever-increasing refinement of those that are already familiar and proven by experience. There is great potential for the development of magnetometry, both to utilise greater sensitivities and also to accelerate the speed of ground coverage. Resistivity should also figure in this process, both allowing much expanded coverage and also exploiting multiprobe methods so as to improve resolution in all three dimensions. Each technique requires careful selection depending on the special demands of individual sites or areas; the more deliberate use of complementary technologies is recommended, and it must be accepted that some modest physical intervention will be repaid by considerable dividends towards the future development both of archaeological and geophysical recording.

Much of the history of archaeological investigation around Stonehenge has, naturally enough, been concerned with studies of individual monuments. The limitations of this 'timid' approach (Bradley 1993, 48) are now widely acknowledged and attention is increasingly being diverted to consideration of the landscape setting within which field monuments are just one manifestation of a diversity of human activities. Geophysical survey, too, has tended in the past to be monument-focused. This will of course continue, but developments taking place now put the methodology at the forefront of landscape exploration, not just of the grander monuments and their groupings and alignments, but of the provocatively empty spaces between.

*Acknowledgements*

The fieldwork that we have discussed above is the accumulated product of years of work by many individuals, including both past and present employees of the Ancient Monuments

Laboratory as well as members of other organisations. We are grateful to all these colleagues for allowing us to use their results. Alister Bartlett in particular is a veteran of the Stonehenge area and we are grateful to him and Tony Clark for sharing results of their more recent work there. We would also like to thank John Gater and Chris Gaffney of Geophysical Surveys of Bradford who, with their colleagues, have surveyed very substantial areas of the landscape and allowed us to quote from and illustrate some of their results. Permission to do so was kindly provided by their client, the Highways Agency. Ted Flaxman is thanked for taking the initiative with pond barrows and for allowing us to refer to and illustrate some of his preliminary results; John Trust provided the radar data. At the Ancient Monuments Laboratory we would like to acknowledge warmly the enthusiasm and contributions to fieldwork and data processing by Mark Cole, Peter Cottrell, and Paul and Neil Linford. Stevan Noon and Tom Williams, placement students from Bradford University, helped as well. Nick Burton and Mark Cole are thanked for their help with the figures. We have benefited from discussions with several archaeologists including Richard Bradley, Aubrey Burl, Christopher Chippindale, Tim Darvill, Andrew Lawson, Mike Pitts and Julian Richards. We are grateful to the National Trust and the owners of Durrington Walls for allowing us to work on their land.

# References

AITKEN, M.J. 1974: *Physics and Archaeology* (Oxford, 2nd ed.).

ALLEN, M.J. and GARDINER, J. 1994: Stonehenge: limited test augering. Wessex Archaeology report 30506 (unpublished).

ASHBEE, P., BELL, M. and PROUDFOOT, E. 1989: *Wilsford Shaft: Excavations 1960–62* (London, Engl. Heritage Archaeol. Rep. No. 11).

ASPINALL, A. 1992: New developments in geophysical prospection. In Pollard, A.M. (ed.), *New Developments in Archaeological Science* (London, Proc. Brit. Acad. 77), 233–44.

ATKINSON, R.J.C. 1979: *Stonehenge* (Harmondsworth).

BARTLETT, A.D.H. 1988a: Geophysical survey at Coneybury Henge, Amesbury, Wiltshire, 1980. Ancient Monuments Laboratory Reports Series 169/88 (unpublished).

BARTLETT, A.D.H. 1988b: Geophysical surveys for the Stonehenge Environs Project. Ancient Monuments Laboratory Reports Series 170/88 (unpublished).

BARTLETT, A.D.H. 1990: In Richards, J. 1990.

BARTLETT, A.D.H. 1993: Stonehenge, Wiltshire: report on archaeogeophysical survey of Western Approach corridors (unpublished).

BARTLETT, A.D.H. 1994: Stonehenge Visitor Centre: report on geophysical survey of Countess Roundabout Site and Access Corridor (unpublished).

BARTLETT, A.D.H. and CLARK, A.J. 1991: Stonehenge Visitor Centre Environmental Assessment Report: report on geophysical survey (unpublished).

BARTLETT, A.D.H. and CLARK, A.J. 1993: Stonehenge, Wiltshire The Lesser Cursus: report on archaeogeophysical survey (unpublished).

BARTLETT, A.D.H. and DAVID, A.E.U. 1982: Geophysical survey of the Stonehenge Avenue. In Pitts, M.W., On the Road to Stonehenge: report on investigations beside the A344 in 1968, 1979 and 1980. *Proc. Prehist. Soc.* 48, 90–3.

BEWLEY, R., COLE, M., DAVID, A., FEATHERSTONE, R., PAYNE, A. and SMALL, R. 1996: New features within the henge at Avebury, Wiltshire: aerial and geophysical evidence. *Antiquity* 70, 639–46.

BOOTH, A.StJ. and STONE, J.F.S. 1952: A trial flint mine at Durrington, Wiltshire. *Wiltshire Archaeol. Natur. Hist. Mag.* 54, 381–8.

BRADLEY, R. 1993: *Altering the Earth* (Edinburgh, Soc. Antiq. Scotl. Monogr. Ser. No. 8).

CLARK, A.J. 1975: Archaeological prospecting: a progress report. *J. Archaeol. Sci.* 2, 297–314.

CLARK, A.J. 1983a: The testimony of the topsoil. In Maxwell, G.S. (ed.), *The Impact of Aerial Reconnaissance on Archaeology* (London, CBA Res. Rep. 9), 128–35.

CLARK, A.J. 1983b: Susceptibility and other meters or, how to detect fires in henges. *Curr. Archaeol.* 86, 93.

CLARK, A.J. 1986: Archaeological geophysics in Britain. *Geophysics* 51, 1404–13.

CLARK, A.J. 1996: *Seeing Beneath The Soil* (London, 2nd ed.).

CLEAL, R.M.J., WALKER, K.E. and MONTAGUE, R. 1995: *Stonehenge in its Landscape: Twentieth Century Excavations* (London, Engl. Heritage Archaeol. Rep. 10).

COLE, M. 1995: Vespasian's Camp, Amesbury, Wiltshire. Report on geophysical survey, August 1995. Ancient Monuments Laboratory Reports Series 44/95 (unpublished).

CRAWFORD, O.G.S. 1929: Durrington Walls. *Antiquity* 3, 49–59.

DEPARTMENT OF THE ENVIRONMENT 1990: *Planning Policy Guidance Note 16: Archaeology and Planning* (PPG 16) (London).

ENGLISH HERITAGE 1995: Geophysical Survey in Archaeological Field Evaluation. *Research and Professional Services Guideline* No. 1.

ENTWISTLE, R. and RICHARDS, J. 1987: The geochemical and geophysical properties of lithic scatters. In Brown, A.G. and Edmonds, M.R. (eds), *Lithic Analysis and Later Prehistory* (Oxford, BAR Brit. Ser. 162), 19–38.

FAßBINDER, J.W.E. 1994: *Die magnetischen Eigenschaften und dei Genese ferrimagnetischer Minerale in Böden im Hinblick auf die magnetische Prospektion archäologischer Bodendenkmäler* (Verlag M.L., Leidorf, Buch an Erlbach).

FAßBINDER, J.W.E. and IRLINGER, W.E. 1994: Aerial and magnetic prospection of an eleventh to thirteenth century motte in Bavaria. *Archaeol. Prospection* 1, 65–9.

FLAXMAN, E.W. nd: A radar survey of pond barrows (unpublished).

FOWLER, M.J.F. 1996: High-resolution satellite imagery in archaeological application: a Russian satellite photograph of the Stonehenge region. *Antiquity* 70, 667–71.

FOWLER, M.J.F. and CURTIS, H. 1995: Stonehenge from 230 kilometres. *AAARGnews* (Newsletter of the Aerial Archaeology Research Group) 11, 8–16.

GATER, J.A. 1987: Report on geophysical survey: Stonehenge Cursus, Wiltshire (unpublished).

GRINSELL, L.V. 1957: Archaeological gazetteer. *Victoria County History of Wiltshire* 1(2) (Oxford).

GSB 1992a: Report on geophysical survey: A303 Amesbury to Berwick Down. Report No. 92/03 (unpublished).

GSB 1992b: Report on geophysical survey: A303 Amesbury to Berwick Down Survey II. Report No. 92/82 (unpublished).

GSB 1993: Report on geophysical survey: A303 Amesbury to Berwick Down Survey III. Report No. 93/128 (unpublished).

GSB 1994: Report on geophysical survey: A303 IV Brown Route Options. Report No. 94/67 (unpublished).

HARDING, P. 1988: The chalk plaque pit, Amesbury. *Proc. Prehist. Soc.* 54, 320–7.

LINFORD, N.T. forthcoming: Report on the geophysical survey at Boden Vean, Cornwall, including an assessment of the micro-gravity technique for the location of suspected archaeological void features.

MEATS, C. and TITE, M.S. 1995: A ground penetrating radar survey at Rowbury Copse banjo enclosure. *Archaeol. Prospection* 2, 229–36.

NOEL, M. 1992: Multielectrode resistivity tomography for imaging archaeology. In Spoerry, P. (ed.), *Geoprospection in the Archaeological Landscape* (Oxford, Oxbow Monogr. 18), 89–99.

PAYNE, A. 1994: Stonehenge: 20th century excavations project. Report on geophysical surveys 1993–4. Ancient Monuments Laboratory Reports Series 33/94 (unpublished).

PAYNE, A. 1995: Geophysical surveys at Stonehenge 1993–4. In Cleal, R.M.J., Walker, K.E. and Montague, R. 1995.

PAYNE, A. and WHITE, D. 1988: Stonehenge Cursus, Wiltshire: report on magnetometer survey at the eastern end of the Cursus 1988. Ancient Monuments Laboratory Reports Series 174/88 (unpublished).

RCHM(E) 1979: *Stonehenge and its Environs* (Edinburgh).

RICHARDS, J. 1990: *The Stonehenge Environs Project* (London, Hist. Build. Monuments Comm. Archaeol. Rep. 16).

SCOLLAR, I., TABBAGH, A., HESSE, A. and HERZOG, I. (eds) 1990: *Archaeological Prospecting and Remote Sensing* (Cambridge).

SHEEN, N.H. and ASPINALL, A. 1994: A simulation of anomalies to aid the interpretation of magnetic data. In Lockyear, K. and Wheatley, D. (eds), *Computer Applications and Quantitative methods in Archaeology 1993* (Oxford, BAR).

STOVE, G.C. and ADDYMAN, P.V. 1989: Ground probing impulse radar: an experiment in archaeological remote sensing at York. *Antiquity* 63, 337–42.

STUKELEY, W. 1740: *Stonehenge: A Temple restored to the British Druids* (London).

SZYMANSKI, J.E. and TSOURLOS, P. 1993: The resistive tomography technique for archaeology: an introduction and review. *Archaeologia Polona* 31, 5–32.

TITE, M.S. 1972: *Methods of Physical Examination in Archaeology* (London and New York).

UCKO, P.J., HUNTER, M., CLARK, A.J. and DAVID, A. 1990: *Avebury Reconsidered from the 1660s to the 1990s* (London).

WAINWRIGHT, G.J. and LONGWORTH, I.H. 1971: *Durrington Walls: Excavations 1966–1968* (London, Rep. Res. Comm. Soc. Antiq. London 29).

*Proceedings of the British Academy*, **92**, 115–144

# Environment and Land-use:
# The Economic Development of the
# Communities who Built Stonehenge
# (an Economy to Support the Stones)

## MICHAEL J. ALLEN

THE STONEHENGE LANDSCAPE is one which has drawn the attention of antiquarians and archaeologists for centuries and, not surprisingly, this chalk landscape is one of the best studied archaeological landscapes in the country. With the exceptions of the Dorchester (Woodward 1991; Wainwright 1979; Allen 1994; Allen in Smith *et al.* 1997, 277–83) and Avebury areas (Smith 1965; Evans *et al.* 1993; Whittle 1991; 1993; Powell *et al.* 1996), it is a landscape which has received more detailed and structured palaeo-environmental enquiry by the mapping and recording of soils, analysis of land snails, faunal remains, charcoal, charred seeds and pollen, than almost any other (Table 1; but also see Allen 1994, table 52). This is the result of the interest aroused by Stonehenge as a monument, the surrounding landscape as an entity with other major sites such as Durrington Walls (Wainwright and Longworth 1971), Woodhenge (Evans and Wainwright 1979), and also to the recent large-scale English Heritage funded programmes published as the *Stonehenge Environs Project* (Richards 1990) and *Stonehenge in its landscape* (Cleal *et al.* 1995).

The strength and resolution of palaeo-environmental interpretation within any study area is largely based on the density of datasets. Unlike Evans's (1975) generalised interpretations which are based on just a few sites from which he was able to extrapolate general conclusions for all of southern England, recent work from several specific areas on the chalklands of southern England, of which the Stonehenge landscape is one, now enable palaeo-environmental interpretation of the landscape mosaic *within* these landscapes. As the resolution of interpretation relies, not on the number of datasets, but their density within the area of study, a simple calculation of this density enables a quasi-quantitative 'confidence' rating to be made (Table 2; Allen 1994, table 52) from which it can be seen that the Stonehenge landscape features highly. The density of datasets within each area is calculated and multiplied by 100 to give a relative information factor, or dataset content factor which gives some indication of the quantity of data behind the resolution of interpretation in each area and, therefore, some level of confidence we may place on the resolution of those interpretations (Table 2).

Despite this relative wealth of study, the detailed understanding of the 80 sq km area around Stonehenge, defined to the west and east by the Till and Avon valleys respectively (Fig. 1), is surprisingly weak and sparse when broken down into the newly defined chrono-

**Table 1.** Summary of the main elements of the palaeo-environmental database

| **MESOLITHIC** | | **8100–7100 cal BC** |
|---|---|---|
| monument types: | none | |
| artefacts: | scattered flint tools | |
| THE EVIDENCE | | |
| *At Stonehenge:* | | Post-pits in carpark |
| *Environmental evidence:* | | |
| • | Avon Valley | pollen |
| • | Stonehenge carpark post-pits | pollen and snails |
| *Archaeological finds:* | | |
| • | Few flints scattered across the area | |
| **PRE-PHASE 1** | **Early–Middle Neolithic** | **4000–3000 cal BC** |
| monument types: | Causewayed enclosures and long barrows | |
| artefacts: | Plain bowl pottery | |
| THE EVIDENCE | | |
| *At Stonehenge:* | | single cow-sized bone |
| *Environmental evidence:* | | |
| • | Stonehenge buried soil | pollen and snails |
| • | Coneybury Anomaly | snails, charcoal, seeds and bones |
| • | Robin Hood's Ball pits | snails, charcoal and bones |
| • | Amesbury 42 long barrow | snails |
| • | King Barrow Ridge pits | snails, charcoal, seeds and bones |
| • | Durrington Walls OLS | pollen and snails |
| *Other Archaeological sites:* | | |
| • | Long barrows | |
| • | at Robin Hood's Ball | pottery scatter |
| • | along King Barrow Ridge | pottery scatter |
| **PHASE 1** | **Middle Neolithic** | **2950–2900 cal BC** |
| monument types: | transitional, few monuments, Cursuses | |
| artefacts: | Peterborough Ware | |
| THE EVIDENCE | | |
| *At Stonehenge:* | | excavation of ditch and Aubrey Holes |
| *Environmental evidence:* | | |
| • | Stonehenge | pollen, snails and bones |
| • | Greater and Lesser Cursus | snails and seeds |
| • | OLS at Durrington Walls | snails and bones |
| • | Coneybury pits | snails and bones |
| *Other Archaeological sites:* | | |
| • | Durrington Walls settlement | |
| • | Robin Hood's Ball | pottery scatter |
| • | King Barrow Ridge/Coneybury | pottery scatter |
| • | Wilsford Down | pottery scatter |
| • | Stonehenge Down | pottery scatter |

| **PHASE 2** | **Late Neolithic** | **2900–2400 cal BC** |
|---|---|---|
| artefacts: | Grooved Ware | |
| monument types: | Henges | |
| THE EVIDENCE | | |
| *At Stonehenge:* | | construction of the timber settings |
| *Environmental evidence:* | | |
| • | Stonehenge | pollen, snails and bones |
| • | Coneybury Henge | snails, charcoals, seeds and bones |
| • | Ratfyn | snails |
| • | Durrington Walls henge | bones and charcoal |
| *Other Archaeological sites:* | | |
| • | Chalk Plaque Pit | |
| • | ?Woodhenge | |
| • | east of King Barrow Ridge | pottery scatter |
| • | Stonehenge Down | pottery scatter |

| **PHASE 3** | **Late Neolithic–Early Bronze Age** | **2550–1600 cal BC** |
|---|---|---|
| artefacts: | Beaker pottery | |
| monument types: | Round barrows, palisade features | |
| THE EVIDENCE | | |
| *At Stonehenge:* | | construction of stone settings and Avenue |
| *Environmental evidence:* | | |
| • | Stonehenge | pollen, snails and bones |
| • | many barrows | snails and soils |
| • | Upper fills Coneybury | snails, seeds and bones |
| *Other Archaeological sites:* | | |
| • | Woodhenge | |
| • | Stonehenge Down | pottery scatters |
| • | Robin Hood's Ball | pottery scatters |
| • | Normanton | pottery scatters |

logical phases of the construction of Stonehenge (Allen and Bayliss 1995). Nevertheless, by reviewing the data provided in both the *Stonehenge Environs Project*, hereafter called *SEP* (Allen *et al.* 1990; Carruthers 1990; Gale 1990; Maltby 1990), and the *Stonehenge in its landscape* volume (see especially Cleal and Allen 1995), the development of organisation and community farming that made possible the construction of the ever more complex monument of Stonehenge by prehistoric communities can be illustrated. In doing this, the inadequacies of the datasets can be realised and, more significantly, the inadequate chronological parameters of the palaeo-environmental information drawn from the landscape around Stonehenge recognised when compared with the high chronological resolution for the construction of the monument, as supplied by the recent large radio-carbon dating programme (Allen and Bayliss 1995).

This paper will, therefore, not address the question of *why* farmers of the Stonehenge communities felt they *needed* to build this edifice, as Bradley has (1993, 9 on), but of *how* those communities became *enabled* to build it. This paper has two objectives; first to show that some interpretation and answers of a more strictly cultural, or conventional,

**Table 2.** Comparison of the density of environmental datasets in chalkland archaeological landscapes and the calculation of a 'confidence factor'

|  | No. of data-sets | Km$^2$ of chalk in study area | Density (datasets÷ Km$^{2)}$ | Confidence Factor (density × 100) |
|---|---|---|---|---|
| Dorchester area | 12 | 35 | 0.343 | **34.3** |
| Stonehenge | 17 | 54 | 0.315 | **31.5** |
| Winchester area | 3 | 16 | 0.187 | **18.7** |
| Avebury | 20 | 130 | 0.154 | **15.4** |
| Isle of Wight | 9 | 64 | 0.140 | **14.1** |
| Strawberry Hill, Wilts | 1 | 10 | 0.100 | **10.0** |
| Lewes area, Sx | 9 | 106 | 0.085 | **8.5** |
| Kent | 3 | 1500 | 0.002 | **0.2** |

archaeological nature can be provided through the archaeological enquiry of palaeo-environmental analyses which extends ideas outlined elsewhere (Cleal and Allen 1995, 484), and second, to suggest a framework for future structured palaeo-environmental enquiry within the area, while appreciating and highlighting weaknesses in the present datasets.

My contention is that in order to understand how communities survived and operated in the past it is necessary to examine more than just the obvious foci of attention; thus to understand Stonehenge we need to understand the communities and landscape surrounding the monument. This does not require the engendering of environmental determinism, but certainly the philosophy of environmental possibilism is embraced (i.e. that environments limit, but do not necessarily cause, patterns of human behaviour: Hardesty 1977, but see also Bell and Walker 1992, 8). It was, after all, the landscape around Stonehenge that contained the farmland which produced food to support both the local communities and the economic base which enabled these communities to provide the organisation and labour force to build, rebuild, modify and remodel the monument of Stonehenge. The interpretations derived from palaeo-environmental analyses enable us to examine and reconstruct the physical and economic arena within which prehistoric communities acted and interacted.

Bradley states that landscape history cannot be studied using an intellectual structure formed almost entirely around artefacts (Bradley 1978, 2) and here, by examining the evidence from the Stonehenge area, an attempt is made to show that it is possible to provide answers and explanation for purely 'cultural' activity via palaeo-environmental enquiry. Environmental archaeology is ideally suited to analysing the landscape; especially now that this discipline has progressed beyond being merely a technique for compiling floral, faunal and climatic sequences and has proved itself as a means to interpret past human activity (Evans 1975).

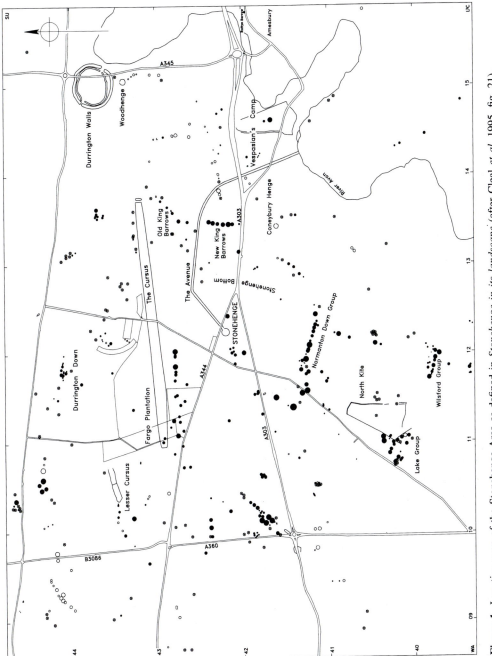

**Figure 1.** Location map of the Stonehenge Area as defined in *Stonehenge in its landscape* (after Cleal *et al.* 1995, fig. 21).

## The evidence

Most of the major environmental analyses have been undertaken recently and therefore, unlike some of the archaeological information from antiquarian sources, we can be confident in the identification and integrity of these datasets. It is still necessary, however, to interrogate the precise contexts from which some of these datasets originate. This is especially applicable to the faunal assemblages, which are often summarised by site rather than period (Richards 1990), and to the unquestioned acceptance and use of the radiocarbon determinations for the area which underpin the chronological framework for all interpretations of change and development.

Most of the palaeo-environmental information comes from archaeological excavations. With few exceptions, the assemblages of charred seeds, charcoal and faunal remains are small. Where faunal assemblages are larger (e.g. Coneybury 'Anomaly', Stonehenge Ditch), they are associated with single feasting events (Coneybury) or specific disposal (Stonehenge) and are not, therefore, representative of the usual farming and hunting economy. Nevertheless these environmental data (seeds, charcoal and bones) have usually been recovered from specific, dated contexts. In contrast, the evidence of the 'environmental landscape' and changing nature of the vegetation structure has largely been examined through the analysis of stratified sequences of land snails from ditches, such as at Stonehenge itself (Evans 1984) and Coneybury Henge (Bell and Jones, in Richards 1990, 154–8). Pollen sequences are especially rare on the chalkland, and a Boreal to Sub-boreal (Mesolithic–Neolithic) combined pollen and snail sequence from a Mesolithic post-pit at Stonehenge (Scaife 1995; Allen 1995) is therefore of prime importance, but enables the examination of only the environment of the earlier local prehistoric landscape nearly four millennia before any of the familiar monuments came into being. Recent work in the Avon floodplain has produced a long pollen sequence (Scaife forthcoming), the base dating from the seventh millennium BC (7950–7030 cal BC, GU-3239, 8460±200 BP). This does not record a complete vegetation record. Apart from the base, no other horizons or vegetation changes have been dated and thus the long vegetation history cannot be accurately correlated with monument building and archaeological events within the broader landscape with any acceptable degree of confidence.

A programme of broader non-site analysis of colluvial sequences (cf. Bell 1983) was unsuccessful because, surprisingly, it failed to identify such deposits in the Stonehenge landscape (Richards 1990, 210–11); an absence confirmed by recent augering (Allen 1994, 268–9, fig. 56). Such a lack of colluvium is anomalous in both Wessex (Allen 1992) and the chalklands of southern England (Bell 1983; Allen 1991). This lack of colluvial deposits, which are considered largely to be a result of human activity, is strange in view of the pre-eminent long history of activity in this area. This has puzzled, and continues to puzzle, a number of authors (Bell 1986; Richards 1990, 210–11; Allen 1991, 51–4; Cleal and Allen 1995, 484), but recent trenching on Coneybury Hill did expose shallow colluvial sequences, the new land snail analyses from which are presented here (Table 3).

**Table 3.** Land snail data from Coneybury Hill colluvial sequence (Tr 3100)

| Sample | 3130 | 3129 | 3121 | 3122 | 3123 | 3124 | 3125 | 3126 | 3127 | 3128 |
|---|---|---|---|---|---|---|---|---|---|---|
| Context | 3107 | 3106 | 3105 | 3104 | 3103 | 3103 | 3102 | 3102 | 3101 | 3101 |
| Depth (cm) | spot | spot | 75–90 | 62–75 | 52–62 | 46–52 | 36–46 | 24–36 | 12–24 | 0–12 |
| Wt (g) | 1500 | 1500 | 1500 | 1500 | 1500 | 1500 | 1500 | 1500 | 1500 | 1500 |
| MOLLUSCA | | | | | | | | | | |
| Pomatias elegans (Müller) | – | – | + | – | – | + | 1 | – | – | – |
| Pupilla muscorum (Linnaeus) | – | – | – | 1 | 1 | 2 | 1 | 1 | – | – |
| Vallonia costata (Müller) | – | 1 | + | – | – | – | 3 | 4 | – | – |
| Vallonia excentrica Sterki | 1 | – | – | 1 | – | 5 | 18 | 30 | 1 | 1 |
| Limacidae | – | – | – | – | – | – | – | 1 | – | 1 |
| Cecilioides acicula (Müller) | 13 | 7 | – | 19 | 23 | 63 | 56 | 31 | 7 | 3 |
| Candidula intersecta (Poiret) | – | – | – | – | – | – | 12 | 27 | 3 | 4 |
| Candidula gigaxii (L. Pfeiffer) | – | – | – | – | – | – | 1 | 1 | 2 | 2 |
| Cernuella virgata (Da Costa) | – | – | – | – | – | – | 3 | – | 6 | 2 |
| Helicella itala (Linnaeus) | 2+[2] | – | 2 | 2 | 2 | 12+[1] | 4 | 5 | – | 1 |
| Taxa | 3 | 1 | 1 | 3 | 2 | 3 | 8 | 7 | 4 | 5 |
| TOTAL | 3 | 1 | 2 | 4 | 3 | 19 | 43 | 69 | 12 | 10 |

Totals in [ ] are modern specimens which retain their periostricum.

# The chronological limitations of the data

Palaeo-environmental data that provide evidence for *change* and *development* in a landscape are probably some of the most important. Such data can be gained from long pollen sequences (e.g. Avon Valley and Stonehenge carpark post-pits), snail sequences from ditches and other sediment traps (e.g. Stonehenge, Cursuses, and pits), or colluvial and alluvial deposits (e.g. Figheldean, Allen and Wyles 1993; and Coneybury Hill, see below).

It is, however, often difficult to integrate and relate the changing evidence provided by palaeo-environmental sequences from these ditches, pits, and colluvial and alluvial deposits with any specific episodes of monument building or other specific archaeological events. Cleal demonstrates this in her attempt to correlate the mollusc sequences from the Stonehenge and Coneybury ditches (Cleal *et al.* 1995, 163). Often, only the construction date is known for pits and ditches of monuments which merely relates to snail-poor sequences from the primary fills. This only provides the date of the *start* of a land-use history depicted in sequence which may, albeit possibly intermittently, extend over several millennia. In fact it is this very longevity that is the attraction of these sequences in examining land-use change and development.

The limitations of such weakly dated sequences immediately becomes apparent when attempting to correlate these interpretations with the tighter chronological resolution provided by recent programmes of $^{14}$C results obtained from monumental sites in the area. Although these limitations cannot be immediately overcome, they can begin to be resolved in part by the careful examination of archive records of the occurrence of datable artefacts (mainly pottery) from ditch fills, in order to provide a tighter chronology for many of the sequences than have been recorded in previous publications. By combining evidence from these artefactual and ecofactual assemblages with the results of the radiocarbon programmes it is now possible to begin to obtain both spatial and chronological resolution across much of the Stonehenge landscape. For instance, by the examination of the distribution of diagnostic sherds in the upper fills of the Coneybury Henge, the important molluscan sequence can be related to the events in other sites and, *inter alia*, attempt to relate this environmental event more confidently with the other events in the area.

The writer is aware of the weaknesses in the chronological relationship between some of the palaeo-environmental sequences and undated monuments, on the one hand, and the tightly-dated sequence at Stonehenge (Allen and Bayliss 1995; Bayliss *et al.*, this volume) on the other. For each phase of construction at Stonehenge, the main sites and nature of the environmental evidence utilised in these discussions is summarised (Table 1), in order to enable both easy reference to the relatively large and diverse spectrum of data. It will also aid critical re-examination of this interpretation should further radiocarbon dates or other information contradict the phases into which environmental datasets and monuments have been placed (Table 1, Fig. 2).

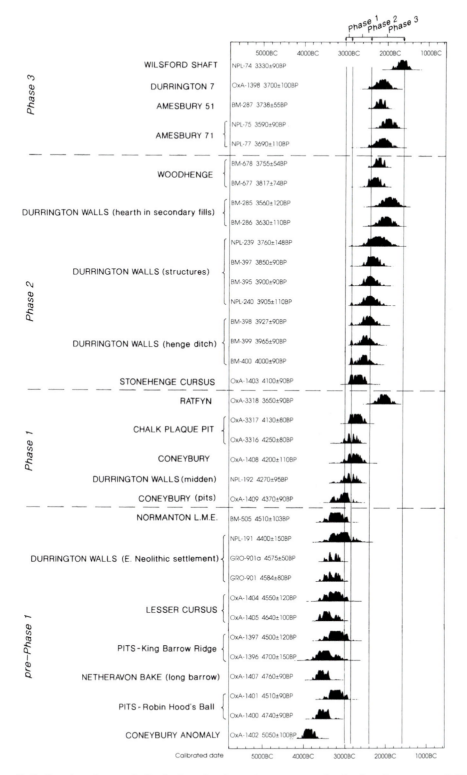

**Figure 2.** Radiocarbon dates and distributions for the main monuments in the Stonehenge area, divided chronologically by the developmental phases of Stonehenge itself.

# The economics behind the building of Stonehenge

Many of the environmental data, and local interpretations of those data, are published elsewhere. Where they have been used in interpretations in this paper, they are referenced in tables by the phases defined for Stonehenge itself (Cleal *et al.* 1995) for convenience of cross-reference (Table 1). This paper, therefore, reviews much of the previously published evidence, but places it within the chronological framework provided by the new phasing of Stonehenge itself. A few new, additional, analyses are included, particularly where major monuments have previously failed to produce palaeo-environmental sequences, or where previous radiocarbon dates are open to question, as at, for instance, the Stonehenge Cursus.

By these means maps of the development and pattern of the utilisation of the land-scape can be drawn (Plates 2–5). Unlike those presented in the Stonehenge Environs Project (Allen *et al.* 1990, fig. 155), which were academically strict in depicting inter-pretation only around the location where datasets occurred, in this paper the reconstruc-tions attempt to be more holistic, and are not just based on specific datasets (viz. Allen *et al.* 1990, fig. 155), but also use evidence of local topography, artefact and monument distributions, as well as educated, informed postulation, to complete an impression of the entire Stonehenge landscape.

The construction of the Stonehenge monument that we see today required consider-able community and collaborative effort. The development of the monument from a simple enclosure ditch to one containing a complex of timber settings was achieved over an extended period of *c*.500 years. Four and a half millennia prior to this, however, Mesolithic communities were erecting unusual 'monuments' in the same area (see below).

In its earliest phase (Phase 1; *c*.3000 cal BC), Stonehenge, as a simple causewayed or segmented enclosure ditch, is not unusual in the chalk landscape, as can be seen by the presence of other communal monuments such as the Earlier Neolithic enclosure at Robin Hood's Ball and contemporaneous monuments of the Lesser and Stonehenge Cursuses. Using Startin's calculations (1982) a labour force of about 45 strong could have constructed the causewayed ditch at Stonehenge in about 5 weeks (working a 50 hour week with *c*.7 hours of daylight).

In its second major phase (Phase 2; 2900–2400 cal BC), the ditch enclosed a complex of timber settings which are essentially undefined (Cleal *et al.* 1995). They may have been considerably more complex than a simple series of wooden, even embellished, posts (see Gibson 1994). Stonehenge was not unique even within its local area; the henge monu-ments at Durrington and Woodhenge in the Avon valley and that at Coneybury were all built with timber structures. Furthermore the construction at Stonehenge, apart from the erection of timber posts, need not have required a large work-force for an extended period of time.

It is only in its final and most prolonged phase (Phase 3; 2550–1400 cal BC), that the stone monument is unique. The construction of the stone monument required a much larger work-force over an extended period to complete even individual elements of this setting; far more than in earlier phases the construction required transport, retrieval, planning, management and engineering skills (see Richards and Whitby, this volume). It is the extent and scope of this design and the management of it that is unique and which is emphasised by the recent rephasing and radiocarbon programme which show the continued development, modification and re-modelling of the stone settings over a period of more than one millennium.

In this last phase the construction of, for example, the sarsen settings (phases 3ii and 3iii) would require a minimum work-force of 600 over 58 weeks, again based on figures given by Startin and Bradley (1981) and estimated on the basis of a 50 hour week. This makes many assumptions: that Startin and Bradley's calculations are broadly correct (they differ significantly from Renfrew 1973), that sarsen settings were constructed as a single event, and that the work-force was deployed continually to a single plan for over a year. It does not take into account any other external, climatic, social or political factors. This, however, need not worry us, as the main points are to demonstrate first, that this stage of the monument required manpower on a significantly different scale than in earlier phases (both Startin and Bradley's, and Renfrew's calculations demonstrate this) and that this required the deployment of an extensive work-force operating over, in terms of the farming year if nothing else, a large time period, and secondly, the continued necessity of the local community, or communities, having the organisational framework (cf. Renfrew 1973) and a sufficiently sound economic basis to allow them, as required, to provide shelter and provision for a large and economically non-productive work-force.

The details of analysis and previous interpretations are adequately presented elsewhere (*SEP* and *Stonehenge in its landscape*, Cleal *et al.* 1995). What follows is a summary of the development of the landscape and economic base of the area in relation to the phases of construction and building of Stonehenge defined by Cleal *et al.* (1995), in order to highlight the main points. Limited new analyses and data are presented where appropriate.

## Mesolithic; human activity in a wildwood landscape, 8100–7100 cal BC (Plate 1)

It may seem strange to begin by briefly discussing the nature of the vegetation structure and the environment around Stonehenge at a time some four millennia before even the first dated evidence at the Monument itself. Nevertheless the presence of people at this time indicates the longevity of use of the area, and may provide us with some possible reasons why this location was later chosen for the construction of the Monument.

The downland, supporting thick brown earths or argillic brown earths, was covered with open hazel and pine woodland (Allen 1995; Scaife 1995). Within a cleared area of this at least four pine posts, cut from the local woodland, were erected upright in deep post-pits in the eighth millennium BC (Plate 1). Parallels for these upright posts can be drawn from herding facades, or even totemic poles, both of which are used by North American hunter-gatherer communities existing in a 'Boreal-type' environment. Care must be taken not to over-speculate, but if the poles do represent a formal display such as a series of 'totem' or symbolic ceremonial posts, then it is of interest to note that where such items occur in native American civilisations, they are erected as a mark of respect for past chiefs and that their locations form arenas of ritual and dance, rather than a focus for settlement and domestic activities. Dancing would leave little obvious trace in the archaeological record. A number of radiocarbon dates belonging to the eighth millennium BC, and the character of the vegetation, independently suggest that these features must belong to this period, despite the fact that no Mesolithic artefacts were associated with any of the excavations (Vatcher and Vatcher 1973; Allen 1995), or within the vicinity (Wymer 1977).

It is not known how widespread was the clearance of the pine and hazel woodland in the area of Stonehenge, and pine charcoals were even recovered from unstratified layers within the Monument itself (Gale, in Cleal *et al.* 1995, 461). Nevertheless, it is possible to suggest that this activity instigated an irreversible change in the local vegetation history. Vegetation composition was not static, but gradually changed in response to wider climatic development. The local regeneration and vegetation succession to woodlands of Sub-boreal climes may have rendered permanent differences in the areas which had already been cleared. If so, it is possible that this area supported a modified vegetation, slightly different from that in the immediate surrounding area even as much as four millennia later. This may, therefore, have played a part in the choice of the location of Stonehenge as it is possible that a vegetation of less dense, open woodland, or even grassland, might have been an attractive location. It may also have provided evidence of the presence of the forefathers, and meaning to antecedents at this location. We can only speculate.

## Pre-Phase 1: Early to Middle Neolithic; taming the wildwood, 4000–3000 cal BC (Plate 2)

Despite the evidence for a Mesolithic presence at the site of Stonehenge itself, this place was not a centre of activity in the Early to Middle Neolithic. There is no evidence of the large-scale plain bowl pottery scatters, or an early causewayed enclosure, as seen at Robin Hood's Ball (Cleal *et al.* 1995, fig. 252), nor even of occasional finds of plain bowl or the siting of a long barrow.

There is, however, evidence of activity over most of the area (Plate 2; Cleal *et al.* 1995, fig. 252), from which a number of radiocarbon dates have been obtained (Fig. 2). Within this period we can see the construction of the Robin Hood's Ball causewayed enclosure and the erection of numerous long barrows, for which a date of 3780–3640 cal BC (OxA-1407, 4760±90 BP) has been obtained from Netheravon Bake. A large scatter of plain bowl wares centres on the enclosure and on a group of dated Neolithic pits at Robin Hood's Ball (Table 1, Plate 2). Other pottery finds occur on Coneybury Hill and King Barrow Ridge.

Despite the lack of artefactual activity at Stonehenge itself, the shallow buried soil beneath the bank contained pollen which indicates an open grassland environment, at least in the locality of the site (Scaife in Allen 1995, 61). Snails from a thin 'poorly differentiated' layer, also under the bank and 'lacking clear horizons' (Evans 1984, 7), certainly corroborate this (Evans, op. cit., zones A and B). Recent augering confirmed the presence of a buried thin rendzina soil (Allen 1995, 60–1).

Much of the environmental evidence, particularly land snails (e.g. Netheravon Bake, Amesbury 42 etc.), indicates open grazed grassland, but the strong bias in the database must be borne in mind. Samples have been consistently taken from archaeological sites, and therefore are biased towards areas of *known disturbance* and human modification of the natural vegetation. Without hillwash or pollen sequences which can be confidently related to this period, there is little else upon which to rely. Charcoals, however, indicate woods of elm, ash, oak, hazel and yew, and limited faunal remains suggest the herding of cattle and possibly some sheep, management of pigs and hunting of deer and aurochs in the woodland and of beaver and fish in the rivers.

The environmental evidence may be biased towards open grazed grassland, but it cannot be denied that large tracts, though by no means all, of the Stonehenge landscape were clear-felled. Much of the chalkland, and presumably the river valleys, however, would still have been considered as 'wildscape'. The character of the woodland, which we assume to have been relatively widespread, changed as areas were locally clear-felled and subsequently allowed to regenerate. This resulted in a complex mosaic of vegetation types with areas of ancient denser woodland, light open mixed hazel and oak woodland and clear-felled areas of shrubs and grassland for grazing, browse, cultivation and occupation.

Overall this evidence seems, irrefutably, to indicate clearance with browse and graze for cattle, sheep and deer. The few cereal remains recovered indicate that crops were cultivated, but probably in small plots, while feasting events (e.g. Coneybury 'Anomaly'), situated in small woodland clearings, were more concerned with meat consumption.

This biodiversity of vegetation types allowed great diversity in the economy of the local population; limited farming would have encouraged more permanent foci of activity; the woodlands enabled pannage as well as hunting and cultivation and collection of plants (see Moffett *et al.* 1989). The mosaic of vegetation types this created was not static; it changed continually through natural regeneration and succession, and through localised human exploitation. Although the overall pattern generally remained constant, the detail of any specific area may not have. Continued small-scale activities of not wholly sedentary populations contributed to this increasing local biodiversity.

# Phase 1: Middle Neolithic; the siting of the monument in its landscape, 2950–2900 cal BC (Plate 3)

The site chosen for the Monument may have been influenced by a number of factors including immediate antecedent activity or long-past activity, as suggested above. It is also possible, as discussed above, that previous human activities may have manifested themselves in permanent and obvious changes in the vegetation pattern resulting in a different local ecological regime with its own floral and faunal characteristics. This would mark an area as different from its surroundings, and may have made the site immediately, or superficially, more attractive; particularly if it was realised this difference was due to the actions of previous communities—the ancestors. Many monuments were constructed in places that had already acquired special significance (Bradley 1991; 1993, 45)—perhaps the Mesolithic presence and placing of upright pine poles at Stonehenge was a part of that earlier, special significance.

## *The landscape*

Although in radiocarbon terms it is now possible to tie the digging of the Stonehenge Ditch to a very tight period of about 50 years at the beginning of the third millennium BC (Bayliss *et al.*, this volume), in order to understand contemporaneous environmental data it is necessary to consider a broader date range of 3500–3000 BC. Otherwise there would be no dated, strictly contemporaneous, information to consider.

Much of the environmental evidence (snails) again indicates open grazed grassland, but the same inherent biases exist in our datasets. At Stonehenge itself Evans's detailed analysis indicates an established grazed downland in his zone A from the base of the Stonehenge Ditch, and beneath the bank (Evans 1984). Buried soils from the later monuments of Durrington Walls (Evans, in Wainwright and Longworth 1971) and Woodhenge (Evans and Jones 1979) also probably refer to this period, and these too indicate an established grazed downland.

The Lesser Cursus can be considered to be broadly contemporary with this phase in terms of its general architectural form (Gibson 1994), pottery (Raymond in Richards 1990, 82–3), and radiocarbon dates (Fig. 2). Multiple molluscan analyses by Entwistle (in Richards 1990, 88–93) produced only sparse Neolithic assemblages from basal deposits (see Entwistle in Richards 1990, tables 37–42 presented in microfiche 1, D5–10). Most of the molluscan sequences, although they depict some spatial variation along the length of this monument (op. cit., 93), refer to undated ditch silting episodes, possibly in the Late Neolithic but, more likely, in the Bronze Age.

The Stonehenge Cursus, which is closer to the Monument, has neither satisfactory radiocarbon dates nor anything in the way of environmental evidence. The radiocarbon date on an antler recorded from the base of the ditch by J.F.S Stone (1947), of 2910–2460 cal BC (OxA-1403, 4100±90 BP see Fig. 2) is considered erroneous as Richards indicates that the antler may have come from an intrusive feature (Richards 1990, 96) and

PLATE 1

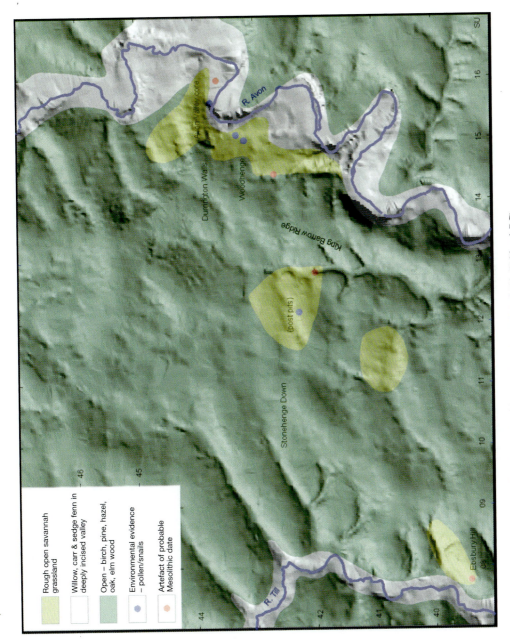

Legend:

- Rough open savannah grassland
- Willow, carr & sedge fenn in deeply incised valley
- Open – birch, pine, hazel, oak, elm wood
- Environmental evidence – pollen/snails
- Artefact of probable Mesolithic date

Map labels: Avon Valley core, R. Avon, Durrington Walls, Woodhenge, King Barrow Ridge, (post pits), Stonehenge Down, R. Till, Etsbury Hill

Grid references: SU, 16, 15, 14, 13, 12, 11, 10, 09, 08, 46, 45, 44, 42, 41, 40

Vegetation and land-use in the Stonehenge landscape in the Mesolithic (8100–7100 cal BC)

PLATE 2

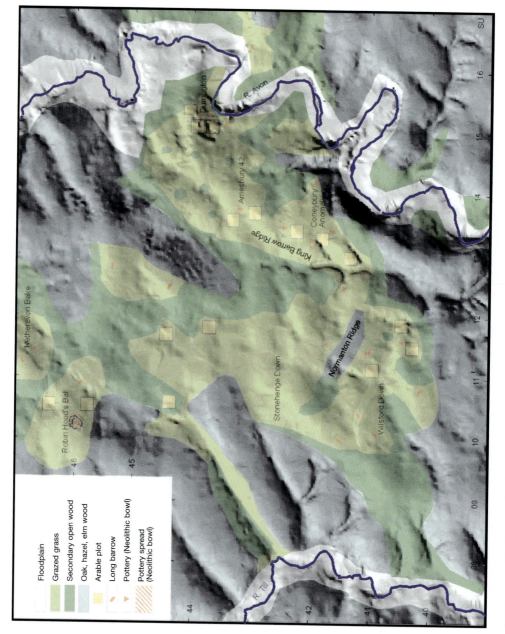

Vegetation and land-use in the Stonehenge landscape in the Early to Middle Neolithic; pre-phase 1 (4000–3000 cal BC)

PLATE 3

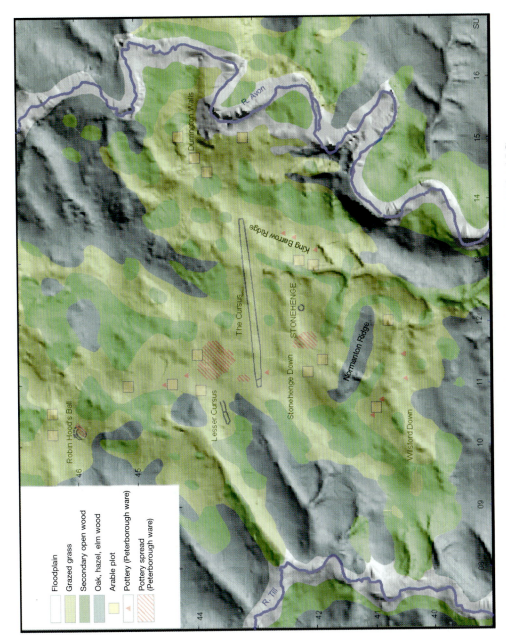

Vegetation and land-use in the Stonehenge landscape in the Middle Neolithic; phase 1 (2950–2900 cal BC)

PLATE 4

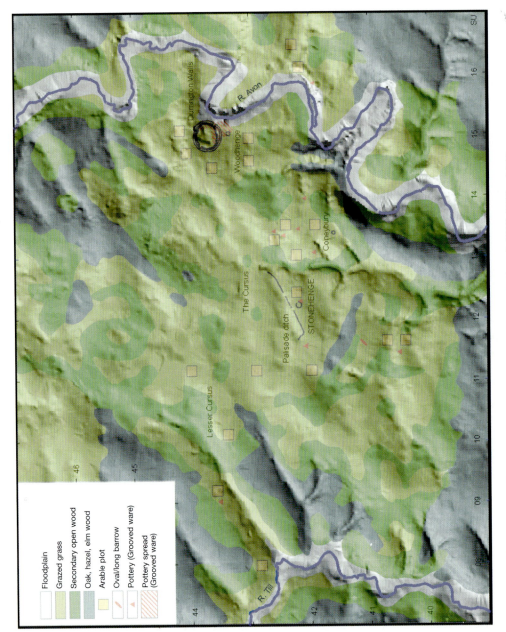

Vegetation and land-use in the Stonehenge landscape in the Late Neolithic; phase 2 (2900–2400 cal BC)

PLATE 5

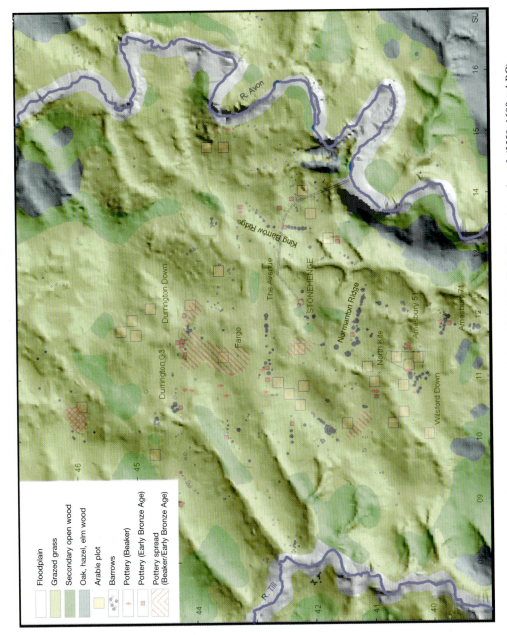

Vegetation and land-use in the Stonehenge landscape in the Late Neolithic/Early Bronze Age; phase 3 (2550–1600 cal BC)

the date does not make sense in terms of the monument's relation with other sites in this area (Cleal and Allen 1995). This cursus is generally considered to be contemporary with the Lesser Cursus, and certainly not significantly later as suggested by the radiocarbon evidence. Although columns of samples were taken for molluscan analysis, the decalcified nature of the deposits in a section through Fargo Wood and the low numbers in a second section at the Larkhill track (Richards 1990, 93, 95, tables 45 and 46 presented in fiche 1, D14 and E1) precluded meaningful interpretation. In an attempt to rectify this a ditch section, fortuitously exposed by a tree fall during the same event that damaged many of the barrows in the King Barrow Ridge making sections there available for examination (Cleal and Allen 1994), was recorded and sampled (Fig. 3).

The basal molluscan assemblages, although low in shell numbers (Table 4), indicate that the construction and early ditch silting history of the Cursus occurred in an established open grazed environment. Possible hints of local cultivation can be seen in the base of the secondary fills (Fig. 3), from which charred caryopses of *Triticum dicoccum* (emmer) were recovered from the mollusc samples (ident. J. Ede).

This general picture is therefore clearly biased towards clear-felled and grazed downland. Nevertheless it is evident that this landscape was a rich and diverse mosaic of habitats (Plate 3). The few charcoal records include oak, hazel, *Prunus*, Pomoideae and maple (Gale 1990, 252–3), indicating some open, probably secondary, woodland.

Many of the clearings seen in the Earlier Neolithic had become both larger and more permanent, with established grazed grassland (Plate 3), especially along the King Barrow Ridge (snails beneath the barrows) and banks of Durrington Walls, Woodhenge and Stonehenge itself. The close cropped nature of the vegetation structure indicated by the snails suggests that the grassland was under relatively rigorous grazing, probably by cattle and sheep, but also possibly deer. This is confirmed by the sparse bone evidence which also included aurochs (Lesser Cursus) and pig.

We can also speculate that within these open areas some arable cultivation occurred in plots of land, as charred grains of *Triticum dicoccum/spelta* (emmer/spelt) and indeterminate cereals have been recovered from Robin Hood's Ball, King Barrow Ridge, Coneybury Hill and the Stonehenge Cursus.

## Phase 2: Late Neolithic; landscape change or continuity?, 2900–2400 cal BC (Plate 4)

Environmental evidence for phase 2 is largely limited to the two long and important snail sequences from the ditches of the Coneybury Henge (Bell and Jones 1990) and Stonehenge (Evans 1984), and can be augmented by information from beneath the banks of Durrington Walls and Woodhenge. With less confidence it may also be possible to ascribe the mollusc sequence analysed from the secondary ditch fills of earlier monuments (e.g. Lesser and Stonehenge Cursuses) to this phase.

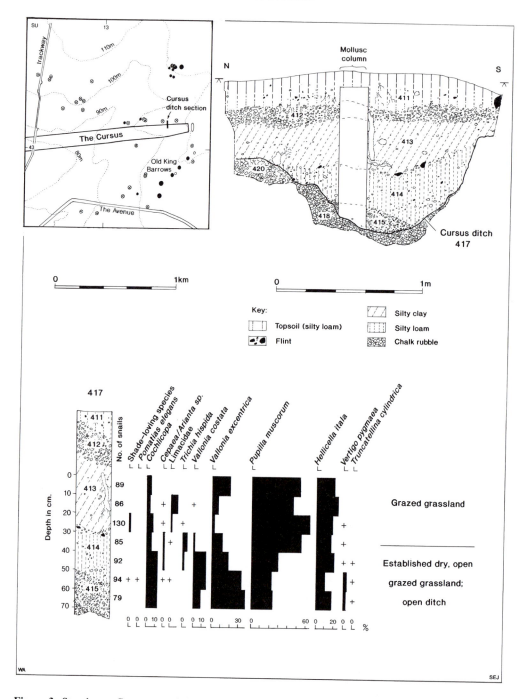

**Figure 3.** Stonehenge Cursus, sampled ditch section, and mollusc histogram.

**Table 4.** Land snail data from the Stonehenge Cursus

| Feature | Stonehenge Cursus [417] | | | | | | | | | Stonehenge Cursus [409] | | | | | | |
|---|---|---|---|---|---|---|---|---|---|---|---|---|---|---|---|---|
| Sample | 2025 | 2026 | 2027 | 2028 | 2029 | 2030 | 2031 | 2032 | 2033 | 2035 | 2036 | 2037 | 2038 | 2039 | 2040 | 2041 |
| Context | 418 | 419 | 421 | 421 | 421 | 421 | 421 | 421 | 422 | 415 | 415 | 414 | 414 | 413 | 413 | 413 |
| Depth (cm) | spot | spot | 55–65 | 45–55 | 35–45 | 25–35 | 15–25 | 10–15 | 0–10 | 60–70 | 50–60 | 40–50 | 30–40 | 20–30 | 10–20 | 0–10 |
| Wt (g) | 1500 | 1500 | 1500 | 1500 | 1500 | 1500 | 1500 | 1500 | 1500 | 1500 | 1500 | 1500 | 1500 | 1500 | 1500 | 1500 |
| MOLLUSCA | | | | | | | | | | | | | | | | |
| Pomatias elegans (Müller) | – | – | + | – | – | 1 | – | – | – | + | 1 | – | – | 2 | – | – |
| Cochlicopa lubrica (Müller) | – | – | – | – | – | – | – | – | – | 3 | 2 | 3 | – | – | – | – |
| Cochlicopa spp. | – | + | – | – | – | – | – | – | – | 6 | 9 | 8 | 5 | 9 | 3 | 4 |
| Truncatellina cylindrica (Férussac) | – | – | – | – | – | – | – | – | – | 1 | 1 | 1 | 1 | – | – | – |
| Vertigo pygmaea (Draparnaud) | – | – | + | – | – | – | – | 2 | 5 | 2 | 4 | 1 | 1 | 2 | – | – |
| Pupilla muscorum (Linnaeus) | 2 | 12 | 3 | 4 | 3 | 10 | 16 | 16 | 17 | 18 | 21 | 27 | 46 | 82 | 37 | 46 |
| Vallonia costata (Müller) | 2 | 7 | 1 | – | – | – | – | – | – | 7 | 13 | 13 | 2 | – | 1 | – |
| Vallonia excentrica Sterki | 1 | 5 | 2 | – | 1 | 3 | 14 | 21 | 14 | 29 | 31 | 17 | 10 | 4 | 12 | 18 |
| Ena obscura (Müller) | – | – | – | – | – | – | – | – | – | – | 1 | – | – | – | – | – |
| Punctum pygmaeum (Draparnaud) | 1 | – | – | – | – | – | – | – | – | – | – | – | – | 2 | – | – |
| Vitrina pellucida (Müller) | – | – | – | – | – | – | – | – | 1 | – | – | – | – | – | – | – |
| Oxychilus cellarius (Müller) | – | – | – | – | – | – | – | – | – | – | 1 | – | – | – | – | – |
| Limacidae | – | – | – | – | 1 | 1 | 1 | 1 | – | – | – | – | 1 | 3 | 8 | – |
| Euconulus fulvus (Müller) | – | 1 | – | – | – | – | – | – | – | – | – | – | – | – | – | – |
| Cecilioides acicula (Müller) | – | – | – | – | 3 | – | 1 | – | 1 | – | – | – | – | 1 | – | – |
| Clausilia bidentata (Ström) | – | – | – | – | – | – | – | – | – | – | – | – | – | – | – | – |
| Candidula intersecta (Poiret) | – | – | – | – | – | – | 1 | 2 | 2 | – | – | – | – | – | 1 | 2 |
| Candidula gigaxii (L. Pfeiffer) | – | – | – | – | – | – | – | 1 | 1 | – | – | – | – | – | – | 1 |
| Cernuella virgata (Da Costa) | – | – | – | – | – | – | – | – | – | – | 1 | – | – | – | 1 | 2 |
| Helicella itala (Linnaeus) | 1 | 5 | 1 | 2 | 3 | 5 | 6 | 10 | 2 | 13 | 9 | 18 | 14 | 23 | 21 | 16 |
| Helicellids | – | – | – | – | – | – | – | – | 3 | – | – | – | – | 1 | – | – |
| Trichia hispida (Linnaeus) | – | – | – | 1 | – | – | – | – | 1 | – | 1 | 2 | 4 | 1 | 1 | – |
| Cepaea/Arianta spp. | – | – | – | – | – | – | – | – | – | – | – | 2 | 2 | – | – | – |
| Taxa | 5 | 5 | 4 | 3 | 4 | 5 | 5 | 7 | 8 | 7 | 11 | 9 | 9 | 11 | 10 | 7 |
| **TOTAL** | 7 | 30 | 7 | 7 | 8 | 20 | 38 | 53 | 46 | 79 | 94 | 92 | 85 | 130 | 86 | 89 |

Coneybury was constructed in a recently cleared opening in the woodland, which was probably contemporary with Evans's zones C and D from the secondary fills of the Stonehenge Ditch. John Evans suggested that these indicate regeneration of a woodland or scrub cover; however, although the molluscan analysis is not questioned, the nature of the analysed deposits have been (Cleal *et al.* 1995, 163). Caution should therefore be expressed in interpreting this as an abandonment phase. Nevertheless, at Durrington Walls and Woodhenge the evidence is less ambiguous; an open countryside is evidenced in the mollusc data by the presence of the monuments themselves, and the large Grooved Ware pottery scatters (Plate 4; Cleal and Allen 1995, fig. 254). The secondary fills of both Cursus monuments (if they can be related to this phase) suggest open grazed downland but also arable activity. In contrast, Kennard lists a mixed snail assemblage from the Grooved Ware pit at Ratfyn, probably suggesting ungrazed grassland and localised scrubby vegetation (Kennard 1935).

Economic evidence is limited, but deer and pig are present in the assemblages from King Barrow Ridge (Maltby in Richards 1990), and cattle and sheep/goat were present as well as deer and pig in the Chalk Plaque Pit (Maltby in Harding 1988). The large assemblage from Durrington Walls confirms the presence of these species and indicates the keeping of relatively large herds of cattle (Harcourt in Wainwright and Longworth 1971) which can utilise both browse and graze.

There is, therefore, unfortunately, comparatively little evidence of land-use and economy of the Stonehenge area in the second half of the fourth millennium BC and it is difficult to map the *development* which occurs during phase 2 in any detail (Cleal and Allen 1995, 481). What evidence there is, tends to indicate an expansion of the utilised and farmed area in which more emphasis may have been placed upon cereal cultivation. Nevertheless, both grazed downland and woodland for pannage and its animal and floral resources were important elements in the economy.

## Phase 3: Late Neolithic–Early Bronze Age; the Beaker Period; an economy to support the stones, 2550–1600 cal BC (Plate 5)

During the millennium of the time of the stone settings (phase 3), there is a wealth of archaeological evidence from the Stonehenge area. One only has to glance at the distribution maps of the archaeology (see Cleal *et al.* 1995, fig. 255; Richards 1990, fig. 159) to recognise this. The environmental data are also more extensive.

*Evidence*

The barrows in the cemetery along King Barrow Ridge and at Amesbury were constructed in well-established short-grazed downland. Those on King Barrow Ridge were actually constructed of turves cut from a large area of downland (Allen and Wyles 1994).

Stonehenge was also in pasture; evidence from the upper fills of the Ditch (Evans 1984, zone F) and Mesolithic post-pits (local mollusc zone 3) in the carpark (Allen 1995) confirm this. A more restricted range of species is represented in the charcoals (Gale 1990, table 136) and includes oak, hazel, Pomoideae and *Prunus* suggesting that where woodland survived it was, in the main, more open secondary and scrubby woodland. At this time too, the presence of cereal remains increases and most of the charred cereals from Coneybury come from the later fills which we can probably ascribe to this phase by virtue of the distribution of Beaker pottery in them (Ellison in Richards 1990, 146–8; Cleal *et al.* 1995, 163 and archive). At this site, it must be admitted that renewed activity, as indicated by the pottery in the upper fills of the ditch, the evidence of meat consumption (bones) and high numbers of cereal remains, seems somewhat incongruous in view of Bell and Jones's emphatic evidence of woodland regeneration and the description of the fills as colluvial which is probably contemporaneous with this feasting. Again, there are the same obvious difficulties in reconciling these two apparently conflicting sets of evidence as Cleal had in interpreting the evidence from the Stonehenge Ditch. Hints of a similar history can be seen from the ditch fills of the Amesbury 42 long barrow (Entwistle in Richards 1990, 105–9), but in the Beaker period the disturbance here may be a result of either the clearance of this vegetation or cultivation in the vicinity.

Molluscan evidence indicates that apart from Coneybury Hill, many other areas were not only in open downland (e.g. Stonehenge Ditch and upper fills of Mesolithic post-pits) but that they were in areas under cultivation. Evidence comes from beneath the Amesbury 71 barrow (Kerney in Christie 1964), from which there is also physical evidence of pre-barrow ploughing or rip-arding in the form of parallel scores in the chalk (Christie 1967, 347). The North Kite, in particular, although established in a pastoral landscape, probably existed in a mixed arable and pastoral one (Allen in Richards 1990, 191–2). Further evidence for tillage comes from the colluvial fills described in the upper fills of many ditches, and their included molluscs; sites include both Cursus monuments and the Durrington 3 barrow (Allen *et al.* n.d.).

Colluvium itself is somewhat enigmatic in its distribution. Investigations in valley locations at the Winterbourne Stoke Cross Roads (W17),[1] The Diamond on Wilsford Down (W18), Durrington Down (W19), two locations in Stonehenge Bottom (W20 and W22), a side valley of Stonehenge Bottom (W21), the Cursus Valley (W22) and 'The Deep Hole' at Greenland Farm (W26) all failed to identify colluvium which could be sampled by excavation and exposed for mollusc analyses (cf. Bell 1983). I have suggested that this lack of colluvium in many valleys may be due to either the intensive arable use of this landscape resulting in the flushing out of deposits (Allen 1991), or the continuous presence of grassland in some areas preventing its formation in the first place (Cleal and Allen 1995, 484). Although colluvium, which is a prime indicator of deforestation or cultivation (Bell 1983; Allen 1992), is not present in many of the valleys in the Stonehenge

[1.] 'W' numbers are the site codes referenced in *Stonehenge Environs Project* (Richards 1990).

area, there are deep deposits of this period at Figheldean (Allen and Wyles 1993) and at Durrington Walls. At the latter we can be sure that some must belong to this period as it post-dates the timber structures, and some pre-date the Iron Age settlement which extends from the Packway (where the Iron Age chalk-cut ditches are 2.1 m deep) into Durrington Walls itself, north of the northern circle, where the ditches are cut *through* colluvium and only occur as 0.3 m deep cuts in the chalk (Wainwright and Longworth 1971, 309–15). Nearer Stonehenge, colluvium also occurs in a small dry valley on Coneybury Hill, precisely in an area of known occupation and suspected arable activity at this time.

### Colluvial sequence at Coneybury Hill

During evaluation work on Coneybury Hill a shallow (0.75 m) colluvial brown earth sequence was recorded at the top of a minor tributary of the Stonehenge Bottom dry valley, immediately south of the New King Barrows and about 450 m north of the Coneybury Henge (Wessex Archaeology 1993). Augering provided a profile of the valley sequence (Fig. 4) and, although not a great depth of colluvium, it is significant in view of the lack of such deposits recorded elsewhere within the Stonehenge area and especially as this tributary leads into Stonehenge Bottom above a point investigated by Bell (Richards 1990, 210–11). Beneath the stone-free, weakly calcareous colluvium was a deposit highly reminiscent of a relict ancient soil, probably a calcareous brown earth. Whether this is an *in situ* old land surface, or an earlier phase of erosion is not certain. However, it is possible that it represented a horizon of possible Neolithic date and may be contemporary with evidence for Grooved Ware activity discovered in the immediate area as a result of the same evaluation exercise. The stone-free and non-calcareous nature of the colluvium overlying this 'soil' would normally be taken to indicate the erosion of earlier soils (i.e. Neolithic/Bronze Age—cf. Allen 1992). However, the presence of later prehistoric (Iron Age) pottery in the lowest colluvial horizons indicates the stripping of all former soils from this minor valley at least by this time. The presence of former deeper, weakly calcareous soils can be considered relatively unusual this late in prehistory (cf. Allen, op. cit.), but local parallels can be found in the colluvial sequences recorded both within, and on the footslopes of, Vespasian's Camp (Allen 1994; Allen in Hunter-Mann 1999).

The Mollusca from the Coneybury Hill colluvium (above) (Table 3) are typical in that they indicate tillage. That from the buried soil suggests pasture. There is no evidence for the woodland elements seen in Bell and Jones's assemblages from Coneybury Henge itself.

### Cultivated fields

The evidence discussed above can be seen as an indication of arable activity alongside the herding of sheep and cattle. Cultivation occurred on plots of land large enough to

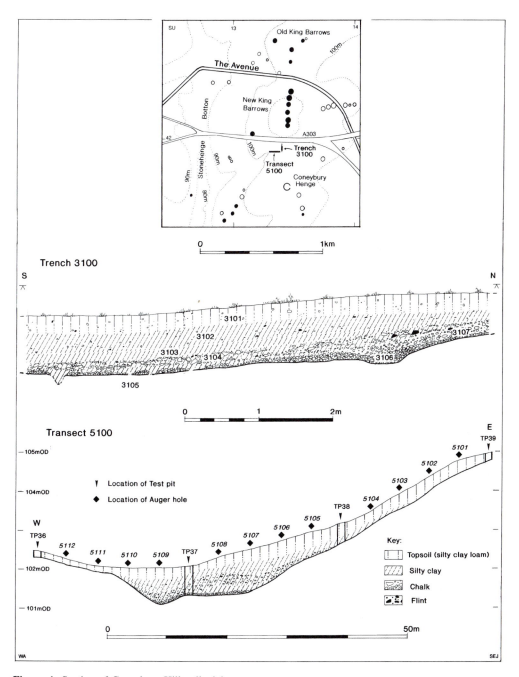

**Figure 4.** Section of Coneybury Hill colluvial sequence.

cause soil erosion on a reasonable, but highly local, scale. The fact that some areas of the landscape have been partitioned off (North Kite) may also suggest demarcation or protection of larger arable areas from herded animals.

In the post-monument phase (i.e. Middle and Later Bronze Age) large areas of field systems existed (see Cleal *et al.* 1995, fig. 187; Richards 1990, fig. 160) and are still evident as lynchets. For them to be present at this time suggests soil erosion, and thus cultivation, of most of these areas in previous periods, and enables it to be suggested that many may have been cultivated during Stonehenge phase 3. The apparent lack of a formalised field system, however, may be a combination of both the lack of a necessity to delineate large tracts of land, as seen in the Later Bronze Age (e.g. linear ditches, Bradley *et al.* 1994), and the fact that any formal field systems had not yet acquired established physical boundaries in the form of lynchets.

This evidence, together with that of pottery scatters which are probably some of the most extensive in southern England (see Plate 5) suggests both that farming populations were well-established locally and also, although we have no physical excavated evidence, were *living* locally.

During Stonehenge phase 3 we have no evidence of the nature of houses or buildings, and to a large extent we do not know what we are looking for even if it survives. The fact that the soils may have been considerably thicker (postulated to be about 1 m thick in the Mesolithic) enables us to suggest that post-holes for timbers may hardly have needed to penetrate the chalk. This, coupled with the known physical loss of the Chalk, calculated by Drewett (1977, 205) as being up to 0.8 m, suggests that little is likely to survive. The extensive flint and, more specifically, Beaker and Early Bronze Age pottery scatters are our most tangible evidence for large areas of domestic settlement. With the exception of Robin Hood's Ball, these all cluster around Stonehenge on Stonehenge Down, Durrington Down and Normanton Down.

## Discussion: farmers and the development and use of farming

### Ritual and community

It should be evident that this argument takes as its basis the assumption that communities operating within the Stonehenge environs had the power, 'finance' and economic wealth with which to employ a work-force to construct the magnificent edifice that today lies in ruins on Salisbury Plain. I believe, as do Gardiner and Cleal (forthcoming), that this landscape should not be viewed as a 'ritual landscape', if indeed such exists (see Cooney and Gardiner forthcoming), that is, a landscape largely concerned with exclusion and non-domestic activity. Undoubtedly, ritual and 'religious' activities and rites played an important role in the area, and some elements of communities had the political power and control to manage the construction of major edifices of stone and timber and chalk, but they are only one element in a diverse social landscape, which provides rich, if not as physically obvious, evidence for the utilitarian, everyday activities of the communities living within it.

It is through the consideration of the environmental evidence and interpretation of the development of the human impact on this specific landscape, that we can address the question of the *economic* basis upon which Stonehenge was built.

## Farming communities, not just farmers

It has been suggested above that, during phase 3, there is a definite shift from a landscape dominated by grazing to one of mixed arable and pasture and a greater emphasis on the cultivation of cereals than in previous phases. Critically, however, the balance of arable and pasture is unresolved. Nevertheless, this trend towards an economy more reliant on farming, with both permanent pasture and cultivation, and thus sedentism, is demonstrable by the time of the inception of phase 3. Any immediate-return system (i.e. hunting, foraging and farming) requires the potential for mobility and contrasts with delayed-return systems (Woodburn 1982), which by virtue of their more specialised economy, lead to less mobility and enable or require social institutions leading to rank and status in a stratified society with centralisation, as argued by Whittle (1981). We can see the full development of farming communities from a more diverse hunter, gatherer, collector, forager economy, labelled by Hayden as 'accumulators' (1990), which also included farming, at the time of the stone settings. By this time, we can see a point in which the communities were using some cereals as an integral, but not major, part of their economy. Where previously, the loss of a cereal crop by crop failure or other factors would not be important, in the Early Bronze Age once its cultivation had become a specialism and was an integral part of the economy, the loss of an annual yield would have been more profound. This increasingly heavier reliance on cereals contributes to the increased permanency of settlement and increased residence time in the area, but when undertaken through tribal or chiefdom societies provides the assurance of community safeguards and gives importance to place and time. Meillassoux contends that farming therefore instils a sense of the past, while at the same time necessitating judicious planning for the future (1972; 1981).

With this, too, came increasing sedentism (Allen in Cleal *et al.* 1995, 169) which is represented by the large foci of pottery scatters. This mixed farming economy and cereal cultivation required community management and the investment of labour with delayed returns, concomitant with labour-intensive episodes of ground preparation, sowing and harvesting. With a delayed return on labour expenditure and the necessity for storage facilities, this economy not only provided a mechanism for an organised, and potentially hierarchical or stratified society, but also enabled the deployment of relatively large numbers of the community during agricultural non-intensive or slack times of the year. It also allowed the possibility, through management and control, of producing a surplus with which to enable the provision of the non-economically productive group of the community who, instead of being engaged in agricultural practices, could be directed towards the building of large-scale, economically extravagant, communal monuments. Thus physical wealth, reflected in the presence of portable objects in some of the contemporaneous barrows, together with the availability of, possibly seasonal, labour, may be contributing factors to, and might be formally displayed by, the construction of the monument itself.

It is perhaps no surprise, therefore, that it is when we can see the formation of an economy that might enable the community to have social order/hierarchy, and the potential to both empower and deploy a work-force, that we see the beginning of the stone construction at Stonehenge. This is not invoking environmental determinism, but surely is a prime example of environmental possibilism.

The argument is not, therefore, that more intensive exploitation, specialisation and agricultural tasks *require* a significant work-force, but that such sedentary communities are more prone to have both a larger population, through their more sedentary lifestyle making procreation and child rearing easier, *and* they have the potential to sustain that increased population.

These ideas are not new, for Renfrew presented them over 20 years ago (1973) and they have been current in much of the archaeological literature since (e.g. Whittle 1981; Bradley 1991; 1993; Sherratt 1990, etc.). However, the environmental database at Stonehenge now provides evidence and argument for the pattern of development of that economic base; i.e. the economic mechanism to enable a stratified society to build a monument of this scale.

## Proposals for the future

It is evident from this review of the development of social farming through the phases that, despite this being one of the most intensively studied archaeological landscapes in the United Kingdom, our environmental database is frighteningly small. There are very few good domestic assemblages of bones that are not biased by placed items or single event (feasting) deposits, and few charred cereals and charcoals with which to examine the detail of interpretation we now wish to attempt for this area. In this respect the Danebury project, located only some 30 km distant, and dealing with a period one millennium later, is a fine example of where just such assemblages of plants and bones are being acquired. The resolution of our understanding of the changing land-use is relatively poor, in particular with respect to the balance of arable and pasture with the economies of any phase. Any interpretation presented is necessarily weakened because of this, and thus isolating this balance must be one of the priorities in analysis and information collection from further fieldwork programmes.

With larger assemblages, we can be more critical of the *context* and date of this information, rather than the date of the site as a whole. In so doing, perhaps we can move away from tables where data are presented solely on location (i.e. excavated site), because of the relatively low numbers of recorded items, to the examination, through greater numbers of recovered items, of properly chronological separated assemblages.

This then leads to questions of

**1** chronologies

and **2** contemporariety.

As much of the data comes from deposits (ditch fills) that are not well dated, it is critical that both the fills and included environmental datasets from any new excavations are closely dated. This may require excavation of larger proportions of ditches and not just of simple slot-dug sections to recover artefacts. It may also require a rigorous policy of acquiring and examining material from these fills for radiocarbon dating (as for Stonehenge itself, Bayliss *et al.*, this volume; Allen and Bayliss 1995). If, then, groups of contexts are dated or related to close ceramic affinities this can be related to the plant, bone or snail assemblages, providing a more accurate ascription of time.

However, in order to examine development within a *landscape*, it is necessary to ensure that datasets can be related between sites to ensure contemporariety or succession. Here again the careful and considered use of radiocarbon dating programmes is called for. Although it must be admitted that the programme from Stonehenge was large, expensive, and was rigorously interrogated, it is not absolutely necessary to employ similarly large dating programmes at other monuments. However, in order to achieve comparability between palaeo-environmental databases from sites to enable the fine-grained mosaic of land-use history to be obtained, it is imperative that well-dated chronologies are obtained for *all* the main monuments in our defined study area.

With the publication of both *SEP* and *Stonehenge in its landscape* it has, at last, been possible to go some way to examining both the landscape and the monument. We can now only really progress significantly by the acquisition of both larger, and better dated, environmental assemblages. The addition of continued small-scale analyses, such as the recent work summarised here from the Lesser Cursus and Coneybury Hill, no longer make a significant contribution to our understanding of the use of the landscape as a whole, only of specific individual locations within that landscape.

*An outline programme for the future*

- selected medium-scale excavations of a number of sites to obtain closely dated environmental data, especially from buried old land surfaces
- an attempt to acquire data which relate to the domestic animal and crop husbandry with an aim of defining the relative importance of each for any designated phase/period
- acquisition and careful dating of long sequences of non-site environmental data (pollen from alluvial sequences and snails from suitable colluvial sequences)
- a radiocarbon dating programme to enable the construction of detailed site chronologies (to relate to events and environmental datasets), and enabling the comparison or absolute sequence and contemporariety between sites.

# Concluding comments

Stonehenge and the surrounding area is, of course, a wonderful and special landscape, but it is not isolated from everyday life and it is the latter that I have concentrated on because it provides the evidence for the economy within which the monument was built and sustained.

Both Startin and Bradley's (1981) and Renfrew's (1973) calculations show that the construction of Stonehenge was achievable by a finite number of people over relatively short time scales. Nevertheless this large working population needed to be fed, clothed and housed. What the environmental data show is that the Stonehenge landscape was capable of sustaining such a population through a mixed agrarian economy, including relatively widespread arable cultivation (Plate 5), and through the evident flocks of sheep and herds of cattle. Thus, in a landscape with a reducing biodiversity and communities increasingly managing resources, we have the opportunity not only for the large-scale deployment of labour, but also of a hierarchical or stratified society, and one with wealth to trade, barter and impress other communities. This rich mixed farming economy under-pinned communities in the region providing the community wealth and enabling it the luxury of engaging many of its folk in activities not related to the acquisition of food and vitals for the stomach but for food for the mind, head and heart.

The following points may be made by way of conclusion.

**1**   The development of farming communities with a mixed agrarian economy and less necessity for mobility occurs at the same time as the requirement of a significantly increased manpower to construct the phase 3 monument.

**2**   There is evidence for large-scale settlement immediately adjacent to the Stonehenge triangle in the form of large and extensive pottery scatters (Allen and Cleal 1995, figs 253–5). The argument that there is no domestic settlement in the area may be simply the result of the fact that we do not know exactly what we are looking for, as structural evidence for the Late Neolithic/Early Bronze Age everywhere is extremely sparse (see Gardiner 1996). Further, that even if substantial Neolithic domestic structures were built (see Wyke Down, Cranborne Chase, Dorset), they may have left relatively limited traces and since investigations involved with the *Stonehenge Environs Project* concentrated largely on plough-damaged monuments and did not excavate the centre of any of the defined Neolithic pottery scatters, it is not surprising that no domestic struc-tural evidence was recovered.

**3**   There is evidence for utilitarian activity during all three phases of construction, but the environmental evidence, independent of any cultural remains, clearly shows that the work-force must have resided in the local landscape, and was fed, clothed, sheltered and cared for within the local community rather than being 'bus-ed' in on a regular basis.

**4**   This idea therefore contradicts any suggestions of exclusion from the landscape (e.g. Barrett 1994; Thomas 1991; Richards 1984; Garwood, pers. comm.). Archaeologists' reasons for suggesting exclusion relate to their own twentieth century perception of the importance of the monument; however, it seems somewhat profane to exclude the communities who may have revered or used it from the area around it.

*Acknowledgements*

It has been a marvellous collaborative experience being involved in the production of the *Stonehenge in its landscape* volume, which stimulated the ideas presented here. It is a pleasure to acknowledge Ros Cleal, Alex Bayliss, Becky Montague, Karen Walker, Linda Coleman and Julie Gardiner for their enthusiastic collaboration and fruitful discussion. This paper, however, has particularly benefited, and been improved, by comments from Richard Bradley and Julie Gardiner. Figures 1, 3 and 4 were drawn by Liz James (Wessex Archaeology) and Plates 1–5 were computer-generated by Karen Nichols and could only have been achieved with the considerable help given by Linda Coleman (Wessex Archaeology) and David Batchelor, Nick Burton and Jon Vallender (Central Archaeological Services).

# References

ALLEN, M.J. 1991: Analysing the landscape: a geographical approach to archaeological problems. In Schofield, A.J. (ed.), *Interpreting Artefact Scatters; contributions to ploughzone archaeology* (Oxford), 39–57.

ALLEN, M.J. 1992: Products of erosion and the prehistoric land-use of the Wessex chalk. In Bell, M.G. and Boardman, J. (eds), *Past and Present Soil Erosion; archaeological and geographical perspectives* (Oxford), 37–52.

ALLEN, M.J. 1994: *The land-use history of the southern English chalklands with an evaluation of the Beaker period using environmental data: colluvial deposits as environmental and cultural indicators* (Unpubl. Ph.D. thesis, Univ. Southampton).

ALLEN, M.J. 1995: Chapter 4; Before Stonehenge. In Cleal, R.M.J., Walker, K.E. and Montague, R. 1995, 41–62.

ALLEN, M.J. and BAYLISS, A. 1995: Appendix 2: The radiocarbon dating programme. In Cleal, R.M.J., Walker, K.E and Montague, R. 1995, 511–38.

ALLEN, M.J., ENTWISTLE, R. and RICHARDS, J. 1990: Molluscan studies. In Richards, J.C. 1990, 253–8.

ALLEN, M.J., HEATON, M. and RICHARDS, J. n.d.: The salvage excavation of round barrow Durrington G3 (Salisbury, Wessex Archaeology, unpubl. report).

ALLEN, M.J. and WYLES, S.F. 1993: The land-use history: the molluscan evidence. In Graham, A.H. and Newman, C., Recent excavations of Iron Age and Romano-British enclosures in the Avon Valley. *Wiltshire Archaeol. Natur. Hist. Mag.* 86, 45–50.

ALLEN, M.J. and WYLES, S.F. 1994: The contemporary land-use and landscape of the King Barrows as evidenced by the buried soils, pollen and molluscs. In Cleal, R.M.J. and Allen, M.J. 1994, 76–81.

BARRETT, J.C. 1994: *Fragments from Antiquity; the archaeology of social life in Britain, 2900–1200BC* (Oxford).

BELL, M.G. 1983: Valley sediments as evidence of prehistoric land-use on the South Downs. *Proc. Prehist. Soc.* 49, 119–40.

BELL, M.G. 1986: Archaeological evidence for the date, cause and extent of soil erosion on the chalk. *J. South East Soils Discussion Group (SEESOIL)* 3, 72–83.

BELL, M.G. and JONES, J. 1990: Land mollusca [Coneybury]. In Richards, J.C. 1990, 154–8.

BELL, M.J. and WALKER, M.J.C. 1992: *Late Quaternary Environmental Change: physical and human perspectives* (Harlow).

BRADLEY, R.J. 1978: *The Prehistoric Settlement of Britain* (London).

BRADLEY, R.J. 1991: Monuments and Places. In Garwood, P., Jennings, D., Skeates, R. and Toms, J. (eds), *Sacred and Profane* (Oxford, Oxbow Monogr. 32), 135–41.

BRADLEY, R.J. 1993: *Altering the Earth; the origins of monuments in Britain and continental Europe* (Edinburgh, Soc. Antiq. Scotl. Monogr. 8).

BRADLEY, R., ENTWISTLE, R. and RAYMOND, F. 1994: *Prehistoric Land Divisions on Salisbury Plain; the work of the Wessex Linear Ditches Project* (London, Engl. Heritage Archaeol. Rep. 2).

CARRUTHERS, W.J. 1990: Carbonised plant remains. In Richards, J.C. 1990, 250–2.

CHRISTIE, P.M. 1964: A Bronze Age barrow on Earl's Farm Down, Amesbury. *Wiltshire Archaeol. Natur. Hist. Mag.* 59, 30–45.

CHRISTIE, P.M. 1967: A barrow-cemetery of the second millennium BC in Wiltshire, England. *Proc. Prehist. Soc.* 33, 336–66.

CLEAL, R.M.J. and ALLEN, M.J. 1994: Investigations of tree-damaged barrows on King Barrow Ridge and Luxenborough Plantation, Amesbury. *Wiltshire Archaeol. Natur. Hist. Mag.* 87, 54–88.

CLEAL, R.M.J. and ALLEN, M.J. 1995: Chapter 10: Stonehenge in its landscape. In Cleal, R.M.J., Walker, K.E and Montague, R. 1995, 464–94.

CLEAL, R.M.J., WALKER, K.E. and MONTAGUE, R. 1995: *Stonehenge in its Landscape: twentieth century excavations* (London, Engl. Heritage Archaeol. Rep. 10).

COONEY, G. and GARDINER J.P. forthcoming: Ritual landscapes; proceedings of the 60th anniversary conference of the Prehistoric Society, Dublin 1995.

DREWETT, P.L. 1977: The excavations of a neolithic causewayed enclosure on Offham Hill, East Sx, 1976. *Proc. Prehist. Soc.* 43, 201–42.

EVANS, J.G. 1975: *The Environment of Early Man in the British Isles* (London).

EVANS, J.G. 1984: Stonehenge – The environment in the Late Neolithic and Early Bronze Age and a Beaker-age burial. *Wiltshire Archaeol. Natur. Hist. Mag.* 78, 7–30.

EVANS, J.G. and JONES, H. 1979: The land Mollusca. In Wainwright, G.J. 1979.

EVANS, J.G., LIMBREY, S., MATÉ, I. and Mount, R. 1993: An environmental history of the upper Kennet Valley, Wiltshire, for the past 10,000 years. *Proc. Prehist. Soc.* 59, 139–95.

EVANS, J.G. and WAINWRIGHT, G.J. 1979: The Woodhenge excavations. In Wainwright, G.J. 1979, 71–4.

GALE, R. 1990: Charcoals. In Richards, J.C. 1990, 252–3.

GARDINER, J. 1996: Early farming communities in Hampshire. In Hinton, D.A. and Hughes, M. (eds), *Archaeology in Hampshire: a framework for the future* (Winchester, Hampshire County Council), 6–12.

GARDINER, J.P. and CLEAL, R.M.J. forthcoming: Places and Perspectives: the view from Stonehenge. In Cooney, G. and Gardiner, J.P (eds) forthcoming.

GIBSON, A. 1994: Excavations at the Sarn-y-bryn-caled cursus complex, Welshpool, Powys, and the timber circles of Great Britain and Ireland. *Proc. Prehist. Soc.* 60, 143–223.

HARDESTY, D.L. 1977: *Ecological Anthropology* (New York).

HARDING, P. 1988: The chalk plaque pit, Amesbury. *Proc. Prehist. Soc.* 54, 320–7.

HAYDEN, B. 1990: Nimrods, piscators, pluckers and planters: the emergence of food production. *J. Anthropol. Archaeol.* 9, 31–69.

HUNTER-MANN, K. 1999: Excavations at Vespasian's Camp Iron Age Hillfort, 1987. *Wiltshire Archaeol. Natur. Hist. Mag.* 92, 39–52.

KENNARD, A.S. 1935: Report on the Mollusca from Pit 5. In Stone, J.F.S., Some discoveries at Ratfyn, Amesbury and their bearing on the date of Woodhenge. *Wiltshire Archaeol. Natur. Hist. Mag.* 47, 55–67.

MALTBY, M. 1990: The exploitation of animals in the Stonehenge Environs in the Neolithic and Bronze Age. In Richards, J.C. 1990, 247–9.

MEILLASSOUX, C. 1972: From reproduction to production. *Economy and Society* 1, 93–105.

MEILLASSOUX, C. 1981: *Maidens, Meal and Money. Capitalism and the Domestic Economy* (Cambridge).

MOFFETT, L., ROBINSON, M.A. and STRAKER, V. 1989: Cereals, fruits and nuts: charred plant remains from Neolithic sites in England and Wales and the Neolithic economy. In Milles, A., Williams, D. and Gardner, N. (eds), *The Beginnings of Agriculture* (Oxford, BAR Brit. Ser. 496), 243–61.

POWELL, A., ALLEN, M.J. and BARNES, I. 1996: *Archaeology in the Avebury area: the Kennet Valley Foul Sewer* (Salisbury, Wessex Archaeol. Rep. 8).

RENFREW, C. 1973: Monuments, mobilization and social organisation in neolithic Wessex. In Renfrew, C. (ed.), *The Explanation of Cultural Change* (London), 539–58.

RICHARDS, J.C. 1984: The development of a Neolithic landscape in the environs of Stonehenge. In Bradley, R. and Gardiner, J., *Neolithic Studies* (Oxford, BAR Brit. Ser. 133), 177–87.

RICHARDS, J.C. 1990: *The Stonehenge Environs Project* (London, Hist. Build. Monuments Comm. Archaeol. Rep. 16).

SCAIFE, R.G. 1995: Boreal and Sub-boreal chalk landscape: pollen evidence. In Cleal, R.M.J., Walker, K.E. and Montague, R. 1995, 51–5.

SCAIFE, R.G. forthcoming: Avon valley floodplain sediments: the pre-Roman vegetational history. In Cleal, R.M.J., Allen, M.J. and Newman, C., An archaeological and environmental study of the neolithic and later prehistoric landscape of the Avon Valley and Durrington Walls environs. *Wiltshire Archaeol. Natur. Hist. Mag.*

SHERRATT, A. 1990: The genesis of megaliths: ethnicity and social complexity in Neolithic northwest Europe. *World Archaeol.* 22, 147–67.

SMITH, I.F. 1965: *Windmill Hill and Avebury; excavations by Alexander Keiller 1925–1939* (Oxford).

SMITH, R.J.C., HEALY, F., ALLEN, M.J., MORRIS, E. and BARNES, I. 1997: Excavations along the route of the Dorchester by-pass, 1986–8 (Salisbury, Wessex Archaeol. Rep. 11).

STARTIN, D.W.A. 1982: Prehistoric earthmoving. In Case, H.J. and Whittle, A.W.R. (eds), *Settlement Patterns in the Oxford Region: excavations at the Abingdon causewayed enclosure and other sites* (London, CBA Res. Rep. 44), 153–6.

STARTIN, B. and BRADLEY, R. 1981: Some notes on work organisation and society in prehistoric Wessex. In Ruggles, C.L.N. and Whittle, A.W.R (eds), *Astronomy and Society in Britain during the period 4000–1500 BC* (Oxford, BAR Brit. Ser. 88), 289–96.

STONE, J.F.S. 1947: The Stonehenge Cursus and its affinities. *Archaeol. J.* 104, 7–19.

THOMAS, J. 1991: *Rethinking the Neolithic* (Cambridge).

VATCHER, F. de M. and VATCHER, L. 1973: Excavation of three post-holes in Stonehenge Carpark. *Wiltshire Archaeol. Natur. Hist. Mag.* 68, 57–63.

WAINWRIGHT, G.J. 1979: *Mount Pleasant, Dorset: Excavations 1970–1971, incorporating an account of excavations undertaken at Woodhenge in 1970* (London, Soc. Antiq. Rep. 37).

WAINWRIGHT, G.J. and LONGWORTH, I.H. 1971: *Durrington Walls: excavations 1966–1968* (London, Rep. Res. Comm. Soc. Antiq. London 29).

WESSEX ARCHAEOLOGY 1993: Stonehenge Visitor Centre, Wiltshire, Site 12: A303 footbed; archaeological evaluation (Salisbury, Wessex Archaeology, unpubl. client report W639a).

WHITTLE, A.W.R. 1981: Later Neolithic society in Britain: a re-alignment. In Ruggles, C.L.N. and Whittle, A.W.R (eds), *Astronomy and Society in Britain during the period 4000–1500 BC* (Oxford, BAR Brit. Ser. 88), 297–342.

WHITTLE, A.W.R. 1991: A Late Neolithic complex at West Kennet, Wiltshire, England. *Antiquity* 65, 256–62.

WHITTLE, A.W.R. 1993: The Neolithic of the Avebury area; sequence, environment, settlement and monuments. *Oxford J. Archaeol.* 12, 29–54.

WOODBURN, J. 1982: Egalitarian societies. *Man* 17, 431–45.

WOODWARD, P.J. 1991: *The South Dorset Ridgeway; survey and excavation 1977–1984* (Dorchester, Dorset Natur. Hist. Archaeol. Soc. Monogr. Ser. 8).

WYMER, J.J. 1977: *Catalogue of Mesolithic sites in England and Wales* (London, CBA Res. Rep. 21).

*Proceedings of the British Academy*, **92**, 145–166

# Remembered and Imagined Belongings: Stonehenge in its Traditions and Structures of Meaning

## ALASDAIR WHITTLE

### Introduction

THIS PAPER ATTEMPTS to ascribe meanings to Stonehenge, especially in its main phase of lithic monumentality, by considering the monument in relation to: its contemporary setting; the tradition of sacred monuments, circular and other, to which it belonged; the layouts of successive phases; the materials from which it was formed; and the patterns of approach and experience which the monument may have engendered. The monument, like other major monuments of the Later Neolithic of the third millennium BC, belonged to a sacral landscape, not to a major settlement concentration. These required the contribution of people from wide areas around. Stonehenge expressed the power of the past in its continuing use of circular form, and sought to make eternal both an ancient tradition of reverence for spirits and ancestral beings and a contemporary social practice of intense ceremonialism. Properties or qualities must be envisaged for the constituent materials, from chalk and timber to stone; different treatments of significant stones are noted. Layouts may have symbolised inclusion and exclusion, unity and division; the three-dimensional nature of the monument is also emphasised, and considered as a possible cosmological model of a hierarchy of spirits. Stonehenge had to be approached and experienced in predetermined ways, both from the surrounding landscape and within the monument itself. Rearrangements of the stone phase indicate how crucial it was to builders and users to make the internal settings fully propitious, for in those details much of the power of the monument may have resided.

# The contemporary setting

Now that every Stonehenge, to invert the famous dictum of Jacquetta Hawkes (Hawkes 1967, 174), is getting the age it deserves, it can be seen that the great stone phases of the monument belong not to the Early Bronze Age as previously supposed (e.g. Atkinson 1979; Pitts 1982; Chippindale 1993; Richards 1990), but to the Later Neolithic (Cleal *et al.* 1995). The recent programme of radiocarbon dating has been crucial. Four determinations are available, one for the sarsen circle and three for the sarsen trilithons, which together constitute the elements of the redefined site phase 3ii. Their overall span is long, from about 2800 to 1700 BC, but if the older determination BM-46 is set aside, a shorter range is indicated between 2800 and 2200 BC, with a date more or less in the middle of the third millennium BC likely for phase 3ii (Cleal *et al.* 1995).

Such a dating takes the great stone phases of Stonehenge back in time, thus removing them from a horizon—the Early Bronze Age—in which most other manifestations of monumental construction had ceased, and placing them in a horizon—the Later Neolithic —in which monuments of many kinds were still being built, both in the Stonehenge area and far beyond. Whatever the nuances of the local sequence, the great stone settings of Stonehenge now more obviously belong with Coneybury, Durrington Walls and Woodhenge, and possibly with the Stonehenge Cursus, if its radiocarbon dating is to be taken at face value, which is highly uncertain (Richards 1990; and see Wainwright and Longworth 1971). The great feats of Stonehenge also become contemporary or near-contemporary with other prodigies of collective labour, such as to the south the complex around Dorchester, Dorset, including Mount Pleasant, Maumbury Rings, and Greyhound Yard (Wainwright 1979; Bradley 1976; Woodward *et al.* 1993); or to the north Marden in the Vale of Pewsey (Wainwright 1971) or Avebury, Silbury Hill and the West Kennett palisade enclosures in the upper Kennet (Smith 1965; Pitts and Whittle 1992; Whittle 1997). To this short list of constructions of excessive zeal have to be added others, no less important locally and regionally, on lesser though often still impressive scales, such as to the south the Knowlton complex close to the older Dorset cursus (Barrett *et al.* 1991; Tilley 1994), or sites in the river valleys to the north, for example in the upper Thames (Case and Whittle 1982; Whittle *et al.* 1992; Barclay *et al.* 1995) or the Nene, Ouse and other valleys to the east (see Parker Pearson 1993). Nor are such groupings of monuments confined to the south of the country; they extend far north and west, to the Orkneys and to Ireland (e.g. Ritchie 1984; Parker Pearson and Richards 1994; Stout 1991).

The great stone settings of Stonehenge therefore find their place in a much wider sacred geography in the third millennium BC. In few areas has it proved possible to document an abundant settlement or occupation record. Around Stonehenge itself, the Environs Project was able to show a gradual opening of woodland through time, and scatters of worked flint. The latter can perhaps be categorised into 'industrial' and 'domestic' zones, but neither is accompanied by evidence for substantial subsoil structures (Richards 1990). Even where built structures can be documented in this horizon, as on the Orkneys, sites like Skara Brae and Barnhouse may themselves be special locales, and not represent the occupations of everyday existence (Parker Pearson and Richards 1994). Two implications follow. First, the milieu to which Stonehenge belonged was still probably, many centuries after the inception of the Neolithic, one of relative mobility, of social flux in the sense of the coming and going of people. Stonehenge cannot be envisaged as lying at the heart of a local or regional concentration of population. Secondly, Later Neolithic monuments belonged to and reinforced a tradition begun earlier in the Neolithic in which built constructions anchored collective allegiance to place against the tide of individual or small-group settlement mobility. They rooted identities in chosen locales, often the scene for intense ceremonialism and social interaction, and provided also a fixed point for the residence of or access to spirits and ancestors, real and imagined. (In the discussions which follow, I refer to ancestors in a generalised way; the term can cover imagined or abstract ancestors, remembered people, or indeed shadowy figures from remote pasts, like the Silver Race of Hesiod, with whom little direct connection was sensed: Whittle 1996; Whitley 1995.) The land was framed by notions and zones of sanctity, with holy areas at its core.

This was part of the means by which the Neolithic phenomenon was brought into being in the first place. Why it should have continued to develop on the scale witnessed in the Later Neolithic remains open to debate. Many models of varying theoretical background have sought to give essentially socio-political explanations, from chiefdoms through ritual authority structures to Eliadean prescriptive structures (e.g. Renfrew 1973; Thorpe and Richards 1984; Garwood 1991; Bender 1992). It has been suggested that the rituals managed through a site like Stonehenge could have maintained social divisions by making them part of a timeless social order (Bradley 1991). But since, setting aside minor assemblage variability, there is little evidence for social differentiation other than the monuments themselves (one of a series of issues raised in this paper which need fuller discussion elsewhere), an alternative is to envisage slower histories of change, dominated by reference to the ancestral past and cycles of ancestral time (Whittle 1996; Whittle 1997). Rather than a straightforward trajectory of social differentiation within each community through the Neolithic and into the Later Neolithic horizon, I envisage a milieu in which people in different areas were conscious of both the pasts and the achievements of their neighbours, and in which emulation took the form of rivalry for sanctity. There is individuality in the forms that monumentality took—thus in the Middle Neolithic, nothing quite like the Dorset cursus, and in the Later Neolithic nothing quite like either Stonehenge or Silbury Hill to its north—and that diversity and the scale of the enterprises can be sought in part in the nature of the wider context.

## Traditions of sacred circularity

Neolithic monuments had many forms and many points of reference. In central southern England, the first constructions were long barrows and chambered tombs, predominantly of rectangular or trapezoidal form, which were connected with the treatment of the ancestral spirits and the ancestral dead, and referred probably to the earlier great timber longhouses of the first generations of the Neolithic in central and western Europe. Elsewhere, in the north and west, more circular mounds are evident from early stages of the Neolithic, perhaps with reference points in forager shell middens or forager and Early Neolithic habitations. Circular ditched and banked enclosures appeared in southern Britain slightly later, in the mid to later fourth millennium BC, themselves again already with a past, rooted in ditched enclosures of central and western Europe, from the late sixth millennium BC onwards (Whittle 1996). Causewayed enclosures were complex arenas of social interaction, in which a great range of concerns was played out. As well as dealings with spirits, ancestors and the dead, as at long barrows and chambered tombs, there were also social concerns, for the businesses of production, consumption, and sharing, relations with neighbours, and attitudes to animals and nature (Edmonds 1993; Whittle and Pollard 1997). No one enclosure need be seen as exactly like any other, and the nature of deposition varied from individual episode to episode, over a span of generations, but all these locales shared, more or less, in the strong symbolism of circularity. Circular layout referred to past history (earlier continental enclosures) and perhaps contemporary social practice (structures and site layouts), served to both exclude and include, and worked to present space and time both as endless and finite.

The tradition established did not remain unaltered. Other monuments predicated on physical and conceptual progression and movement were added to the repertoire in the Middle Neolithic (Bradley 1993; Tilley 1994). But circular form remained important in the Later Neolithic. Stonehenge phase 1 and Flagstones, Dorchester (Cleal *et al.* 1995; Woodward and Smith 1987; cf. Bradley 1991) show the tradition in transmission to greater formality, which found its fullest expression in the layouts and elevations of monuments like Durrington Walls, Avebury and Mount Pleasant. The uses of Later Neolithic enclosures cannot be seen as the same as earlier ones, but it is likely that they too, just like their predecessors, carried a baggage of memory from a distant past. It is no accident, therefore, that Stonehenge phases 1 and 2 of the new chronology (leaving aside for these purposes whether they can be thus separated) should retain circular form, and refer to the past in the form of depositions of animal bone, some of it itself old, and cremated human remains. Whatever lay in the centre of Stonehenge phases 1 and 2, visitors had to pass a familiar external ditch, and move through a zone given to the dead and ancestral practice. We can think of such movement, perhaps, as serving to transcend time, even before the site had reached its greatest monumentality.

## Contemporary circles

It is not a new idea that the stone phases of Stonehenge mimicked timber constructions (e.g. Atkinson 1979), but with the revised chronology, the relationship becomes closer.

The stone constructions at the heart of Stonehenge in phases 3ii-3v parallel more or less contemporary constructions in timber in two ways. First, there is the technical and laborious imitation in stone of woodworking techniques, such as mortice and tenon, tongue-and-groove jointing, and perhaps some effort at reproducing the texture of adzed surfaces, for example in the treatment of stone 16 in the sarsen circle (Fig. 1). Secondly, and in the light of the revised chronology perhaps even more striking, is the transmutation into stone of the idea of circular layout seen in so many timber structures of the contemporary Later Neolithic. The sarsen circle is just over 30 m in diameter; with the Y and Z Holes, the diameter of the central setting is over 50 m. These figures straddle the recurrent diameters of timber settings, such as locally the South and North Circles within Durrington Walls and Woodhenge, and further afield Site IV within Mount Pleasant

**Figure 1.** Dressing marks on the side of stone 16 in the sarsen circle. Photo: Robin Skeates.

(Wainwright and Longworth 1971; Wainwright 1979; for other figures, see Gibson 1994). Both Stonehenge 3ii-3v and more or less contemporary timber structures were three-dimensional structures. In the latter, the largest post-holes usually belong to the inner of several concentric rings (e.g. circle 2E in the second phase of the South Circle at Durrington, which is second to central: Wainwright and Longworth 1971); in Stonehenge, the sarsen trilithon rises highest, above more or fewer outer and inner rings depending on whether Y and Z Holes are counted or not. The three-dimensional timber structures had axis and directionality planned into them (Pollard 1992; Pollard 1995; Thomas 1993), just like the more famous alignment of Stonehenge. We do not know whether any of the complex timber structures were roofed; my own view is that the details of deposition suggest bare poles (cf. Richards and Thomas 1984). Plausible reconstructions can be offered for both possibilities (Musson 1971; Parker Pearson 1993, fig. 58). But in either case, the situation is that Stonehenge 3ii-3v transcribes the essence of contemporary timber forms, whether bare, lintelled poles, or roofed structures. It makes eternal, at the heart of a circular space sanctified by tradition, memory, the dead, ancestral practice and transcended time, a contemporary social practice which was also rooted in the use of circular space and circular structures. Part of the business of using timber structures involved directed movement, which I discuss further below, and deposition of food remains and artefacts. In this last point, there does seem to be difference. The excavations to date within Stonehenge have not shown anything comparable, for example, to the platform, midden and post-surround depositions seen in the Durrington Walls South Circle. Possibly the axe carvings on the sarsen circle could be a commemoration of something similar. Most of the carvings are low down (admittedly perhaps for other, practical reasons), and they appear from our knowledge so far to be concentrated, principally on the east and north-west sides of the sarsen and trilithon circles (Cleal *et al.* 1995, 30–2); those on the east (stones 29, 3, 4, 5 and 53) outnumber those to the north-west (stones 57 and 23). Uncannily, such a concentration on the east side can also be seen within the depositions and features of the Durrington South Circle, Woodhenge and the Sanctuary (Richards and Thomas 1984; Pollard 1992; Pollard 1995).

Another dimension of the elevation of Stonehenge can be considered. The stone settings are markedly stepped (Fig. 2), a visual aspect which if anything becomes more dominant at a distance from the monument, certainly including the approach from the north-east along the line of the Avenue. Could this too have meaning, and if so, how could we begin to engage with such a possibility? One starting point might be that many belief systems in non-western society involve a hierarchy of spirits and beings. The most powerful spirits and beings are often conceptualised as belonging in the air, above the moral as well as physical domain of humans. The corollary is that they are often taken for granted in daily life, much of day-to-day concern being with lesser spirits, clan ancestors, ghosts, witches, fetishes, spells and the like (Sahlins 1968). Another starting point might be the hieroglyph of stepped form shown in the Pyramid Texts of third millennium BC Egypt, which represents a primeval mound as earth symbol arising from the watery

**Figure 2.** The stepped profile of Stonehenge (from the south). Photo: Robin Skeates.

chaos of creation (Jenkins 1980, 148 and fig. 116). Strikingly, the earliest pyramid, of Dhoser at Saqqara, of around 2700 BC, has stepped form. The parallel is distant in space but not far removed in time. It may be more relevant to the mound idea so elaborated at Silbury Hill, and I have pursued its interpretations and yet other starting points for insight into earth symbolism elsewhere (Whittle 1997); but if Silbury Hill and Stonehenge 3ii-3v have become closer in time, it is worth considering the possible connections. Different parts of connected ritual practice may be played out over time and space (Leach 1976, 27). I suggest therefore that we could think of the three-dimensionality of Stonehenge as both symbolising a hierarchy of spirits and celestial beings and drawing on a set of ideas current in the third millennium BC to do with the earth and creation.

## Materials: the language of stones

While the transport of materials to Stonehenge, bluestones from further away to the west and sarsen from within Wessex, has long attracted attention (Atkinson 1979; Thorpe *et al.* 1991), rather less thought has been given to Neolithic materials and their meanings. With reference to Stonehenge, this has been taken up only by Bender (1992). Her treatment is brief (Bender 1992, 744–6), but in emphasising what she calls the indivisibility of nature and culture, she notes the possible connotations of stone, earth and chalk. This paper attempts to expand her initial suggestions.

In the Neolithic people placed their dead at the feet of large timbers and stones, and conducted an intense ceremonialism in spaces defined by digging into the earth. It is barely conceivable that chalk, earth, timber and stone did not have ascribed meaning as metaphoric or metonymic symbols (cf. Leach 1976). Two examples from the ethnographic record illustrate some of the possibilities. For the Zafimaniry, shifting cultivators in Madagascar, especial importance was attached to the properties of wood, which was used for fires and houses, and associated metaphorically with the development of people, the bones of ancestors and other symbolic transformations (Bloch 1992; Bloch 1993). For Aborigines in western Arnhem Land in northern Australia, stone tools have had aesthetic and symbolic value (Taçon 1991). Hardness, durability, and colour have been valued. Stone tools have been associated with particular social roles, for example those of initiated males, and with the beginnings and final resting places of Ancestral Beings, who in other guises framed the whole landscape. The symbolism of the Neolithic axe may draw on similar values and a connection with its source within the earth itself (Whittle 1995). The very earliest stones set up in western Europe, the *menhirs* of Brittany, may have mirrored axe form (Thomas and Tilley 1993).

While there is much to say about timber, and the transmutation from timber to stone that Stonehenge pre-eminently presents needs to be kept in mind (perhaps in some way linked to the long history of the site prior to the erection of stones: Joshua Pollard, pers. comm.), it is sensible to concentrate here on stone. Stone has obvious properties of hardness and durability, and its texture and colour normally give it a distinctive character. Sarsen in Wessex would presumably have been derived from deposits where it lay partially buried, as in modern-day locations in the dry valleys of north Wiltshire; bluestones may have been quarried. Sarsen and other stones elsewhere in the country were used to frame houses of the dead and the ancestors (though interestingly the nearest stone chambered tombs to the Stonehenge area itself are those of the Avebury area: Grinsell 1957, map II). Stone may have stood metonymically for the earth (a point also emphasised by Colin Richards, pers. comm.) and metaphorically in part for the ancestors. By the middle and late phases of the Neolithic in both Britain and Ireland and Brittany, when rows of standing stones come to prominence (Burl 1993), it seems implausible to regard them purely literally as inanimate settings; these were powerful symbols, steeped in basic notions of the past and the earth.

Particular stones may have been ascribed special meaning. There have been tentative suggestions that variation in height and shape among the sarsen stones at Avebury may have been to do with representation of gender difference (Smith 1965; Burl 1979; cf. Bender 1992, 745). These stones, like most in other sites of both the Earlier and Later Neolithic, were not shaped or dressed. There is, however, one candidate for deliberate selection: stones with a bevelled top. There are examples of this kind of form in earlier

**Figure 3.** The Cove, North Inner Circle, Avebury. Photo: Richard Atkinson.

**Figure 4.** The Stones of Stenness, Orkney. Photo: author.

monuments, such as at Cairnholy I in south-west Scotland. There the stone facade of a Clyde cairn rose symmetrically to its highest on either side of the entrance; one of the left side stones had a bevelled top (Piggott and Powell 1949). Perhaps the pronounced tilt of roofstones in portal dolmens and some court graves around the Irish Sea is something to do with the same idea, whatever it may have meant. The bevelled top recurs in the Later Neolithic, for example in the Cove of the North Inner Circle at Avebury and the Stones of Stenness in Orkney (Smith 1965; Ritchie 1976; Figs 3–4). In the Orkneys at least, this is the result of natural cleavage, though the base of such stones appears to be roughly dressed (information from Colin Richards and Niall Sharples). Such stones are often oriented to the east; a natural form is given meaning by selection and placement. A similar pattern might be seen in the more irregular tops of stones of the outer circle inside Avebury, though the pattern there is not wholly regular. Behind this might lie either a specific meaning or a general sense of propitiousness based on body side (left:right) or horizon orientation (west:east).

What of the language of stones at Stonehenge itself? The stone settings juxtapose and alternate the exotic or distant but smaller (bluestones, however derived from southwest Wales) and the more local but larger (sarsens). Both elements are used to inscribe, in the end, a complete and a broken circle. The sarsen circle is not only linked by its continuous lintel, both uprights and lintels being shaped, but presents strong visual unifor-

**Figure 5.** The sarsen circle. Photo: Wessex Archaeology.

**Figure 6.** Lintels of the sarsen circle. Photo: Richard Atkinson.

mity (Figs 5–6). The view down the line of the Avenue from the centre of the monument would originally have been past both Slaughter Stone and Heelstone (and others), both pointed-top stones and the latter perhaps with some resemblance to a bevelled-top stone.

Within the central setting, there is not quite the same unity in the trilithons, but rather an internal or alternating rhythm (Figs 7–18). The initial observation (the germ of which I owe to our former undergraduate Gwyn Maurice) is that the surfaces and dressing of the trilithon uprights are not identical. Proceeding clockwise, of the pair 51 and 52 (Figs 7–10), the inner face of 52 is rather pocked by natural unevennesses (noticeable in profile as well as face-on: Cleal *et al.* 1995, figs 294 and 297), while the inner face of 51 is smooth; 52 is also slightly more bulky, which the ground plans more or less faithfully reflect (e.g. Cleal *et al.* 1995, fig. 97), though the pair are otherwise well matched in a front-on view (Cleal *et al.* 1995, pl. 2.4). Of pair 53 and 54 (Figs 11–14), 53 is notice-ably smoother on its inner face, which bears some of the best known axe carvings, while 54 has a series of natural pockmarks down its inner edge adjacent to 54; both outer faces are dressed to some extent, but the rear of 54 is far less symmetrical and much more bulbous (Cleal *et al.* 1995, pls 4.3 and 6.3). As far as we can tell, both 55 and 56, the central and highest pair, were more or less equally well dressed, though 55 is notice-ably broader, and perhaps also thicker, than stone 56 (Fig. 15).

**Figure 7.**   The inner faces of trilithon pairs 51 and 52 (left) and 53 and 54 (right), from the north-east, inside the monument. Photo: Wessex Archaeology.

**Figure 8.** The inner faces of trilithon pairs 51 and 52 (left) and 53 and 54 (right), from the west. Photo: Robin Skeates.

**Figure 9.** Detail of the inner faces of stones 51 (left) and 52 (right). Photo: Richard Atkinson.

**Figure 10.** The outer faces of trilithon pairs 51 and 52 (right) and 53 and 54 (left), from the south-east. Photo: Wessex Archaeology.

**Figure 11.** The inner faces of stones 53 (left) and 54 (right). Photo: Wessex Archaeology.

**Figure 12.** The outer faces of stones 53 (right) and 54 (left), from the east. Photo: Richard Atkinson.

**Figure 13.** The outer faces of stones 53 (right) and 54 (left), from the south. Photo: Richard Atkinson.

**Figure 14.** Side view of stone 54. Photo: Richard Atkinson.

**Figure 15.** The sarsen trilithons, from the west, with stone 56 in the centre, in front of the fallen stone 55.
Photo: Robin Skeates.

In the next pair, 57 and 58, there is also a lack of matching; relative to the north-easterly axis of the monument or to the plan seen from above as a whole, the placement is reversed compared to the other side of the trilithon horseshoe, but seen from the inside on the ground the same sidedness is maintained (Figs 16–18). Stone 57 is the smoother on both inner and outer faces, in addition having a very pronounced bevelling down its innermost front edge, while both the front and back of 58 have natural fissures and irregularities (Cleal *et al.* 1995, fig. 103 and pl. 2.2, inner faces, and fig. 101, outer faces). It is difficult to bring the last pair, 59 and 60, into the picture, since 59 is both fallen and broken, though it might be hazarded that stone 60 (Fig. 18) was the bulkier of the pair (Cleal *et al.* 1995, pl. 6.2).

**Figure 16.** The inner faces of stones 57 (left) and 58 (right). Photo: Wessex Archaeology.

**Figure 17.** The outer faces of stones 57 (right) and 58 (left). Photo: Wessex Archaeology.

**Figure 18.** Side view of stone 57; stone 60 to the extreme right in the background. Photo: Wessex Archaeology.

What can this lack of matching imply? It may be argued that it has no significance at all, given the uneven surfaces of sarsen in its natural state and the presumed rarity of the very largest stones available. On the other hand, the sarsens of the sarsen circle are more even, and there too the more fissured faces appear to be on the outside. The pattern in the trilithon horseshoe just described is striking. It suggests that some kind of principle of opposition or combination was being expressed, between smooth and rough, shaped and natural, and slim and bulky. There are rhythms to the placings. Looking from the inside (turning always to face the stones), smooth, shaped and slim are on the left, rough, natural and bulky are on the right. Standing outside the trilithon horseshoe, say a little to the north-east with one's back to the sarsen circle, there is reversal, since smooth, shaped and slim are the closer in the pairs on the left-hand or south-east side, while on the right-hand or north-west side, those stones are the further away in the pairs. The central pair, 55 and 56, which may not fit the pattern of the other four trilithons, could have acted as a pivot in this alternation.

## Approaching and seeing: orientation and the body

The layout of the trilithon horseshoe could be taken to show two dimensions of meaning. First, the individual stones incorporated into the overall structure could speak for and stand for different values, conceived as either opposed or complementary. The practice of smoothing stones, and hence an interest in textures and finishes (a reminder I owe to Ian Kinnes), had existed since at least the beginning of the Neolithic in the form of polished stone and flint axes (well illustrated in Clarke *et al.* 1985). At Stonehenge, we can hardly recover the meanings of such textures, though I have hinted at interest in the relationship between nature and culture.

It is hard to resist bringing in another cross-cultural analogy, that left and right, defined by the human body, could be the focus for a sense of orientation and especially propitiousness. There is no cross-cultural regularity, however, in which side is chosen to stand for the propitious. In the context of Neolithic Brittany, it has been suggested that the left side and movement to the left were propitious (Thomas and Tilley 1993), while the Mapuche Indians of Chile, to take a recent example more or less at random, associate the right with among other things good, life, day, health, ancestral spirits and abundance, and the left with evil, death, night, sickness, evil spirits and poverty (Faron 1976). The repositioning of the bluestones in phases 3ii-iv (Cleal *et al.* 1995) may indicate how important it was to get the appropriate sense of propitiousness right, down to the last details such as whether particular bluestones should be jointed or not.

Secondly, the mirror-like placements and the reversals obtainable by shifting from inside to outside or *vice versa* strongly imply physical movement around and within the monument. I set aside for the purposes of this discussion (because they are such wide issues) whether this was restricted to a group of people or available to all who chose to participate, and the question of whether detailed knowledge accompanied every such presumed movement. Movement is significant in two ways. It further serves to unite the stone setting of Stonehenge with the interiors of timber structures in other Later Neolithic monuments, in which it has been suggested there was also directed movement (Thomas 1991; Thomas 1993; Pollard 1992; Pollard 1995). It also serves to reveal a more extensive human involvement in the experience of the monument, and to link the monument to its wider setting.

There has been much discussion of orientation of another kind, the relationship of the monument to horizons and the rising and settings of the moon and sun (summarised best in Chippindale 1993; Burl 1987). Such discussions have centred on a static view outwards from the stone setting, with little allowance for movement within and around it, or for approaches to and departures from it, thus denying the sense of progression, physical and symbolic, which some other Neolithic monuments may imply (e.g. Tilley 1994, on the Dorset cursus). To be understood, Stonehenge had to be experienced by movement. The layout of the stone setting, like that of timber structures, perhaps required circlings and recirclings by people, as suggested by the use of the circle shape itself, by the ambiguity of personal orientation in terms of left and right and front and back, and by the evident reference of the monument to the movement of moon and sun around the circles of the horizons and heavens.

The general orientation of Stonehenge phase 3ii-v, including the existence of the Avenue, also implies directionality. Experience within and experience outside need not be separated, movement linking both, with ambiguity or reversal always present. In approaching the monument along the course of the Avenue from the Avon, most of the major older monuments lay to the right (roughly speaking the north). The three-dimensionality of the stone setting is thus given a further point of reference as the observer approached. Could this sidedness have been carried into the experience of the monument itself, following the details set out above? One possibility is that the sarsen trilithon horseshoe could have provided a calendar of significant moonsets and sunsets through the year (Burl 1987, fig. 12). This involves principally the pairs of stones 59 and 60 and stones 55 and 56. To a centrally placed observer the major northern moonset is visible between stones 59 and 60, while the midsummer sunset is obscured by stone 59; the midwinter sunset is visible between stones 55 and 56, but the major southern moonset is obscured by stone 55. It is possible that this further reinforces the significance of the left-hand stones when seen from within the circle, though admittedly those on the south-east side are not brought into this picture.

The Avenue need not be claimed as the only way to approach or depart from Stonehenge, nor need patterns have been static through time (Darvill, this volume). It has been suggested that by the Early Bronze Age round barrow groups were placed around more or less fixed radii centred on the monument, which may imply a strong sense of circularity and perhaps circular movement in the landscape around (Woodward and Woodward 1996). It is possible that Early Bronze Age practice merely fixes what was an earlier tradition of paths (cf. Bender 1992).

## Summary and conclusion

The symbolic power of Stonehenge was manifold. The monument belonged to an ancient tradition of circular sites, which had long been peopled by spirits, ancestors and the dead as well as by the living, and commemorated by intense participatory ceremonialism involving amongst other things feasting and deposition. It drew on a basic symbolism of the circle, which served both to include and exclude, to separate and unite. It made permanent in stone a more or less contemporary form of structure normally built in timber, itself associated with great circular earthworks and other contexts. The contemporary was made timeless, in what may have been a tradition conceived as timeless. The form of the stone settings might also have stood as some kind of earth metaphor, seen in different form to the north in Silbury Hill, and the stepped elevation of the stone setting, as well as mimicking the great timber structures of the Later Neolithic, might also have symbolised a hierarchy of spirits or gods in the heavens above mortal life.

The stones themselves may have carried meaning. Stones themselves had long been used, especially in connection with the dead and the ancestors. Stones were treated at Stonehenge in part as though they were timbers, the axe carvings picking out zones which were probably also significant in timber structures for deposition. At Stonehenge, a distinction is possible between not only local and exotic materials, but also textures, surfaces and treatment or dressing. This in its turn may suggest movement within and around the monument, bringing direct experience to the fore as opposed to static or passive observation, and serving to link experience within the stones to the experience of approaching, leaving or circling. Movement into the monument was past ditch, bank and Aubrey Holes, which also made reference to the past, through an ancient kind of layout, remains of the dead and an old style of deposition.

Stonehenge drew on the past, while its central form echoed something from the present. It united people, directly through bodily movement, with their ancestors, spirits and the earth, made present in the stones and speaking through the stones, in a timeless frame of reference. It made the future possible by suspending the past.

If this is anywhere near the remembered and imagined belongings of Stonehenge in the Later Neolithic, we should celebrate its difference from our own world, while reflecting that central ideas of the kind explored above are not in themselves more strange or less powerful than the beliefs in parthenogenesis and resurrection at the heart of Christianity. Our view of Stonehenge has been too scientific and too socio-political (cf. Kehoe 1974; Wrigley 1989). The contemporary social context of the Later Neolithic should not be excluded, but it needs further discussion elsewhere. My belief is that the sacred settings of Stonehenge cannot easily or plausibly be reduced to ideological device serving sectional interest. The last dimension of the power of Stonehenge was that it was believed in— even if not fully understood—by all.

*Acknowledgements*

Variously for information, discussion and criticism, I am very grateful to Tim Darvill, Ian Kinnes, Gwyn Maurice, Joshua Pollard, Colin Richards, Niall Sharples, Julian Thomas, James Whitley and Ann Woodward. For help with illustrations thanks are due to Julie Gardiner, Robin Skeates and John Morgan.

# References

ATKINSON, R.J.C. 1979: *Stonehenge* (Harmondsworth, revised ed.).

BARCLAY, A., GRAY, M. and LAMBRICK, G. 1995: *Excavations at the Devil's Quoits, Stanton Harcourt, Oxfordshire, 1972–3 and 1988* (Oxford, Oxford University Committee for Archaeology).

BARRETT, J.C., BRADLEY, R. and GREEN, M. 1991: *Landscape, monuments and society: the prehistory of Cranborne Chase* (Cambridge).

BENDER, B. 1992: Theorising landscapes, and the prehistoric landscapes of Stonehenge. *Man* 27, 735–55.

BLOCH, M. 1992: What goes without saying: the conceptualization of Zafimaniry society. In Kuper, A. (ed.), *Conceptualizing society* (London), 127–46.

BLOCH, M. 1993: Domain-specificity, living kinds and symbolism. In Boyer, P. (ed.), *Cognitive aspects of religious symbolism* (Cambridge), 111–19.

BRADLEY, R. 1976: Maumbury Rings, Dorchester: the excavations of 1908–1913. *Archaeologia* 105, 1–97.

BRADLEY, R. 1991: Ritual, time and history. *World Archaeol.* 23, 209–19.

BRADLEY, R. 1993: *Altering the earth* (Edinburgh, Society of Antiquaries of Scotland).

BURL, A. 1979: *Prehistoric Avebury* (New Haven and London).

BURL, A. 1987: *The Stonehenge people* (London).

BURL, A. 1993: *From Carnac to Callanish: the prehistoric stone rows and avenues of Britain, Ireland and Brittany* (New Haven and London).

CASE, H.J. and WHITTLE, A.W.R. (eds) 1982: *Settlement patterns in the Oxford region* (London, CBA).

CHIPPINDALE, C. 1993: *Stonehenge complete* (London, 2nd ed.).

CLARKE, D.V., COWIE, T.G. and FOXON, A. 1985: *Symbols of power at the time of Stonehenge* (Edinburgh).

CLEAL, R.M.J., WALKER, K.E. and MONTAGUE, R. 1995: *Stonehenge in its landscape: twentieth century excavations* (London, Engl. Heritage Archaeol. Rep. 10).

EDMONDS, M. 1993: Interpreting causewayed enclosures in the past and present. In Tilley, C. (ed.), *Interpretative archaeology* (Oxford), 99–142.

FARON, L.C. 1976: Symbolic values and the interpretation of society among the Mapuche of Chile. In Middleton, J. (ed.), *Myth and cosmos: readings in mythology and symbolism* (Austin), 167–84.

GARWOOD, P. 1991: Ritual tradition and the reconstitution of society. In Garwood, P., Jennings, D., Skeates, R. and Toms, J. (eds), *Sacred and profane* (Oxford, Oxford Univ. Comm. Archaeol. Monogr. 32), 10–32.

GIBSON, A. 1994: Excavations at the Sarn-y-bryn-caled cursus complex, Welshpool, Powys, and the timber circles of Great Britain and Ireland. *Proc. Prehist. Soc.* 60, 143–223.

GRINSELL. L.V. 1957: Archaeological gazetteer. In Pugh, R.B. and Crittall, E. (eds), *A history of Wiltshire, volume 1, part 1* (London), 21–279.

HAWKES, J. 1967: God in the machine. *Antiquity* 41, 174–80.

JENKINS, N. 1980: *The boat beneath the pyramid: King Cheops' royal ship* (London).

KEHOE, A.B. 1974: Saints of Wessex? *Antiquity* 48, 232–3.

LEACH, E. 1976: *Culture and communication: the logic by which symbols are connected* (Cambridge).

MUSSON, C.R. 1971: A study of possible building forms at Durrington Walls, Woodhenge and The Sanctuary. In Wainwright, G.J. and Longworth, I.H. 1971, 363–77.

PARKER PEARSON, M. 1993: *Bronze Age Britain* (London, English Heritage).

PARKER PEARSON, M. and RICHARDS, C. 1994: Architecture and order: spatial representation and archaeology. In Parker Pearson, M. and Richards, C. (eds), *Architecture and order: approaches to social space* (London), 38–72.

PIGGOTT, S. and POWELL, T.G.E. 1949: The excavation of three chambered tombs in Galloway. *Proc. Soc. Antiq. Scotl.* 83, 103–61.

PITTS, M.W. 1982: On the road to Stonehenge: report on the investigations beside the A344 in 1968, 1979 and 1980. *Proc. Prehist. Soc.* 48, 75–132.

PITTS, M. and WHITTLE, A. 1992: The development and date of Avebury. *Proc. Prehist. Soc.* 58, 203–12.

POLLARD, J. 1992: The Sanctuary, Overton Hill, Wiltshire: a re-examination. *Proc. Prehist. Soc.* 58, 213–26.

POLLARD, J. 1995: Inscribing space: formal deposition at the Later Neolithic monument of Woodhenge, Wiltshire. *Proc. Prehist. Soc.* 61, 137–56.

RENFREW, C. 1973: Monuments, mobilization and social organization in Neolithic Wessex. In Renfrew, C. (ed.), *The explanation of culture change: models in prehistory* (London), 539–58.

RICHARDS, C.C. and THOMAS, J.S. 1984: Ritual activity and structured deposition in later Neolithic Wessex. In Bradley, R. and Gardiner, J. (eds), *Neolithic studies* (Oxford, BAR), 189–218.

RICHARDS, J. 1990: *The Stonehenge Environs Project* (London, Hist. Build. Monuments Comm. Archaeol. Rep. 16).

RITCHIE, G. 1984: Ritual monuments. In Renfrew, C. (ed.), *The prehistory of Orkney* (Edinburgh), 118–30.

RITCHIE, J.N.G. 1976: The Stones of Stenness, Orkney. *Proc. Soc. Antiq. Scotl.* 107, 1–60.

SAHLINS, M. 1968: *Tribesmen* (Englewood Cliffs, New Jersey).

SMITH, I.F. 1965: *Windmill Hill and Avebury* (Oxford).

STOUT, G. 1991: Embanked enclosures of the Boyne region. *Proc. Roy. Ir. Acad., Section C* 91, 245–84.

TAÇON, P.S.C. 1991: The power of stone: symbolic aspects of stone use and tool development in western Arnhem Land, Australia. *Antiquity* 65, 192–207.

THOMAS, J. 1991: *Rethinking the Neolithic* (Cambridge).

THOMAS, J. 1993: The politics of vision and the archaeologies of landscape. In Bender, B. (ed.), *Landscape: politics and perspectives* (London), 19–48.

THOMAS, J. and TILLEY, C. 1993: The axe and the torso: symbolic structures in the Neolithic of Brittany. In Tilley, C. (ed.), *Interpretative archaeology* (Providence and Oxford), 225–324.

THORPE, I.J. and RICHARDS, C. 1984: The decline of ritual authority and the introduction of Beakers into Britain. In Bradley, R. and Gardiner, J. (eds), *Neolithic studies* (Oxford, BAR), 67–84.

THORPE, R.S., WILLIAMS-THORPE, O., JENKINS, D.G. and WATSON, J.S. 1991: The geological sources and transport of the bluestones of Stonehenge, Wiltshire, UK. *Proc. Prehist. Soc.* 57(2), 103–57.

TILLEY, C. 1994: *A phenomenology of landscape* (Oxford).

WAINWRIGHT, G.J. 1971: The excavation of a late Neolithic enclosure at Marden, Wiltshire. *Antiq. J.* 51, 177–239.

WAINWRIGHT, G.J. 1979: *Mount Pleasant, Dorset: excavations 1970–1971* (London, Society of Antiquaries).

WAINWRIGHT, G.J. and LONGWORTH, I.H. 1971: *Durrington Walls: excavations 1966–1968* (London, Rep. Res. Comm. Soc. Antiq. London 29).

WHITLEY, J. 1995: Tomb cult and hero cult: the uses of the past in Archaic Greece. In Spencer, N. (ed.), *Time, tradition and society in Greek archaeology* (London), 43–63.

WHITTLE, A. 1995: Gifts from the earth: symbolic dimensions of the use and production of Neolithic flint and stone axes. *Archaeologia Polona* 33, 247–59.

WHITTLE, A. 1996: *Europe in the Neolithic: the creation of new worlds* (Cambridge).

WHITTLE, A. 1997: *Sacred mound, holy rings. Silbury Hill and the West Kennet palisade enclosures: a Later Neolithic complex in north Wiltshire* (Oxford).

WHITTLE, A., ATKINSON, R.J.C., CHAMBERS, R. and THOMAS, N. 1992: Excavations in the Neolithic and Bronze Age complex at Dorchester-on-Thames, Oxfordshire, 1947–52 and 1981. *Proc. Prehist. Soc.* 58, 143–201.

WHITTLE, A. and POLLARD, J. 1997: Windmill Hill causewayed enclosure: the harmony of symbols. In Edmonds, M. and Richards, C. (eds), *Social life and social change: papers on the Neolithic of Atlantic Europe* (Glasgow), 233–50.

WOODWARD, A.B. and WOODWARD, P.J. 1996: The topography of some barrow cemeteries in Bronze Age Wessex. *Proc. Prehist. Soc.* 62, 275–91.

WOODWARD, P.J., DAVIES, S.M. and GRAHAM, A.H. 1993: *Excavations at the Old Methodist Chapel and Greyhound Yard, Dorchester, 1981–1984* (Dorchester, Dorset Natural History and Archaeology Society).

WOODWARD, P.J. and SMITH, R.J.C. 1987: Survey and excavation along the route of the southern Dorchester by-pass, 1986–1987—an interim note. *Proc. Dorset Natur. Hist. Archaeol. Soc.* 109, 79–89.

WRIGLEY, C.C. 1989. Stonehenge from without. *Antiquity* 63, 746–52.

*Proceedings of the British Academy*, **92**, 167–202

# Ever Increasing Circles:
# The Sacred Geographies of Stonehenge
# and its Landscape

## TIMOTHY DARVILL

## Introduction

THE GREAT STONE CIRCLE standing on the rolling chalk downland of Salisbury Plain that we know today as Stonehenge, has, in the twentieth century AD, become a potent icon for the ancient world, and the focus of power struggles and contested authority in our own. Its reputation and stature as an archaeological monument are enormous, and sometimes almost threaten to overshadow both its physical proportions and our accumulated collective understanding of its construction and use. While considerable attention has recently been directed to the relevance, meaning and use of the site in the twentieth century AD (Chippindale 1983; 1986a; Chippindale *et al*. 1990; Bender 1992), the matter of its purpose, significance, and operation during Neolithic and Bronze Age times remains obscure. The late Professor Richard Atkinson was characteristically straightforward when he said that for questions about Stonehenge which begin with the word 'why': 'there is one short, simple and perfectly correct answer: We do not know' (1979, 168).

Two of the most widely recognised and enduring interpretations of Stonehenge are, first, that it was a temple of some kind; and, second, that its orientation on the midsummer sunrise gave it some sort of astronomical role in the lives of its builders. Both interpretations, which are not mutually exclusive, have of course been taken to absurd lengths on occasion. During the eighteenth century, for example, William Stukeley became obsessive about the role of the Druids at Stonehenge (Stukeley 1740). And, in our own century, some of the careful astronomical observations by Sir Norman Lockyer (1909) have been expanded and contorted into almost comical claims about prehistoric calculators and Neolithic computers by Gerald Hawkins in his book *Stonehenge decoded* (Hawkins 1966). It has to be said, however, that both Stukeley and Hawkins appear almost credible when compared with some of the really fanciful interpretations of the site.

In this paper I would like to re-visit questions about the meaning and purpose of Stonehenge by using the perspectives of sociology and social archaeology to look again at the interpretation of the site as a temple and the idea that astronomical alignments were embodied in the design of the structures. A key concept in this, and one that I shall return to several times over, is that of cosmology—the science or theory of the universe held by a given society. I will refer to the archaeological manifestation of a cosmology as a 'sacred geography'.

Defining the question though is far easier than knowing where to start in answering it. I could begin with the celestial bodies occupying the sky above Stonehenge, or the countryside in which the site is set, or the stones and objects recorded there, or even the holes, ditches and pits that were dug there. In due course I will come to discuss all of these, but the place I would really like to start is in the minds and collective consciousness of the individuals and communities who were responsible for the design, construction and use of that most strange thing we now call 'Stonehenge'. By starting with people and societies—surely the only proper focus of archaeology—it is easy to develop a critical understanding of three inhibiting preconceptions which apply particularly to Stonehenge: sites, succession, and science.

First, the idea of the archaeological site has been around a long time but probably represents the single biggest impediment to interpretative thinking in the discipline. The problem is especially acute when the scenes and edges of arbitrarily located archaeological investigations become confused with patterns of activity in the past. People's lives have never been confined to specific sites: they live, work, and move about within much bigger environments which are essentially continuous and infinitely expandable both horizontally and vertically. Moreover, as Colin Renfrew has argued, it is not only the physical environment that is of importance to archaeologists, the cognitive background of past communities is also critical (Renfrew 1982).

Second, succession presents two pit-falls for the unwary. First is the idea that a series of superimposed structures imply steps or stages of development towards the ultimate form represented, as if the builders were trying to achieve something that required several attempts. The way that Stonehenge is presented sometimes gives that impression. Second, is the idea that successive stages were built by people who thought the same way and conceived of the world around them in the same way. In long sequences such as we find at Stonehenge the number of intervening generations precludes the possibility that those concerned with the construction and use of the early stages had the same feelings and thoughts as those concerned with the final use of the site.

Third, science as we know it today, is, in archaeological terms, a recent phenomenon grounded mainly in Western Christian positivist philosophy. Descriptive geometry or astronomy provide useful ways of expressing or communicating relationships and observations. But the fact that today's models map onto designs and arrangements set out by prehistoric communities does not mean they used the same models, still less that they had any theoretical understanding of the laws and principles that we believe underlie the behaviour of the things we observe. In the first edition of his book on Stonehenge, Professor Richard Atkinson cautioned that, at Stonehenge, 'things were aligned *roughly and approximately*' (Atkinson 1956, 89; original emphasis), a statement he retains in all subsequent editions. The same point was reiterated time and again by speakers at the Royal Society and British Academy Seminar on *The place of astronomy in the ancient world* held in London in December 1972 (Hodson 1974), and was made yet again by a number of speakers at the symposium reported in this volume (and see Chippindale 1986b).

Freedom from these three constraints on thinking about the past has many implications. First and foremost, however, it allows a view of prehistoric people who are free to move about in their world unfettered by the boundaries of our imposed ideas of sites. They are intellectually empowered to build things up, change them or knock them down again for their own purposes. And they are at liberty to organise and express their thoughts about the world as they choose. However, before turning to see how these implications affect our interpretations of Stonehenge and its surroundings, I would like briefly to review four important concepts which underpin the way in which a sacred geography can be built up: space, place, landscape, and structuration.

## Space, place and structuration

The words 'space' and 'place' are in widespread common usage, often interchangeably. Yet in a more technical usage these two words express important concepts which have been explored in some detail by the American geographer Yi-Fu Tuan (1977). He sees space as an essentially abstract concept which we apply to everything which is outside one's self. In this sense, space is continuous, it has no edges, but it can be measured or scaled if so desired in almost any plane. Today, we are familiar with the measurement of space in feet or metres, miles or kilometres, in horizontal and vertical planes. But people divide space up in many different ways. There are no universals, although cross-cultural studies suggest that in many societies the human body in upright position is used as the basic map from which subdivisions of space are developed, for example: front and back, up and down, left and right (Fig. 1). The words may change between societies but the basic concepts remain as body-referenced sectors of space become associated with other ideas such as the future and the past, good and evil, light and darkness, the sacred and the profane. Lefebvre (1991) has reviewed the way that conceptual systems based on the human body affect the production of space, while Sennett (1994) considers the relationship between the ideas relating to the human body and the use of space and the constructions that are created in such space at different periods of history.

In modern times the magnetic compass and a coordinate system based on the notional subdivision of the globe by latitude and longitude, or some other local grid, allows individuals to orientate themselves and others so that there is standardisation in the way space is divided up. Coordinate systems have also been developed to map the heavens (Newton

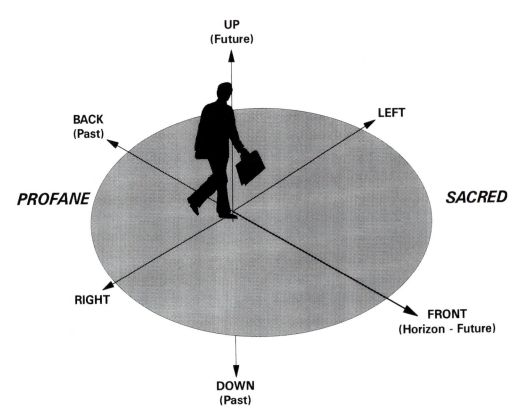

**Figure 1.** Notional categorisation and mapping of space relative to the human body in upright position. (After Tuan 1977, fig. 2, with additions.)

1974). In the absence of the magnetic compass and other calibrated recording devices, other coordinate systems have to be developed and these may be derived from terrestrial or cosmic patterns.

Perhaps the most important characteristic of space is that it is always there; it always has been and always will be even though it is partitioned and subdivided in different ways. Thus even today we can enter and move through the same space that prehistoric people moved through.

The abstract nature of 'space' can be contrasted with the very concrete nature of 'place'. A place is somewhere special, specific, time-dependent, and socially recognised. A sense of place involves an engagement with a certain tract of space which is not simply defined in a coordinate system but is given meaning and value which can be appreciated and understood by those who experience it. As Tuan suggests (1977, 33), every aspect of a place tells a story which may be real or mythical, but always serves to give meaning and relevance. Thus while we can move through the same spaces as Neolithic people, we can never recapture the sense of place that Neolithic people knew.

A close relative of the concept of 'place' is that of 'landscape'; indeed many would see a landscape as a grossly extended place or a network of connected places (Bender 1993). In this, a landscape is not a physical thing, simply a tract of space or an environment, but rather a construction in people's minds based on a set of values, meanings and understandings which are developed in response to what they see around them, what they feel, what they are told, what they remember or think they remember, and their socialisation (Cosgrove 1985; Cosgrove and Daniels 1988; Ingold 1993; Schama 1995). The idea of both place and landscape are closely linked to perception, experience, and engagement, and embrace widely applicable themes about the relationship between people, the realm of ideas and values, and the world that groups and individuals create for themselves to live in.

It is this relationship between what people do and the world they create for themselves that lies at the heart of the fourth matter to touch on here, the process of structuration. Initially developed by the Cambridge sociologist Anthony Giddens, structuration theory provides a means of analysing social action: what people actually do, why they do it, and what the consequences are. This is not the place for a full analysis of structuration theory, but, quite simply, structuration involves patterning or recurrence in the way people do things and relate to one another across space and through time (Giddens 1984). This, Giddens argues, comes about because of fixed rules, resources and structures in society which both constrain and enable people to carry on the business of everyday life, while at the same time reproducing itself (i.e. society) over and over again. A key element of this is a duality between 'structure' as the things which give form to social life and 'interaction' which relates to the relationships between individuals. Set between these two elements, and relating them together, is what Giddens refers to as 'modality', an important element of which is an 'interpretative scheme' or those aspects of an individual's stock of knowledge that is applied reflexively to make accounts of things, offer reasons, and explain actions (Giddens 1984, 29).

Giddens' general theory of structuration, originally developed to deal with contemporary social phenomena, can usefully be modified and extended for application in an archaeological context by identifying the consequences (experiences and tangible/physical outputs) of structure and interaction with social action and material culture respectively. By the same token, interpretative schemes can be closely identified with cosmologies or widely held belief systems. Figure 2 shows in schematic form how such an archaeologically orientated theory of structuration might work. People act against the background of an interpretative scheme of the world, facilitated by their needs, desires and resources, and implemented in the light of socially accepted norms and rules. The outcome is experience and products of various sorts, which in turn relate to the reproduction of the system which both constrains and enables action. In contrast to Giddens' original scheme, this model is cyclical. Its momentum is maintained by the push-pull effect of two sets of influences: on one side there are social structures which significate, dominate and legitimate action; on the other side, social interactions which allow communications,

# *STRUCTURE*

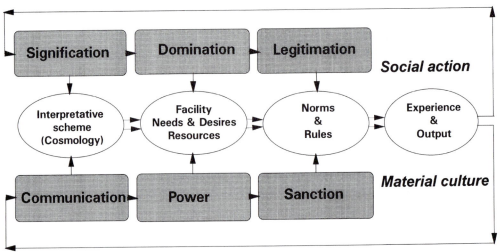

# *INTERACTION*

**Figure 2.** Diagram showing the influence of 'Structure' and 'Communication' on social action and the development of material culture. (Based on Giddens 1984, fig. 2, with substantial modification and additions.)

provide power, and impose sanctions.

The relevance of structuration theory developed in this way to archaeology is two-fold. First, it recognises that the outputs of social action include what archaeologists term material culture which, in this revised model, represent adjuncts to the psychological satisfaction or otherwise of the actor or actors. Second, is the way that the idea of structuration provides a direct connection between belief systems about the world, the way people think, and what they actually do. Thus the power of the model is the way it provides a general theory of society which is applicable at a number of different levels.

Structuration has particularly important implications for exploring the organisation and partitioning of space. As we have already seen, people are free to move about according to socially defined rules and norms. Every area of space can therefore be identified with a series of socially constituted values and meanings because the space itself is categorised or compartmentalised in the minds of its inhabitants or users. This is what gives rise to the definition of value and meaning in places and landscapes. Structuration theory suggests that such compartmentalisation will be based on general interpretative schemes. Conceptual divisions may be significated and made to dominate action through the construction of boundaries, markers, or the distribution of things and associations (and see Tuan 1977). Communication means that people can read these meanings like the words of a book or the signs beside the road, and develop an understanding of the power of the place or landscape they are in. Some categories superficially appear functional and straightforward: field, pasture, house, or burial ground. But behind these simplistic descriptions there are usually more deeply embedded understandings which reveal themselves as emotions and feelings: burial grounds that mix images of darkness with the spirits of the ancestors; woods that disorientate and confuse; springs that give new life and link the land of the living to a supernatural world beyond; rivers that metaphorically represent the passage of time and the cycle of life itself.

The values or meanings attributed to different parts of the environment dictate the way that people relate to it, move about within it, and what actually happens there. These represent the legitimation or sanctioning of action through norms and rules.

Numerous anthropological studies illuminate the way in which space is conceptualised and subdivided in a range of societies so as to produce socially meaningful places and landscapes. They also highlight the way that physical objects (i.e. material culture) relate to concepts of space and place. Studies such as those of the Trobriand Islanders by Glass (1988), or the Pirá-Paraná Indians of Colombia by Hugh-Jones (1979), are particularly relevant, and, along with others, serve to amplify aspects of the cross-cultural links between space, place, landscape and structuration which are particularly relevant to archaeological analysis in general, and the problem of Stonehenge in particular. Two deserve mention here.

First, the categorisation of space is generally systematic and the rules which inform the understanding of each category (i.e. an interpretative scheme) are often founded in a received cosmology. Wheatley (1971) describes the cosmological basis for the planning of ancient Chinese cities, Coe (1993, 174–90) the layout of Maya ceremonial centres in central America, and, rather controversially, Bauval and Gilbert (1994) look at the arrangement and cosmological referencing of the pyramids at Giza in Egypt. On the basis of these and many other studies, the equation between interpretative schemes or cosmologies and structure in the archaeological evidence is no surprise, and should, as Ian Hodder has advocated (1987), be considered an integral and essential part of archaeological inquiry.[1]

Second, is a recognition that the categorisation of space is often 'nested' in the sense that arrangements apply at several different levels simultaneously as interpretative schemes impinge on almost every dimension of life. Thus, for example, patterning in the sub-division, arrangement, and meaning of space may, at the same time, be found in the decorative schemes applied to material culture, the arrangement of spaces and disposition of activities in the home, the layout of a settlement, and patterns of behaviour in the landscape as a whole. This means that if patterns can be detected strongly at one level they may also be applicable at others.

---

[1.] Fashion is an important factor here. In recent decades it has not been fashionable to interpret archaeological remains by reference to cosmological systems, but Humphrey Case has kindly drawn my attention to Mortimer's assertion (1905, 298) that the Huggate Wold barrows in former East Yorkshire were laid out to represent the seven stars in Charles' Wain in the constellation of Ursa Major.

## Stonehenge and its landscape

Archaeological investigations and surveys of the space occupied by Stonehenge and the area around about are legion: indeed it is one of the most intensively studied areas of Britain if not northern Europe. Among recent surveys drawn upon here, special mention may be made of the work by the Royal Commission on the Historical Monuments of England during the 1970s (RCHM 1979), the Stonehenge Environs Survey carried out by Wessex Archaeology in the early 1980s (Richards 1990), and the various studies carried out in the early 1990s contained in the first Environmental Statement prepared for the Stonehenge Conservation and Management Program (Darvill 1991). Twentieth century excavations at Stonehenge itself have recently been published (Cleal *et al.* 1995) and the revised chronology and phasing presented in that report is used here with only minor modification. Figure 3 shows a chart which summarises the approximate chronological duration of the main dated monuments in the area.

The following analysis does not follow the conventional phasing of prehistory, or of any particular excavated site in the Stonehenge area. Rather, following a social perspective, interest focuses on the changing patterns of evidence, the archaeological structuration as just explained, and, by implication, the changing cosmologies which underpinned everything. The chronological framework is that of calibrated radiocarbon ages expressed as calendar years.

### The early years

Theoretically, the Stonehenge environment began to be parcelled up and structured from the time of the first settlement. When this was is not exactly known, although it is generally presumed to have been during the early post-glacial period, perhaps as early as the ninth or tenth millennium BC. The very low density of flintwork of that period recovered from the area suggests that settlement was not intensive hereabouts, but this does not mean that no-one cared about the area. Specific places were already being identified for attention by the seventh millennium BC when a series of at least four posts, perhaps decorated and painted like the totem poles of native North American societies, were set up in the area which is now used as the Stonehenge car-park (Vatcher and Vatcher 1973; Cleal *et al.* 1995, 43–7). These posts were not necessarily all contemporary, and could indeed represent the periodic confirmation of something special about the place. Three of the post-holes have a general alignment roughly east-west, but the fourth, some distance away, is not on the same line. Care must be exercised in using this evidence as it is far from clear that a complete picture has yet been recovered. What is interpreted as a tree-hole was found at the western end of the line of three post-holes (A-C), more or less in line with them. Little has been made of this, and it remains undated, but its position relative to the posts and its spatial association with them makes it tantalising to speculate that this was in fact the thing that gave significance to the place. There is nothing odd

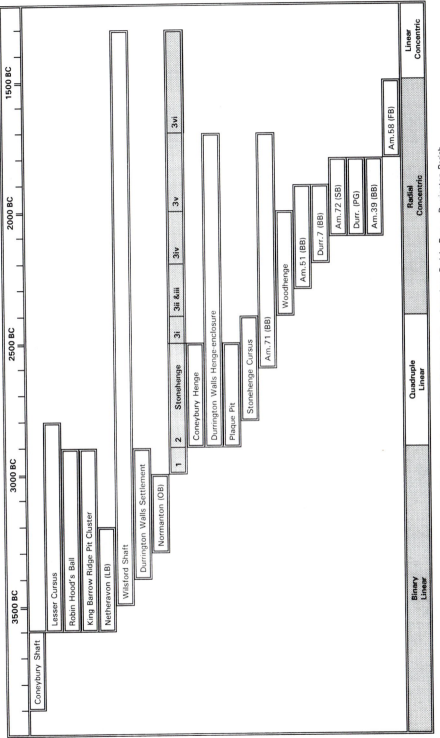

OB = Oval Barrow;   BB = Bowl Barrow;   FB = Fancy Barrow;   SB = Saucer Barrow;   PG = Pit Grave;   Am. = Amesbury Parish;   Durr. = Durrington Parish

**Figure 3.** Chart showing the relative dating of key archaeological monuments mentioned in the text.

about considering an essentially natural thing as being the most important feature of a place. Such a case has been argued by Christopher Tilley in respect of the Mesolithic flint scatters on Bodmin Moor, Cornwall, which, he believes, indicate an interest in the natural rock outcrops or tors on the moor (Tilley 1994; lecture to IFA conference 13th April 1995).

The post-holes in the Stonehenge car-park are some 200 m away from where Stonehenge was later constructed, and while they may indicate a general signification of the area it would be hard to argue that they significate the space later used for Stonehenge itself. Sadly, little of the central area of Stonehenge has been sufficiently fully investigated to know what might have attracted people to imbue this space with meaning. Whether there was a special tree, unusual rock, or more posts on the site cannot be determined because of the poor dating and virtual absence of stratigraphic control over most of the internal features. There is no reason, however, why some of the post-holes conventionally assigned to Phase 2 of the monument could not have been considerably earlier. The possibility of what, in traditional terminology, would be called Mesolithic features representing the first signification of a place which continued in use through into the Neolithic should occasion little surprise in the context of the social model already outlined. Indeed Mesolithic features and finds at sites which are recognisably important through the construction of substantial monuments during Early and Middle Neolithic times are well-known and widespread, as illustrated by Hazleton North long barrow, Gloucestershire (Saville 1990, 240), Gwernvale long barrow, Powys (Britnell and Savory 1984, 136), and the Billown enclosures and Killeaba cemeteries in the Isle of Man (Darvill 1996b, 48).

### Fourth millennium BC

During the fourth millennium BC (*c*.4000–3000 BC) the range of recorded activity around Stonehenge becomes greater and the organisation of space has sharper focus. Figure 4 shows the distribution of recorded sites which fall into three main groups.

First there are shafts or holes dug into the ground. The earliest of these, dating to 3980–3708 BC (OxA-1402) is the Coneybury anomaly on Coneybury Hill to the east of Stonehenge. Excavation proved this to be a flat-bottomed pit, 1.25 m deep and 1.9 m in diameter (Richards 1990, 40–61). The primary deposit contained abundant animal bones suggestive of a major episode of butchery in which at least ten cattle, several roe deer, one pig, and two red-deer were processed. The remains of beaver and a fish were also present. Fragments of over 40 pottery vessels, and flint tools used for cutting, emphasise the possible role of this site in feasting. Other pit groups have been excavated on King Barrow Ridge and Vespasian's Ridge (Richards 1990, 65), but potentially the most remarkable shaft of the period is the Wilsford Shaft to the south-west of Stonehenge, 30 m deep and up to 1.8 m in diameter (Ashbee *et al.* 1989). Although generally regarded as being of Bronze Age date, the ten radiocarbon dates accord exactly with their stratigraphic

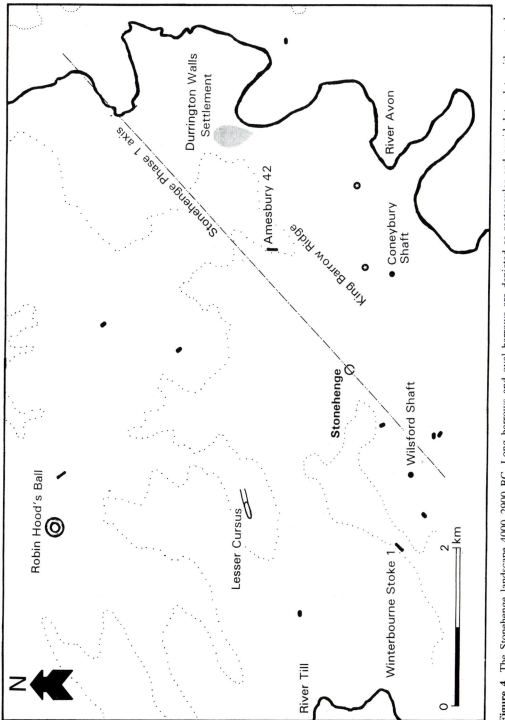

**Figure 4.** The Stonehenge landscape 4000–2900 BC. Long barrows and oval barrows are depicted as rectangular and ovoid dots; dots with central star-symbols indicate pit clusters.

sequence, beginning with a date of 3510–3345 BC (OxA-1089) on wood from the remains of a bucket in the bottom of the shaft.[2]

The second group of monuments are linear structures which include three long barrows (Amesbury 42, Figheldean 27, and Winterbourne Stoke 1), seven oval barrows, and the so-called Lesser Cursus which is a two-phase monument more reminiscent of a long mound or bank barrow than a cursus (cf. Bradley 1983).[3] The larger monuments in this group tend to lie on higher ground at intervals of 2.0–2.5 km, although the smaller examples are more unevenly distributed. All share the fact that they have a single dominant axis inherent to their form, but there is little commonality of alignment between them.

The third group of sites comprises enclosures and settlements. To the north-west of Stonehenge is Robin Hood's Ball, a typical Wessex-style causewayed enclosure with two rings of boundary ditches encircling a maximum of about 3 ha (Thomas 1964). No certain entrance is known, but a scatter of worked flints and pits dating to the period 3200–3000 BC has been found to the north (Richards 1991, 74). Of broadly similar date is the spread of occupation debris below the bank of the henge-enclosure at Durrington Walls, although the full context and extent of this material is not known (Wainwright and Longworth 1971, 192–3).

The earliest earthwork enclosure at Stonehenge (Phase 1) was constructed around the turn of the fourth millennium BC at a time when many of the sites already mentioned were ancient and beginning to fall out of use. Stonehenge 1, dating to the period *c.*2950–2900 BC, comprises a roughly circular enclosure about 100 m in diameter, bounded by a bank, external ditch, and small outer counterscarp bank. Inside the main bank, and broadly concentric with it, was a ring of 56 post-holes which are now believed to have held upright timber posts (Cleal *et al.* 1995, 102–7). In the portion of the earthwork boundary that has been excavated there was an 11–13 m wide gap in the enclosure earthwork to the north-east, a gap about 3–5 m wide opening to the south, and perhaps a third gap, later blocked, about 2–3 m wide, opening to the south-west. The ring of 56 internal posts does not recognise any of these three gaps, although the spacing of the posts would not have hindered movement through the gaps if that was their purpose.[4] There may also have been other post-holes in and around the monument, for example some of those within and beyond the north-east entrance.

In its construction and design, Stonehenge 1 seems to incorporate a number of features which accord with earlier traditions. The ditch, for example, was constructed as a series of segments divided from one another by causeways in the same fashion as the boundaries at Robin Hood's Ball. In the ditch were a series of deposits of animal bones, some of which were already several centuries old by the time they were deposited. As at cause-

---

[2.] The Neolithic age of the site was cogently argued by Mark Knight at a meeting of the Neolithic Studies Group held in the British Museum on 13th November 1995.

[3.] See Grinsell 1957 for list of these sites with notes.

[4.] There is always a danger in uncritically interpreting gaps as entrances.

wayed enclosures, the ditch terminals were identified for special attention. Both terminals for the north-east gap had fires in, and abundant antlers. The south entrance had cattle jaw bones on either side, while the putative south-western entrance had a cattle skull in the terminal of ditch segment 23 on its west side. Whether there were any engravings on the ditch walls, as at the comparable enclosure discovered at Flagstones, Dorset (Woodward 1988), is not known. Equally, however, the design of Stonehenge 1 prefigures later structures in its circular form and the construction of a post-ring around the inside of the bank.

The largest of the gaps in the boundary earthwork opens to the north-east with its axis on an azimuth of $c.46°33'$ taken from the centre of the enclosure (Atkinson 1982, 111). In the early 1960s Mr C.A. Newham suggested that the early phase of Stonehenge had been related to the observation of lunar phenomena (1972, 20–2) and this has been followed and developed by Aubrey Burl (1987, 64–80) and others. The arguments, however, are weak (Atkinson 1982, 111). They are based on the ascription to Phase 1 of all the post-holes in and around the north-east entrance, the acceptance that the pattern of post-holes genuinely represents attempts to determine moonrise positions, and the recognition that out of the eight defining directions of the moon's movements over an 18.6 year cycle only one could easily be observed through the north-east entrance and even then not along what appears to be the axis of the monument at that time. Moreover, with the re-phasing of the Heel Stone and other outliers (Cleal et al. 1995) there are no certain markers which would allow lunar events to be observed (cf. Burl 1991 on lunar alignment of the Heel Stone).

Other explanations should be considered, among them the possibility that the earthwork enclosure was not related to the observations of the heavens at all, but was instead built in a form which symbolically represented the surrounding landscape in which its users lived. Figure 5 shows one possible interpretation, placing Stonehenge at the centre of a roughly circular space about 10 km across. The size of the space was determined by simply projecting the main axis of Stonehenge 1 north-east until it encountered a substantial natural boundary or feature, in this case the course of the river Avon. As can be seen, the river Avon enters and leaves this large space in exactly the same relative position as the north-east and south gaps occur in the earthwork at Stonehenge itself. Perhaps the juxtaposition of the river in actual space and the position of the entrances within the physically constructed space at the monument is coincidental, but it is notable that when standing within Stonehenge it feels as if one is at the centre of a circular landscape edged with hills as well as in a circular monument edged by a bank. Moreover, the area enclosed within the wider landscape neatly incorporates most of the fourth millennium BC monuments in the immediate neighbourhood of Stonehenge.

Some support for a terrestrial interpretation of the design of Stonehenge 1 comes from reviewing again the disposition of other monuments (Fig. 4). A dispersed pattern of activity is apparent, what little evidence for settlement there is being in the form of pottery finds which concentrate in the south and east along the valley of the river Avon (Cleal

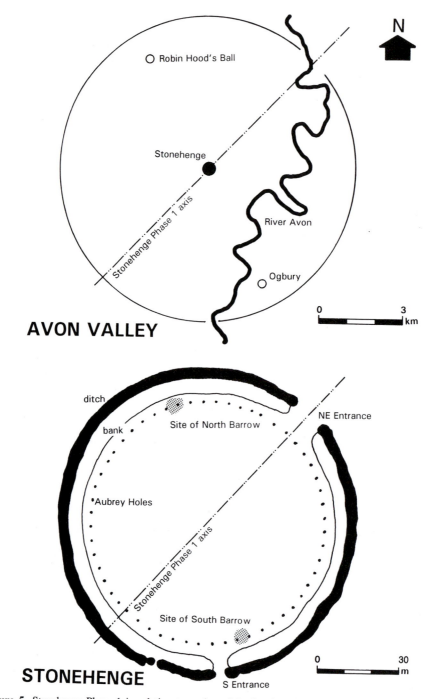

**Figure 5.** Stonehenge Phase 1 in relation to a plan of the local environment. (Stonehenge after Cleal *et al.* 1995, fig. 36.)

*et al.* 1995, fig. 252). Barrows, burial monuments, and the putatively ceremonial enclosure at Robin Hood's Ball lie towards the west and north. In this pattern Stonehenge stands more or less in the centre, constructed in an area which the poverty of fourth millennium BC cultural material suggests was not intensively used. But absence of cultural material does not mean it was an unimportant place as numerous anthropological studies testify (Carmichael *et al.* 1994). Memories of earliest significance, perhaps represented archaeologically by the tree and early post-holes noted above, may have structured behaviour in the sense that the hill-slope on which Stonehenge stands was the only appropriate place for the construction of the new enclosure. Until that time the 'centre' of these people's world had not been elaborated in an archaeological sense. Like other existing monuments, it had a single dominant axis.

It is tempting to speculate that, in symbolic terms, the axis of all these fourth millennium BC monuments was seen as a river, in this case the river Avon. It is easy to speculate on the sort of legends and creation myths that could underpin such an interpretation, not least stories of the colonisation of the area, or the place of the ancestral homeland.[5] If the river was important then its representation in the design of Stonehenge should be no surprise (cf. Fig. 2).

Other things might be important too. The ring of posts represented by the Aubrey Holes (Cleal *et al.* 1995, 102–7) is an unusual feature. Its explanation, like that of the construction of the monument as a whole, should perhaps be set in the general social context of the turn of the third millennium BC. Alasdair Whittle has argued that this was a period of considerable change, with the abandonment and destruction of earlier sites, the localised regeneration of woodland, population increases, and widespread stress on available resources (1978; 1981). The fourth millennium BC was also the period when the natural woodland cover of the Stonehenge area was being cleared away to leave a mosaic of open grassland and light woodland in the main settlement areas, wildwood all around. If Stonehenge is a symbolic or metaphorical representation of its landscape then, for the users of the site, perhaps the posts and bank represent the edge of the 'world' where the uncleared forest began and the hills rise up beyond.

The evidence from Stonehenge then does not have to be forced into a cosmological order based on lunar events; it can more easily be set against a terrestrial cosmology based on the landscape rather than the heavens and perhaps originally derived from the myths and legends of earlier hunter-gatherer communities who first occupied the area. A simple linear binary system would accommodate the patterning present, whether or not the symbolism of this axis is derived from the river. Such an axis, which perhaps Stonehenge sits astride in the real landscape, may have symbolically separated one sector from the other and perhaps created a series of simple binary oppositions as part of an interpretative scheme: the living separated from the dead, beginning from end, light from dark, summer from winter.

[5.] See by way of illustration Hugh-Jones (1979) for riverside communities in Amazonia.

*Early third millennium BC*

The early pattern of structuration at Stonehenge did not last long. Over a period from about 2900 BC through to 2400 BC (Phases 2 and 3i) the ditches were deliberately filled to the point where their course would have been lost from view in places. The bank also became reduced as it provided the main source of infill material. Included within this refilling are human burials and cremations. The posts which stood in the Aubrey Holes were probably removed, and timber structures and various alignments of posts constructed in the central area.

Activity around the north-east entrance was especially intensive. Professor Atkinson argued that after his Phase I, the north-east entrance was made wider by infilling the eastern ditch terminal and removing the former bank for a distance of *c.*8 m (1979, 73). This allowed the axis of the monument to shift 5° east onto the rising midsummer sun and the Avenue to be constructed with a neat junction onto the remains of the earlier enclosure boundary. Recent work suggests that the ditch filling was part of a more wide-spread phenomenon around the whole circuit, and that the Avenue was not added until later (Cleal *et al.* 1995, 139–40). Nevertheless, although the details of the sequence have changed, the realignment of the primary axis is clear enough.

Some of the post-settings in the interior and around the entrance are perhaps early manifestations of the revised solar alignment. Particularly relevant are features 3364 and 3362 flanking the centre of the site as these may define the place from which observations could be made. It is possible that the Heel Stone (Stone 96) and its neighbour Stone 97 were set up at this time and from the centre of the enclosure would have acted like a gun-sight to the midsummer rising sun (Pitts 1982; Burl 1991; 1992). The chronology and phasing of construction is vague, but other stones may also have been positioned outside the entrance area to fix the line of the solar axis. The four Station Stones (91–94) forming a rectangular setting inside the former enclosure can tentatively be assigned to Phase 2 or 3i; probably the earlier. Many supposed alignments have been based on these stones, the only very convincing ones being across each of the short axes of the rectangle onto the midsummer and midwinter solstices. All the others hinge on the use of other (sometimes hypothetical) markers, and/or the absence of any features in the centre of the monument which would have blocked views along the alignments. It is, however, note-worthy that two of the Station Stones are enclosed within ditches (sometimes called barrows): if Stonehenge 1 is correctly identified as a representation of its landscape, then the two enclosed stones correspond almost exactly to the relative position of Robin Hood's Ball and Ogbury in the real landscape.[6]

During Stonehenge 3i the solar axis is established for the first time as a stone struc-ture in the centre of the site. This is the Bluestone Circle (Fig. 6). Again, recent work

---

[6.] Ogbury Camp is a rather large hilltop enclosure of uncertain date, although in its visible form may reasonably be regarded as Iron Age. In the centre are slight traces of an earlier enclosure which might possibly be of Neolithic date. See Crawford and Keiller (1928, 150-2) for plan and photograph.

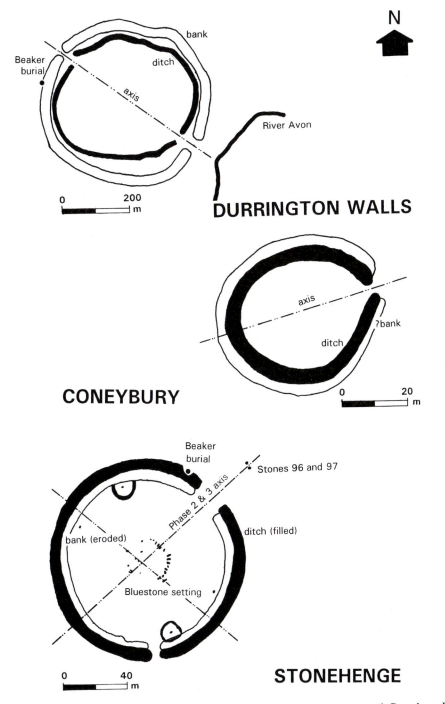

**Figure 6.** Stonehenge Phase 3i compared with Durrington Walls Henge-enclosure and Coneybury Henge. (After: Cleal *et al.* 1995, fig. 66; Wainwright and Longworth 1971, fig. 2; Richards 1990, fig. 97.)

has cast doubt on the geometrical regularity of the circle as originally proposed by Atkinson, Cleal and collaborators concluding that it may have been set out as a semi-circle or even a three-sided open rectangular arrangement with rounded ends (Cleal *et al.* 1995, 188). What is, however, clear is the elaboration of the putative entrance between R38 and R1 with a line of up to five stones flanking the entrance whereas the remainder of the circuit is marked by pairs of stones. This entrance follows the midsummer sunrise axis. Also important is the probable presence of a large stone, possibly the Altar Stone, in feature WA3639 directly opposite the entrance to the Phase 3i setting. The Altar Stone, which measures 4.9 m by 1 m by 0.5 m thick has never been fully investigated because it lies partly under the fallen remains of the Great Trilithon (Stones 55 and 156). Rather unusually, however, the Altar Stone is made of a micaceous sandstone believed to come from south-west Wales and is the only certain block of such stone known at Stonehenge (Cleal *et al.* 1995, 29).

The visual appearance of the Phase 3i setting remains speculative, although the presence of a number of cut and shaped bluestones around the site hints that it may have been more spectacular than its archaeological footprint might suggest. Lintelled structures around some of the perimeter is certainly possible, and the tongued and grooved stones may suggest an elaborate focal screen of some sort.

Stonehenge was not the only site receiving attention at this time. Much else was happening in the surrounding landscape and Stonehenge became the focus of a more tightly clustered ring of sites than in previous centuries (Fig. 7).

The Stonehenge Cursus was built about 1 km north of Stonehenge around 2700 BC.[7] One of the longer cursus in Britain with a length of about 3 km, the two ends are inter-visible on the ground, but because its central section crosses a shallow valley (Stonehenge Bottom) the ends are not always visible from within. At the east end is an earlier long barrow. The cursus is not straight, but subdivisible into three straight segments set slightly off-line to one another (Stone 1948; Christie 1963).[8] Projecting the line of the cursus east-wards there is a standing stone (the Cuckoo Stone), removed from its original position in relatively modern times. Beyond this again, on the same alignment, is Woodhenge, probably established around the middle of the third millennium BC.

North of Woodhenge is Durrington Walls, a massive henge-enclosure 490 m by 468 m with opposed entrances to the NW and SE. The south-eastern entrance opens to the river Avon. Radiocarbon dates suggest that the enclosure was first constructed 2800–2400 BC (Wainwright and Longworth 1971).

Of more or less the same date is Coneybury Henge to the south-east of Stonehenge. This small henge is only 40 m across along its greatest axis (Richards 1990, 109–58). Other monuments in the area include pits containing Grooved Ware, and burial monu-

---

[7.] One radiocarbon date is available: 2878–2502 BC (2150±90 bc OxA-1403)

[8.] The alignment of the cursus WSW to ENE means that on the equinox in March and September the sunrise and sunset can be viewed along its length, but since the idea of the equinox is generally regarded as a recent observational phenomenon it is here disregarded as being significant for prehistoric patterning.

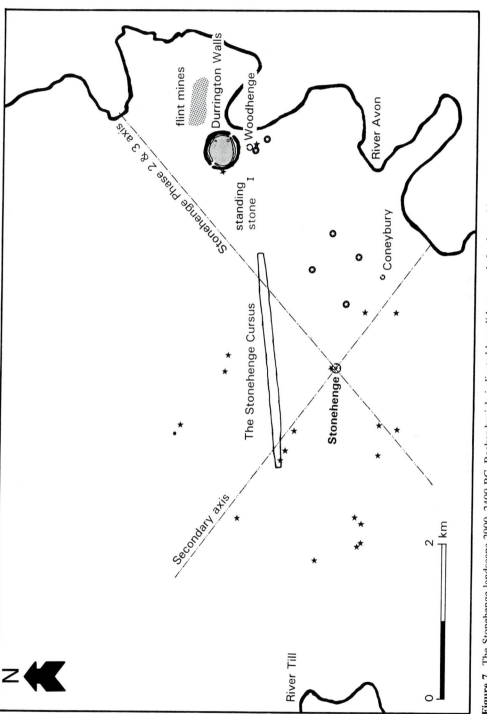
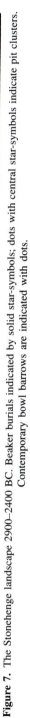

**Figure 7.** The Stonehenge landscape 2900–2400 BC. Beaker burials indicated by solid star-symbols; dots with central star-symbols indicate pit clusters. Contemporary bowl barrows are indicated with dots.

ments associated with Beaker pottery. Some flint mines are known to the north-west of Durrington Walls, and are also probably of this period (Booth and Stone 1952).

The midsummer sunrise axis is the most obvious axis visible at Stonehenge (Atkinson 1982), but it is not the only one. There are four key positions in the solar cycle: midsummer sunrise and sunset, and midwinter sunrise and sunset. The angle between midsummer sunrise and midwinter sunrise is about 80°, the same as between midwinter sunset and midsummer sunset. Risings are to the east, settings to the west. Thus the midsummer sunrise (here called the primary axis), can be projected backwards to the south-west where it aligns on the midwinter sunset. The secondary axis, roughly south-east to north-west, is more difficult to identify than the primary axis because of the rather partial plan of the Phase 3i settings. However, there are two unusual features belonging to this phase, WA3654 to the north-west and WA2321 to the south-east. Both are large stone-holes, although the stones that were set in them were removed in subsequent phases. WA2321 stands immediately outside the defined line of the bluestone setting; the same may also apply to W3654. The axis created by these two features bisects the primary solar axis at 80° near the notional centre of the bluestone setting (see Cleal *et al.* 1995, fig. 80). Moreover, the same north-west to south-east axis is well represented at Durrington Walls where it is marked by the alignment of the two main entrances into the enclosure.

This simple solar scheme, more or less in the form of a cross with a primary and secondary axis, can be projected onto the landscape (Fig. 7) outwards from Stonehenge to create two potentially significant axes defining four quarters. One interesting feature of this is the way that the projected alignments intersect the line of the cursus at just the places where its width changes slightly: it is narrower at the ends compared with the central part.

The linear quadruple partitioning of space also finds expression in the distribution of monuments and artefacts. The eastern sector contains sites which have been associated with feasting (Durrington Walls and Coneybury Henge). As Table 1 shows, the highest proportion of Beaker Age burials (58%) lie in the western sector. By contrast, over 85% of Grooved Ware findspots lie in the eastern sector (Table 2), while 62% of Beaker pottery findspots lie in the north and west sectors. Flint-mining and extensive flint-knapping are known only in the eastern and southern sectors.

Further support for the four-fold partitioning of space can be found in the decoration applied to artefacts of the period and later. Figure 8 shows a small selection. The engraved chalk plaque from a pit beside the A303 near King Barrow Ridge has a rather angular

**Table 1.** Distribution of Beaker burials in the area around Stonehenge by quarter

|                | North | East | South | West |
|----------------|-------|------|-------|------|
| Beaker burials | 8%    | 16%  | 16%   | 58%  |
|                | (1)   | (2)  | (2)   | (7)  |

**Table 2.** Distribution of pottery types in the area around Stonehenge by quarter

|                     | North       | East        | South       | West        |
|---------------------|-------------|-------------|-------------|-------------|
| Peterborough Style  | 18%<br>(4)  | 22%<br>(5)  | 35%<br>(8)  | 25%<br>(6)  |
| Grooved Ware        | 0%<br>(0)   | 85%<br>(12) | 15%<br>(2)  | 0%<br>(0)   |
| Beaker Pottery      | 21%<br>(7)  | 13%<br>(4)  | 25%<br>(8)  | 41%<br>(13) |

outline to its depiction of intersecting axes (Fig. 8A). Later pieces, including the beaker from Wilsford G62 barrow (Fig. 8D) and the goldwork from Bush Barrow (Fig. 8B and C), show a lozenge-shaped depiction of the same thing. The larger of the two Bush Barrow lozenges is especially interesting as Alexander Thom and others have claimed it was a template or map for the construction of Stonehenge (Thom *et al.* 1988); here it is argued the piece was designed in the light of broader inherited ideas about the organisation of space.[9]

Individual sites around Stonehenge also perpetuate one or other of the significant solar axes. Durrington Walls, for example has the south-east to north-west axis, while Coneybury has a midsummer sunrise axis adjusted to accommodate the different configuration of hills. Both Stonehenge and Durrington Walls are known to have Beaker Age burials on the outside of their boundaries (Evans 1984; Wainwright and Longworth 1971, fig. 2), interestingly both to the right of anyone approaching the entrance from the outside (cf. Fig. 6).

Overall, therefore, a common set of arrangements and alignments seem to have significance in the landscape as a whole, in the layout and design of sites of the period, and in the motifs used for the decoration of some objects.

An interest in solar events seems to be common to all these patterns, and represents the only uncontested astronomical alignments at Stonehenge itself. Interest in the sun became common over much of Europe during the mid third millennium BC. This might in part be attributed to the adoption of Beakers and the ideas associated with them. So-called gold 'sun-discs' are among the earliest objects bearing solar imagery to achieve a wide circulation (Case 1977). However, solar cosmology also occurs in non-Beaker contexts too. Colin Richards (1993) has examined its implications with reference to a range of dwellings, sacred structures, henges and tombs in Orkney. He found a high correspondence between architectural form and a putative central place of the sun in the lives of the communities who built the structures. In Ireland the developed passage graves of the Boyne Valley embody solar alignments: Newgrange, for example, was constructed

---

[9.] Burgess (1980, 113) assigns the Bush Barrow grave goods to early metalworking Stage VI, equivalent to Reinecke A2 in Europe, and spanning the early second millennium BC.

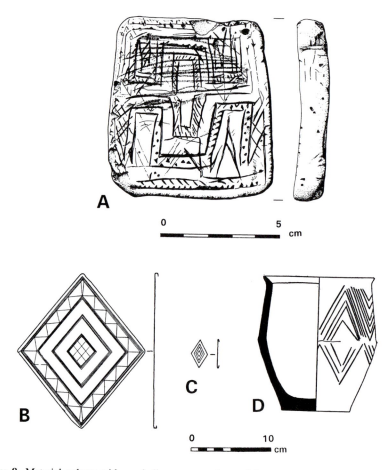

**Figure 8.** Material culture with symbolic representations of linear quadruple structuring of space. A: Chalk plaque from King Barrow Ridge, Amesbury. B and C: Gold lozenges from the Bush Barrow (Wilsford cum Lake G5), Wilsford. D: Beaker from the primary burial in bowl barrow Wilsford cum Lake G62, Wilsford. (A after Harding 1988, fig. 2; B-D after Annable and Simpson 1964, items 135, 168, and 177.)

about 3291–2929 BC (GrN-5462) in such a way that the midwinter sunrise illuminated the central chamber (O'Kelly 1982, 122–5). Passage grave art, especially the circles and radial line motifs (Shee Twohig 1981, 107), may include solar imagery, a position not necessarily diminished by Dronfield's (1996) interpretations which suggest a link with altered states of consciousness and the desire to provide a symbolic means of access between real and supernatural worlds.

As for earlier patterns it is impossible to get at the stories and myths that lie behind the solar cosmologies, even though the main element is visible. The farthest we can go is perhaps the development of patterns of association from the disposition of monuments in the landscape and objects in monuments. In this case, two sectors, the eastern and

**Table 3.** Provisional set of cosmological associations for early third millennium BC Wessex

| | (NORTH) Earth Cold | |
|---|---|---|
| (WEST) Sunset Death Burial places Darkness Winter Fire Cooking | Sun Hearth Transformation | (EAST) Sunrise Life Settlements Light Summer Water Feasting |
| | (SOUTH) Sky Warm | |

western, seem especially significant. The eastern sector was strongly associated with sunrise, new beginnings, life, light, fertility, feasting, water, and the earth. The western sector with sunset, endings, death, darkness, quietness, and the sky. Table 3 provides a provisional summary of these associations in schematic form. Movement between and within different areas may, at certain times at least, have been strictly controlled. If the above pattern of associations has any utility then perhaps the cursus served to structure movement between life and death in the landscape: a pathway for the soul?

*Later third and early second millennia BC*

The patterns established during the early third millennium BC continued for a thousand years or more as the basic elements of a quartering of space became more embedded in the things people did. To it was added another dimension, an interest in concentric patterns which in due course may have taken over from or complemented the four-fold partitioning of space.

At Stonehenge itself the general pattern is at its most clear. Phases 3ii-3vi represent the successive remodelling, perhaps every hundred years or so, of the same basic concepts. It was a process still going on in the years around 1600 BC if the dates from the antlers in Y-Hole 30 are any guide to works that were never finished.

The addition of further stones at the north-eastern entrance in Phase 3iii, and the Avenue in Phase 3iv, must have produced an entry rather similar to the stone-defined passage envisaged by Aubrey Burl (1994) on the basis of excavated stone-holes and antiquarian depictions. If there were indeed stones set at intervals along the Avenue as far as Stonehenge Bottom, as slight anomalies revealed by geophysical surveys suggest (Cleal *et al.* 1995, 506), then there must have been a spectacular approach to the site.

No new alignments seem to have been added to Stonehenge which retained its solar orientation, but at other sites in the area the idea of concentric arrangements becomes more prevalent. Inside Durrington Walls, the Southern Circle was, in its first phase, a modest circular building. This was replaced by a massive timber lodge with six concentric rings of posts and a maximum diameter of 39 m (Fig. 9).[10] Radiocarbon dates put the age of the timbers used for this structure at between 2500 and 2100 BC, two or three centuries later than the construction of the earthwork boundary and perhaps broadly contemporary with Stonehenge 3iv or 3v. Durrington Walls generally takes the secondary axis (see above for the main enclosure) and the South Circle is no exception; the main entrance is to the south-east (Wainwright and Longworth 1971, fig. 84). A study by Colin Richards and Julian Thomas (1984) of the disposition of finds within the excavated section of Durrington Walls revealed differences in the range of material found in the Southern Circle as compared with other contexts on the same site, and that within there were distinctions between the range and quantity of material found in the outer areas as against the inner rings.

The structure inside Woodhenge is not adequately dated, but presumably should be set after the construction of the earthwork enclosure around 2200–2000 BC. It too has six concentric rings of posts. Like Stonehenge it has an axis on the midsummer sunrise (Cunnington 1929, pl. 4). An analysis by Joshua Pollard (1992; 1995) of material found inside Woodhenge shows clear patterning in the deposition of pig bones around and outside of post-hole circuit C, mainly in the south-east and north-east quadrants, and the deposition of carved chalk around post-hole circuit C in the south-east quadrant. Two axes were found at Woodhenge, both on the east side of the axis (Pollard 1992, 223).

In its final form, Stonehenge 3vi also had six concentric rings, although the outer pair (X and Y holes) seemingly never contained stones. Also, the central settings have a horseshoe plan open to the north-east. The numerous axe carvings at Stonehenge are all to the east of the primary solar axis.

The cross and concentric ring patterns are frequently applied motifs on Later Neolithic and Early–Middle Bronze Age artefacts. Figure 10 shows a selection from different phases. Particularly fine are the cross motifs on two beads in a necklace from the G5j barrow: both show in detail the intersection of the sunrise/sunset axes (see Figs 7 and 11) which differs slightly from a simple cross where the axes intersect at right-angles. The same applies to the base of the incense cup from Wilsford G40. This also includes the concentric circles motif. Concentric circles are also present on Grooved Ware pottery of the Durrington Walls sub-style, although rather rarely. At Durrington Walls, six groups of sherds carrying the motif were found, all but one in direct association with Phase 2 of the Southern Circle or its external midden. Three of the groups were in post-holes at the entrance to the structure (Wainwright and Longworth 1971, 140–3). A few sherds were also found at Woodhenge (Cunnington 1929, pl. 26). The pin from the ditch

---

10. Six of these large timber structures have been recorded in England to date, mainly through aerial photography (Darvill 1996a). More no doubt await discovery.

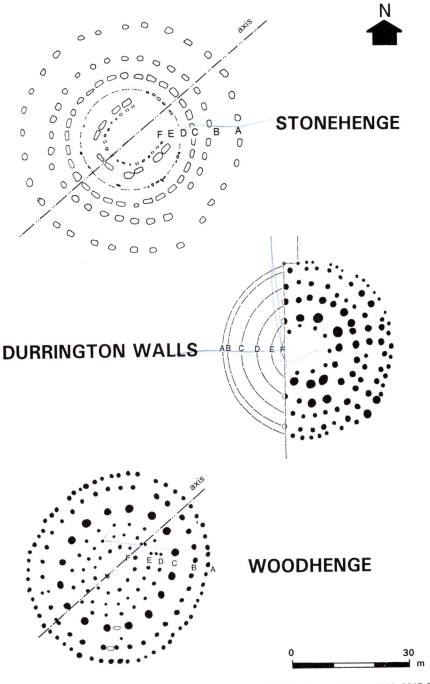

**Figure 9.** Stonehenge Phase 3vi (*c*.2030–1520 BC) compared with Woodhenge (after *c*.2283–2047 BC), and Phase 2 of the Southern Circle at Durrington Walls (after *c*.2580–2147 BC). (Stonehenge after Cleal *et al.* 1995, fig. 257; Durrington Walls after Wainwright and Longworth 1971, fig. 84; and Woodhenge after Wainwright and Longworth 1971, fig. 115.)

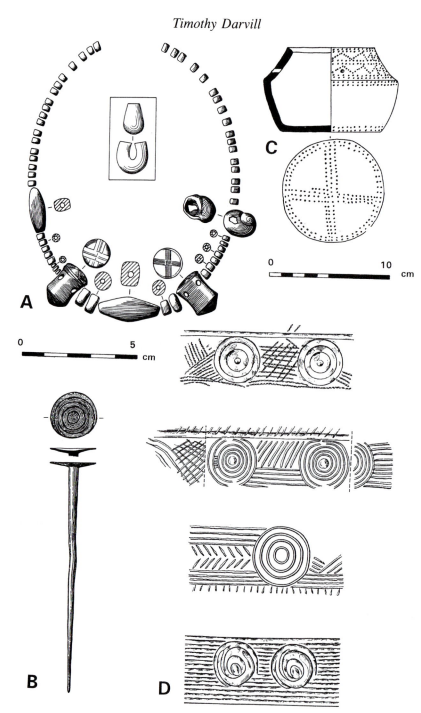

**Figure 10.** Material culture with symbolic representations of radial concentric structuring of space. A: Bead necklace from bowl barrow Shrewton G5j. B: Bronze pin from bell barrow Shrewton G5L. C: Incense cup from bowl barrow Wilsford cum Lake G40, Wilsford. D: Grooved Ware decorative motifs. (A and B after Green and Rollo-Smith 1984, figs 27 and 28; C after Annable and Simpson 1964, item 449; D after Wainwright and Longworth 1971, fig. 29.)

of barrow Shrewton G5L also has the concentric pattern on its head and represents, in chronological terms, the opposite end of the date-range to that just noted from the Grooved Ware. During the second millennium BC, solar imagery was extremely widespread in northern Europe (Coles and Harding 1979, 314).

Applying the radial concentric model of structuration into the broader landscape is fraught with problems, not least because of the huge amount of data which is in large measure undifferentiated by date. Round barrows were constructed in great numbers, mostly within round barrow cemeteries. Links with the past are demonstrated by the fact that some barrow cemeteries included, and perhaps focused on, earlier long barrows; the legitimation of new orders through an appeal backwards in time to the old. In the Winterbourne Stoke Barrow Cemetery the earliest barrow is the long barrow. The later round barrows are set out fairly regularly with one main axis (now marked by a fence line) and a series of outliers. The long barrow has a dominant axis too but it is actually a few degrees west of the later axis. In all, the cemetery contains 20 round barrows including bowl, bell, disc, saucer, and pond barrow forms.

Figure 11 shows a provisional scheme for the late third and early second millennia BC which attempts to show possibilities rather than defined patterns. All the four main sectors established in earlier times now include barrows, while the distribution of settlements has apparently extended westwards. Around Stonehenge itself there seems to be a small area in which barrows were permitted. Beyond is an area where they are absent, the outer edge of which coincides with the distant end of the Avenue in Stonehenge Bottom. Linear barrow cemeteries are common in the third ring out from Stonehenge, while dispersed cemeteries are most numerous in areas beyond. Although these patterns are not as strongly structured as in other periods, research by Ann and Peter Woodward from a completely different starting position has established much the same patterning (Woodward and Woodward forthcoming).

During the early second millennium BC most of the monuments in use during the previous 500 years were abandoned; Stonehenge was an exception. As already noted, settlements became established further to the west than previously and cemeteries further to the east. Gradually, the area around Stonehenge seems to have changed from being arranged as sectors to being structured concentrically, with a ring of major barrow cemeteries positioned to overlook Stonehenge itself with, around and between them, modest settlements. The full implications of the symbolic arrangement of this landscape have yet to be explored. The construction of the Avenue may in this scenario be seen as a replacement for the Cursus, allowing movement on a different axis through the landscape towards Stonehenge, now with death to the right and life to the left; leaving Stonehenge down the Avenue literally involved walking into the sun along the defined alignment with death to the left and life to the right.

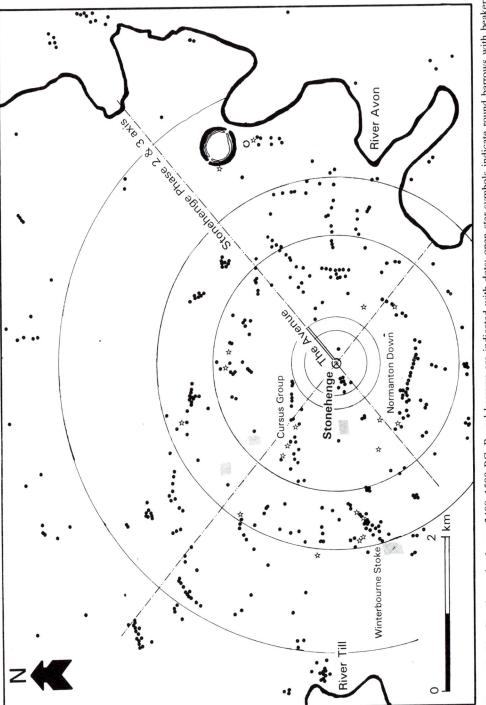

**Figure 11.** The Stonehenge landscape 2400–1500 BC. Round barrows are indicated with dots; open star-symbols indicate round barrows with beaker burials; settlement areas are indicated by stippling.

*Late second millennium BC*

Change continued. In what is conventionally the Middle and Later Bronze Age (*c.*1500–700 BC), the area around Stonehenge became subject to a more diverse range of uses. Stonehenge was not modified much during this period although continued to play a role in people's lives. There is a case to be made for the extension of the Avenue from Stonehenge Bottom to the river Avon at Amesbury around 1000 BC,[11] and this alteration in the relationship between Stonehenge and its landscape may reflect changing belief systems. Richard Bradley (1990, 97–154) has usefully brought together available evidence for an emergent preoccupation with water and wet places during the late second and early first millennia BC in northern Europe (but cf. Case 1991), so the creation of a formal link between Stonehenge and the river Avon should perhaps be seen as an inevitable and natural development. In some respects this could be seen as a return to the associations prevalent 1500 years earlier, but if the focus of attention was the same, the cosmology behind it was almost certainly different.

Burial arrangements also changed. Deverel-Rimbury style urns containing cremation burials are known in small bowl barrows and flat cremation cemeteries connected with round barrow cemeteries. Some barrow cemeteries were extended and a few new round barrows were built. They provide an element of repetition across the landscape, and together they document a continuing link between life and death in the landscape. Settlements are known near Fargo Plantation and elsewhere, and five main blocks of regular aggregate fieldsystem can be identified, perhaps fragments of one or two original systems.

Overall, the area around Stonehenge was extensively, and in places intensively, utilised by the Later Bronze Age. The linear boundaries which criss-cross the area suggest also that its control had been subdivided to the extent that the concentric arrangement had broken down and a more linear subdivision of space established, each such strip incorporating a portion of land in the surrounding valleys as well as the more exposed upland around Stonehenge itself. Figure 12 shows a provisional arrangement. The structuration of space on a linear concentric system may reflect the practical realities of land apportionment in an agrarian society. The decorative schemes on artefacts of the period, especially pottery (Fig. 13), perhaps show concerns with the almost regimental subdivision of land: the decoration on the miniature vessel from Winterbourne Stoke G68 could almost be a stylised map of the fields and boundaries shown on Figure 12.

## Discussion

The four successive phases just described provide a picture of the changing landscape around Stonehenge over a period of some 25 centuries. Throughout that time, as at any

---

[11.] See Cleal *et al.* 1995, 326-7 for summary of the debate.

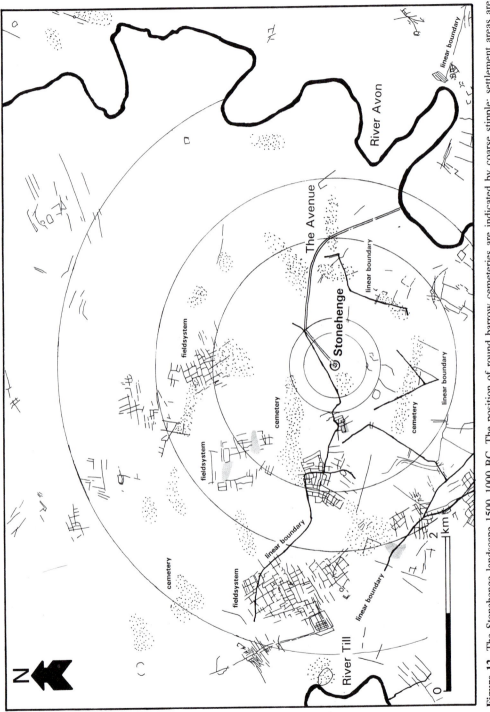

**Figure 12.** The Stonehenge landscape 1500–1000 BC. The position of round barrow cemeteries are indicated by coarse stipple; settlement areas are indicated by fine stipple.

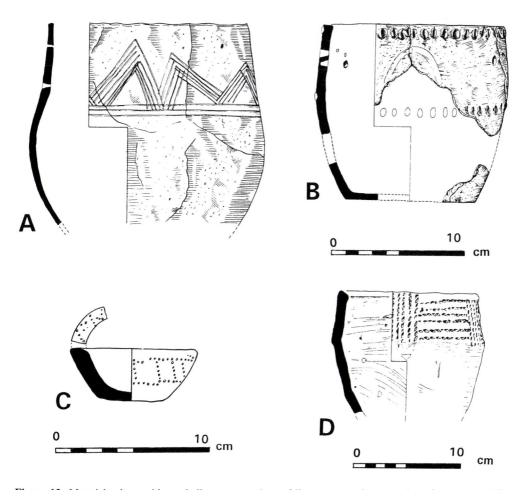

**Figure 13.** Material culture with symbolic representations of linear concentric structuring of space. A and B: Globular and bucket urns from bowl barrow Shrewton G5a. C: Miniature vessel from primary burial in disc barrow Winterbourne Stoke G68; D: Urn from barrow Winterbourne Stoke G46. (A and B after Green and Rollo-Smith 1984, fig. 25; C after Annable and Simpson 1964, item 455; D after Gingell 1988, fig. 34.4.)

other, the values that people attached to different segments of the space all around them were deeply grounded in the cosmologies and belief systems that they held. These would have extended into the realm of explaining their very existence, right from wrong, and many other things too. The structuration inherent in the cosmological schemes used carry through into the domain of material culture and these can be studied archaeologically at many different scales. Indeed, it is only through the investigation of patterns in land-scapes, structures and objects that some of these regularities become evident.

Looking across time two forces can be seen pulling against one another: continuity and modification. Some elements of a structure are selectively retained while others are dispensed with. Figure 14 shows in summary form the progression in stages of the proposed structuring principles that underlie the social use of space. Thus the simple linear binary system of the fourth millennium BC, based perhaps on a terrestrial cosmology involving the separation of life and death, continued to influence sectoring in the landscape during the early third millennium BC. But by this time the sun had become a significator of arrangements and where previously there had been two sectors now there were four.

The sun seems to have remained an important feature of later cosmologies as the formal quartering of space gave way to an increased emphasis on centrality and a concentric mode of differentiation. Separations between life and death became more small-scale and localised. Burial areas influenced the use of space in the Middle and Later Bronze Age as fields and settlements jostled for position in a countryside more crowded than ever before. By the end of the second millennium BC a new linearity was being introduced into the structuration of the landscape, the form of fieldsystems, and the decorative motifs applied to pottery.

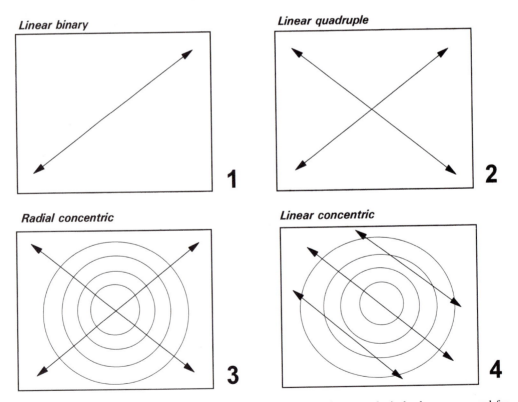

**Figure 14.** Summary of the structuration implicit in the four successive cosmological schemes proposed for the period 3000–1000 BC in central Wiltshire, England.

Throughout these changes there was no one Stonehenge but many. The space was always there but each generation gave it a different sense of place with meanings and values in accord with the ever-changing relationships between themselves and the beliefs they held. The centrality of Stonehenge relative to the lives of local people and the fact that it was reformed as beliefs changed surely endorses the general idea of the site as temple. And for part of its history at least there were a small number of significant astronomical alignments built into its design. However, the process of recurrent structuration is at once both a unique feature of the site and the source of its great mystery: what did relate to what at each of its different incarnations?; how much was retained for ongoing use and how much destroyed?

In the twelfth century AD, Henry of Huntingdon wrote in his history of England that Stonehenge had been erected in the manner of doorways, so that doorway appears to have been raised upon doorway (Chippindale 1983, 20). Turning outwards to look through those doorways at the sacred geography of the site and its surroundings, the picture perhaps subtly changes to one of ever-increasing circles of space, place, and structuration arranged so that each circle appears to have been set within another, their edges often obscured.

*Acknowledgements*

The work of producing this paper has benefited enormously from the assistance of a number of individuals: Nicola King was responsible for the assembly of much of the data on which this study is based; Miles Russell, Jeff Chartrand, and Claire Baker helped with bibliographic and computing queries; Jane Timby helped check the text and prepare the illustrations; and Ann Woodward, Peter Woodward, Barry Cunliffe, Colin Renfrew, and Humphrey Case kindly offered comments and helpful criticism after reading drafts of the main text.

# References

ANNABLE, F.K. and SIMPSON, D.D.A. 1964: *Guide catalogue of the Neolithic and Bronze Age collections in Devizes Museum* (Devizes, Wiltshire Archaeological and Natural History Society).

ASHBEE, P., BELL, M. and PROUDFOOT, E. 1989: *Wilsford Shaft: Excavations 1960–62* (London, Hist. Build. Monuments Comm. Archaeol. Rep. 11).

ATKINSON, R.J.C. 1956: *Stonehenge* (London).

ATKINSON, R.J.C. 1979: *Stonehenge* (Harmondsworth, revised ed.).

ATKINSON, R.J.C. 1982: Aspects of the archaeoastronomy of Stonehenge. In Heggie, D.C. (ed.), *Archaeoastronomy in the Old World* (Cambridge), 107–16.

BAUVAL, R. and GILBERT, A. 1994: *The Orion mystery* (London).

BENDER, B. 1992: Theorising landscapes, and the prehistoric landscapes of Stonehenge. *Man* (ns) 27, 735–55.

BENDER, B. (ed.) 1993: *Landscape: Politics and perspectives* (Oxford).

BOOTH, A.StJ. and STONE, J.F.S. 1952: A trial flint mine at Durrington, Wiltshire. *Wiltshire Archaeol. Mag.* 54, 381–8.

BRADLEY, R. 1983: The bank barrows and related monuments of Dorset in the light of recent fieldwork. *Proc. Dorset Natur. Hist. Archaeol. Soc.* 105, 16–20.

BRADLEY, R. 1990: *The passage of arms. An archaeological analysis of prehistoric hoards and votive deposits* (Cambridge).

BRITNELL, W. and SAVORY, H.N. 1984: *Gwernvale and Penywyrlod: Two Neolithic long cairns in the Black Mountains of Brecknock* (Cardiff, Cambrian Archaeol. Assoc. Monogr. 2).

BURGESS, C. 1980: *The Age of Stonehenge* (London).

BURL, A. 1987: *The Stonehenge people* (London).

BURL, A. 1991: The Heel Stone, Stonehenge: A study in misfortunes. *Wiltshire Archaeol. Mag.* 84, 1–10.

BURL, A. 1992: More about the Heel Stone. *Wiltshire Archaeol. Mag.* 85, 140.

BURL, A. 1994: Stonehenge: Slaughter, sacrifice and sunshine. *Wiltshire Archaeol. Mag.* 87, 85–95.

CARMICHAEL, D.L., HUBERT, J., REEVES, B. and SCHANCHE, A. (eds) 1994: *Sacred Sites, Sacred Places* (London, One World Archaeology 23).

CASE, H.J. 1977: An early accession to the Ashmolean Museum. In Markotic, V. (ed.), *Ancient Europe and the Mediterranean* (Warminster), 18–34.

CASE, H.J. 1991: Review of "The Passage of Arms" By Richard Bradley. *Proc. Prehist. Soc.* 57.2, 232–34.

CHIPPINDALE, C. 1983: *Stonehenge complete* (London).

CHIPPINDALE, C. 1986a: Stoned Henge: events and issues at the summer solstice 1985. *World Archaeol.* 18(1), 38–58.

CHIPPINDALE, C. 1986b: Stonehenge astronomy: Anatomy of a modern myth. *Archaeology* January/February 1986.

CHIPPINDALE, C., DEVEREUX, P., FOWLER, P., JONES, R. and SABASTIAN, T. 1990: *Who owns Stonehenge?* (London).

CHRISTIE, P.M. 1963: The Stonehenge Cursus. *Wiltshire Archaeol. Mag.* 58, 370–82.

CLEAL, R.M.J., WALKER, K.E. and MONTAGUE, R. 1995: *Stonehenge in its Landscape: Twentieth Century Excavations* (London, Engl. Heritage Archaeol. Rep. 10).

COE, M. 1993: *The Maya* (London, 5th ed.).

COLES, J.M. and HARDING, A.F. 1979: *The Bronze Age in Europe* (London).

COSGROVE, D. 1985: Prospect, perspective and the evolution of the landscape idea. *Trans. Inst. Brit. Geogr.* (ns) 10, 45–62.

COSGROVE, D. and DANIELS, S. (eds) 1988: *The Iconography of Landscape* (Cambridge).

CRAWFORD, O.G.S. and KEILLER, A. 1928: *Wessex from the Air* (Oxford).

CUNNINGTON, M.E. 1929: *Woodhenge* (Devizes).

DARVILL, T. (ed.) 1991: *Stonehenge Conservation and Management Project: Environmental Statement* (London, 3 vols).

DARVILL, T. 1996a: Neolithic buildings in England, Wales and the Isle of Man. In Darvill, T. and Thomas, J. (eds), *Neolithic houses in north-west Europe and beyond* (Oxford, Neolithic Studies Group Seminar Pap. 1 and Oxbow Monogr. 57), 77–111.

DARVILL, T. 1996b: *The Billown Neolithic Landscape Project, Isle of Man, 1995* (Bournemouth, School of Conservation Science Res. Rep. 1).

DRONFIELD, J. 1996: Entering alternative realities: Cognition, art and architecture in Irish passage-tombs. *Cambridge Archaeol. J.* 6.1, 37–72.

EVANS, J.G. 1984: Stonehenge – The environment in the Late Neolithic and early Bronze Age and a Beaker-Age burial. *Wiltshire Archaeol. Mag.* 78, 7–30.

GIDDENS, A. 1984: *The constitution of society* (Cambridge).

GINGELL, C. 1988: Twelve Wiltshire round barrows. Excavations 1959 and 1961 by F. de M. and H.L. Vatcher. *Wiltshire Archaeol. Natur. Hist. Mag.* 82, 19–76.

GLASS, P. 1988: Trobriand symbolic geography. *Man* (ns) 23, 56–76.

GREEN, C. and ROLLO-SMITH, S. 1984: The excavation of eighteen round barrows near Shrewton, Wiltshire. *Proc. Prehist. Soc.* 50, 255–318.

GRINSELL, L.V. 1957: Archaeological Gazetteer. In Pugh, R.B. (ed.), *Victoria County History of Wiltshire. Volume 1.1* (London, Institute of Historical Research), 21–279.

HARDING, P. 1988: The chalk plaque pit, Amesbury. *Proc. Prehist. Soc.* 54, 320–6.

HAWKINS, G.S. 1966: *Stonehenge decoded* (London).

HODDER, I. 1987: Converging traditions: The search for symbolic meaning in archaeology and geography. In Wagstaff, M. (ed.), *Landscape and culture* (Oxford), 134–45.

HODSON, F.R. (ed.) 1974: *The place of astronomy in the ancient world* (London, The British Academy).

HUGH-JONES, C. 1979: *From the Milk River: Spatial and temporal processes in Northwest Amazonia* (Cambridge).

INGOLD, T. 1993: The temporality of landscape. *World Archaeol.* 25(2), 152–74.

LEFEBVRE, H. (trans. Nicholson-Smith, D.) 1991: *The production of space* (Oxford).

LOCKYER, SIR N. 1909: *Stonehenge and other British stone monuments astronomically considered* (London).

MORTIMER, J.R. 1905: *Forty years researches in British and Saxon burial mounds of east Yorkshire* (London).

NEWHAM, C.A. 1972: *The astronomical significance of Stonehenge* (Shirenewton).

NEWTON, R.R. 1974: Astronomy in ancient literate societies: Introduction to some basic astronomical concepts. In Hodson, F.R. (ed.), *The place of astronomy in the ancient world* (London, The British Academy), 5–20.

O'KELLY, M.J. 1982: *Newgrange. Archaeology, art and legend* (London).

PITTS, M. 1982: On the road to Stonehenge: report on the investigations beside the A344 in 1968, 1979 and 1980. *Proc. Prehist. Soc.* 48, 75–132.

POLLARD, J. 1992: The Sanctuary, Overton Hill, Wiltshire: a re-examination. *Proc. Prehist. Soc.* 58, 213–26.

POLLARD, J. 1995: Structured deposition at Woodhenge. *Proc. Prehist. Soc.* 61, 137–56.

RCHM 1979: *Stonehenge and its environs* (Edinburgh).

RENFREW, C. 1982: *Towards an archaeology of mind* (Cambridge, Inaugural Lecture).

RICHARDS, C. 1993: Monumental choreography: Architecture and spatial representation in Late Neolithic Orkney. In Tilley, C. (ed.), *Interpretative archaeology* (Oxford), 143–78.

RICHARDS, C. and THOMAS, J. 1984: Ritual activity and structured deposition in Later Neolithic Wessex. In Bradley, R. and Gardiner, J. (eds), *Neolithic Studies. A review of some current research* (Oxford, BAR Brit. Ser. 133), 189–218.

RICHARDS, J. 1990: *The Stonehenge Environs Project* (London, Hist. Build. Monuments Comm. Archaeol. Rep. 16).

RICHARDS, J. 1991: *Stonehenge* (London, English Heritage).

SAVILLE, A. 1990: *Hazleton North. The excavation of a Neolithic long cairn of the Cotswold-Severn Group* (London, Hist. Build. Monuments Comm. Archaeol. Rep. 13).

SCHAMA, S. 1995: *Landscape and memory* (London).

SENNETT, R. 1994: *Flesh and stone. The body and the city in western civilization* (London).

SHEE TWOHIG, E. 1981: *The megalithic art of western Europe* (Oxford).

STONE, J.F.S. 1948: The Stonehenge cursus and its affinities. *Archaeol. J.* 104, 7–19.

STUKELEY, W. 1740: *Stonehenge a temple restor'd to the British Druids* (London).

THOM, A.S., KER, J.M.D. and BURROWS, T.R. 1988: A solar and lunar calendar for Stonehenge? *Antiquity* 62, 492–502.

THOMAS, N. 1964: The Neolithic causewayed camp at Robin Hood's Ball, Shrewton. *Wiltshire Archaeol. Mag.* 59, 1–27.

TILLEY, C. 1994: *A phenomenology of landscape* (Oxford).

TUAN, Y.-F. 1977: *Space and place. The perspective of experience* (London).

VATCHER, F. and VATCHER, L. 1973: Excavations of three postholes in Stonehenge car park. *Wiltshire Archaeol. Mag.* 68, 57–63.

WAINWRIGHT, G.J and LONGWORTH, I.H. 1971: *Durrington Walls: Excavations 1966–1968* (London, Rep. Res. Comm. Soc. Antiq. London 29).

WHEATLEY, P. 1971: *The pivot of the four quarters* (Chicago and Edinburgh).

WHITTLE, A.W.R. 1978: Resources and population in the British Neolithic. *Antiquity* 52, 34–42.

WHITTLE, A.W.R. 1981: Later Neolithic society in Britain: a realignment. In Ruggles, C.L.N. and Whittle, A.W.R. (eds), *Astronomy and society in Britain during the period 4000–1500 BC* (Oxford, BAR Brit. Ser. 88), 297–342.

WOODWARD, A. and WOODWARD, P. forthcoming: The topography of some barrow cemeteries in Bronze Age Wiltshire. *Proc. Prehist. Soc.*

WOODWARD, P. 1988: Pictures of the Neolithic: discoveries from the Flagstones House excavations, Dorchester, Dorset. *Antiquity* 62, 266–74.

*Proceedings of the British Academy,* **92**, 203–229

# Astronomy and Stonehenge

## CLIVE RUGGLES

## Introduction

THE PORTRAYAL OF STONEHENGE in the 1960s and 1970s as an astronomical observatory or computer forms one of the most notorious examples known to archaeologists of an age recreating the past in its own image (Hawkes 1966; Castleden 1993, 18–27; Chippindale 1994, 230–1). Despite persistent popular belief, detailed reassessments of the ideas of C.A. Newham, Gerald Hawkins, Fred Hoyle and others have shown that there is no convincing evidence that, at any stage, constructions at Stonehenge deliberately incorporated a great many precise astronomical alignments, or that they served as any sort of computing device to predict eclipses (Atkinson 1966; Burl 1981; Heggie 1981, 145–51, 195–206). In short, there is no reason whatsoever to suppose that at any stage the site functioned as an astronomical observatory—at least in any sense that would be meaningful to a modern astronomer.

Yet we would be unwise simply to dismiss all astronomical ideas relating to Stonehenge. People within human societies of a very wide range of types perceive certain celestial objects and integrate them into their view of the world, linking them inextricably into the realms of politics, economics, religion and ideology (Thorpe 1981; Ruggles and Saunders 1993a). The material record from Neolithic and Early Bronze Age Britain and Ireland suggests that astronomical symbolism, in the form of rough alignments upon certain horizon rising and setting positions of the sun or moon, was incorporated into a range of prehistoric ritual monuments at various places and times. Evidence comes from certain individual sites, most notably Newgrange with its spectacular midwinter sunrise phenomenon (O'Kelly 1982, 123–5), but most compellingly from trends observed in regional groups of small, similar Bronze Age ritual monuments such as the recumbent stone circles of north-eastern Scotland (Ruggles and Burl 1985) and the short stone rows of western Scotland (Ruggles 1988; Martlew and Ruggles 1996) and the south-west of Ireland (Ruggles 1994). 'Once we have accepted the reality of even the simplest observations . . . the question is no longer one of acceptance or rejection, but simply of degree' (Bradley 1984, 77).

Two questions immediately arise: what exactly do we mean by astronomy, and why should we be interested in it?

In order to assign a useful meaning to the term 'astronomy', it helps to focus on the distinction between the observation of celestial objects and phenomena, and their perception and use (Ruggles and Saunders 1993a, 2–4). The term 'astronomy' will be used here to describe the process of observation, whatever its context, despite the objections of some archaeologists who argue that the very word necessarily implies Western analytical science (e.g. Chippindale 1994, 230),[1] and despite the implicit overtones of twentieth-century Western science that have dogged archaeoastronomy[2] for many years. Perception, on the other hand, is the process of making sense of, and attaching meaning to, certain observations. Different groups or individuals may 'see' the same objects in the sky, but the significance that they attach to them will be influenced by their classification of the natural world and the various ways in which they interact with it. As is familiar to archaeologists, this broader world-view, cosmology, or *cosmovisión* (Broda 1982) will generally bear little resemblance to the principles of Linnaean classification that underlie modern, 'rational' scientific thought.

Why might astronomy be interesting? It is clear from the preceding discussion that evidence relating to what could have been observed, and to what was observed, is essential to the process of developing and improving theories relating to what was perceived. But why should the archaeologist, and in particular the student of Neolithic and Bronze Age Wessex, be interested in the perception of astronomical phenomena? A general answer is that in many, if not virtually all, non-Western world-views celestial phenomena are not separated from terrestrial ones but form part of an integral whole with complex interconnections. The association may often be viewed as closer in nature to modern astrology than modern astronomy. 'A basic feature of traditional rituals and cosmologies [is] their astrological insistence that good fortune on earth can be ensured only by keeping human action fundamentally in tune with observable astronomical events. "On earth as it is in heaven." Again and again, we find this belief that the template for the ancestral "Way" or "Law" lies in the skies' (Knight 1991, 294). Once we tackle questions of people's perceptions of their natural environment as a whole, it would be unreasonable not to consider their perceptions of objects and events in the sky.

An aspect of indigenous cosmologies that is currently receiving a good deal of attention is that of 'sacred geographies'. Many indigenous peoples have a world-view that

---

[1] This objection might seem strange to many astronomers in view of the fact that the word 'cosmology', which is also used as the name of a branch of modern science, is freely used in their own sense by anthropologists without any such reservations.

[2] Although to some archaeologists (e.g. Chippindale 1994, 220) the term 'archaeoastronomy' is inextricably linked with the ideas of Hawkins and Hoyle, the term was not even invented in the mid 1960s, but grew largely from reassessments in the late 1970s of the work of Alexander Thom. Modern archaeoastronomy has grown to encompass multidisciplinary studies of astronomical practice worldwide in the context of diverse social questions (Aveni 1989; Ruggles and Saunders 1993b) and to think less about natural phenomena in themselves and more about the impact of nature upon people (Aveni 1992).

expresses an intimate, spiritual connection between humans and their natural environment. By associating special places (such as prominent landmarks) with particular celestial features and with sacred and secular practices, through myth and oral tradition, the vitality and power of being in a particular place is reinforced. Sacred geographies are evidenced amongst groups as diverse as Aboriginal hunter-gatherers in Australia (Morphy 1991) and the Aztec state in the Valley of Mexico (Broda 1993). Archaeologists are becoming increasingly aware that patterns of human activity within the Neolithic and Bronze Age landscape, including the siting and orientation of public ritual monuments, may well have been structured according to symbolic or cosmological principles (Bradley 1993; Thomas 1991; Tilley 1994), ideas that also apply to the area around Stonehenge (Darvill, this volume). It is in the context of such ideas that astronomy assumes potential importance in the particular context of Stonehenge and its landscape.

Astronomy, then, is an integral part of cosmology, in the anthropological sense. To ignore it in attempts to understand people's perceptions of the Stonehenge landscape is to impose another twentieth-century agenda, one rooted in the backlash to astronomical overload in the 1960s and 1970s; an understandable one maybe, but an unreasonable one nonetheless.

It is not the aim of this paper to attempt new cosmological interpretations but rather to consider certain evidence on the nature of astronomical observations made at Stonehenge, encapsulated in some way in the material record, that may bear directly upon some broader issues of current interest. The available data are not generally of high precision, since they are mostly reconstructed from plans and maps rather than being obtained from first-hand surveys; but, as we shall see, in most cases this is quite adequate for our purposes. The data that will be presented here mostly involve orientations of structures and show how these relate to celestial objects or events visible at or close above the horizon. While the word 'alignment' is retained as a convenience, for example in phrases such as 'the Phase 3 axis is aligned upon midsummer sunrise', its use should not be taken to convey a restrictive view on the nature of use or meaning of such relationships, if any existed at all in prehistoric times (some correlations might, for example, have been meaningful in terms of shadow phenomena rather than direct sighting of the horizon) but rather to give an indication of what could have been seen in a certain direction of possible interest, either on the horizon or above it, or what other effects (such as shadows) might have occurred.

## Prehistoric astronomy: the conceptual framework

Before examining the alignment evidence at Stonehenge it is necessary to clarify certain concepts and assumptions that underlie the critical framework within which we conduct the examination. One of the most fundamental of these is direction. Prehistoric people did not necessarily have a concept of direction as point-azimuth, analogous to ours. There are many examples of directions being perceived as regions (azimuth ranges) rather than points, from pre-Columbian Mesoamerica to Europe in the Middle Ages (Köhler 1989). Even if directions were conceived as point-azimuths, those directions that we consider of special significance, such as the cardinal directions, are not necessarily exactly reflected in other conceptual systems: the Chorti Maya of present-day Yucatan, for example, regard the rise-set directions of the sun on the day of zenith passage as 'east' and 'west', although these are actually several degrees from our cardinal points (Aveni 1980, 40). Thus when looking at alignment evidence it is important to think in terms of events within certain azimuth ranges as well as at particular azimuths.

In considering prehistoric astronomy it is common to apply a 'recipe book' of solar and lunar horizon targets which at minimum consists of the rising or setting sun at the solstices and the most northerly or southerly rising or setting moon at one of the lunar 'standstills' (Fig. 1). After these come the rising or setting sun at the equinoxes, and so on. However, the solar and lunar motions, and hence what might be perceived to be significant about them, have to be approached through concepts that might make sense within a non-Western world-view to someone making observations, very possibly not on any regular basis, and without the benefit of visualisation aids (such as graphs) or sophisticated recording techniques.

Thus in the case of the sun, the solstices are directly observable and their use is widely attested, although their main significance may be not as directions-as-points but as the limits of directions-as-ranges—this can still be seen, for example, amongst traditional Maya groups in modern Mexico (Sosa 1989, 132). The equinox, however, is a concept unlikely to have any meaning outside the viewpoint of modern Western science and its precursors. It is defined by modern astronomers as the time when the sun crosses the celestial equator (see below). Yet the position at which the sun rises or sets on the day of the equinox is inherently indistinguishable from adjacent days, its rising or setting position merely continuing to move rapidly north or south before and afterwards. It is often supposed that importance might have been attached to the mid-point between the solstices. This could either be determined spatially, by halving the distance between the directions (azimuths) of the two solstices, or temporally, by halving the time difference between successive solstices. To do the former with any precision would involve devising a method to mark the solstice positions (perhaps using natural markers on or below the horizon) and determining their mid-point; it also assumes a concept of point-direction. The latter would involve counting the days between two solstices, and then counting half the number of days, which implies the existence of a method of recording numbers up to more than 180 and of halving a large number. While it is not inherently implausible that some prehistoric people could do this if duly motivated—after all, someone was evidently capable of careful planning in order to calculate the number of bluestones and sarsens needing to be transported from afar so as to build Stonehenge 3—the question is whether the concept of a mid-point dividing something into two equal parts, either in space or time, was itself of particular significance or interest. This is far from self-evident.

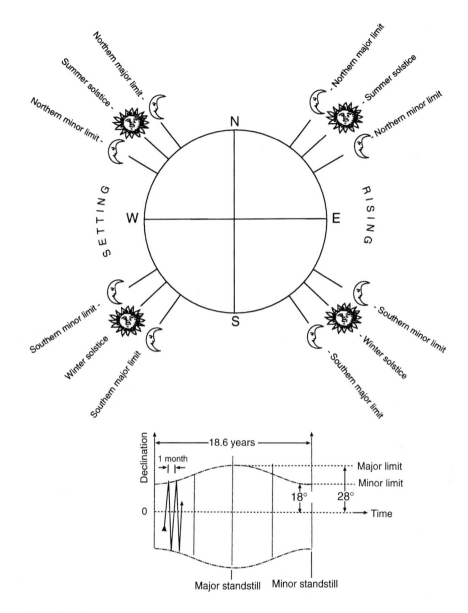

**Figure 1.** A schematic representation of the directions of the 'classic' solar and lunar horizon targets for an observer in southern Britain.

(a) Over the year, the sun rises and sets within the horizon arcs delimited by the solstices. Around the time of major standstill, which occurs every 18·6 years, the moon rises and sets within wider arcs delimited by what are here called the 'major limits', moving between these limits and back again once every month. Around minor standstill, mid-way between these times, the rising and setting positions are confined to the arcs between the 'minor limits'.

(b) The lunar standstills are defined as the times when the limits of the moon's monthly motions themselves reach a limit. After Thom (1971, fig. 2.2).

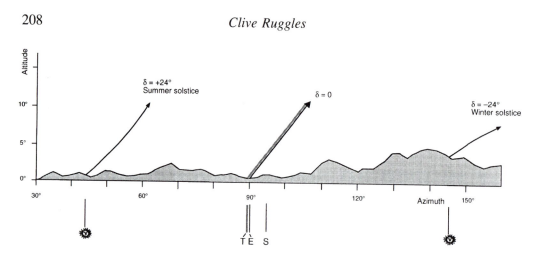

**Figure 2.** Possible 'mid-way' concepts yielding dates approximating to the modern concept of the equinox, for a hypothetical eastern horizon within the British Isles. The spatial mid-point between sunrise at the two solstices (sun symbol) is at *S*; while sunrise halfway in time between the solstices may be anywhere within the shaded area *T*. Sunrise on the day when the sun rises and sets in opposite directions will generally be different again, depending on the altitude of the western horizon. Sunrise at the equinox, corresponding to a declination of 0°, is *E*.

Furthermore, even if one of these mid-points was seen as important, it would not generally yield a date exactly corresponding to our equinox in any case (Fig. 2). A similar argument applies to the suggestion that significance might have been attached to the date when the sun rises and sets in opposite directions (see, e.g. Hoyle 1966, 271–2).

The fundamental point is that these concepts—the spatial mid-point between the solstices, the temporal mid-point between the solstices, and the day on which sunrise and sunset are opposite each other—bear no relationship whatsoever *on the conceptual level* to the modern astronomer's equinox. They have only been sought by modern investigators because they yield dates close to it. Even if any of these concepts was convincingly shown to have been of importance in prehistoric times, this would still not provide evidence that 'our' equinox was conceived and observed. The specificity of the equinox concept to Western science does not generally seem to be appreciated: this is evident, for example, in the remark 'The extremes were evidently what counted; the equinoxes were seemingly of lesser importance to early peoples' (North 1994, 2); and in the claims of equinoctial alignments that are still encountered quite frequently in the archaeoastronomical literature.[3]

The lunar standstills are another concept unlikely to have any meaning outside the framework of Western science. They represent the times when the limit curve of the moon's monthly motions itself reaches a limit, rather than anything directly observable;

---

[3.] This does not, of course, preclude alignments upon sunrise or sunset at particular times of year, perhaps on the occasion of calendrical festivals, and such alignments are widely attested; the point is that our equinox would not occupy any special place in the range of possible festivals.

on the day when a standstill technically occurs the moon might actually rise or set anywhere on the horizon between the two corresponding limits, depending upon its position within the monthly cycle. What *might* be observable at major standstill is that (i) for a period of time, lasting some months, the moon can rise and set unusually far north and south; or (ii) the length of moonlight close to full moon is unusually long. (i) implies an awareness of the positions of the extremes but not necessarily of when the extremes will happen (Ellegård 1981, 105), and no corresponding observation can be made at minor standstill. (ii) may be more important for a community whose only effective illumination during the long winter nights was the moon (Thom 1967, 21). An awareness of this effect has been noted, for example, amongst a modern Irish farming community (Barber 1973, 37).

The northerly and southerly lunar limits have very different characteristics in pragmatic terms. The northerly limit corresponds to the full moon in midwinter, when the presence or absence of a near-full moon makes the difference between a long dark night and an illuminated night. The southerly limit is less consequential; whether or not there is a near-full moon on a short night close to midsummer, astronomical twilight ensures that the night is never very dark. Surprisingly, this important difference between the northern and southern lunar limits is rarely noted. Any symbolism relating to longer moonlit winter nights should relate to the northern major limit.

This discussion could be extended, but the point will already be clear that it may be very misleading indeed to use any 'recipe book' of astronomical targets that seem significant to us. Instead, in considering the possible astronomical significance of any alignment, it is better to quote a *declination* which defines a rising or setting line on the celestial sphere. The declination of any horizon point can be determined from the azimuth, altitude and latitude of the site, and the positions of any (periodic) celestial body at any time in the past can be calculated in terms of declination. By convention, the declination of the celestial north pole is $+90°$, that of the celestial equator is $0°$ and that of the celestial south pole is $-90°$. At the latitude of Stonehenge ($51°·2$), celestial objects with declinations between about $-39°$ and $+39°$ (the exact figures depend upon the horizon altitude in the north and south) will rise and set daily; those with higher declinations will circle in the northern sky, never setting, and those with lower declinations will never rise above the horizon.

In the literature on archaeoastronomy, declinations are often quoted to a precision of $0°·1$ or even greater. However, the quality of the material evidence, together with the fact that the horizon around Stonehenge is relatively close (Cleal *et al.* 1995, 37) and devoid of prominent distant features interpretable as accurate foresights, do not justify considerations of declination to a precision much greater than the nearest degree, or approximately twice the apparent diameter of the sun or moon. To do otherwise is to risk obscuring any intentional, low-level astronomical effects with meaningless detail.

Tables 1–4 give the declinations of some prominent astronomical bodies and events, to aid discussion and interpretation. Table 1 gives the declinations of the solar and lunar

**Table 1.** Declinations of the solar solstices and lunar major and minor limits

| Solar or lunar event | Declination (4000–1500 cal BC) |
|---|---|
| Moon: northern major limit | +28° |
| Sun: summer solstice | +24° |
| Moon: northern minor limit | +18° |
| Moon: southern minor limit | −20° |
| Sun: winter solstice | −24° |
| Moon: southern major limit | −30° |

**Table 2.** Declination of the sun at intervals during the year

| Days from summer solstice | Equivalent Julian calendar date, taking Jun 21 as the solstice | Approximate declination of sun (4000–1500 cal BC) |
|---|---|---|
| 0 | Jun 21 | +24° |
| −27 / +30 | May 25 / Jul 21 | +21° |
| −59 / +61 | Apr 23 / Aug 21 | +12° |
| ±92 | Mar 21 / Sep 21 | 0° |
| −124 / +122 | Feb 17 / Oct 21 | −12° |
| −157 / +153 | Jan 15 / Nov 21 | −21° |
| −184 / +181 | Dec 19 | −24° |

**Table 3.** Limiting declinations of the planets

| Planet | Declination limits (4000–3000 cal BC) | Declination limits (2500–1500 cal BC) |
|---|---|---|
| Mercury | ±31° | ±31° |
| Venus | ±27° | ±26° |
| Mars | ±26° | ±26° |
| Jupiter | ±25° | ±25° |
| Saturn | ±27° | ±26° |

limits already discussed. To a precision of 1° they do not change over the period 4000–1500 cal BC. Table 2 gives the declination of the sun at intervals during the year. Table 3 gives the limiting declinations of the planets; their motions are complex within these limits. Finally, Table 4 gives the approximate declinations of some of the brightest stars, which change significantly over the centuries owing to precession.

The list is not meant to be in any way exhaustive, but merely to give an idea of some of the possibilities. There are examples of people for whom other features in the sky are of greater importance than the brightest stars, such as dark or light patches in the Milky Way (e.g. Urton 1981). Non-periodic events such as novae and comets are not included. Stars at the latitude of Britain rise and set at a shallow angle and are generally not visible until they reach an altitude of several degrees (Schaefer 1993), so care must be taken in postulating stellar relationships.

**Table 4.** Approximate declinations of those of the 22 brightest stars in the sky (magnitude greater than 1·5) that were visible from the latitude of southern Britain at different dates between 4000 and 1500 cal BC, quoted to the nearest degree, and ordered by the declination in 2500 cal BC. Also included are two other formations prominent in northern hemisphere skies: Orion's belt (the declination given is for the centre star, ε Ori) and the Pleiades. Bracketed values represent stars not visible at the date in question

| Star | Apparent magnitude | Brightness ordering | 4000 cal BC | 3000 cal BC | 2500 cal BC | 2000 cal BC | 1500 cal BC | AD 2000 |
|---|---|---|---|---|---|---|---|---|
| Arcturus (α Boo) | −0·1 | 4 | +54° | +49° | +46° | +43° | +40° | +19° |
| Vega (α Lyr) | 0·0 | 5 | +47° | +44° | +43° | +41° | +40° | +39° |
| Deneb (α Cyg) | 1·3 | 19 | +37° | +36° | +36° | +36° | +37° | +45° |
| Capella (α Aur) | 0·1 | 7 | +20° | +26° | +29° | +31° | +34° | +46° |
| Pollux (β Gem) | 1·2 | 17 | +18° | +23° | +25° | +26° | +28° | +28° |
| Regulus (α Leo) | 1·4 | 21 | +22° | +24° | +24° | +24° | +24° | +12° |
| Spica (α Vir) | 1·0 | 16 | +19° | +15° | +13° | +11° | +8° | −11° |
| Altair (α Aql) | 0·8 | 11 | +13° | +10° | +9° | +7° | +7° | +9° |
| Procyon (α CMi) | 0·4 | 8 | −1° | +3° | +5° | +6° | +7° | +5° |
| Pleiades | | | −6° | 0° | +3° | +5° | +8° | +24° |
| Aldebaran (α Tau) | 0·8 | 12 | −11° | −5° | −2° | 0° | +3° | +16° |
| Betelgeuse (α Ori) | 0·8 | 13 | −13° | −8° | −5° | −3° | −1° | +7° |
| Antares (α Sco) | 0·9 | 15 | +2° | −4° | −7° | −10° | −12° | −26° |
| Orion's belt | | | −23° | −17° | −15° | −12° | −10° | −1° |
| Sirius (α CMa) | −1·5 | 1 | −26° | −23° | −21° | −19° | −18° | −17° |
| Rigel (β Ori) | 0·1 | 6 | −31° | −26° | −23° | −21° | −18° | −8° |
| Adhara (ε CMa) | 1·5 | 22 | −37° | −34° | −32° | −31° | −30° | −29° |
| Mimosa (β Cru) | 1·3 | 20 | −30° | −34° | −36° | [−38°] | [−41°] | [−59°] |
| β Centauri | 0·6 | 10 | −29° | −34° | −36° | [−39°] | [−41°] | [−60°] |
| α Centauri | −0·1 | 3 | −31° | −36° | −38° | [−41°] | [−43°] | [−61°] |
| Acrux (α Cru) | 0·9 | 14 | −34° | −38° | [−40°] | [−42°] | [−44°] | [−63°] |

## Evidence for astronomy at and around Stonehenge

Within the conceptual framework and with the background data just described, we can now proceed to evaluate some of the main evidence for astronomy in the archaeological record at and around Stonehenge.

### *The Early Neolithic*

Long barrows have been claimed to provide evidence for symbolic astronomy during this period. Burl (1987, 26–8) has examined 65 examples on Salisbury Plain and finds that their orientations fall consistently between NNE and south. Some of these are shown in Fig. 3. Burl estimates that 52 examples lie within the solar arc, concluding that 'as no fewer than 13 of the 65 barrows face either to the north or south of this narrow arc, it is unlikely that their builders had aligned them on the sun' (ibid., 28). On the other hand, 59 examples lie within the wider lunar arc, from which Burl concludes that 'it seems quite probable that they were intentionally aligned on the rising moon' (ibid.). These conclusions are critically dependent upon the outermost orientations in the sample, and the distinction between 6 out of 65 outside the lunar range and 13 out of 65 outside the solar range seems too small to justify strong support for the lunar hypothesis and rejection of the solar one. Indeed, Castleden (1993, 42) concludes from the same data that the symbolism was solar.

North (1994, 2), on the other hand, suggests that the long barrows were aligned upon bright stars rather than the sun or moon, a theme that is to be developed in a new book on Stonehenge (pers. comm.). He also introduces 'three dimensionality', arguing that the height of a long barrow was important, perhaps acting as a false horizon. This idea may be appealing but the material record can give little support to it because of the state of the monuments that come down to us; there is already a great deal of room for manoeuvre in fitting bright stars to orientations when the date is uncertain (Cooke *et al.* 1977, 130), and the uncertainties in the original heights of the barrows as well as the uncertainties in their precise orientation simply compound this.

Nonetheless, it remains as a possibility that the five southerly-facing barrows that have no solar or lunar explanation might be oriented upon the Southern Cross and Pointers, which in the early fourth millennium cal BC hung a few degrees up in the southern sky (see Table 4) before dawn in early winter, and earlier in the night in late winter and spring, where they would have formed a prominent feature in the landscape. Another possibility, in view of the fact that only one barrow is oriented to the north of the lunar arc[4] and a relatively small number to the north of the solar arc, is that the important thing was to catch the sun or moon climbing in the sky rather than at its actual point of rising, a suggestion also put

---

[4.] The statement that only one barrow is oriented to the north of the lunar arc (Burl 1987, 28) is contradicted by the table (ibid., table 4) where four barrows are listed as being oriented NNE. The azimuth of the northern lunar limit is, by Burl's own estimate, 41°, yet NNE covers the azimuth range 11° to 34°, so at least four barrows would appear to be oriented to the north of the lunar limit. We assume here that the table is in error.

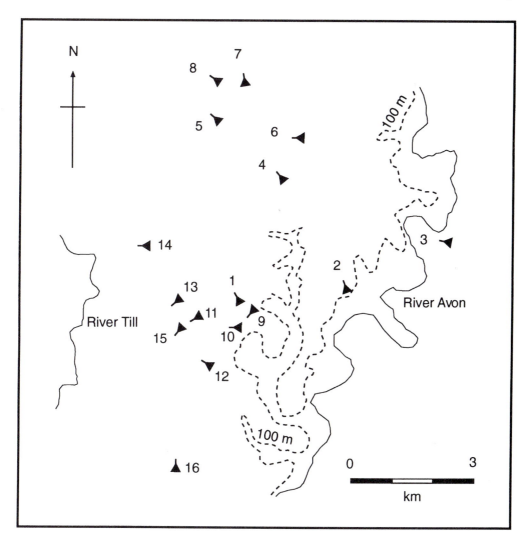

**Figure 3.** The distribution and orientation of long barrows in the vicinity of Stonehenge, after Burl (1987), fig. 3.

forward in the context of the orientations of certain groups of tombs in southern Europe (e.g. Hoskin *et al.* 1995).

Despite the uncertainties in its explanation, the orientation trend amongst the long barrows is unequivocal and further work is needed in order to move towards more convincing explanations. These may well feature the sun, moon or stars but might also invoke symbolism associated with sacred points and features in the natural landscape, the visibility of other long barrows and so on.

*Stonehenge 1*

The first question to arise in the Middle Neolithic is whether the choice of a site for Stonehenge 1 was influenced by any astronomical considerations. It has been suggested that the monument was placed so as to be viewable from a distance (Cleal *et al.* 1995, 476–7), yet its location has no obvious distinguishing features apart from the site itself (ibid., 37). It is possible that survey work might reveal special properties possessed by the actual site and not by other sites in the vicinity. None is known at present.

If the earth bank and ditch were the first features at Stonehenge, preceding the post-holes in the north-eastern entrance and elsewhere (ibid., 109), then the first recognisable orientations at the site were those of the ditch and bank entrances. The horizon declinations of the sides of the north-eastern entrance, and those of the southern causeways, as viewed from the centre, are shown in Fig. 4. The axis through the centre of the north-eastern entrance yields a declination (+27°) close to the northern lunar limit, but the left-hand side is well to the left of the northernmost possible lunar rising position. The sun is just shut out, at least as viewed from the centre of the site, so that Stonehenge 1 does not appear (cf. Burl 1987, 73) to reflect the practice found in the early stone circles of Cumbria (Burl 1988) of having two entrances, one in a cardinal direction and one defining a calendrical event by the rising or setting of the sun.

*Stonehenge 2*

One idea that has persisted since the 1960s and appears in recent literature (Burl 1987, 67–9; Castleden 1993, 54–8) is Newham's (1966; 1993, 20–3) that the entrance causeway post-holes were used to mark moonrises over several 18·6–year cycles, and hence to set up an exact orientation upon the northern lunar limit. Despite this, and despite two different possibilities for the detailed interpretation, the idea is untenable. Newham himself proposed that each of the six rows (across the entrance) represented observations within

**Table 5.** Orientations of entrances in Phase 1 and the possible post-holes in C44, probably attributable to Phase 2, from the centre of the site. The azimuths have been judged from Cleal *et al.* (1995, fig. 36) except for the post-holes in C44, for which ibid. (fig. 66) was used. In this and subsequent tables a horizon altitude of 0°·5 has been assumed throughout for convenience. The quoted declination should be within 0°·5 of the true value for any horizon between 0° and 1° in altitude, and Abney Level measurements taken in May 1996 confirmed that the relevant horizon altitudes vary between 0° 0' and 0° 50'

| From | to | Az | Dec |
|------|-----|----|-----|
| Phase 1/2 centre | 100 terminal | 37 | +30 |
| | mid-line (axis) | 43 | +27 |
| | 1 terminal | 49 | +24 |
| | Southern causeway (mid) | 174 | −39 |
| | Blocked causeway (mid) | 202 | −36 |
| | Post-holes in C44 | 138 | −28 |

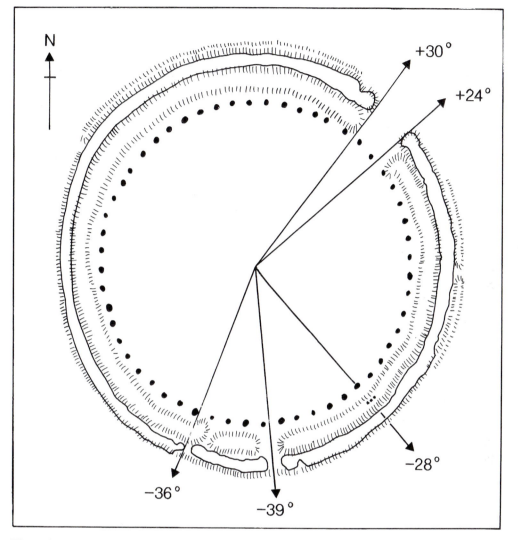

**Figure 4.** Stonehenge 1. Five of the orientations listed in Table 5 are shown together with the horizon declination estimated for a horizon at altitude 0°·5. The orientation of the post-holes in C44 is probably ascribable to Phase 2 but is included here for convenience. Based on Cleal *et al.* (1995, fig. 256). The arrows and 'indicated declinations' on this and later figures are merely intended to help the reader to assess the astronomical potential of a given direction, not to imply that observations were necessarily made of horizon phenomena, nor that they were made from a certain position along the arrow as 'sightline'.

one lunar cycle, of 'successive midwinter full moon risings'. The two problems with this explanation are that such observations should be clustered towards the left-hand (north-west) end, closest to the northern major limit (Heggie 1981, 202) and that the poles would have needed to stand for over 112 years, during which time they would inevitably have

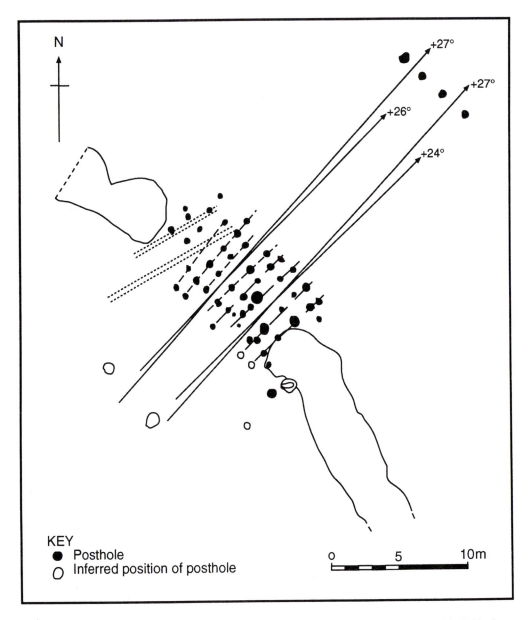

**Figure 5.** The north-eastern entrance during Phase 2. The entrance corridor orientations listed in Table 6 are shown together with the horizon declination estimated for a horizon at altitude 0°·5. Based on Cleal *et al.* (1995, fig. 68).

decayed. This problem forced Burl (1987, 68) to concede that 'perhaps exceptional accuracy was not an important consideration'. The other possible interpretation is that the posts were erected on successive nights or months around a single standstill, but here one runs into the sorts of problems widely discussed in regard to Alexander Thom's 'megalithic lunar observatories', such as the need for extrapolation (Ruggles 1981). Burl points out as confirmatory evidence that the holes on the left-hand (north-west) edge of the grid of post-holes line up with major northern moonrise and those on the right with midsummer sunrise, but the latter seems problematic rather than confirmatory for the lunar theory: why have such a sharp cut-off at midsummer sunrise? This is not 'as could be expected if that was where the observers began their sightings' (Burl 1987, 68), because at midsummer the moon is new, and hence invisible, when it rises in the NE.

The idea that the entrance post-holes represented attempts to fix the lunar orientation of the monument also depends on the assumption that the entrance post-holes pre-dated the north-eastern entrance of the ditch and bank (e.g. Castleden 1993, 54), a scenario that is now considered unlikely but which can not be ruled out (Cleal *et al.* 1995, 109). Castleden (1993, 55) suggests that the post structures blocked access through the north-eastern entrance, which was used for observations outwards, while people accessed the interior of the monument via the (remaining) southern entrance and causeway. Even if the entrance post-holes were not precise markers, and even if they did post-date the bank and ditch, it is still possible to argue that their lunar orientation did have significance and meaning, but possibly within the context of much less organised observations.

The prevailing view from the current archaeological evidence is that the post-holes represent structures that restricted access to the north-eastern entrance down to two narrow 'entrance corridors' (e.g. Cleal *et al.* 1995, 484) (Fig. 5).[5] If it is surmised that the earlier ditch and bank entrance was deliberately aligned upon the limiting moon, it is interesting to see whether any lunar symbolism was preserved in the later structures. The two proposed passageways line up with gaps between the 'A' post-holes further out, and are in the same orientation as the Phase 1 axis, yielding a horizon declination of +27°. These lines do not, however, pass through the centre of the monument, and viewing the passageways from the centre yields orientations further to the east, the right-hand one lining up on the midsummer sunrise. The details are given in Table 6.

**Table 6.** Orientations of the entrance corridors in Phase 2. The azimuths have been judged from Cleal *et al.* (1995, fig. 66)

| From | to | Az | Dec |
|---|---|---|---|
| Phase 1/2 centre | Left corridor to left A-hole gap | 43 | +27 |
| | Right corridor to right A-hole gap | 43 | +27 |
| | Left corridor, from centre | 45 | +26 |
| | Right corridor, from centre | 49 | +24 |

[5.] Another possibility is that they represent no more than a planked bridging structure to protect the entrance while the sarsens were being dragged through prior to their construction (J. Richards and M. Whitby, this volume).

There is one item of evidence that may strengthen the now much weakened idea that the entrance post-holes did have significance in relation to the moon. Three small post-holes were reported under the bank on the south-east side of the monument, in section C44 (see Cleal *et al.* 1995, 94) (Fig. 4). They appear to date to Phase 2, but may date to Phase 1 or even before (ibid., 107). Their orientation from the centre of the Aubrey Hole ring yields a declination of –28°, which is close to southern major moonrise. It is still possible that the ring of Aubrey Holes, these three post-holes, and all the post-holes at the north-eastern entrance pre-date the enclosure (ibid., 107). The possibility that they had a function as markers against which the motions of the moon could be observed (which is different from saying that they functioned as precise markers of the rising positions themselves) is one that can not be entirely discounted.

Finally, Burl (1987) and Castleden (1993, 218–20) have argued that the spatial distribution of deposits of bone, antler and pottery and stone during Phases 1 and 2, in the Aubrey Holes and in the enclosure bank, reflects strong astronomical symbolism. For example, a cluster of nine cremations near Aubrey Hole 14 marks moonrise at the southern lunar limit. Burl (1987, 103) argues that such offerings demonstrate the transition from a lunar to a solar tradition; Castleden (1993, 282, note 78) considers that the moon and sun were worshipped together. Such interpretations are hampered more than most by the lack of evidence from unexcavated parts of the site, and now need to be reassessed in the light of the integrated primary data now published (Cleal *et al.* 1995, ch. 9).

### *Stonehenge 3i/3a*

In relation to the equivocal evidence of lunar symbolism in Phases 1 and 2, the evidence of solar solstitial orientation in Phase 3 is relatively clear cut, at least in relation to the main axis.

Within the bluestone setting of Stonehenge 3i, the Altar Stone, placed on the south-west side, appears to have been the centre of attention. Whether it stood in feature WA 3639 (Cleal *et al.* 1995, 188) or WA 3359 (ibid., 268), or whether there was a pair, it was placed on an axis that yields a declination of +24° to the NE and –24° to the SW (Fig. 6). The axis, while not precisely defined, is precise enough that we can say for certain that stone 97 and the Heelstone straddle it and bracket the midsummer sunrise

**Table 7.** Orientations of the axis and station stone rectangle in Phase 3i/3a. The Phase 3i axis has been estimated from Cleal *et al.* 1995, fig. 80. The station rectangle orientations have been determined from Cleal *et al.* 1995, plan 1 together with fig. 164 (for stone 94) and fig. 165 (for stone 92)

| From | to | Az | Dec |
|------|-----|-----|-----|
| Phase 3 centre | Phase 3i axis to NE | 49 | +24 |
| | Phase 3i axis to SW | 229 | –24 |
| | Phase 3a: 93–94 | 49 | +24 |
| | Phase 3a: 93–91 | 116 | –16 |
| | Phase 3a: 93–92 | 140 | –29 |
| | Phase 3a: 92–91 | 50 | +24 |

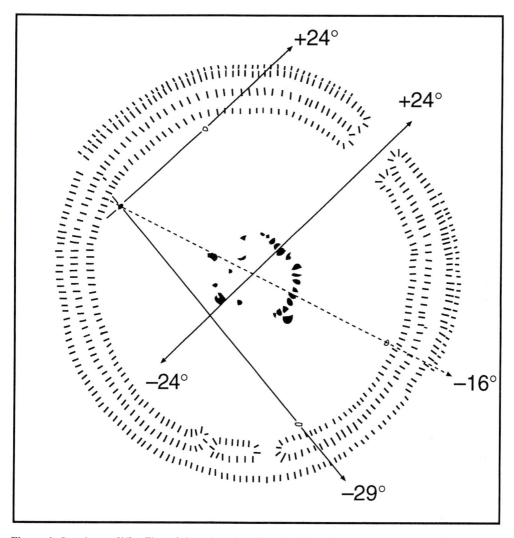

**Figure 6.** Stonehenge 3i/3a. Five of the orientations listed in Table 7 are shown together with the horizon declination estimated for a horizon at altitude 0°·5. They comprise the axis through the Altar Stone in both directions and various alignments between the station stones. Based on Cleal *et al.* (1995, fig. 256).

(Cleal *et al.* 1995, 268–70). The entrance from the NE now leads to a focus in the SW. It is possible that the significant association was the alignment of the Altar Stone in the direction of midwinter sunset, or the play of the light from the rising midsummer sun upon its north-east face, or both.

The station stone rectangle in one direction is aligned with the Phase 3i axis, but in the other direction, to the NW and SE, it is aligned upon declination ±29°, corresponding roughly to major limiting moon rising in the south (full in summer) or setting in the north (full in winter), a fact known since the 1960s. The question here, given that the solstitial axis is taken to be intentional, is whether the coincidence that the moon came very occasionally to rise or set in the direction at right angles to the axis simply passed unnoticed, or whether it was actively exploited. If so, then solar and lunar symbolism was being incorporated side by side.

The question of why the station stones were placed in a rectangle and not a square, has given rise in the past to the tentative suggestion that the WNW-ESE diagonal might have astronomical significance; however its declination, −16°, has no obvious explanation in terms of the sun or moon and in any case the diagonal passed across the centre of the site where it might have been partially obscured by the bluestones, and certainly would have been obscured by the later sarsens (Castleden 1993, 134).

The axis shift at the beginning of Phase 3 is generally assumed to represent a change to solar orientation,[6] but alternative explanations have been put forward. For example, North (priv. comm.) argues that the axis change was made because of precessional drift, which implies that it was the stars, rather than the sun or moon, that were of interest. Is it possible that bright stars were the cause of the axis shift? The question is important because of its bearing on the idea of continuity (see below). The only bright stars visible through the north-eastern entrance in 3000 cal BC were Deneb—which would already be at an altitude of 7° by the time it reached the left-hand side of the entrance, rising to 13° altitude by the time it reached the right-hand side—and Capella, which would rise within the entrance but would probably already have passed to the right before rising sufficiently to be visible. Deneb had only lost a degree in altitude by 2500 cal BC, and Capella would be becoming more visible rather than less so, rendering an axis shift unnecessary. Thus there is no evident reason why observations of bright stars, at least rising in line with the entrance, should motivate an axis change.

### Further developments at Stonehenge 3

At the periphery, there are many uncertainties due to the lack of stratigraphic relationships and reliable sequencing; for example, it is not certain that the Heelstone and stone 97 actually stood together (Pitts 1982, 82). However, it seems reasonable to make the tacit assumption that they did (Cleal *et al.* 1995, 268).

A crucial question at this stage is whether the Slaughter Stone and its companion formed the middle two of a line of four stones placed across the entrance, as argued by Burl (1994, 90) on the basis of a postulated fourth stone to the south-east of the original position of the Slaughter Stone. Burl's argument is disputed by Cleal *et al.* (1995, 285–7).

---

[6.] On p. 20 of the 1995 edition of the English Heritage handbook on Stonehenge and Neighbouring Monuments is the statement that 'the entrance was ... reorientated slightly during the lifetime of Stonehenge to compensate for astronomical variation in the midsummer sunrise over many centuries'. This is erroneous. The variation in the solstice position is too small (only about 30 arc minutes, or the sun's own diameter, over 4000 years) and the axis shift is too great.

They also (ibid., 139) dispute Atkinson's (1979, 73) contention that some 7 m of the ditch to the south-east of the north-east entrance was deliberately backfilled, to bring the width of the earthwork entrance into line with the width of the avenue. Finally, they argue that the two gaps between stones *D* and *E*, and *E* and the Slaughter Stone, mimicked in stone the earlier two narrow passages through the entrance posts.

This new interpretation of the archaeological evidence does not affect the orientation of the 'solar corridor' passing between *E* and the Slaughter Stone, close to *C* and *B*, and between the Heelstone and its companion (Burl 1994, 91–3). It does, however, result in a considerable shift of emphasis, because the entrance along the solar corridor is now one of two (Fig. 7): the second entrance, to the NW, passes between *D* and *E* and has an orientation closer to the old lunar alignment, with declination +27°. Furthermore, the emphasis upon the 'solar corridor' as the central line of the avenue is countered by the fact that between a third and a half of the width of the avenue at its end by the entrance is still blocked by the ditch.

Yet the dramatic effect of midsummer sunrise (Burl 1994, 91) is unaffected. The sarsen circle and horseshoe having been constructed on the same axis as the earlier blue-stone setting, the light of the rising midsummer sun would have passed between the Heelstone and its companion, between *E* and the Slaughter Stone, between stones 1 and 30 of the sarsen circle, and between stones 31 and 49 of the inner bluestone ring, into a space considerably more confined than at previous phases of the monument, in which much of the view of and from the outside world had been cut off by the large sarsens. The result must have been a very exclusive spectacle, in which light and shadow played an important part, the sun's light 'pouring down a thin tunnel of stone like the passage of a chambered tomb' (ibid.). The new archaeological interpretation does not affect this but implies that entrance to the interior was more restricted to people, perhaps empha-sising the exclusivity of the spectacle.

One feature is worthy of comment in Phase 3iv: the anomalous, radial orientation of stone 33e (Cleal *et al.* 1995, figs 117 and 231), which appears to have provided some sort of additional access into the interior (Cleal *et al.* 1995, 486). Its azimuth from the centre is 137° and its declination –27°, close once again to the southern major limit of the moon.

### The Bronze Age barrows

During the Early Bronze Age several dozen round barrows were built within sight of Stonehenge, many of them situated on a ridge forming a 'false horizon' a little over 1 km from the monument (Cleal *et al.* 1995, 35–7). If certain celestial bodies or events were of significance when viewed from Stonehenge, might not some of the most presti-gious barrows be located in relation to those events as seen from Stonehenge? In Figure 8 we show the 'envelope of visibility' formed by this near horizon, together with the barrows, and add a few examples of orientations from Stonehenge to particular barrows showing the declinations of the horizon behind them. The declinations of intermediate

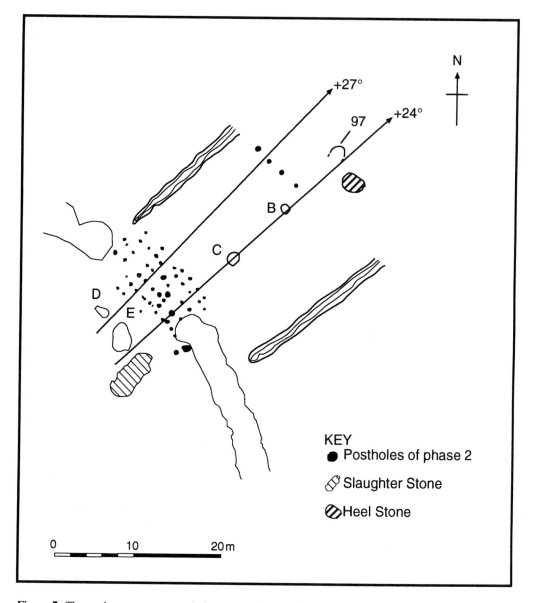

**Figure 7.** The north-eastern entrance during Phase 3. The orientations listed in Table 8 are shown together with the horizon declination estimated for a horizon at altitude 0°·5. They comprise the 'solar corridor' axis and the line through the gap between *D* and *E*. Based on Cleal *et al.* (1995, fig. 156).

barrows can be estimated by extrapolation. There is no obvious evidence that the stretches most thickly populated with barrows occupy particularly noteworthy declination ranges. Is there, then, any evidence that the most flamboyant examples were placed in particular spots that acquired special significance through being aligned with astronomical targets

**Table 8.** Orientations of the 'solar corridor' and other features in Phase 3a-b-c. The axis is determined from Cleal *et al.* 1995, fig. 79. The centre-to-D/E alignment is determined from this in combination with Plan 1

| From | to | Az | Dec |
|------|----|----|----|
| Phase 3 centre | Centre to gap between D and E | 43 | +27 |
| | 'Solar corridor' axis | 49 | +24 |

beyond? The only one marked that has an astronomical correlation of obvious significance is G15, which aligns with the midwinter sunset, but whether this is because of the solstitial alignment, whether it was placed in line with the Stonehenge axis, or whether its position arose through the chance combination of other factors, is unknown.

## Discussion

*Stonehenge astronomy in context*

The preceding discussion has tended to concentrate upon areas where the archaeological evidence bears upon astronomical ideas, in particular reinforcing or modifying existing ideas. But how does the astronomical evidence bear upon archaeological ideas? We briefly identify two areas of current debate where it may have some direct relevance, and then make some suggestions for future research.

The first area of debate is the extent to which Stonehenge emphasised continuity, representing slow-changing ritual practice during a time of otherwise rapid change (Bradley 1991; Cleal *et al.* 1995, 486–7). Can astronomy cast any light on this? It surely has the potential to do so, because authors such as Burl (1987) have emphasised a change from lunar symbolism to solar symbolism, and this could imply that some fundamental changes in ritual practice and tradition accompanied the transition from Stonehenge 2 to Stonehenge 3.

The evidence for intentional lunar orientation of Stonehenge 1 and 2 from the various structures does not seem strong, even if one is prepared to argue that the entrance postholes preceded the ditch and bank, although the evidence from spatial patterns of deposition, when reassessed in the light of the new corpus from the twentieth-century excavations, may bear strongly upon this question. There is certainly no compelling evidence for solar orientation during this period, yet the evidence is quite convincing when we reach Stonehenge 3, especially with regard to the 'solar corridor' into the sarsen circle, despite the uncertainties in much of the archaeological evidence. This does seem to imply that a change in emphasis towards solar symbolism took place at the beginning of Stonehenge 3, and very probably that the change of axis is symptomatic of that change.

Yet there are also hints of continuity. The three post-holes under the bank in C44, the cluster of cremations near Aubrey Hole 14, the NW-SE orientation of the station stone rectangle, and possibly even the reorientation of bluestone 33e, do hint at a persistent

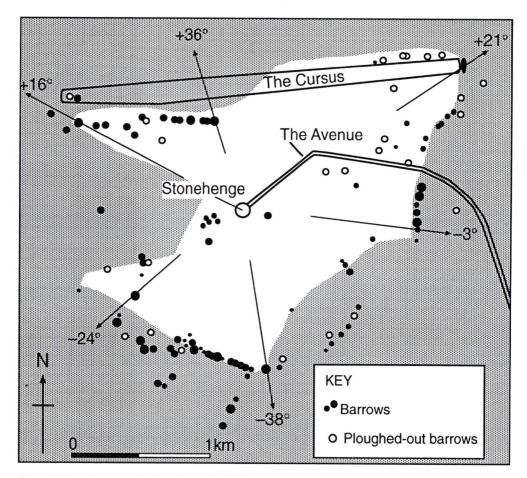

**Figure 8.** Stonehenge 3. The 'envelope of visibility' formed by the near horizon (unshaded) as seen from Stonehenge, showing barrows on and within the near horizon. The orientations listed in Table 9 are shown together with the horizon declination estimated for a horizon at altitude 0°·5. Based on Cleal *et al.* (1995, fig. 21).

interest in orientations aligned upon moonrise within two or three degrees of (and always to the north of, i.e. within the lunar arc) the southern major limit. Likewise, the orientation of the entrance of the Stonehenge 1 ditch and bank, the entrance post-holes with their two passages aligned upon gaps in the A holes, and possibly also the left-hand entrance gap in Phase 3, between stones *D* and *E*, are all aligned within two or three degrees of the northern major limit. Most convincing perhaps is the station stone rectangle, but perhaps also in stone 33e and stones *D* and *E*, come hints that lunar symbolism continued into the latter stages.

The second area of debate might clarify this. The question here is to what extent the later phases of Stonehenge were intended to restrict access, and the social implications of this. As far as astronomical observations are concerned, we can identify different degrees

**Table 9.** Orientations and declinations of selected round barrows as viewed from Stonehenge

| From | to | Az | Dec |
|------|------|------|------|
| S/h centre | (S/h Cursus E end | | |
| | and earlier long barrow) | 56 | +21 |
| | King Barrow Gp S end | 95 | −3 |
| | Norm. Down Gp E end | 168 | −38 |
| | Norm. Down Gp W end (G15) | 230 | −24 |
| | Monarch of the Plain (G55) | 296 | +16 |
| | Cursus barrows, E end (G43) | 340 | +36 |

of accessibility: a moonrise or sunrise, on a particular occasion such as the solstice, might be observable by many hundreds of people, not all within the enclosure. But moonrise or sunrise in relation to nearby markers—moonrise behind the entrance timber posts or sunrise between the Heelstone and its companion—might be directly viewable only by a few individuals inside the enclosure, within a fairly restricted space. And the privilege of witnessing phenomena such as the midsummer sun's light shining along the 'solar corridor' and into the centre of the sarsen monument, or shadow effects at midwinter sunset, might have been available to very few. It can be argued that the nature of astronomical observations gets gradually more exclusive, while access to the interior becomes more controlled (Burl 1987, 205; Cleal *et al.* 1995, 485).

Drawing these threads together suggests some tentative working hypotheses. First, there *was* lunar symbolism in Stonehenge 1 and 2, and there are hints that some of it may have carried through to Stonehenge 3. It was in the form of orientations upon the rising moon within two or three degrees of its major limits, both in the north and south. The posts in the north-eastern entrance did not function as precise markers of lunar rising positions, and they may have served to restrict access through the entrance, but they may also have served as markers against which the moon could be more casually observed.

Second, access to solar phenomena seems to have been restricted. Midsummer sunrise and midwinter sunset light and shadow effects would only have been visible to a privileged few in the interior. Third, this contrast between the generally more public access to lunar phenomena and more restricted access to solar ones is reminiscent of both the small, open ritual monuments such as the recumbent stone circles and short stone rows, built by the score in northern and western Britain and Ireland in the Early Bronze Age, where studies of groups of sites yield statistical evidence of preferential orientation upon the moon; as well as large chambered tombs such as Newgrange and Maes Howe, where solar light phenomena are confined within spaces with restricted access.

Concerning astronomy and Stonehenge, it will be clear that on the basis of the evidence currently available very little can be said with any great degree of confidence. Part of the problem is the nature of astronomical data, which either need to be collected from a large enough group of different cases for trends to be isolated statistically, or specifically to inform—and thereby to reinforce or weaken—a contextual argument. Most archaeologists are not in the habit of collecting declination data as part of field survey; yet any phenomenological study of the landscape is surely enriched by taking account of the appearance of the sky.

*Future directions*

In 1982 Richard Atkinson concluded a review of the astronomy of Stonehenge with the remark that 'only the alignment of the Avenue on the summer solstice sunrise . . . can be accepted with confidence. All other interpretations are open to doubt or to alternative explanations' (Atkinson 1982, 107). Despite a number of new ideas put forward in recent years, generally much more securely founded in the broader archaeological context than were those being reviewed by Atkinson, this remark remains true in broad terms.

Yet the preceding discussion suggests that investigations of astronomical potential could, and should, inform a number of important research questions relating to Stonehenge and its environs. The following programmes of work could be particularly enlightening.

**1** *Monuments in the Early Neolithic landscape.* A systematic study of the siting and orientation of the long barrows, involving the collection of field data on horizon altitudes and declinations and their combination with data on the visibility of and relationship to other human-made and natural features in the terrestrial landscape, would help to establish the place of each monument within the terrestrial and celestial landscape surrounding it, and to determine whether certain astronomical bodies or events were of particular significance. Wider studies of long barrows in the vicinity of the Wessex causewayed enclosures other than Robin Hood's Ball could show whether similar considerations were important elsewhere.

**2** *The siting of Stonehenge and the axial orientation of Stonehenge 1 and 2.* Theodolite surveys exploring the general astronomical potential of the site chosen and of other sites in the immediate vicinity would establish whether any special properties were possessed by the actual site, and if so to which astronomical bodies or events they might have related. This is relevant to the wider issue of whether the choice of location was influenced more by the 'view in' or the 'view out' (Cleal *et al.* 1995, 35). Comparison with the siting of the other circular enclosures and henges in the vicinity could help to establish whether there were any common patterns of preference. Comparison with the orientations of their axes and entrances could cast light on the question of whether the orientation of the north-eastern entrance at Stonehenge 1 and 2 was in fact astronomically influenced, and in particular whether it was related to the moon.

**3** *The change in axis and the solstitial orientation of Stonehenge 3.* Further investigation of the zone outside the ditch in both directions along the Phase 1/2 and Phase 3 axes (the latter is already proposed in English Heritage's suggestions for a long-term programme of investigation—see Cleal *et al.* 1995, 493, item 4.2) could cast new light on the function and significance of the axial orientation, astronomical or otherwise, and the sequence of events marking the change from one to the other. It would also be enlightening to obtain new information from the south-east quadrant to clarify whether a south-easterly direction defined by the sun or moon (the latter hinted at by some of the evidence presented above), or indeed a NW-SE axis, was of particular significance.

**4** *Astronomical factors in patterns of movement and approach.* What did the sky look like as people stood at certain points in the landscape, or moved around in certain ways? Was it important, perhaps, to be in a certain place, or to move in certain ways, at a particular time, when the celestial configuration was right? Was it important, perhaps, sometimes to approach Stonehenge along the avenue at night, when the stars in the sky would have been as prominent as earthly signs of ancestors during the day? Astronomical considerations should inform phenomenological studies. A pilot project might involve survey measurements to establish any prominent astronomical objects or events that could have accompanied an approach to Stonehenge along the avenue.

Throughout its history, and especially in Phase 3, Stonehenge was a focus of intense ceremonialism and is likely to have been imbued with significance and meaning at many levels and in many ways (Bender 1992; Whittle, this volume)—in its shape, form, and texture; in the materials used; in spatial patterns of deposition; in the symbolism of inclusion and exclusion; in patterns of experience and approach; and in notions of cyclical time. Astronomy surely has a place in contextual explanations exploring such meanings.

# References

ATKINSON, R.J.C. 1966: Moonshine on Stonehenge. *Antiquity* 40, 212–16.

ATKINSON, R.J.C. 1979: *Stonehenge* (Harmondsworth, 3rd ed.).

ATKINSON, R.J.C. 1982: Aspects of the archaeoastronomy of Stonehenge. In Heggie, D.C. (ed.), *Archaeoastronomy in the Old World* (Cambridge), 107–16.

AVENI, A.F. 1980: *Skywatchers of Ancient Mexico* (Austin, Texas).

AVENI, A.F. (ed.) 1989: *World Archaeoastronomy* (Cambridge).

AVENI, A.F. 1992: Archaeoastronomy and archaeology. *Archaeoastronomy and Ethnoastronomy News* 6, 1 and 4.

BARBER, J.W. 1973: The orientation of the recumbent-stone circles of the south-west of Ireland. *J. Kerry Hist. Archaeol. Soc.* 6, 26–39.

BENDER, B. 1992: Theorising landscapes, and the prehistoric landscapes of Stonehenge. *Man* 27(4), 735–55.

BRADLEY, R.J. 1984: *The Social Foundations of Prehistoric Britain* (London).

BRADLEY, R.J. 1991: Ritual, time and history. *World Archaeol.* 23(2), 209–19.

BRADLEY, R.J. 1993: *Altering the Earth* (Edinburgh).

BRODA, J. 1982: Astronomy, cosmovisión and ideology in Prehispanic Mesoamerica. In Aveni, A.F. and Urton, G. (eds), *Ethnoastronomy and Archaeoastronomy in the American Tropics* (New York, Annals of the New York Academy of Sciences 385), 81–110.

BRODA, J. 1993: Astronomical knowledge, calendrics and sacred geography in ancient Mesoamerica. In Ruggles, C.L.N. and Saunders, N.J. (eds) 1993b, 253–95.

BURL, H.A.W. 1981: Holes in the argument. *Archaeoastronomy* (Center for Archaeoastronomy) 4(4), 19–25.

BURL, H.A.W. 1987: *The Stonehenge People* (London).

BURL, H.A.W. 1988: 'Without sharp north'—Alexander Thom and the great stone circles of Cumbria. In Ruggles, C.L.N. (ed.), *Records in Stone* (Cambridge), 175–205.

BURL, H.A.W. 1994: Stonehenge: slaughter, sacrifice and sunshine. *Wiltshire Archaeol. Natur. Hist. Mag.* 87, 85–95.

CASTLEDEN, R. 1993: *The Making of Stonehenge* (London).

CHIPPINDALE, C. 1994: *Stonehenge Complete* (London, 2nd ed.).

CLEAL, R.M.J., WALKER, K.E. and MONTAGUE, R. 1995: *Stonehenge in its Landscape: Twentieth Century Excavations* (London, Engl. Heritage Archaeol. Rep. 10).

COOKE, J.A, FEW, R.W., MORGAN, J.G. and RUGGLES, C.L.N. 1977: Indicated declinations at the Callanish megalithic sites. *J. Hist. Astron.* 8, 113–33.

ELLEGÅRD, A. 1981: Stone age science in Britain? *Curr. Anthropol.* 22, 99–125.

HAWKES, J. 1966: God in the machine. *Antiquity* 41, 174–80.

HEGGIE, D.C. 1981: *Megalithic Science* (London).

HOSKIN, M.A., ALLAN, E. and GRALEWSKI, R. 1995: Studies in Iberian archaeoastronomy: (3) Customs and motives in Andalucia. *Archaeoastronomy* no. 20 (supplement to *J. Hist. Astron.* 26), S41–8.

HOYLE, F. 1966: Speculations on Stonehenge. *Antiquity* 40, 262–76.

KNIGHT, C. 1991: *Blood Relations: Menstruation and the Origins of Culture* (New Haven, Connecticut).

KÖHLER, U. 1989: Pitfalls in archaeoastronomy: with examples from Mesoamerica. In Romano, G. and Traversari, G. (eds), *Archeologia e Astronomia* (Rome), 130–6.

MARTLEW, R.D. and RUGGLES, C.L.N. 1996: Ritual and landscape on the west coast of Scotland: an investigation of the stone rows of northern Mull. *Proc. Prehist. Soc.* 62, 117–31.

MORPHY, H. 1991: *Ancestral Connections: Art and an Aboriginal System of Knowledge* (Chicago, Illinois).

NEWHAM, C.A. 1966: Stonehenge: a neolithic "observatory". *Nature* 211, 456–8.

NEWHAM, C.A. 1993: *The Astronomical Significance of Stonehenge* (repr.) (Warminster).

NORTH, J.D. 1994: *The Fontana History of Astronomy and Cosmology* (London).

O'KELLY, M.J. 1982: *Newgrange: Archaeology, Art and Legend* (London).

PITTS, M.W. 1982: On the road to Stonehenge: report on the investigations beside the A344 in 1968, 1979 and 1980. *Proc. Prehist. Soc.* 48, 75–132.

RUGGLES, C.L.N. 1981: A critical examination of the megalithic lunar observatories. In Ruggles, C.L.N. and Whittle, A.W.R. (eds), *Astronomy and Society in Britain During the Period 4000–1500 BC* (Oxford, BAR 88), 153–209.

RUGGLES, C.L.N. 1988: The stone alignments of Argyll and Mull: a perspective on the statistical approach in archaeoastronomy. In Ruggles, C.L.N. (ed.), *Records in Stone* (Cambridge), 232–50.

RUGGLES, C.L.N. 1994: The stone rows of south-west Ireland: a first reconnaissance. *Archaeoastronomy* no. 19 (supplement to *J. Hist. Astron.* 25), S1–20.

RUGGLES, C.L.N. and BURL, H.A.W. 1985: A new study of the Aberdeenshire recumbent stone circles, 2: interpretation. *Archaeoastronomy* no. 8 (supplement to *J. Hist. Astron.* 16), S25–60.

RUGGLES, C.L.N. and SAUNDERS, N.J. 1993a: The study of cultural astronomy. In Ruggles, C.L.N. and Saunders, N.J. (eds) 1993b, 1–31.

RUGGLES, C.L.N. and SAUNDERS, N.J. (eds) 1993b: *Astronomies and Cultures* (Niwot, Colorado).

SCHAEFER, B.E. 1993: Astronomy and the limits of vision. *Vistas in Astronomy* 36, 311–61.

SOSA, J.R. 1989: Cosmological, symbolic and cultural complexity among the contemporary Maya of Yucatan. In Aveni, A.F. (ed.) 1989, 130–42.

THOM, A. 1967: *Megalithic Sites in Britain* (Oxford).

THOM, A. 1971: *Megalithic Lunar Observatories* (Oxford).

THOMAS, J. 1991: Reading the Neolithic. *Anthropol. Today* 7(3), 9–11.

THORPE, I.J. 1981: Ethnoastronomy: its patterns and archaeological implications. In Ruggles, C.L.N. and Whittle, A.W.R. (eds), *Astronomy and Society in Britain During the Period 4000–1500 BC* (Oxford, BAR 88), 275–88.

TILLEY, C. 1994: *A Phenomenology of Landscape* (Oxford).

URTON, G. 1981: *At the Crossroads of the Earth and Sky* (Austin, Texas).

*Proceedings of the British Academy,* **92**, 231–256

# The Engineering of Stonehenge

## JULIAN RICHARDS & MARK WHITBY

## Introduction

Julian Richards

*The experiments*

THE EXPERIMENTS DESCRIBED IN THIS PAPER, and the thoughts which both preceded and arose from them, are the direct result of the involvement of both authors in the production of a BBC programme in 1994. The series, 'Secrets of Lost Empires', examined the greatest and most enduring engineering challenges of the ancient world, among which is the construction of Stonehenge, or more precisely, of the sarsen horseshoe and circle which form the most impressive elements of the stone structures. Within these, the single largest element is the Great Trilithon, now ruinous, but the largest of the individual stone settings, each of which consist of two uprights and one horizontal lintel (Fig. 1). The brief was to demonstrate, using human effort and such technology as could reasonably be expected to have been available to the builders of Stonehenge during the earlier part of phase 3, now dated to between 2550 and 1600 BC (Cleal *et al.* 1995, 167) how this could have been accomplished. The nature of the experiment was dictated by the evidence provided by Stonehenge itself, the sarsen stones, estimated as weighing up to 40 tonnes, for which no convincing evidence for local origin could be produced. A possible source on the Marlborough Downs, some 30 km to the north, was first suggested by Samuel Pepys in 1665 (quoted in Brentnall 1946) and was reaffirmed by Colt Hoare in the early nineteenth century (Colt Hoare 1812, 149–50). After considerable subsequent debate this source appears to be confirmed (Pitts 1982, 119–23; Green, this volume). At Stonehenge pairs of the largest of these stones have been dressed to a more regular shape, jointed in a manner reminiscent of carpentry techniques, raised to a vertical position and capped with lintels of similar stone weighing up to 10 tonnes. The experiment could consequently be seen to consist of three individual tasks. The first was to move an upright,

**Figure 1.** The ruins of the great trilithon. The fallen lintel lies in front of stone 56 with its pronounced tenon. (Copyright: Wessex Archaeology. Photograph: Elaine Wakefield.)

the heaviest of the constituent stones, both on flat ground and up a slope of approximately 1 in 20, the minimum slope estimated as being necessary for human transport from its assumed source to Stonehenge. The second task was to raise the upright to a vertical position, and the third, after placing the second upright in position using modern methods, was to lift the lintel into place.

The brief was not presented to archaeologists but to an engineer (Whitby) who was asked to devise possible methods for accomplishing the specified tasks with an archaeologist (Richards) to provide details of available technology and the archaeological evidence for construction methods.

*Previous experiments and the development of a visual orthodoxy for the construction of Stonehenge*

During this century there has been no shortage of opinion about the means of stone transportation or erection and the consequent labour requirements. Of early authors Stone (1924a and b) offers over-confident solutions accompanied by scale models while, in a flurry of activity in the late 1970's both Garfitt (1979 and 1980) and Hogg (1981) solve the problem diagrammatically. Estimates of labour requirements have shown considerable variation, for example the task of moving stones has been suggested as requiring between 90 individuals for 30 tonnes (Garfitt 1979) to 600 for the steepest parts of the route and the heaviest stones (Startin and Bradley 1981). Atkinson (1956, 115) increases this requirement to 1100 men, rising to 1500 for the steepest parts of the route. Such a wide range seems inconsistent when the motive potential of one person appears to have been estimated at a relatively consistent level. Factors which influence the estimates include perceptions of the vehicle to be utilised, while those produced by some of the earlier authors may have been based on preconceptions that the prehistoric workers were short in stature and therefore provided less motive power than their modern counterparts.

Practical experiments have also been carried out, ranging in scale from the transport of a replica bluestone by Atkinson in 1954 (Atkinson 1956, 107–10) to the considerably more ambitious work carried out in 1991 by Pavel (Pavel 1992). While such experiments clearly have a value in establishing some basic principles of transportation and engineering, they were not carried out with replica stones approaching the full size and weight of the largest sarsens and direct extrapolation from their results is consequently unwise. These experiments should also be viewed in the context of the many and varied methods of moving large stones practised around the world (Smith 1866).

Small-scale experiments, theoretical engineering and imagination have combined to produce a standard orthodoxy for the building of Stonehenge. This is best rendered in graphic form in the reconstruction painting until recently displayed at Stonehenge and which appears in the current site guide book (English Heritage 1995, 26–7). In this reconstruction, stones are transported on sledges running on rollers, are raised from the horizontal by means of what appear to be ropes, sheerlegs and timber props and, finally, lintels are elevated using levers on a crib of interlaced and apparently squared timber. What was offered by the BBC was the opportunity to test these and alternative approaches using full-sized replica components of the largest element of the sarsen horseshoe, the Great Trilithon.

*Archaeological evidence and assumptions*

The dimensions of the surviving intact upright (stone 56) of the Great Trilithon were used to produce two matching reinforced concrete 'stones'. The fallen lintel (stone 156) was similarly replicated. Although mortice holes and tenons were cast into the 'stones', no attempt was made to replicate the original asymmetry of the two uprights (they were clearly of unequal length) or any minor irregularities in their overall shape. Tests suggested that the density of the concrete, calculated as 2380 kg/m$^3$, was very similar to that of sarsen. The weight of each upright was calculated at approximately 40 tonnes and that of the lintel at 10 tonnes.

The profile of the hole for stone 56 has been known since its investigation in 1901 (Gowland 1902) and this profile was used as a directly applicable guide to depth and shape. The recently published results of subsequent investigations (Cleal *et al.* 1995), while providing additional detail for stone 56's hole (op. cit., figs 149–50) suggest that there is little consistency in stone-hole morphology. Beyond the evidence from subsoil features, Stonehenge itself appears to offer few direct clues to the methods involved in stone erection. Antler picks provide an obvious indication of the methods used for hole digging and the evidence for their curation suggests an importance beyond mere functional considerations. The direction of ramping demonstrated by excavated stone-holes suggests whether stones were erected from the 'inside' of the structure or from without. In addition, in the absence of a fully understood internal sequence of construction within phase 3, common sense suggests that within phase 3ii (sarsen circle and trilithons) the horseshoe of sarsen trilithons must have been built before the outer sarsen circle was completed.

Certain assumptions were made concerning the materials and technology available at the time of Stonehenge's construction. Inevitably much evidence is provided by areas with good organic preservation. The ability to fell substantial mature trees and to split and work their timber is well documented from the Earlier Neolithic onwards (Coles *et al.* 1978). Stone tools were readily available for both felling and shaping and are capable of efficiently working green oak. Experiment has shown that longitudinal splitting of substantial straight-grained oak trunks can be successfully achieved using seasoned wooden wedges (J. Keen, pers. comm.). The environmental evidence for the early second millennium BC from the immediate environs of Stonehenge suggests a landscape largely devoid of trees. Woodland, largely managed, may have been restricted to small pockets or to the steeper margins of the adjacent river valleys (Allen in Cleal *et al.* 1995, 168–9) although the evidence from Coneybury Henge (Richards 1990, 154–8) suggests woodland regeneration at this period. In contrast to the sparsely wooded environs of Stonehenge and the similar conditions which can be suggested in the Avebury area (Smith 1984, 117–18) the suggested route of the stones from the Marlborough Downs would provide a far wider resource zone within which quantities of timber from both semi 'wildwood' and from more managed woodland would have been available.

The methodology developed for the experiment depended not only on the use of timber but also on the use of rope. Although evidence for rope, or even for string, is rare within the archaeological record, the Wilsford Shaft, approximately 1.5 km south-west of Stonehenge, provided a remarkable survival. The waterlogged basal deposits of a Middle Bronze Age shaft or well contained fragments of a three-strand cord originally of 7 mm diameter and carefully made from an unidentified bast fibre (Ashbee, Bell and Proudfoot 1989, 62–5). Although this cord has been suggested as having a breaking load in the region of 250 kg, the planned experiments clearly required a more substantial rope (rope is greater than 1 in., 25 cm in diameter). An experimental length of rope made from the bast of coppiced Small Leaved Lime (*Tilia Cordata*) was made by Jake Keen of the Cranborne Ancient Technology Centre. The bark was retted and the fibres were then plaited into strands, three of which were themselves plaited together to make a comparatively simple rope. The length of the component bast fibres (over 4 m) and their strength, combined to produce a rope which only broke at its weakest point, where looped, at a breaking strain of 980 kg. Although, for health and safety reasons, modern but traditionally made hemp ropes were used for the construction tasks, this experiment demonstrated the practicality of producing ropes capable of withstanding the forces required.

## Engineering solutions

Mark Whitby and Julian Richards

*Moving the stones*

The approach to moving large stones is inevitably dictated by their size, and solutions require modification as size increases. Atkinson (1956, 109–10) demonstrated that a small stone (weighing approximately 1.5 tonnes) could be dragged using a simple sledge across level smooth grass using a team of 32 haulers. Above this size it is possible that stones of up to 4 tonnes in weight could be carried by teams of up to 100 people grouped around a litter. Beyond this weight, however, the need to develop an economy of effort would seem to dictate that a more efficient system be developed.

Such systems will depend on how many stones are to be transported and how far, the nature of the terrain to be crossed and the maximum available labour force. It is quite feasible that a system which predominantly used brute force could be used when moving a heavy stone over a short distance. But the moving of 40 tonne stones over a distance of 30 km would surely have provoked serious consideration of a means that economised on labour, made the best use of the community and exploited the resources and skills available.

In the case of the Stonehenge sarsens, the terrain over which they were moved varies from the firm undulating chalk of the Marlborough Downs and Salisbury Plain to the level, but potentially wetter Vale of Pewsey. There are several suggestions for the precise route of the stones, the most enduring published by Atkinson (1956, fig. 4) and still broadly accepted 40 years later (English Heritage 1995, 16). Whatever the precise route, the varied nature of the terrain, with undulating topography and potentially wet areas, helps to dictate the approach to the development of a method of transportation. In this development a number of ideas were considered including the use of rollers, forming a timber cylinder around the stone and rolling it, 'crabbing' the stone along using levers and the use of ice as a medium across which the stone could be slid.

The orthodox method using rollers to move the stones was considered but rejected. Subsequent experiments in moving the 10 tonne lintel proved that it is a practical system, but has limitations. The direction of the stone is difficult to control on all but the most level ground and the method involves high risk as rollers have to be placed ahead of the moving object. As the load goes up, the system becomes prone to binding as the weight of the whole load will at times bear on only one or two of the rollers due to unevenness either in the rollers or in the ground surface. The latter can be overcome by running the rollers on a flat, possibly timber track, and the former by selecting rollers of a uniform diameter. However, directional control remains an issue, as any roller placed out of true to the track will cause the load to veer off.

Having rejected the use of rollers, consideration was given to sliding the stone. Ice is recorded as a suitably slippery surface employed in China but the climate of Late Neolithic Britain, combined with the porosity of the chalk across which the majority of the route passes, would render it an inconsistent and infrequently available surface. Other substances were considered; mud for which there is evidence of use in Egypt, powdered chalk, clay, mixtures of these and tallow. The latter, produced from animal fat, has been used until relatively recently to lubricate slipways for the launching of ships and was consequently thought to be the most suitable.

A system was devised, extrapolating from the technology employed in ship launching, that utilised an oak sledge on which the 40 tonne stone was lashed. The sledge consisted of a single slab of oak approximately 5 m long, 1 m wide and 300 mm deep, with a chamfered leading edge. A rectangular section keel was attached to the underside of the sledge (Fig. 2). The overall unladen weight of the sledge was estimated at 1 tonne. The sledge was set on a slipway, consisting of pairs of approximately 200 mm square section timber rails. These were set 750 mm apart and laid end to end to create a route, along which the stone on its sledge could be hauled. With the slipway timbers set into the ground, a firm base was provided, as well as side restraint that would hold the timbers, and hence the whole system, in position. For the purposes of this experiment the topsoil was removed and the rails laid on solid chalk. Examination of the chalk surface after five passes of the loaded sledge and the removal of the rails revealed no trace of surface compaction. The route of such a trackway would appear to be archaeologically invisible. The keel in the bottom of the sledge, running in between the inside faces of the timber rails, was intended to ensure that the sledge and its load remained on the slipway.

Investigations were made into lubricants for the slipway, with serious consideration being given to both 'mud' and tallow, but ultimately a proprietary Shell grease was

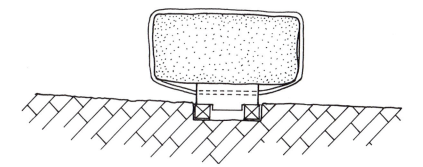

**Figure 2.** Cross section of sledge, rails and stone.

selected. This was readily available, is used on modern slipways, and has properties similar to tallow, but with a slightly lower coefficient of friction. Small-scale tests were carried out to check the feasibility of such a system, as the process requires a large bearing area between sledge and rails in order that the grease is not displaced by the pressure of the sledge.

Estimates of the coefficient of friction for the grease were 0.05, meaning that on level ground, a 40 tonne stone and sledge would require just over 2 tonnes of pulling force to move it. To pull it up the 1 in 20 slope dictated by the experiment would require an additional 2 tonne pulling force, increasing the total to 4 tonnes.

Conversely, to run the stone down a 1 in 20 slope should, in theory, require no effort at all. In both cases, however, an initial force would be required to set the stone in motion and break the sticking effect that came from the grease being forced out under the static weight of the resting stone. For the uphill pull it was estimated that this would momentarily increase the force required to 6 tonnes.

The use of draught animals, specifically oxen, to provide motive power was considered. Received wisdom was that oxen were difficult to work with and were unco-operative in teams unless trained together. Their use was therefore beyond the limits of this experiment but the possibility should not be ignored.

Estimates for the (human) labour requirements were based on the assumption that an individual can pull with a maximum force equivalent to their own weight. For the purposes of calculation an average weight of 60 kg was assumed but the actual average was estimated as being closer to 75 kg (approximately 12 stone). Experiments using a dynamometer with teams of eight confirmed this but suggested that allowances had to be made for increased inefficiency as teams grew larger. Reducing their combined efficiency to 50% it was estimated that a team of 200 individuals would be required. This figure would obviously be reduced by using heavier individuals or by increasing co-ordination of effort.

Although 200 individuals were estimated to be required and this number volunteered, only 130 were eventually available for the experiment. The volunteer group was of mixed sexes, ages and physical strength and can perhaps be suggested as providing a cross section of modern, if not prehistoric, society. For the purpose of moving the stone the group was divided into four teams, each strictly disciplined and co-ordinated by a single supervisor. Movement down the 1 in 20 slipway was initiated and maintained using 60 people (Fig. 3). This movement required a constant but lighter effort to maintain motion, indicating a frictional force slightly greater than the 0.05 that was estimated. However, returning the stone uphill required an extraordinary effort from all the volunteers assisted by the engineering staff.

Initially the stone was impossible to move, due to the combined friction load and the sticking force. To break the latter, the stone was rocked by two teams of four people using levers on either side of the leading edge, while the rest of the team maintained the tension on the ropes. Once freed the stone could be hauled at a slow walking pace up the 30 m long slipway by all 130 available volunteers. During the one-day period of the transportation experiment, the stone was hauled in total 150 m, twice uphill and three times down. Clearly the main limitation to this method is the length of slipway prepared and available but, if sufficient were laid, it was considered that it would have been feasible to move up a steady 1 in 20 slope for a distance in excess of 1 km in a day. On level ground or downhill a distance of 10 km a day could be achieved.

During the experiment approximately 50 kg of grease was used, with fresh applica-

**Figure 3.** The upright pulled downhill. (Copyright: BBC.)

tions on the track for each pull. Were tallow to have been used, with its higher coefficient of friction (approximately 0.1), it is estimated an additional 70 people would have been required, making a total of 200.

*Raising the uprights*

This part of the experiment involved raising one of the 40 tonne uprights to vertical in a stone-hole (prepared by machine excavation) the profile of which was based on that of stone 56 excavated by Gowland. The assumption was made that the stone was inserted from the ramped side of the hole.

Most published diagrams and illustrations of raising the stones to vertical show various systems whereby the stone is levered up from its top end, or hauled up using ropes on a timber 'A' frame (see for example Atkinson 1956, 128; English Heritage 1995, 26–7). Both systems would require a lifting force of at least 20 tonnes, some 3.5 times greater than the maximum 6 tonne force generated by the team of 130 volunteers. Whilst the 'A' frame could give some considerable mechanical advantage and levers could be used to generate lifting force, both systems lack the necessary control that would ensure that the stone could be inserted into the hole without sliding forward on tilting and jamming against its front face. Precise positioning of the stone would be of critical importance as its recovery from a partially inserted position would have been extremely difficult. A system was required which allowed the stone to rotate to an angle of 70 degrees from the horizontal, to clear the front face of the stone-hole and finally to drop the remaining short distance into the bottom of the hole (Fig. 4).

The approach that was adopted recognised that for the stone to rotate successfully into the hole, it would require a hard 'pivot point' on which to rotate. An alternative means of generating the force required to rotate the stone was also sought. The most suitable pivot point that could be envisaged was one of stone and initial thoughts were that the upright could be notched in order to hook over the pivot stone as it rotated. The present appearance of the upright sarsens at Stonehenge does not support this concept which was eventually modified to one where the front of a wooden sledge, to which the upright was tightly lashed, provided the 'notch'. The pivot 'stone', triangular in section and reminiscent of some of the wedge-shaped stones in the sarsen circle, was made of reinforced concrete and was set immediately adjacent to the stone-hole, the line of the sloping face of which extended up through the sloping side of the pivot stone (70 degrees from the horizontal). A ramp of crushed stone (representing a chalk ramp) laid to a slope of 1 in 20 was constructed behind the pivot stone, and timber rails, identical to those employed in the moving experiment, were laid on its surface.

Trial models suggested that the pivot was best set 1500 mm above the ground level, so that the stone, bearing in mind it was heavier at its 'bottom' end due to its shape, was not in danger of overbalancing either forward when near to the horizontal or backwards once tipped to an angle of 70 degrees. The stone was placed on a sledge (smaller but of

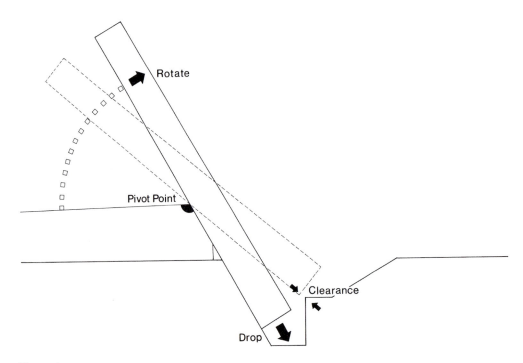

**Figure 4.**

similar principle to that used in the stone-moving experiment) on the ramp with its centre of gravity positioned to the rear of the pivot point. In order to provide force to assist with the rotation of the stone, timber rails were placed along its length and on these was placed a small wooden sledge to which were lashed six, 1 tonne concrete blocks. The principle of this method was that the near horizontal stone could be pivoted using the weight of the 'tilting stones' (Fig. 5) as they reached the tip of the stone overhanging the hole. A weight of six tonnes was calculated to be required for a pivot point set 1500 mm above the ground surface. The stone was lashed to the sledge in such a position that theoretically, on completion of its rotation through 70 degrees, the leading edge of the sledge would engage with the lip of the pivot stone. The stone would then be held momentarily in this position before breaking free of its lashings and dropping into the base of the hole. Once positioned, the sledge containing the tilting stones was gently pulled along its slipway by a small team of less than 50 people, with brake ropes attached in order to ensure that it could not be rapidly pulled off the edge of the stone. As the bundle of tilting stones reached the bottom of the 40 tonne stone, their weight caused it to overbalance, pivot on the front edge of the sledge, and rotate through 70 degrees. As this happened, the 6 tonne bundle of stones slid off the end of the stone (Fig. 6) onto the ledge in the stone-hole in front (Fig. 7), the sledge broke away from its lashings and the stone neatly dropped into the hole.

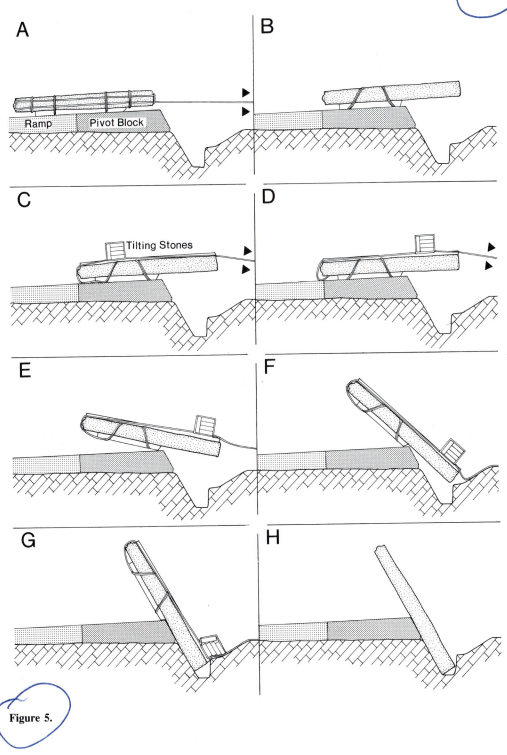

A

Ramp  Pivot Block

B

C

Tilting Stones

D

E

F

G

H

**Figure 5.**

**Figure 6.** The tilting process; 'tilting stones' about to fly off the end of the stone. (Copyright: Sue Lobb.)

The success of this element of the experiment exceeded all expectations as the stone came to rest at a greater angle than the 70 degrees to the horizontal which was expected. This was due to the effect of the tilting stones accelerating off the end of the stone, creating momentum in the entire system. This resulted in the stone rotating beyond 70 degrees and being prevented from settling back against the sloping edge of the pivot stone by the sledge. This had broken free of its lashings as intended but unpredictably had come off the pivot point and slipped down between the stone and the pivot stone.

With the stone now at an angle of over 70 degrees to the horizontal it was now considered that it would be an easy task to pull to vertical using systems similar to those shown in conventional illustrations. However, it was calculated that a force of 10 tonnes would still be required. The team of 130 had generated a pulling force estimated at between 4 and 6 tonnes, and whilst increasing the numbers of people was one solution, ways were sought to maximise the force generated by the available team. A system was adopted whereby a timber 'A' frame was used as a lever, with the force of the team multiplied by attaching the ropes from the stone to a point one third of the way up the 'A' frame and attaching the hauling ropes to the top of the frame (Fig. 8). This had the effect of multiplying the force of the team exerted on the stone by three, from 4 to a maximum of 12 tonnes. Before the team could put this into effect, they were allowed

**Figure 7.** The upright and the 'tilting stones' as they came to rest. (Copyright: Julian Richards.)

to attempt a direct pull, thus proving that there were some things that they couldn't do as they had, by this time, begun to believe that they were superhuman.

Using the 'A' frame lever (Fig. 9), it was possible to crank the stone slowly to vertical, packing between the stone and the pivot stone after each pull. Blocks were initially placed between the stone and pivot stone, and as the stone neared vertical, crushed rock was inserted between the stones.

Larger packing stones such as those used by the builders of Stonehenge are more practical as a packing medium than using crushed stone as the latter can escape

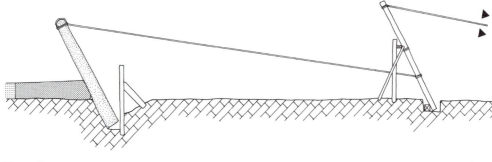

**Figure 8.**

**Figure 9.** 'A' frame used as a lever to assist with the pull to upright. (Copyright: BBC.)

around the side to the front of the stone, frustrating attempts to raise it to a vertical position.

A useful function of the steepness of the rear face of the stone-hole is that it leaves a small wedge to be infilled, much more able to hold the stone upright than a hole with a shallower face. There is also less tendency for the fill material to escape as the stone tips back against it.

The second upright was placed using a 100 tonne crane.

*Raising the lintel*

Although the engineering solution for raising the lintel involved the use of a ramp, the opportunity was also taken to test the conventional 'crib' method.

CRIB METHOD

The timber 'crib', essentially a platform of alternating horizontally laid timbers, has often been suggested as the method by which the lintels were raised. Some illustrations show a plank decking on which workers use levers to raise alternate ends of the lintel, which are then supported before the process continues. This method was tested using a platform of railway sleepers (Fig. 10) and demonstrated that the lintel could be raised quite satisfactorily. Each end of the stone could be raised by the depth of a railway sleeper (approximately 150 mm). The process of levering was shown to be quite easy and swift, with considerably more time being taken to raise the remainder of the platform up to the corresponding level. Once the platform had reached a height above which a direct downward pull could not be applied to the ends of the levers, then they could only be operated by means of ropes. Operated in this way the levers were prone to slipping. The

**Figure 10.** The use of the timber 'crib' and levers to raise the lintel. (Copyright: Julian Richards.)

consequent risk to their operators could have been minimised either by notching the levers where they passed over their pivot blocks, or by employing safety ropes to prevent them falling from the platform. The advantages of this method lie in its comparatively simple material requirements and in the ease with which the platform can be erected and dismantled for reuse. The construction of a platform of sufficient size to provide an adequate and stable working surface (say 9 m long and 3 m wide to a maximum height of 6 m) would require approximately 2600 m of timber of square section or diameter 250 mm. The squared timber could be provided by approximately 200 trunks 4.5 m long and 1 m in diameter while the round section timber would be easier to obtain and work and, if rudimentarily notched, would create a structure of some stability. Whatever section the constituent timbers, the structure could be stabilised by tying it in through the gap between the upright sarsens.

RAMP METHOD

The method devised for raising the lintel (Fig. 11) is essentially a variation on the ramp method suggested by a number of previous authors (e.g. Stone 1924a) and tested at a considerable scale by Pavel (Pavel 1992). A 30 degree scaffolding ramp was constructed, intended to represent one built of timber and earth, but with due regard to

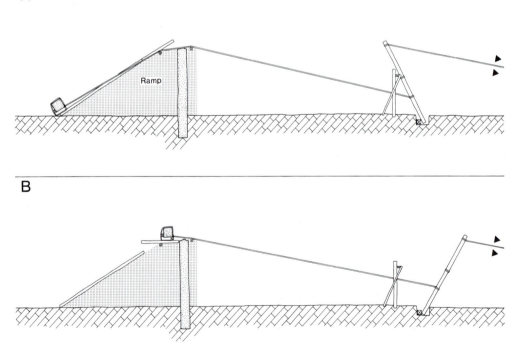

**Figure 11.**

health and safety. A slipway of three parallel wooden rails (similar to those used in the preceding elements of the experiment) was built on the ramp up which the lintel was to be hauled, lashed to a sideways running wooden sledge. The sledge was that used for the raising of the upright, now running at 90 degrees to its original direction of travel and consequently with additional notches cut to engage the three rails. At the point at which the angled ramp joined the horizontal decking around the top of the uprights, the final section of the rails projected the 30 degree ramp angle. The rails here were designed to break as the stone reached this point, allowing it to slide the final horizontal distance of 1.5 m into a position just in front of the two uprights. The level of this was such that it was set to clear the top of the tenons on the upright stones, by running off the slipway onto two greased blocks set on top of the stones.

It was calculated that the force required to haul the 10 tonne lintel up the greased slope of 30 degrees was approximately 6 tonnes, achievable with the full team of 130, who, using the 'A' frame lever, had generated a pulling force of 12 tonnes. Using the same system and with a reduced team of 90 people (this was the third weekend and numbers were falling), the lintel on its sledge was hauled up the ramp, at each stage being tied back and the 'A' frame reset (Fig. 12). Once teething problems with both lashing and with the sledge binding on the rails had been overcome, the lintel was raised in about 3 hours. However, in pulling up the ramp, the lintel had drifted out of line with the tenons and was 100 mm out of position. Over 4 hours was then spent coaxing the stone over that final short distance using levers, a process that illustrated some of the problems and risks of working with levers 'up in the air', and the logic of the tenons as locating devices. The hemispherical tenons cast into the replica stones were too tight a fit in the corresponding mortice holes and should have been similar to the pointed example on stone 56.

The trilithon was then complete and the removal of the ramp allowed the scale of the complete structure to be appreciated (Fig. 13). Even allowing for the fact that stone 55 never possessed the grace of its companion upright the completed trilithon was a structure of considerable power and elegance.

## Conclusions

### Julian Richards & Mark Whitby

*The results and validity of the experiments*

The experiments, inevitably involving some moments of anxiety and carried out with the awareness that the end product was intended to be a television programme, were both enjoyable and informative. Between engineer and archaeologist some divisions of opinion were identified and some remain amicably unresolved. While not suggesting that the methods devised and implemented were the only ones possible for the construction of Stonehenge, alternatives to the standard orthodoxy have been devised, tested and proved feasible.

**Figure 12.** The use of a ramp to raise the lintel. (Copyright: Julian Richards.)

**Figure 13.** The completed trilithon. (Copyright: BBC.)

It has been clearly demonstrated that a 40 tonne load (one major upright or three or four lintels) can be moved up a slope of 1 in 20 with a minimum labour force of approximately 130. Allowances for the lower friction coefficient resulting from the use of lubricants available to the original builders suggest that the motive power of approximately 200 individuals would be required. The experiment demonstrated that movement down a 1 in 20 slope required only 60 individuals, suggesting that approximately 100 would be a more realistic 'prehistoric' figure. Many previous theoretically derived estimates of human power requirements now seem to have been over cautious and there seems no reason why alternative methods of transportation should not produce similar figures to those derived from the recent experiments.

What was required by this task, and by the other elements of the experiment described above, was a considered approach to the problem to be solved and an investment in infrastructure. Both the sledge and the rails are simple, robust and capable of reuse, their construction well within the capabilities of Neolithic woodworkers. It could be argued that continued use would improve the efficiency of the combined sledge and rails and that the recent experiment was carried out during the 'running in' period of the replicated equipment.

The solution devised for the raising of the upright may, to some, be seen as over complicated, or perhaps over engineered. There are sound reasons, however, why the method currently most frequently presented in graphic form requires reappraisal and the recent experiment introduced only one novel concept, that of the employment of weights to assist with the tilting process. The requirement for some form of ramp to elevate the bottom end of the stone to be erected has previously been recognised and a logical extension of this requirement is the provision of a solid pivot point to provide additional control as the stone swings over. The leading edge of an earth ramp would not provide sufficient rigidity and, although this could be provided by a substantial timber revetment, one made of stone would perhaps be more stable.

Moving the upright to vertical from its position of rest within its stone-hole may seem the simplest part of the overall process, but proved difficult. These difficulties, and the necessity of employing an 'A' frame to multiply the effort applied on the ropes, demonstrated that insufficient direct force could have been applied by employing shear legs as often suggested. The Spanish windlass (involving twisting paired ropes by means of a pole inserted between them) which was required in order to take up slack in the ropes may be unnecessary if ropes are stretched and appropriately treated before use.

The two methods of raising the lintel, ramp and 'crib', were both shown to work, although only the former was carried through to completion. Other methods should now be evaluated in terms of their material and labour requirements.

*Implications for labour requirements* (J.R.)

The experiments described above addressed parts of the overall task of building one element of Stonehenge. They have provided the first data empirically derived from the movement and erection of full-sized components, data which should consequently be capable of providing a greater insight into the labour requirements of the monument as a whole, or at least for the sarsen structures. The intention of estimating labour requirements is not to attempt to inject some false precision into the overall monumental task, but rather to place it in perspective with contemporary structures and to suggest a reasonable time frame within which it could have been completed.

The building of the sarsen structures which, although now redated, are essentially the 'Beaker Monument' discussed by Startin (1983), involves a number of identifiable tasks, each with its own specific problems, solutions and consequent labour requirements.

EXTRACTION

Stones at their source, to judge from surviving but possibly atypical examples, would have required not quarrying but possibly partial excavation to free them from their surrounding matrix of colluvial deposits and soil. A direct lift or sliding a short distance would then have been required in order to place them on the sledge. The excavation and lifting/dragging, activities focused on a specific area, would have required large numbers of people for short periods of time. Alternatively, this task would have been made considerably less labour intensive if the stones had already been selected, extracted and possibly raised for use in an existing structure. The Avebury area is certainly one in which there was, by the Later Neolithic, some experience of moving and raising large stones, for example those used in the construction, if not the blocking, of the West Kennett long barrow (Piggott 1962).

TRANSPORT

Without a precise understanding of the route from the source of the sarsens (at *c*.150 m OD) to Stonehenge (at *c*.100 m OD) it must suffice to say that the route undulates. It has been demonstrated that moving the largest of the stones uphill would have required approximately 200 people, while easier gradients and smaller stones will obviously lessen the labour requirement. It therefore seems likely that, if a team of 200 is required for specific aspects of the transportation process, a team of this size would have been available throughout. Averaging gradients suggests that a 40 tonne stone could be moved over 30 km in 12 days with 200 people, perhaps less time with the trackway installed for the complete route. The possibility that the route was not only defined but that rails or alternative structures were laid for its entire length should not be discounted. The material requirements can be placed in context by those estimated for the construction of the timber platform to raise the lintel (above p. 246) and by the quantities of timber used in broadly contemporary monuments in the Avebury area. Here the construction of the West Kennett palisade enclosure (Whittle 1991) demonstrates no shortage of mature timbers and, as already noted, the route itself provides a corridor along which timber resources were presumably widely available. A continuous track does not seem impossible in the context of Neolithic trackway construction in the Somerset Levels (Coles and Coles 1986) and would allow for the movement of several stones simultaneously, using the full complement of 200 to move the largest stone where gradient required such effort, splitting into smaller teams to move additional stones on easier gradients. There may be advantages in a smaller stone travelling in convoy with a large example as the former could be used to overcome the sticking effect shown to bind sledge to rails when at rest, effectively to 'bump start' the larger stone.

If it is accepted that unquantifiable but not excessive time is spent in preparing the infrastructure for transport, then the figure given above for the movement of a single 40 tonne stone can be used to calculate that the 80 or so sarsens, with a combined unshaped weight of at least 1300 tonnes, could have been moved in approximately 100,000 person/days. If 200 people is the optimum team size then 500 days would have been required suggesting that the stones could have been transported within two years, or, if transportation was a part-time, possibly seasonal activity, comfortably within a decade.

The components of the sarsen structures at Stonehenge show a remarkable uniformity of scale and proportion, even if some has been achieved through careful tooling. It seems inconceivable that the building of the structures was started before the stones had all been selected and most likely transported to site. This seems to suggest a concerted short period of prospection, identification, extraction and transport.

SHAPING

This aspect of the overall task was not addressed by the recent experiments and remains one of the most difficult to quantify in terms of both method and labour requirement. The accepted method of shaping is by means of stone hammers or 'mauls' but whatever the method employed, the volume of material removed in the case of each stone is incalculable as consequently are the labour requirements.

RAISING

At Stonehenge itself the requirements for both resources and labour would have been concentrated although the latter could have been considerably reduced by employing methods similar to those demonstrated in the recent experiments.

Once delivered to site, the majority of the required effort would have been directed towards the preparation of stone-hole and ramp, positioning the stone and installing the ropes and mechanisms for tilting. The availability on site of a range of sizes of sarsens, and, at this time, the bluestones, would have facilitated a number of tasks. Ramps could have been built around a core of stones, firmer and easier to move into place and subsequently remove than volumes of earth or chalk.

The preparation, tilting and hauling to upright could have been achieved by a maximum team of approximately 150 people (the number required to pull the largest stones to vertical). Given the variety of scale and duration of the constituent tasks within this phase of the buildings programme, a team of this size could probably have accomplished the raising of all of the uprights within a period of 120 days (18,000 person/days).

PLACING THE LINTELS

The labour requirements for this task depend on the method employed. Considerable effort is required for the construction of a ramp, although once in place the lintel can be raised quickly, certainly within a single day, by around 90 people. In contrast, the crib requires little preparation once the timbers are available, but is a slower process, taking a team of around 20 people one day to raise each lintel a distance of 1 m. Using the lowest labour requirements, the raising of the 35 lintels can be estimated as having taken a team of 20 145 days (2900 person/days).

OVERALL REQUIREMENTS

What is suggested by the figures above is that, given a tremendous concentration of effort, the sarsen structures at Stonehenge could have been built within a period of 3 years. Such a short time scale seems unlikely as the construction of a monument such as Stonehenge cannot have been an impulsive gesture and must have involved considerable planning and social organisation. The 200 individuals estimated as being required for the most focused and labour intensive of the tasks represent the undeniable element of a labour requirement that may be far more substantial and extensive. The building of Stonehenge provides evidence of an extraordinary degree of social cohesion and of co-operative effort on more than a local basis. Its stones, both sarsens and the bluestones now accepted as having been deliberately transported from the Presceli mountains (Green, this volume; Scourse, this volume) show a monument of national significance at the time of its construction.

*Stonehenge as construction site* (J.R.)

It is unlikely that the scale and intensity of construction at Stonehenge would have left no physical trace. Within the earthwork enclosure the timber settings, only recently documented in a comprehensible manner and interpreted largely within the intellectual framework imposed by Stonehenge (Cleal *et al.* 1995, 140–52) may have had a more prosaic function. The profusion of predominantly unphased post-holes within the stone settings cannot all be organised into convincingly circular ceremonial structures (op. cit., fig. 70). Phase 2 includes both the timber settings on the main causeway (op. cit., figs 67–8) and evidence of 'the deliberate backfill of some parts of the ditch with clean chalk' (op. cit., 115). Phase 3 involves the introduction into the ditched enclosure of around 1300 tonnes of sarsen, together with the smaller bluestones, but from which direction? If in the direction in which they were to be raised then they would either have to be introduced over the ditch and bank or manoeuvred within the enclosure. The former would seem more practical but would involve temporary backfilling of the ditch and a coincident breaching of the bank. There appears to be evidence of the former and the bank has been insufficiently examined to identify breaches and subsequent reinstatement. The other possibility is that either for practical or ceremonial reasons, the main entrance was utilised. This would have required reinforcement of the fragile causeway in order to prevent its eventual erosion. Can the timber settings on the causeway be interpreted as the remains of post-based plank surfaced bridging structures or are they simply ceremonial? The evidence is ambiguous, but alternatives to monotheistic interpretations should also receive consideration.

*The future direction of experimentation* (M.W. & J.R.)

The constraints of experimentation within a filming schedule inevitably meant that many avenues of research were identified but not followed. Alternative vehicles and tracks for stone transport may be suggested and studies of lubricants should examine the properties of a wide range of substances available in prehistory. Experiments in rope making should continue and should involve the use of other types of fibre. Other methods of raising the uprights may be suggested, while those appropriate for raising the lintel continue to provoke debate amongst the authors. While one (Richards) still favours the timber crib method, the other feels that a variation of the method described by Hogg (1981) may be quicker and more efficient. Hogg suggests rocking stones about a central pivot placed between the paired uprights (Fig. 14), a method which in principle is described as being used in the construction of pyramids (Fitchen 1986, 230).

The methods of construction employed at Stonehenge will no doubt continue to exercise the imagination of both archaeologists and engineers. It would be preferable if their practical skills could also be exercised. After the completion of the experiment the trilithon was dismantled (by crane) and its components were donated to English Heritage. They are currently (1996) in store on the Salisbury Plain Training Area. Their fate is undecided but it has been assumed that they will eventually be re-erected at an appropriate venue. Far from being a static monument to a single experiment, the authors would prefer to see the replica stones used in a dynamic way, available for further experimentation to anyone with an idea to test and the resources to carry it through in safety. The stones are unlikely to be replicated again in a manner suitable for robust use and once permanently raised both they and the ideas that they generated will end up set in concrete. An annual Stonehenge trilithon raising (preferably timed for completion on 21st June) could also prove to be a considerable visitor attraction.

*Postscript*

'The engineer who designed Stonehenge, and devised the methods by which the work of erection might be carried out, must have been a man of extra-ordinary ability – the Archimedes

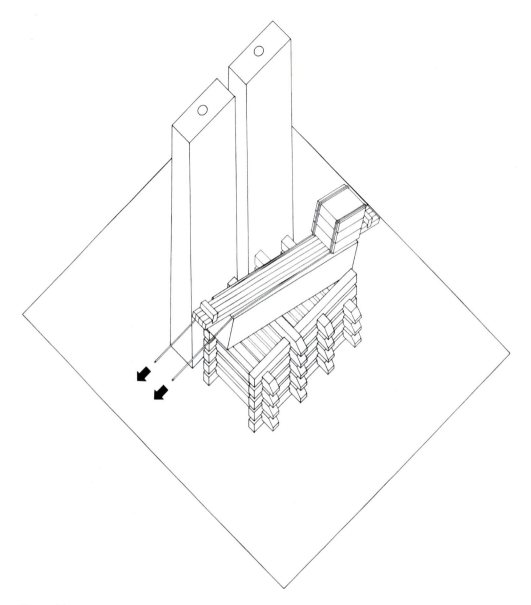

**Figure 14.**

of his time... He was perhaps the man from whom the legend of Merlin had a remote origin ... He was probably a foreigner – "a wise man from the east'" (Stone 1924a, 447).

The experiments described in this paper are of the late twentieth century, a time when the overwhelming force of the machine age appears to have rendered obsolete the skills and ingenuity of our forbears. Those involved in the experiment feared that any degree of success would somehow diminish the achievements of the original builders, or contribute to a gradual demystification of Stonehenge. This was far from the case. The experiments gave all who participated, and, it is to be hoped, the viewers of the television programme, an increased respect for those who laboured with antler picks, split timbers, twine ropes and maybe unwilling beasts, to construct the most enduring and celebrated achievement of our prehistoric past.

*Acknowledgements*

The authors would like to thank the BBC for making these experiments possible and for allowing what had previously been a paper exercise to become exciting reality. Thanks are due to the producers, Cynthia Page and Robin Brightwell and to all the film crew who showed considerable patience. Roger Hopkins, the third member of the team, made the timber crib experiment possible and provided valued criticism of our efforts. Mr Robert Lawton allowed his land to be used for the experiments and Robin and Gill Swanton provided the opportunity to experiment with sarsens. Jake Keen's practical help and experience of ancient technology were invaluable. Thanks are due to Laings Construction, to Desmond Mairs and Robert Sellars of Whitby and Bird and to Mike O'Rouke who kept the volunteers in order. To our respective colleagues with whom we have discussed the work, our thanks and the acknowledgement that the remaining flaws are our responsibility. The drawings (with the exception of Fig. 14 (Whitby and Bird)) are by Rob Read. Finally, we must thank all the volunteers whose efforts moved and raised the stones.

# References

ASHBEE, P., BELL, M. and PROUDFOOT, E. 1989: *Wilsford Shaft: Excavations 1960–62* (London, Engl. Heritage Archaeol. Rep. 11).

ATKINSON, R.J.C. 1956: *Stonehenge* (London).

ATKINSON, R.J.C. 1961: Neolithic engineering. *Antiquity* 35, 292–9.

BRENTNALL, H.C. 1946: Sarsens. *Wiltshire Archaeol. Mag.* 51, 419–39.

CLEAL, R.M.J., WALKER, K.E. and MONTAGUE, R. 1995: *Stonehenge in its Landscape: Twentieth Century Excavations* (London, Engl. Heritage Archaeol. Rep. 10).

COLES, B. and COLES, J.M. 1986: *Sweet Track to Glastonbury* (London).

COLES, J.M., HEAL, S.V.E. and ORME, B.J. 1978: The use and character of wood in prehistoric Britain and Ireland. *Proc. Prehist. Soc.* 44, 1–46.

COLT HOARE, R.C. 1812: *The Ancient History of South Wiltshire* (London).

ENGLISH HERITAGE 1995: *Stonehenge and Neighbouring Monuments* (London).

FITCHEN, J. 1986: *Building construction before mechanisation* (Cambridge, Mass.).

GARFITT, J.E. 1979: Moving the stones to Stonehenge. *Antiquity* 53 no. 209, 190–4.

GARFITT, J.E. 1980: Raising the lintels at Stonehenge. *Antiquity* 54 no. 211, 142–4.

GOWLAND, W. 1902: Recent excavations at Stonehenge. *Wiltshire Archaeol. Mag.* XXXIII No. XCIX (1903–4), 1–62.

HOGG, A.H.A. 1981: Another way to lift the Stonehenge lintels. *Antiquity* 55 no. 214, 131–2.

PAVEL, P. 1992: Raising the Stonehenge lintels in Czechoslovakia. *Antiquity* 66 no. 251, 389–91.

PIGGOTT, S. 1962: *The West Kennet Long barrow: excavations 1955–6* (London).

PITTS, M.W. 1982: On the road to Stonehenge: report on the investigations beside the A344 in 1968, 1979 and 1980. *Proc. Prehist. Soc.* 48, 75–132.

RICHARDS, J.C. 1990: *The Stonehenge Environs Project* (London, Hist. Build. Monuments Comm. Archaeol. Rep. 16).

RICHARDS, J.C. 1991: *Stonehenge* (English Heritage).

SMITH, A.C. 1866: Methods of moving colossal stones, as practised by some of the more advanced nations in antiquity. *Wiltshire Arch. Mag.* X No. XXVIII (1866–7), 52–60.

SMITH, R.W. 1984: The ecology of neolithic farming systems as exemplified by the Avebury region of Wiltshire. *Proc. Prehist. Soc.* 50, 99–120.

STARTIN, B. 1983: The labour involved in the construction of the Beaker Monuments at Stonehenge (unpublished typescript).

STARTIN, B. and BRADLEY, R. 1981: Some notes on work organisation and society in Prehistoric Wessex. In Ruggles, C.L.N. and Whittle, A.W.R., *Astronomy and Society in Britain during the period 4000–1500 BC* (Brit. Archaeol. Rep. 88), 289–96.

STONE, E.H. 1924a: The method of erecting the stones of Stonehenge. *Wiltshire Archaeol. Mag.* XLII No. CXL, 446–56.

STONE, E.H. 1924b: *The stones of Stonehenge* (London).

WHITTLE, A. 1991: A late neolithic complex at West Kennet, Wiltshire, England. *Antiquity* 65, 256–62.

*Proceedings of the British Academy,* **92**, 257–270

# The Provenance of Rocks used in the Construction of Stonehenge

## C. P. GREEN

## Introduction

THE FACT THAT THE WIZARD MERLIN was invoked to explain the construction of Stonehenge and the supposed carriage of its stones from Ireland suggests that already in the mediaeval period visitors to the site had realised that there is no obvious local geological source for any of the building materials used in its construction. Certainly, as soon as we have the written accounts of enquiring visitors, a striking feature of their observations is their recognition that the provenance of the stones is problematic. Perhaps the earliest written reflection on this point is that of Hermann Folkerzheimer, a Swiss visitor to England in the mid sixteenth century. Writing home in 1562 after riding out from Salisbury to look at Stonehenge he reports that the stones '. . . are of an uncommon size almost every one of which, if you should weigh it would be heavier even than your whole house'. Yet they stand, he says '. . . in a very extensive plain at a great distance from the sea, in a soil which appears to have nothing in common with the nature of stones or rocks' (Chippindale 1983).

## The geology of Stonehenge

### The Monument

There are two groups of rock types represented in the visible monument at Stonehenge. The principal building material is sarsen stone, of which 53 specimens remain at Stonehenge today though it seems likely that there were originally at least 85 sarsens in the structure. Sarsen stone is a silicified sandstone which is found not as a continuous geological stratum but as scattered blocks resting on the Chalk in southern England. Sarsen stone is the product of silicification affecting beds of sand in the Lower Tertiary geological formations that overlie the Chalk and are now mainly preserved in the Hampshire and London Basins (Curry 1992). An important subsidiary building material at Stonehenge is a group of predominantly volcanic rocks, collectively known as the bluestones. In many cases these can be matched in specific geological outcrops in South Wales (Thorpe *et al.* 1991). There are 43 recorded bluestones at Stonehenge. Thirty three of these remain above ground level today and a further ten have been identified as stumps below the ground surface. The configurations in which the bluestones were originally used suggest that there may once have been a further 36 bluestones present at Stonehenge.

*Foundations and tools*

In addition to the stones forming the visible monument at Stonehenge, rock was used in its construction to wedge the upright stones firmly in their holes. Numerous sarsen blocks were employed for this purpose, but also blocks of Chilmark ragstone of Portlandian age and glauconitic sandstone derived from the Upper Greensand of Albian age. These rock types have their nearest outcrop at a distance of some 20 km to the south of Stonehenge, in the Upper Jurassic and Lower Cretaceous formations of the Vale of Wardour (Fig. 1). Stone was also the material used by the builders of Stonehenge to prepare and dress the monoliths. Large numbers of mauls or hammerstones have been found in excavations at Stonehenge. In 22 separate excavations, mainly those of Gowland (1902) and Hawley (1921–1928), at Stonehenge, for which detailed records of the stone debris are published, 447 stone mauls and hammerstones, or fragments, are recorded. Almost all the mauls and hammerstones are made from sarsen. Many are made from the same type of sarsen as the monoliths, but there are also substantial numbers made from a distinctive type of sarsen which is very densely cemented by microcrystalline silica and in consequence of exceptional toughness. This type of sarsen occurs as cobbles and small boulders in the river gravels of Wessex and occasionally as isolated blocks lying on the ground surface. A few possible mauls and hammerstones of exotic rock types have been recorded, including a small boulder of ignimbritic tuff-lava described by Kellaway (1991) and of probable Welsh origin. It seems unlikely that such a stone would have been brought from such a distant source simply to be used as a maul, so it may originally have had some other function before being tried, probably unsuccessfully, as a maul and then finally discarded. Other stone artefacts that have been recovered in excavations at Stonehenge are mainly flint tools but also include objects made of chalk and tools made from rocks entirely foreign to the Wessex region.

*Waste*

As well as the stones and stone tools used in the construction of Stonehenge, there are in the immediate vicinity of the monument huge quantities of stone waste. This consists of chips and fragments of almost all the rock types that can be identified in the structure or have been found in use as hammerstones and mauls. In the 22 excavations referred

**Figure 1.** South Wiltshire – location map.

to above, over 11,500 stone fragments were recorded, including nearly 4,000 pieces of sarsen from a single location in the Avenue between the Heel Stone and the Slaughter Stone (Hawley 1925). Some of this material was probably produced during the several stages of construction and rearrangement affecting the stones during a period of some 1500 years in Late Neolithic and Bronze Age times (Pitts 1982). However, bearing in mind the possible disappearance from the site of perhaps sixty or seventy stones from the total number originally used, some of the waste undoubtedly relates to the robbing of material at various times since the monument fell into disuse in the prehistoric period.

# Source areas

The geological problems, which have been a subject of debate for more than 250 years, concern the provenance and history of the geological materials that are found at Stonehenge. When the site of Stonehenge was first chosen in the prehistoric period, was all or some of this material already present close to the site, brought there in the more remote past by natural agencies? Or was it brought to Salisbury Plain from a variety of distant sources by the people who built Stonehenge?

*Minor rock types*

The large number of sarsen hammerstones found at Stonehenge, particularly the tougher variety, can only be explained convincingly in terms of systematic search along river beds and at natural exposures over a large area. The use of Chilmark ragstone and Upper Greensand sandstones also argues for the exploitation of a recognised and accessible local resource, albeit 20 km away. There is certainly no natural process in the history of land-form development in south Wiltshire that could have transported blocks of Jurassic and Lower Cretaceous rock from the low ground within the Vale of Wardour northward, and upward, onto Salisbury Plain. Thus it can be shown that some of the smaller pieces of rock used in the construction of Stonehenge had been selected on the basis of partic-ular qualities and had been systematically collected and brought to the site from an area having a radius of at least 20 km. This is an important observation, because it establishes a pattern of social organisation and resource use which has implications for an under-standing of the stones forming the monument itself. These present two separate problems —the provenance of the sarsens and the provenance of the bluestones.

*Sarsens*

The sediments in Wessex and elsewhere in southern England, affected by the silicifica-tion process that produced the sarsen stone are all of Lower Tertiary age. Both the sediments themselves and the silicification process appear to be no later than the earliest Eocene and thus mainly Palaeocene. There has been very little modern work on the petrology or the original stratigraphic position of the sands forming sarsen stone. Their assignment to the Palaeocene Reading Formation is based largely on the fact that sands regarded as having suitable characteristics of composition and texture have occasionally been recognised in that formation (Whalley and Chartres 1977). Work on the diagenetic fabric of sarsen (Summerfield and Goudie 1980) suggests that the process of silicifica-tion was identical with that observed in modern silcretes forming in semi-arid sub-trop-ical environments. This finding is consistent with what is known about the depositional environment and palaeoclimatic conditions of the Reading Formation.

Palaeocene sediments, represented by the Reading Formation, are present both in the

Hampshire Basin, extending northward almost as far as Salisbury, and in the London Basin, extending westward to the north of the Vale of Pewsey (Fig. 2). In the intervening area, which includes the whole of Salisbury Plain and the site of Stonehenge, Palaeocene sediments *in situ* are absent except for a possible outlier on the summit of Sidbury Hill, some 20 km north and east of Salisbury and consisting of a shingle of well-rounded flint pebbles.

The Reading Beds probably once extended across the whole of this region. There is however good evidence (Green 1985) that in the area occupied by Salisbury Plain they had already been removed prior to the Middle Eocene and been replaced by sediments of Middle Eocene age. Small remnants of these Middle Eocene sediments are preserved on the summits of the Chalk on the western edge of Salisbury Plain, and in a large solution pipe in the Chalk at Clay Pit Hill, near Chitterne, about 12 km to the west of Stonehenge. Similar sediments are also present on the Chalk at Martinsell Hill, to the north of the Vale of Pewsey. The Middle Eocene age of these sediments is demonstrated by the composition of the pebble beds which matches closely the highly distinctive composition of the Agglestone Grit in the Middle Eocene of Dorset (Green 1985). The composition and sedimentology of the Middle Eocene outlier at Cley Hill, near Warminster on the western edge of Salisbury Plain, also suggest that the summit there, and neighbouring summits at a similar altitude are remnants of a Middle Eocene erosional surface (Green 1969). These summits rise above the general level of the Chalk summits in south Wiltshire, which themselves represent a polycyclic erosional surface of low relief that formed in the later part of the Tertiary period (Green 1974). The present river valleys cut deeply into this surface and are the product of dissection during the Quaternary. This history shows that the relief of Salisbury Plain has been reshaped repeatedly since the Palaeocene and that in consequence there is little likelihood that any sarsen stone will have survived in the immediate vicinity of Stonehenge at the time that its construction was undertaken.

The present-day distribution of sarsen stones in Wiltshire fully supports this interpretation of Tertiary landform development. The survey of sarsen stones in Wessex as a whole, initiated by the Society of Antiquaries (Bowen and Smith 1977), showed that in Wiltshire to the south of the Vale of Pewsey, sarsen stones in whatever condition of preservation are few in number and small in size. There is no record from south Wiltshire, apart from the stones at Stonehenge, of a sarsen with a long dimension greater than 5.0 m, and most of the recorded stones are very much smaller. In addition, apart from cobbles noted in river gravels, no numerous scatters of sarsen stone occur in south Wiltshire, and at only 11 sites were groups of even as many as two or three sarsens found together in circumstances adjudged to be undisturbed. At a further 28 sites single sarsens were recorded in apparently undisturbed situations. In south Wiltshire, sarsen is also rarely found incorporated in prehistoric structures (18 cases recorded), or used as a building material in the historic period (17 cases recorded). Where it has been put to use, in almost all cases only a few small stones are present.

The scarcity and meagre dimensions of the sarsen stones in south Wiltshire give no

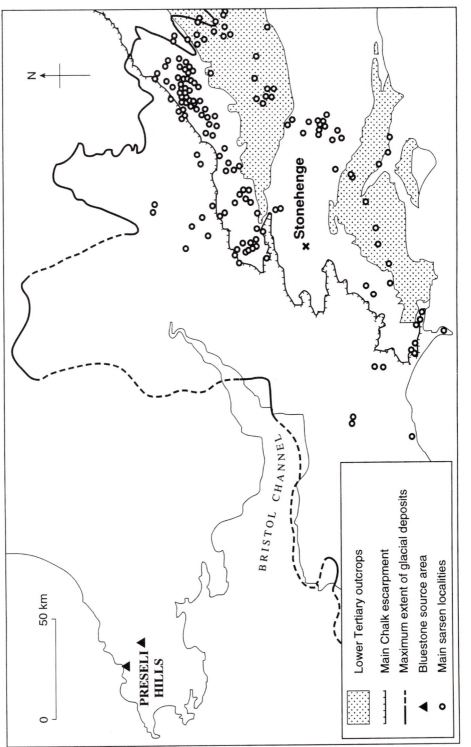

**Figure 2.** Stonehenge – the geological setting. Main sarsen localities based on Summerfield and Goudie (1980); extent of glacial deposits based on IGS Quaternary Map of the UK (1977) and Gilbertson and Hawkins (1978); bluestone source areas based on specific identifications in Thorpe *et al.* (1991).

indication of a likely source for the stones used in the construction of Stonehenge. The sarsen stones at Stonehenge are exceptional even in the context of areas where sarsens are numerous and large. Summerfield and Goudie (1980) indicate that in general the upper end of the size range for sarsens in southern England is represented by 'boulders with long axes of 4 to 5m'. Clark *et al.* (1967) found that 77 per cent of the boulders at Fyfield Down, near Marlborough, one of the best known and most extensive sarsen spreads, had long dimensions of less than 1.5 m. The largest stones at Stonehenge are those used in the central trilithon of the inner horseshoe. The surviving upright, stone 56, is over 9.0 m in total length and is estimated to weigh about 50 tonnes. The other sarsens in the horseshoe and circle are from 6.0 m to 7.0 m in length and each weigh approximately 25 tonnes. Sarsens of this size are nowhere common, and it seems probable that the Stonehenge examples were carefully selected in an area where sarsens were plentiful. The most likely source area is the Marlborough Downs, where many thousands of sarsens remain today, despite prolonged commercial exploitation in the nineteenth and early twentieth centuries. It is interesting to note however that in an exploratory study of the heavy mineralogy of sarsen fragments from Stonehenge, Howard (1982) found that the Stonehenge material differed from sarsen collected in the Marlborough area. A fuller investigation of sarsen mineralogy seems very desirable as a possible means of pinpointing the source area of the Stonehenge sarsens. If, as still seems most likely, the Stonehenge sarsens came from the Marlborough area, it follows that the builders who incorporated these very large stones into Stonehenge had the social organisation and technical facilities to move them over a distance of approximately 40 km.

*Bluestones*

Thirty-three bluestones remain visible at Stonehenge today. There are 28 examples of dolerite, all but three of these being the so-called spotted dolerite, four examples of rhyolite and one example of sandstone, namely the Altar Stone. A further ten bluestones are known to survive as stumps below the ground surface. Two of these are spotted dolerites, five are volcanic ashes, two are sandstones and one is a rhyolite. It has long been understood that all these stones are totally foreign to the Stonehenge area. Successive petrological investigations (Maskelyne 1878; Thomas 1923; Thorpe *et al.* 1991) have had the effect of narrowing down the source area from which these rocks can be shown to have come. The most recent work (Thorpe *et al.* 1991) involved the sampling of 15 of the dolerite monoliths and all four of the visible rhyolite monoliths. Thorpe *et al.* also analysed nine dolerite fragments, 13 rhyolite fragments and one sandstone fragment, all derived from previous excavations at Stonehenge.

All the dolerite samples were shown by Thorpe *et al.* (1991) to come from a small area in the eastern Preseli Hills, within a radius of not more than 1.5 km and possibly of as little as 0.5 km. The rhyolites were shown to have a rather more scattered provenance. Ten of the samples could be referred to an area lying within the same 1.5 km radius as the dolerite samples, two were referred to outcrops lying about 8 km from the edge of the dolerite distribution, and three were tentatively referred to outcrops further afield on the north coast of Pembrokeshire. One of the rhyolites remained unidentified and the last was referred in general terms to '? Pembrokeshire'. The sandstone sample was identified as a Palaeozoic sandstone from South Wales. It might be a fragment from a former sandstone monolith, now present only as a buried stump. It could not be matched with the Altar Stone, also a sandstone and the largest of the bluestones. The Altar Stone was not sampled by Thorpe *et al.* but a careful visual examination led them to suggest that it also comes from the Palaeozoic outcrop in South Wales, possibly from the Senni Beds in the Old Red Sandstone.

## Transport of the bluestones

The problem that remains to be discussed is whether these rocks from south-west Wales were brought to Stonehenge by the people who used them there, or were they found in prehistoric times on Salisbury Plain having reached there in the remoter past through some natural agency. The long distance transport of stone during the Neolithic period has long been recognised and the ritual or ceremonial significance of selected rock types in Neolithic society is now generally appreciated (Clarke, Cowie and Foxon 1985; Edmonds 1995). The widespread dispersal of stone artefacts from highly specific source outcrops is well attested. The use of stone brought from a distance in the fabric of ceremonial structures is relatively uncommon, but where it does occur it seems to be associated with particularly ambitious structures such as the elaborate passage tombs at Newgrange and Knowth in Ireland (Mitchell 1992) and the great menhir and ornamented dolmen at Locmariaquer in Brittany (Thomas 1923).

In relation to the bluestones of Stonehenge, the only plausible natural agency capable of transporting them from South Wales to Salisbury Plain would seem to be glacial ice, as proposed originally in connection with the Stonehenge stones by Judd (1902) and more recently claimed by Kellaway (1971, 1991) and Thorpe *et al.* (1991). In general, where ice has penetrated into an area, it brings with it rock debris from the outcrops over which it has passed, and this debris is left behind when the ice disappears. This rock debris commonly comprises material of all sizes up to and including substantial boulders. It may occur where it was left by the ice, as a spread or scatter of glacial material, or it may subsequently suffer erosion and be found incorporated into later sediments. The case for a glacial origin of any of the Welsh rocks on Salisbury Plain is totally unsupported either by the character of the bluestones themselves or by the Quaternary geology of the area. In the following paragraphs, the evidence on Salisbury Plain is reviewed and certain key problems are re-examined.

*Limited diversity of bluestone rock types*

An ice sheet advancing from the Irish Sea basin, across South Wales and into southern England would cross the outcrop of a great variety of durable rock types, which ought therefore to be represented in any glacial deposit on Salisbury Plain. The Stonehenge bluestones display no such variety. Their detailed petrology shows that they come from a small area in south-west Wales.

*Absence of glacial deposits on Salisbury Plain*

No one has ever claimed to recognise glacial deposits *in situ* on Salisbury Plain, and no boulder, petrologically similar to any of the bluestones of Stonehenge has ever been recorded in a natural context anywhere south or east of the Bristol Channel. It has been suggested however (Bartenstein and Fletcher 1987; Thorpe *et al.* 1991) that the present-day absence of rocks on Salisbury Plain reflects the clearance of agricultural land in the late eighteenth and early nineteenth centuries and that before this clearance not only sarsen but also volcanic rocks were present as boulders scattered over the surface of the Plain. The sole basis for this suggestion appears to be an account of Salisbury Plain written by the French geologist De Luc (1811) following visits to the area between 1777 and 1809. The suggestion that volcanic rocks were to be seen on Salisbury Plain in the late eighteenth century is obviously highly significant. However in a careful reading of De Luc it is clear that the reference to volcanic rocks in the passage describing Salisbury Plain (De Luc 1811, vol. III, 461) relates not to field observations on Salisbury Plain but is a reference to superficial geological deposits described by Playfair in the Midland counties of England 'beginning from about Worcester and Birmingham and proceeding north-east through Warwickshire, Leicestershire, Nottinghamshire, as far as the south of Yorkshire' (De Luc 1811, vol. III, 463). The absence of volcanic rocks from Salisbury Plain in the eighteenth century is in fact perfectly evident from the records of those who were best acquainted with Stonehenge and Salisbury Plain at that time. Both Stukeley and Cunnington recognised that the bluestones at Stonehenge had come from distant source areas. Had volcanic rocks been present in any sort of natural context on Salisbury Plain in the eighteenth century, such careful observers would undoubtedly have recognised the possibility of a local source for the volcanic material.

*The Bowls Barrow bluestone*

In an archaeological context and away from the source area in South Wales, the only example of a substantial bluestone outside the Stonehenge setting is a large boulder of spotted dolerite, now in Salisbury Museum, which is currently regarded (Cunnington 1924) as having been found by William Cunnington, together with a quantity of sarsen boulders, during an excavation of Bowls Barrow near Heytesbury on Salisbury Plain in 1801.

Bowls Barrow is a long barrow and appears therefore to represent a cultural tradition that flourished several hundred years before the earliest recognised appearance of the blue-stones at Stonehenge. If the accepted provenance of this stone is correct, then the Bowls Barrow spotted dolerite is either of glacial origin, or it indicates a cultural link between South Wales and Wiltshire that pre-dates the incorporation of the bluestones into Stonehenge. However, there is an element of doubt regarding the provenance of the dolerite boulder now in Salisbury Museum. The documentary record is less than completely satisfactory.

The stone in Salisbury Museum came to light in the 1920s in the grounds of Heytesbury House as the result of enquiries being made at that time by B.H. Cunnington (1924), the great-grandson of William Cunnington. These enquiries, which included corre-spondence with the Hon. Mrs Hamersley who had lived at Heytesbury House for many years during the nineteenth century, demonstrated two significant facts about the stone. Firstly, the stone had been in the grounds of Heytesbury House since before 1860; and secondly, the stone was known to the household at Heytesbury House as 'The Stonehenge Stone'.

That the stone discovered in the grounds of Heytesbury House in the 1920s might be a stone found by William Cunnington in Bowls Barrow in 1801 has been inferred on the basis of two pieces of evidence. Firstly, William Cunnington lived in Heytesbury in a house only a few hundred yards from the place where the stone was found in the grounds of Heytesbury House. Secondly, there is Cunnington family correspondence which has a bearing on the facts (Cunnington 1924). On 18th July 1801, William Cunnington wrote to his patron H.P. Wyndham of Salisbury. The letter comes down to us in the form of a copy made at the time of writing by Cunnington's daughter Elizabeth. Cunnington describes the excavation at Bowls Barrow. He reports that the core of the barrow consisted of 'a ridge of large sarcen (*sic*) stones'. There is a note at this point written on this copy of the letter, in Cunnington's own hand, 'the stones are about 28lbs to 200lbs weight'. The letter continues, 'The stones that composed so large a part of this ridge over the bodies are of the same species as the very large stones at Stonehenge.' At this point there is a further footnote to the manuscript in Cunnington's own hand, 'Since writing the above I discovered amongst them the Blue hard stone ye same as the upright stones in ye inner Circle at Stonehenge.' The letter then goes on to describe sarsen stones in general, 'They are often found just under the turf in the vallies in our Downs. They have the appearance of very old landmarks. I have brought away ten to my house.'

There are several points of particular interest in this copy of Cunnington's letter. Firstly, this letter contains the only reference in Cunnington's papers and publications to the discovery of bluestone at Bowls Barrow, despite the obvious potential significance in terms of linking the construction of Stonehenge to the people whose burial rites included inhumation in long barrows. Secondly, Cunnington's note about the discovery of blue-stone at Bowls Barrow is related within the letter to his account of discovering a core of large stones within the barrow. It is not related to his record of bringing ten stones to his house in Heytesbury. It seems unlikely that he should have selected stones to bring away to his house and not noticed that one of them was a bluestone. His note says nothing about the size or form of the bluestone he discovered at Bowls Barrow. Thirdly, Cunnington's note on the weights of individual stones forming the core of Bowls Barrow indicates a range from 28 lb. to 200 lb. (12.7–90.8 kg). The bluestone in Salisbury Museum, on the basis of its dimensions and the specific gravity of the minerals comprising dolerite, must weigh at least 300 kg and possibly as much as 400 kg. Is it likely that Cunnington would not have noted either on his letter to Wyndham, or elsewhere, the exceptionally large size of the bluestone had it come from Bowls Barrow?

Thus we have no record from Cunnington's own time that a boulder of bluestone weighing over 500 lb. was found in Bowls Barrow, let alone brought away to Heytesbury. While all we know about the bluestone now in Salisbury Museum is that it was in the grounds of Heytesbury House before 1860, and that it was known there as 'The Stonehenge Stone'. There must therefore be at least some doubt about the provenance of the bluestone in Salisbury Museum. Is it in fact a stone from Stonehenge brought to Heytesbury House at some unknown time in the past, prior to 1860? B.H. Cunnington (1924) believed that 'it has certainly been dressed on its faces and is not a rough block as quarried'. Its dimensions and shape are consistent with it having been part of a stone in the bluestone horseshoe at Stonehenge and this is a possibility that could be explored more fully.

William Cunnington's tantalising record of finding bluestone in Bowls Barrow cannot be dismissed but is less problematic if his find was of a relatively small piece or pieces. His account does not indicate an exact rock type, which may therefore have been either dolerite or rhyolite. In either case, implements using these materials are known from the Early Neolithic onward and finds of such material in Early Neolithic contexts either as artefacts or even as raw material (Edmonds 1995) are therefore possible.

One further item of documentary interest is a letter written by William Cunnington's grand-daughter, Elizabeth, in 1864, in which she describes the garden of her grandfather's house in Heytesbury and recalls that 'a circle of blocks of stone from Boles Barrow near Imber was placed round a weeping ash at the end of the lawn'. Thus there is confirmation of the record in her grandfather's correspondence that stones were indeed brought from Bowls Barrow to Heytesbury. A search in the 1920s by B.H. Cunnington in the garden of William Cunnington's house at Heytesbury produced only three sarsen stones.

*Quaternary terrace gravels*

Not only is there no evidence of glacial deposits *in situ* on Salisbury Plain, there is no trace of glacially-derived material in the Quaternary deposits of the rivers draining the area. Around Salisbury and in the valley of the river Avon to the south, there are river terraces representing stages of valley development from the earliest Quaternary to the present day (Clarke and Green 1987). If glacial ice brought far-travelled rocks into the catchments of these rivers at any time during the Quaternary, it seems certain that examples of those rocks will be present in the terrace sediments.

In a study (Green 1973) of over 50,000 pebbles from 28 sites, representing at least seven separate stages within the terrace succession, not one pebble was found that could not have come from existing pre-Quaternary outcrops within the present-day catchments of the rivers. The bulk of the material is either flint from the Chalk or chert from the Upper Greensand. The small suite of other durable rock types, mainly quartz, can be matched in the Middle Eocene sediments, described above, that survive as small outliers on Salisbury Plain.

This situation is very different from the one that prevails in the terrace sediments of rivers where the catchment is known to have been glaciated. It is now widely accepted that the catchment of the river Thames was glaciated in the pre-Anglian Pleistocene and that rock types in pre-Anglian terrace gravels which are foreign to the present-day catchment of the river are of glacial derivation. Such rock types may form as much as 50 per cent of the 11.2 mm to 16.0 mm fraction of pre-Anglian gravels of the Thames, and in general form between 30 and 45 per cent of the total in this size fraction (Green *et al.* 1982).

## Conclusion

The geological and geomorphological arguments outlined in this paper show as conclusively as the present evidence permits that the bluestones found at Stonehenge were not brought to Salisbury Plain by glacial ice. It follows that they were carried there by the people who incorporated them into Stonehenge. In some respects this appears a less challenging undertaking than the transport of the sarsens from the Marlborough Downs. Although the distance is greater and a sea voyage has been deemed likely (Atkinson 1979), the bluestones are substantially smaller than the sarsens and their transportation would seem to be well within the capabilities of societies that could contemplate the technical and organisational achievements represented by such monuments as Silbury Hill and Avebury.

## References

ATKINSON, R.J.C. 1979: *Stonehenge: archaeology and interpretation* (Harmondsworth).

BARTENSTEIN, H. and FLETCHER, B.N. 1987: The stones of Stonehenge – An ancient observation on their geological and archaeological history. *Zeitschrift fur deutsche geologische Gesellschaft* 138, 23–32.

BOWEN, H.C. and SMITH, I.F. 1977: Sarsen stones in Wessex: the Society's first investigations in the Evolution of the Landscape Project. *Antiq. J.* 57, 185–96.

CHIPPINDALE, C. 1983: *Stonehenge complete* (London).

CLARK, M.J., LEWIN, J. and SMALL, R.J. 1967: The sarsen stones of the Marlborough Downs and their geomorphological implications. *Southampton Res. Ser. Geogr.* 4, 3–40.

CLARKE, D.V., COWIE, T.G. and FOXON, A. 1985: *Symbols of power at the time of Stonehenge* (Edinburgh).

CLARKE, M.R. and GREEN, C.P. 1987: The Pleistocene terraces of the Bournemouth-Fordingbridge area. In Barber, K.E. (ed.), *Wessex and the Isle of Wight, Field Guide* (Cambridge, Quaternary Research Association).

CUNNINGTON, B.H. 1924: The 'Blue Stone' from Boles Barrow. *Wiltshire Archaeol. Natur. Hist. Mag.* 42, 431–7.

CURRY, D. 1992: Tertiary. In Duff, P.McL.D. and Smith, A.J. (eds), *Geology of England and Wales* (London, The Geological Society).

DE LUC, J.A. 1811: *Geological Travels. Volume III. Travels in England* (London).

EDMONDS, M. 1995: *Stone tools and society* (London).

GILBERTSON, D.D. and HAWKINS, A.B. 1978: The Pleistocene succession at Kenn, Somerset. *Bull. Geol. Survey Great Britain* No. 66, 1–41.

GOWLAND, W. 1902: Recent excavations at Stonehenge. *Archaeologia* 58, 37–105.

GREEN, C.P. 1969: An Early Tertiary surface in Wiltshire. *Trans. Inst. Brit. Geogr.* 47, 61–72.

GREEN, C.P. 1973: Pleistocene river gravels and the Stonehenge problem. *Nature* 243, 214–16.

GREEN, C.P. 1974: The summit surface on the Wessex Chalk. In Brown, E.H. and Waters, R.S. (eds), Progress in Geomorphology. *Inst. Brit. Geogr. Spec. Publ.* 7, 127–38.

GREEN, C.P. 1985: Pre-Quaternary weathering residues, sediments and landform development: examples from southern Britain. In Richards, K.S., Arnett, R.R. and Ellis, S. (eds), *Geomorphology and soils* (London).

GREEN, C.P., MCGREGOR, D.F.M. and EVANS, A.H. 1982: Development of the Thames drainage system in Early and Middle Pleistocene times. *Geol. Mag.* 119, 281–90.

HAWLEY, W. 1921: The excavations at Stonehenge. *Antiq. J.* 1, 19–39.

HAWLEY, W. 1922: Second report on the excavations at Stonehenge. *Antiq. J.* 2, 36–51.

HAWLEY, W. 1923: Third report on the excavations at Stonehenge. *Antiq. J.* 3, 13–20.

HAWLEY, W. 1924: Fourth report on the excavations at Stonehenge. *Antiq. J.* 4, 30–9.

HAWLEY, W. 1925: Report on the excavations at Stonehenge during the season of 1923. *Antiq. J.* 5, 21–50.

HAWLEY, W. 1926: Report on the excavations at Stonehenge during the season of 1924. *Antiq. J.* 6, 1–25.

HAWLEY, W. 1928: Report on the excavations at Stonehenge during 1925 and 1926. *Antiq. J.* 8, 149–76.

HOWARD, H. 1982: A petrological study of the rock specimens from excavations at Stonehenge, 1979–1980. In Pitts, M.W. 1982, 104–24.

JENKINS, G. and JENKINS, J. 1993: The Stonehenge 'bluestones' enigma: how to test the glacial hypothesis. *Geol. Today* 9(3), 87.

JENKINS, G., JENKINS, J. and WILLIAMS-THORPE, O. 1994: de Luc's Salisbury Plain in 1780 and 1810, and the rocks of Stonehenge. *Geol. Today* 10(3), 95–6.

JUDD, J.W. 1902: Note on the nature and origin of the rock fragments found in the excavations made at Stonehenge by Mr Gowland in 1901. In Gowland, W. 1902, 106–18.

KELLAWAY, G.A. 1971: Glaciation and the stones of Stonehenge. *Nature* 232, 30–5.

KELLAWAY, G.A. (ed.) 1991: *The Hot Springs of Bath* (Bath).

MASKELYNE, N.S. 1878: Stonehenge: the petrology of its stones. *Wiltshire Archaeol. Natur. Hist. Mag.* 17, 147–60.

MITCHELL, F. 1992: Notes on some non-local cobbles at the entrance to the passage-graves at Newgrange and Knowth, county Meath. *J. Roy. Soc. Antiq.* 122, 128–45.

PITTS, M.W. 1982: On the road to Stonehenge: report on investigations beside the A344 in 1968, 1979 and 1980. *Proc. Prehist. Soc.* 48, 75–132.

SUMMERFIELD, M.A. and GOUDIE, A.S. 1980: The sarsens of southern England: their palaeoenvironmental interpretation with reference to other silcretes. In Jones, D.K.C. (ed.), *The shaping of southern England* (London).

THOMAS, H.H. 1923: The source of the stones of Stonehenge. *Antiq. J.* 3, 239–60.

THORPE, R.S., WILLIAMS-THORPE, O., JENKINS, D.G. and WATSON, J.S. 1991: The geological sources and transport of the bluestones of Stonehenge. *Proc. Prehist. Soc.* 57, 103–57.

WHALLEY, W.B. and CHARTRES, C.J. 1977: Preliminary observations on the origin and sedimentological nature of sarsen stones. *Geologie en Mijnbouw* 55, 68–72.

*Proceedings of the British Academy,* **92**, 271–314

# Transport of the
# Stonehenge Bluestones:
# Testing the Glacial Hypothesis

## J. D. SCOURSE

## Introduction

IN 1923 THOMAS PUBLISHED his seminal paper on the provenance of the Stonehenge 'bluestones' and, in unequivocally attributing the majority of them to source outcrops in the Preseli Hills of Pembrokeshire, highlighted the improbability that the stones could have been transported to Salisbury Plain by ice (Fig. 1), an hypothesis suggested earlier by Judd (1902). This led Thomas to invoke human transport, either overland or by a combined sea/overland route, from Preseli to Stonehenge, an explanation which has subsequently become widely accepted by both the archaeological and geological fraternities: 'There can be no question of the stones having been carried even part of the way towards southern England by ice during the Pleistocene period, and their appearance at Stonehenge can only be explained as the result of deliberate transport by man' (Atkinson 1979, 105).

In 1971, however, Kellaway highlighted a body of evidence pertaining to possible glaciation of southern England unavailable to Thomas in the 1920s, and in doing so explicitly supported Judd's earlier contention that the Stonehenge 'bluestones' were glacial clasts transported from Preseli by ice and subsequently used by prehistoric man in the construction of the monolith. In a series of later papers, Kellaway (Kellaway *et al.* 1971, 1975; Hawkins and Kellaway 1971) developed this model further, claiming extensive glaciation of not only southern England, but also of the Celtic Sea and English Channel. Despite widespread criticism of this model in the 1970s, Kellaway has recently revived the glacial hypothesis (1991a, 1991b), albeit in slightly altered form, and his earlier ideas have been invoked by another group advocating glacial transport (Thorpe *et al.* 1991). The glacial hypothesis is therefore very far from having been convincingly falsified, and for a significant minority it remains the favoured explanation: 'There is infinitely more evidence to

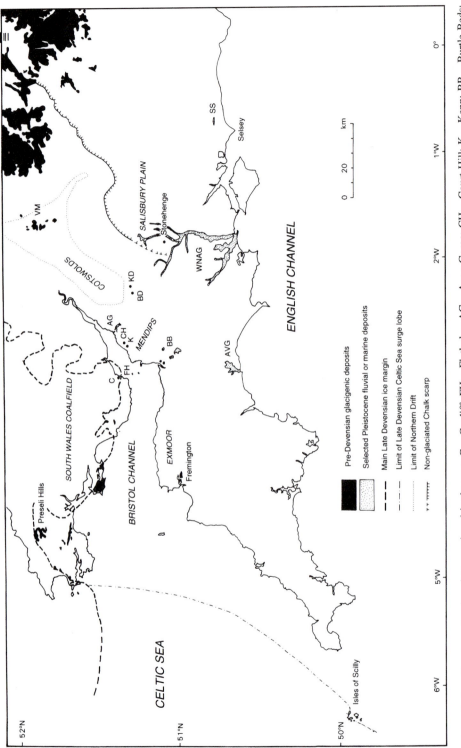

**Figure 1.** Location map showing sites mentioned in the text. C – Cardiff; FH – Flatholm; AG – Avon Gorge; CH – Court Hill; K – Kenn; BB – Burtle Beds; AVG – Axe Valley gravels; BD – Bathampton Down; KG – Kings Down; WNAG – Wylye, Nadder and Avon gravels; SS – Slindon Sands; VM – Vale of Moreton.

support the theory of ice transport than there is support for the great contemporary myth of long-distance haulage by the Beaker people' (John 1984, 38).

## The Stonehenge 'bluestones' and their source

'Bluestone' is a 'bag' term to describe all the non-local rock lithologies found in and around the stone settings at Stonehenge. The term is thought to have arisen as a means of distinguishing between the lighter-coloured sarsen 'greywethers' which have a demonstrably local origin as Tertiary silcrete (Thorpe *et al.* 1991), and the more far-travelled stones which generally have a darker appearance (Fig. 2). The major bluestones total in number around 80 (Atkinson 1979), but excavations since the early nineteenth century have recovered a very large number of bluestone fragments from in and around the site (Cunnington 1824; Maskelyne 1878; Judd 1902; Thomas 1923; Thorpe *et al.* 1991). It is now widely accepted, following the detailed petrological investigations of the larger bluestones and fragments by Judd (1902), Thomas (1921, 1923) and Thorpe *et al.* (1991), that four main lithologies are represented at the site.

The most common of these is a distinctive spotted dolerite (formerly termed 'diabase'), the 'spotting' representing white or light-coloured feldspar phenocrysts; some of the dolerites are, however, unspotted. Other igneous rocks include banded rhyolite/ignimbrite and some pyroclastic varieties, whilst the Altar Stone (Fig. 2) and one fragment (Thorpe *et al.* 1991) are pale green micaceous sandstone. Clearly it is critical that the sources of these lithologies can be located with some confidence as this informs any debate as to the means of their transport to Stonehenge.

Ramsey (in Ramsey *et al.* 1858) first suggested that some of the Stonehenge bluestones might derive from a source in the Lower Silurian of north Pembrokeshire, but he mentioned other possibilities including North Wales. Though Judd (1902) provided accurate petrological descriptions of the rock types represented, he remained agnostic as to any possible source. Thomas (1921, 1923) was the first to identify possible source outcrops with confidence. He attributed the pale green micaceous sandstone of the Altar Stone to the Old Red Sandstone of either the Senni Beds (Glamorgan) or the Cosheston Group (Pembrokeshire). He supported Ramsey's attribution of the spotted diabases to northern Pembrokeshire, and identified a source for the banded rhyolites at Carn Alw in the Preseli Hills. All three main bluestone lithologies he therefore attributed to Pembrokeshire, and all igneous varieties to a specific district at the eastern end of the Preseli Hills.

In their recent comprehensive petrological and geochemical analysis of the bluestone materials, Thorpe *et al.* (1991) have refined still further the provenance of the spotted dolerites to three sources in a small area in the eastern Preseli Hills (Fig. 3). They also attribute the rhyolites to four sources within the Preseli district and other (unidentified) locations in Pembrokeshire, and the Altar Stone and sandstone fragment to two locations within the Palaeozoic of south-west Wales. There is therefore strong evidence from all the petrological

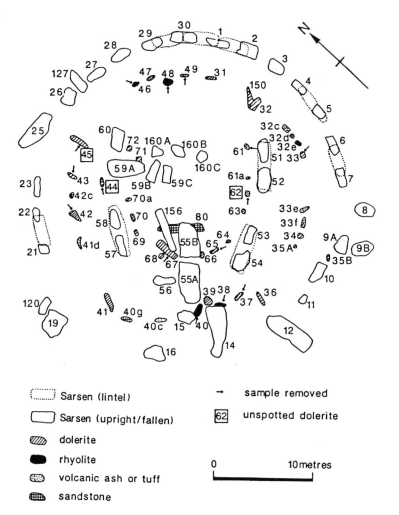

**Figure 2.** Plan of the central stone settings at Stonehenge from Thorpe *et al.* (1991, fig. 1), after Newall (1959), Chippindale (1987) and Atkinson (1979), showing the petrology of the stones and stone locations. All dolerites are spotted except stones 44, 45 and 62. The Altar Stone is number 80. Stone numbering follows Atkinson (1979) and Thorpe *et al.* (1991). (Copyright: the Prehistoric Society.)

investigations undertaken for a Preseli origin for the igneous bluestones, and a wider Pembrokeshire source for the sandstones and possibly some of the rhyolites. Though the banded rhyolites/ignimbrites could potentially come from a variety of other localities far from Pembrokeshire, the assemblage of bluestone lithologies can be found together within a relatively small area of south-west Wales lending further support to this as the likely source area. Apart from some further discussion on the provenance of the banded rhyolites/ignimbrites in relation to glacial flow lines (see below), for the remainder of this paper it will be assumed that Pembrokeshire, and specifically the Preseli Hills, is the bluestone source.

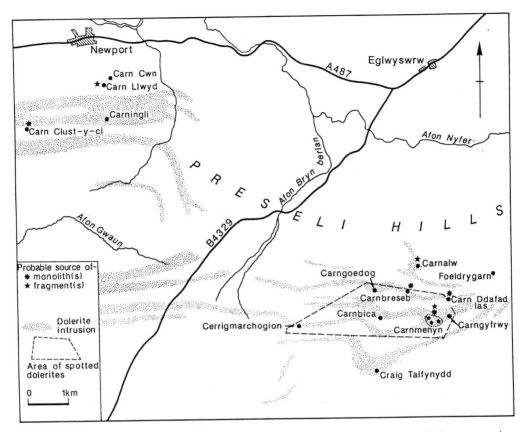

**Figure 3.** Map of the Preseli Hills showing location of important outcrops of spotted dolerites representing sources for the Stonehenge monoliths and fragments, from Thorpe *et al.* (1991, fig. 8). The three outcrops surrounded by a dotted line are all part of the Carnmenyn outcrop. Approximate extent of the dolerites after Evans (1945). Map base is after Evans (op. cit.) and Bevins *et al.* (1989). (Copyright: the Prehistoric Society.)

The purpose of this paper is to review critically the glacial hypothesis for the transport of the Stonehenge bluestones from their source in Preseli to Salisbury Plain. Despite the apparent intractability of this problem, the hypothesis can be tested with reference to existing published observational and modelling data from a variety of sources. To the glaciologist or glacial geologist faced with this problem there are four main questions requiring positive answers if the hypothesis is to remain unfalsified:

1   Are glaciers capable of transporting clasts of the mass of the Stonehenge bluestones over the 213 km required?

2   Do any undressed bluestone clasts demonstrate morphological and/or surface microwear features consistent with clasts from modern glacial environments?

3   Is there any stratigraphical and/or geomorphological evidence to support the contention that Salisbury Plain has been glaciated?

**4**   Are there other ice flow indicators between Preseli and Wiltshire consistent with this proposed flow trajectory, and, given the regional evidence for glaciation, is such a trajectory consistent with the physics of ice movement?

After reviewing the evidence cited in support of the glacial hypothesis, the paper will address each of these questions in turn, with particular attention given to the two most recent expositions of the glacial hypothesis (Thorpe *et al.* 1991; Kellaway 1991a, 1991b).

## The glacial hypothesis: a review

Judd (1902) was the first to suggest that the non-local (bluestone) lithologies found in and around Stonehenge might have been transported by ice to Salisbury Plain. Though he was not specific as to their sources, Judd was impressed by the diversity of lithologies represented, and suggested that prior to weathering on site this diversity had probably been greater: '. . . the "bluestones" now remaining at Stonehenge probably represent only the hardest and most durable of the materials employed, many stones of soft and fissile character having disappeared entirely, owing to the action of the weather and the assaults of the relic-mongers . . .' (op. cit., 115–16). This diverse assemblage suggested to him a similarity with glacial drifts in other districts, though he recognised that the 'southern limit of boulder clay' was usually placed by geologists 'well to the north of Wiltshire' (op. cit., 117). He cited the fact that scattered boulders often occur well to the south of this limit, and that the 'sheets of boulder clay which now cover so large a part of the country are merely relics of a formerly much more widely spread formation' (op. cit., 117). He claimed that the gravels of the rivers draining Salisbury Plain contain many foreign rocks derived from the formerly more widely distributed glacial deposits. Other foreign material he suggested had been removed for incorporation into more recent constructions.

Judd was also impressed by the copious bluestone fragments found in and around the Stonehenge site when compared with the sparse representation of the local sarsen material in the same contexts. This convinced him that the bluestones were dressed, and hence reduced in volume and mass, on site, and that this argues against the stones having been transported by man: 'The comparative paucity of fragments of sarsen-stone . . . points to the conclusion that these large monoliths were selected for their size and shape, and then rudely trimmed *at the spots where they were found*' (Judd's italics, p. 115). As for the bluestones, '. . . it is no less obvious that they were for the most part chipped into the required forms and dressed *near the place of their erection*' (Judd's italics, p. 115).

Many of the essential points raised by Judd in this first exposition of the glacial hypothesis are repeated in later versions. These include the diversity of the lithological assemblage, the suggestion of former extensive glaciation of the Wiltshire Downs now only represented by *remanié* boulders many of which have been removed since the construction of Stonehenge, and the glacial source for the far-travelled material contained in the river gravels draining the Wiltshire Downs. Subsequent versions also emphasise the quantity of bluestone fragments discovered on site, and draw the conclusion that the undressed bluestones are therefore unlikely to have been transported by man.

Thomas (1923) critically reviewed Judd's hypothesis and found it wanting: '... there is no evidence of glacial drift on Salisbury Plain as would of necessity have been left by any ice-sheet capable of transporting the masses of rock in question' (op. cit., 252). He argued that '... there is the clearest evidence that ... the ice-front lay only just south of the present coast-line of Pembrokeshire, and that ice as a solid mass never crossed the Bristol Channel to Devon and Cornwall ...' (op. cit., 252). He accepted that ice crossed Pembrokeshire in a south-easterly direction as a lobe of the Irish Sea ice-sheet but that '... the front of this ice-sheet never reached across or far up the Bristol Channel' (op. cit., 254). In thus rejecting the glacial hypothesis Thomas famously raised in detail possible mechanisms of human transport.

Thomas' arguments against the glacial hypothesis and in favour of human transport proved influential, and it was not until 1971 that the glacial hypothesis was revived by Kellaway. Immediately prior to publication of this paper, Kellaway had become aware of new evidence pertaining to the glaciation of southern England, in particular the discovery of impressive glacigenic sequences at Court Hill and Kenn near Clevedon in north Somerset during the construction of the M5 motorway (Hawkins and Kellaway 1971). Supported by other evidence from South Wales, these data led Kellaway (1971) to speculate that the bluestones were transported to Stonehenge during the 'Anglian' glaciation (Table 1) from Pembrokeshire in west-east flowing ice which entered the Somerset lowlands from the Bristol Channel and continued eastwards to Salisbury Plain (Fig. 4). He distinguished this from a later Wolstonian glaciation (Table 1) which was more limited in extent and represented by the new sites in and adjacent to the Somerset lowlands.

Apart from the glacigenic sequences exposed at Court Hill and Kenn near Clevedon, Hawkins and Kellaway (1971) also identified other evidence of glaciation, including possible glaciofluvial meltwater channels (Avon Gorge, Rickford Coombe, Limpley Stoke) and the occurrence of far-travelled pebbles on hilltops in the Bristol-Bath district (Bathampton Down, Kingsdown). These high-level gravels were interpreted as glacial in origin, and in another paper (Kellaway et al. 1971) the steepening and subsequent cambering of slopes in the same area were attributed to glacial erosion: '... the effect of glaciation has been to produce abnormally steep slopes either by direct glacial action or erosion by meltwater of rocks which may at some time have been frozen' (op. cit., 26).

In his 1971 paper Kellaway speculated that during the 'Anglian' the '... great flow of ice which passed over Pembrokeshire was constricted as it moved up channel, confined on the north by the high ground of the South Wales Coalfield, and on the south by Exmoor and the Brendon Hills' (op. cit., 30; Fig. 4). This glaciation was also said to be responsible for the deposition of the Plateau Gravel or Northern Drift of the Cotswolds and north Oxfordshire (Sandford 1926), an interpretation repeated in Kellaway et al. (1971):

**Table 1.** Summary of Quaternary stage names, ages and correlation with deep-sea oxygen isotope record. Adapted from Bridgland (1994)

| Age (in thousands of years) | UK stage names (NW European equivalents in parentheses) | $^{18}O$ stage | Climatic status |
|---|---|---|---|
| | Holocene or Flandrian | 1 | temperate |
| 10 | | | |
| | Late Devensian (Late Weichselian) | | |
| 18 —Last Glacial Maximum (LGM) | | 2 | cold |
| 26 | Middle Devensian (Middle Weichselian) | 3/4 | boreal-cold |
| 71 | Early Devensian (Early Weichselian) | 5a–5d | boreal-cold |
| 122 | Ipswichian (Eemian) | 5e | temperate |
| 128 | ?Wolstonian (late Saalian) | 6 | cold |
| 186 | | 7 | temperate |
| 245 | ?Wolstonian (mid Saalian) | 8 | cold |
| 303 | | 9 | temperate |
| 339 | ?Wolstonian (early Saalian) | 10 | cold |
| | Hoxnian (Holsteinian) | 11 | temperate |
| 423 | Anglian (Elsterian) | 12 | cold |
| 478 | Cromerian Complex | 13–21 | |

during the Anglian glaciation the Northern Drift '... ice-sheets may have made contact with or diverted other masses of ice moving eastward from Wales and the Bristol Channel' (op. cit., 25). They suggested that at the maximum of the glaciation '... the great Northern Drift ice-sheets extended across Oxfordshire towards the Chilterns and to the south-west across Berkshire as far as the Chalk escarpment' (op. cit., 25). They review the Chalky Boulder Clay found in the Vale of Moreton (Fig. 1; Bishop 1958) and attribute this, and associated glaciofluvial gravels and glaciolacustrine sediments, to the same event. In this paper Kellaway *et al.* (1971) therefore clearly suggest confluence of the 'Northern Drift

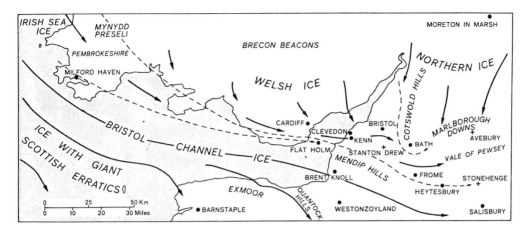

**Figure 4.** Flow lines of 'Anglian' ice as suggested by Kellaway (1971, fig. 2). Kellaway (1971) suggests that Exmoor might have formed a small centre of ice accumulation, and that the Mendip and Cotswold Hills were overridden at the height of the glaciation. (Reprinted with permission from *Nature*, copyright (1971) Macmillan Magazines Ltd.)

ice-sheet' with a glacier moving eastwards from the Bristol Channel towards Salisbury Plain during the Anglian.

In the 1971 paper Kellaway suggested that the Anglian glaciation also involved extensive glaciation of the Celtic Sea and English Channel causing the emplacement of large erratic boulders on the shore platform of Cornwall, Devon and the Channel coast and the deposition of the Burtle Beds of the Somerset lowlands and the Slindon Sands of Sussex (Fig. 1). This thesis was developed in a later paper (Kellaway *et al.* 1975) in which the flat featureless seabed abutted by clifflines, palaeovalley systems and enclosed deeps of the English Channel were attributed to glacial erosion, though in this review a 'Saale' age was preferred for this extensive glaciation (Table 1). During this event morainic material was said to be deposited at Selsey which caused the impounding of 'Lake Solent', and '... the great mass of ice passed over the Pembrokeshire uplands' and '... being deflected by Exmoor turned eastwards up the Bristol Channel, filled the Somerset lowlands, burying all but the highest parts of the Mendips and filling the gaps leading southwards to the Hampshire Basin and the English Channel coast' (op. cit., 205).

This series of papers therefore postulated extensive Pleistocene glaciation of southern England, the Celtic Sea and the English Channel, including the transport of the Stonehenge bluestones from Pembrokeshire to Salisbury Plain. Though Kellaway's thesis received some limited support from Briggs (1976a, 1976b, 1977), mainly concerning the former distribution of erratics, Kellaway's views were widely criticised during the 1970s, and Briggs' support was itself refuted (Shotton 1976). Green (1973) tested the glacial hypothesis by examining the lithology of Pleistocene gravels in the Wylye, Nadder and Avon valleys (Fig. 1). If Salisbury Plain had been glaciated then these rivers would have carried the outwash from the glaciers. In 1902 Judd had claimed evidence to support this case. In fact these gravels are composed of materials derived from outcrops within the existing catchments (Chalk flint, Upper Greensand chert and sandstone). Green found small quantities of other ultimately far-travelled lithologies (vein quartz, quartzites, grits, cherts) but these are all present in local Tertiary formations. Unlike the terrace gravels of the undoubtedly glaciated Thames basin, at no point is there a sudden influx of relatively large far-travelled material. Green's conclusion was therefore unequivocal: 'The complete lack of glacially derived material in the Pleistocene river gravels of the Wylye, Nadder and Avon seem to show conclusively that the "Anglian" ice never invaded the basins of these rivers, and that the outwash of the Wolstonian ice was never tributary to them. "Anglian" ice cannot therefore be invoked to explain the presence of large and medium sized Welsh rocks . . . at Stonehenge . . . The problem of the introduction of these rocks to this area remains unsolved' (op. cit., 216).

Aside from the specific instance of Stonehenge, Kellaway's wider views on extensive glaciation, particularly of the English Channel (Kellaway *et al.* 1975), were also criticised. Kidson and Bowen (1976) made the point that 'foreign' boulders are not always evidence of glaciation. Some on the Channel coast have turned out in fact to be very local (Reid 1892) whilst other undoubtedly far-travelled boulders can be attributed to sea-ice or icebergs, or even to ships' ballast. They argue that there are no glacigenic sediments to support the geomorphological interpretation of former ice, as the Slindon Sands or the gravels of the Hampshire Basin are demonstrably not glaciofluvial in origin. Kidson and Bowen conclude: 'In our view all the facts adduced in favour of glaciation are capable of alternative interpretation. Though they may seem to have some substance collectively, all can be dismissed when examined individually, for deposits may be ambiguous indicators of process and different processes may produce similar landforms' (op. cit., 8).

The essence of Kellaway's (1971) argument, and the criticisms of it during the 1970s, remain relevant because in the most recent investigation of this problem by Thorpe *et al.* (1991) this argument is again given prominence. These authors address the objections originally raised against the glacial hypothesis by Thomas (1923), and argue that these objections are now weaker in the light of subsequent glaciological observations and recent evidence pertaining to glaciation of the critical area between Pembrokeshire and Wiltshire; much of this latter evidence derives directly from the earlier papers of Kellaway. They also emphasise the significance of some early observations by de Luc (1811) concerning the clearance of scattered boulders from Salisbury Plain between 1780 and 1805 (Bartenstein and Fletcher 1987) which they claim supports Judd's (1902) contention of a former widespread cover of glacially transported material across the Wiltshire Downs.

Kellaway has himself recently restated his conviction that the bluestones were transported by ice, but there are significant differences between this new synthesis (1991a, 1991b) and his earlier views. Rather than invoking ingress of ice from the Bristol Channel during the 'Anglian', he now prefers possible transport from a more northerly direction during a Pliocene glaciation at 2.47Ma. He questions the exclusively south-west Welsh origin for the material and raises the possibility of sources from further north in Wales; particular prominence is accordingly given to a discussion of a boulder of ignimbrite which is similar to Ordovician rocks from Snowdonia. His earlier view that the high-level gravels at Bathampton and Kingsdown (Hawkins and Kellaway 1971) are glacial in origin he reinterprets as Pliocene fluvial or glaciofluvial gravels of the 'Southampton River' (= Solent river; Gibbard and Allen 1994) flowing south-south-eastwards from head-waters in Wales: '. . . if they [the high-level gravels] have not been glacially transported and deposited (and there is no evidence for this), then they are almost certainly of fluvioglacial or fluviatile origin . . . No ice scratched rocks have been found' (Kellaway 1991a, 225). Meltwater associated with the Pliocene glacial event was '. . . localized along a route roughly coinciding with the palaeovalley of the Southampton River and this would account for the restriction of Welsh rocks to the Heytesbury-Stonehenge belt' (Kellaway 1991b, 255; Fig. 5). He therefore interprets the bluestones as having been transported down the Solent river in a glaciofluvial context: 'We do not know to what extent the Pliocene glaciation and the penetration of ice carrying the bluestones of Stonehenge affected its [the Solent River] development, but it may well have contributed much melt-water during deglaciation. Much depends on the interpretation of the Stonehenge erratics in the sense that though morainic in origin, they may have been carried for some consid-erable distance downstream in floating ice' (Kellaway 1991a, 228).

There are therefore significant differences between these two most recent expositions of the glacial hypothesis. Thorpe *et al.* (1991) argue for derivation from Pembrokeshire in a Pleistocene west-east ice flow which draws heavily on Kellaway's earlier ideas (1971; Kellaway *et al.* 1975), whilst Kellaway (1991a, 1991b) questions the Pembrokeshire source and prefers a more northerly glaciation during the Pliocene with the bluestones them-selves representing glaciofluvially or river ice transported clasts. Thorpe *et al.* (1991) have themselves drawn this distinction; they comment that a more northerly source is '. . . inconsistent with the evidence for derivation of Stonehenge bluestone monoliths from Preseli and we propose that these were transported by glacial action through the Bristol Channel' (op. cit., 147–8). Also implicit in the two discussions is a difference in the mode of glacial transport, Thorpe *et al.* (1991) preferring transport of the bluestones as 'free boulders' on the surface of the ice (supraglacial transport) whereas Kellaway (1991a, 1991b) emphasises the significance of striations and faceted surfaces which would imply subglacial abrasion.

## Testing the glacial hypothesis

*Entrainment and transport of large boulders by glaciers*

The largest of the bluestone boulders at Stonehenge has a weight of the order of four tons (Atkinson 1979). There are no natural agencies capable of transporting boulders of this size over the distances required in a single trajectory other than by glacier.

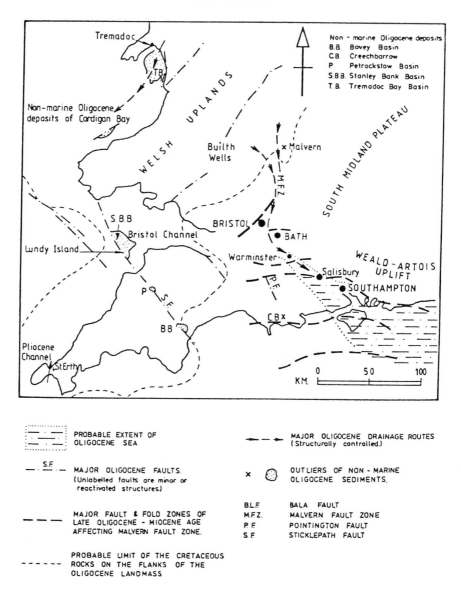

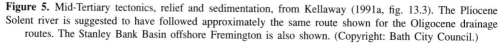

**Figure 5.** Mid-Tertiary tectonics, relief and sedimentation, from Kellaway (1991a, fig. 13.3). The Pliocene Solent river is suggested to have followed approximately the same route shown for the Oligocene drainage routes. The Stanley Bank Basin offshore Fremington is also shown. (Copyright: Bath City Council.)

Gravity-driven mass movements on slopes and even flood flows in high energy river channels are capable of entraining and transporting particles of this mass but only over very short distances and always exclusively downslope. Thorpe *et al.* (1991) suggest supraglacial entrainment and transport for the Stonehenge bluestones. Citing Flint (1955) they argue that 'free boulders' derived from nunataks may have dimensions measured in tens of metres and that they can be found tens of kilometres from source. They argue that the Stonehenge bluestones were derived by mass movements from bedrock sources forming nunataks in the Preseli district, and then transported supraglacially the entire distance from Pembrokeshire to Salisbury Plain.

There are many analogous situations described in the glacial geological literature. Glaciers are known to be able to transport individual boulders up to $10^5$ tonnes in weight over thousands of kilometres, often irrespective of topographic constraints. Both the mass and trajectory distance of such erratics are orders of magnitude greater than the Stonehenge case. One of the most famous of all glacial erratics is the Big Rock of Okotoks in Alberta, Canada. This large quartzite mass of some 120,000 tonnes is derived from the Jasper area from the west side of the North American continental divide. It is believed to have been dumped from an ice-free peak (nunatak) onto the surface of the Cordilleran ice cap and transported supraglacially east to the foothills near Calgary as part of the Foothills Erratic Train (Stalker 1976). The mode of entrainment and transport of this erratic, and its trajectory over significant topographic features, is similar to that suggested by Thorpe *et al.* (1991) for the emplacement of the Stonehenge bluestones. Though there is a net downs-lope gradient of some 250 m between the Preseli source, at around 350 m OD, and Stonehenge, at 102 m OD, the proposed route (Fig. 4) would involve ice flow over topographic features as low as –50 m OD in the Bristol Channel and up to 320 m OD in the Mendips and uplands of north Somerset.

In warm-based situations, where the basal ice is at the pressure melting point, glaciers move by basal sliding and internal deformation (Fig. 6). Where the basal ice is below the pressure melting point it is frozen to the bed and basal sliding is inhibited; in this situation the ice moves by internal deformation alone (Paterson 1981). Internal deformation, or strain ($\dot{\varepsilon}_s$) at a point within the glacier is determined by shear stress ($\tau$) and a constant related to temperature (A; Glen Flow Law; Glen 1955):

$$\dot{\varepsilon}_s = A\,\tau^n \tag{1}$$

where n is a constant (creep exponent). Strain increases as shear stress and temperature increase. The basal shear stress ($\tau_b$) in turn is described by:

$$\tau_b = \rho_i\,g\,h\,\sin\alpha_s \tag{2}$$

where h is ice thickness, $\alpha_s$ is the gradient of the ice surface, $\rho_i$ is the density of ice and g is gravitational acceleration (Fig. 6). This equation (2) is sometimes known as the 'driving stress' equation (Drewry 1986) since it describes the forces required to induce motion by strain deformation in a glacier. Shear stress increases as ice thickness and gradient increase, so ice flow is controlled not by topographic constraints at the bed but by the slope of the ice surface. It follows that, in situations where indicator erratics have been transported by ice across topographic obstacles, the maximum slope of the ice surface was discordant with bed topography. There are therefore theoretical grounds to explain

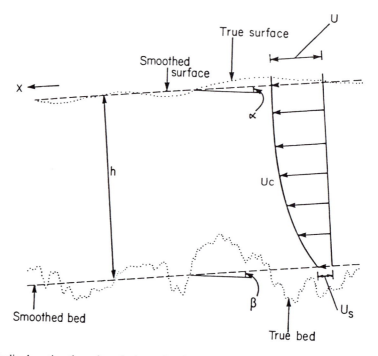

**Figure 6.** Idealised section through a glacier or ice-sheet, from Drewry (1986, fig. 1.6). Actual ice and bed surfaces are shown dotted whilst the parallel slab approximation is shown dashed (with slopes α and β). A velocity profile is illustrated defining total surface velocity (U), creep ($U_c$) and basal sliding ($U_s$). Ice thickness is given by h. (Copyright: Edward Arnold, London.)

the transport of the bluestone erratics over the topographic obstacles posed by the Preseli to Wiltshire route assuming the ice surface was close to the elevation of the source outcrops.

The upper limit on the size of a supraglacial boulder capable of being transported by a glacier is imposed by the size (areal extent, thickness) and velocity of the glacier in relation to the mass of the boulder. The addition of a large superincumbent mass to the ice load will increase normal stress which will increase shear stress ($\tau_b$) and thus internal deformation ($\varepsilon_s$). Whilst it is possible theoretically to define critical threshold mass for a given glacier, such situations in nature are not common because it is unusual for individual blocks to approach the critical threshold mass as single coherent boulders without first fracturing into smaller particle sizes. This reduction in particle size occurs during gravity-driven mass movements, such as rock-falls, as potentially unstable rock masses exceed the limiting equilibrium on exposed bedrock faces and move to the glacier surface below. Most modern observations of mass movements from nunataks onto glacier surfaces consist of aggregations of individual particles well below the critical threshold mass.

Such supraglacially-derived material is often very coarse and angular (e.g. Lawson 1979; Boulton 1978), the absence of finer material resulting from meltwater removal and lack of abrasion. Supraglacial diamicts are typically sandy, pebbly/bouldery muds of heterogeneous grainsize often enriched in weak lithologies and far-travelled material (Eyles 1983). The enrichment in weak lithologies is consistent with Judd's (1902) view that the main bluestone types represent only the most resistant representatives of a formerly much more diverse but differentially weathered assemblage.

The transport distances of erratics are dependent on the mode of entrainment and routeway, supraglacial, englacial or subglacial, followed by the particle during ice movement. The interpretation that the Stonehenge bluestones were transported supraglacially has an important glaciological implication which relates to transport. If sediments are added to a glacier surface in the accumulation area they will be rapidly buried in the ice and englacial transport will ensue (Fig. 6); if added in the ablation area they will tend to remain at the surface (Drewry 1986). This implies that the Preseli district was already coincident with the ablation area of the glacier concerned and therefore located towards the margin of the ice mass. In this case the equilibrium line altitude (ELA) must have been greater than 350 m, the elevation of the Preseli Hills.

In terms of the mode of entrainment and transport, the mass of the Stonehenge erratics and the transport distance, the situation envisaged by Thorpe *et al.* (1991) is consistent with glacial geological observations and glaciological theory, but such a model would imply entrainment and deposition within the ablation area of the glacier concerned.

*Surface microwear and particle shape*

It has been noted that supraglacially-derived and transported particles are often very angular. This contrasts markedly with subglacial clasts which are characteristically sub-angular to sub-rounded as a result of clast-clast and clast-bed abrasion in the often debris-rich basal ice (e.g. Lawson 1979; Fig. 8); such subglacially transported clasts are also characteristically striated and faceted as a result of abrasion, and often as a result assume overall 'bullet' or 'blunt-nosed' shapes. It is obviously difficult to compare the majority of the Stonehenge bluestones with such clast characteristics because any surface dressing will have removed any original surface microwear features and changed the overall shapes of boulders. However, there is a body of evidence pertaining to such characteristics from a few apparently undressed Stonehenge bluestones which demands analysis.

Thorpe *et al.* (1991) note that the question of how many of the bluestones have been dressed remains controversial, but that many appear unworked and some, including nos 46 (rhyolite), 47 and 31 (both spotted dolerites) '. . . have rounded shapes consistent with natural boulders' (op. cit., 105–7). Despite the lack of apparent dressing none of these existing boulders has been reported to have any characteristically glacial features. However, Kellaway (1991b) does refer to striated erratics having been excavated at Stonehenge: '. . . a few have been striated and were therefore regarded by some archaeologists as being of glacial origin' (op. cit., 267). Kellaway notes that at the time of Colonel Hawley's excavation at Stonehenge in the 1920s a number of igneous and

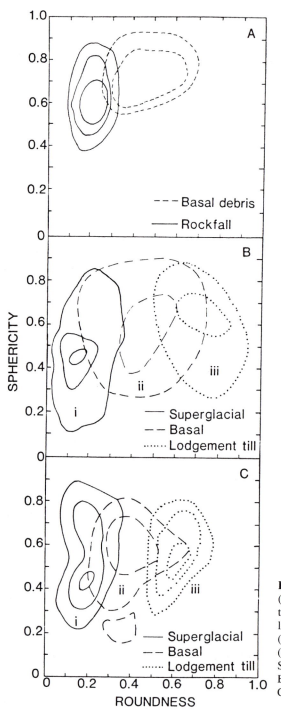

**Figure 8.** Roundness and sphericity of clasts (based on Krumbein's index) for material in transport in basal ice, supraglacial ice and in lodgement till, from Drewry (1986, fig. 7.13). (A) Samples from Breidamerjökull, Iceland (Boulton 1978). (B) Søre Buchananisen, Svalbard (Boulton 1978). (C) Grinnel Ice Cap, Baffin Island, Canada (Dowdeswell *et al.* 1985). Contours are at 5, 10 and 15% of data per 1% area. (Copyright: Edward Arnold, London.)

metamorphic rocks of Welsh origin were discovered: 'A few of these carried striations which appeared to be of glacial origin' (op. cit., 267). He draws attention to the discussion comments by Dale and Engleheart after Hawley's 1921 excavation report: '. . . one piece was striated, and he [Engleheart] thought they were all of glacial origin' (Engleheart 1921, 40). Thorpe *et al.* (1991) quote a letter written by Kellaway to the authors: 'In 1969–71 I came into contact with Mr R S Newall . . . who told me that during Col. Hawley's excavations in the early twenties he drew attention to the appearance of rocks resembling glacial erratics. Hawley would have none of it, but Newall preserved some of this material for nearly half a century, before passing it to me for consideration' (op. cit., 107–8). Kellaway (1991b) figures this boulder, which is an Ordovician ignimbrite, similar to those from Snowdonia; it is clear from the photographs that this is a sub-angular to sub-rounded, faceted and bleached clast. What is less clear from the photographs are the claims that the boulder is striated, and that one side has been partially worked. Kellaway not only uses the evidence of this single boulder to support the glacial hypothesis, but also implicitly emphasises its North Wales source to argue for ice transport from a more northerly direction. Though Thorpe *et al.* (1991) were clearly aware of the existence of this boulder, they were unable to trace it, and they make no mention of Kellaway's reference to striae.

Given the nature of the derivation of this ignimbrite boulder, with the implication of suppression in Kellaway's letter, the integrity of the evidence deriving from it should be discounted unless and until reliable evidence is forthcoming as to its original context at Stonehenge. If, for the sake of argument, the evidence from this particular boulder, and the other largely circumstantial evidence for other striated boulders at Stonehenge (Engleheart 1921), is accepted as reliable, then a number of implications follow.

The presence of striations associated with faceted surfaces implies subglacial transport in a warm-based glacier. The potential for erratic transport in this situation is quite different from the supraglacial situation envisaged by Thorpe *et al.* (1991) and discussed above. If particles are either entrained subglacially by quarrying (Laitakari 1989), or derived supraglacially in the accumulation area and then descend to the subglacial zone (Fig. 7), then erratic survival and transport distances are a function of ice velocity and time in relation to crushing and fracturing of particles during ice flow (Donner 1989).

There is now a huge literature on erratic transport and dispersal generated as a result of studies related to ore prospecting, particularly in the shield areas of Canada and the Baltic (Shilts 1976; Eyles 1983). The detailed study of erratic trains and fans has been an essential requirement for ore prospecting in these areas as the distribution of ore-bearing erratics has been demonstrated to be an effective means of identifying valuable source rocks. The database on erratic transport paths is therefore extremely good and is of direct relevance to the Stonehenge bluestone problem. Donner (1989) has compared transport distances of Weichselian (Table 1) subglacially-entrained erratics in central Finland with those on the margins of the Baltic shield. In central Finland transport

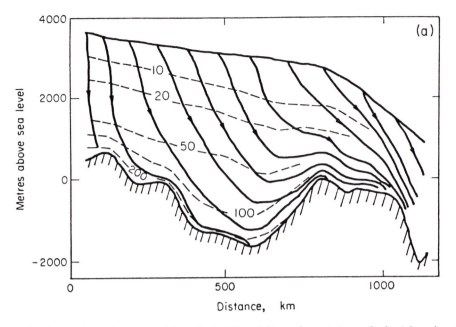

**Figure 7.** Computed steady-state particle paths (solid) and lines of constant age (broken) in units of 1000 years along a flow line in the Antarctic ice sheet from Vostok to near Wilkes, from Paterson (1981, fig. 10.6a) adapted from Budd *et al.* (1971). (Copyright: Pergamon Press, Oxford.)

distances from source are very short (usually <10 km). Pertunnen (1977) has noted that indicator erratics increase exponentially in the direction of ice movement as the ice flows over the source outcrop, and then decrease exponentially away from the distal contacts. 'Half-distance values', the distances at which the frequencies of the rock types are halved from the frequencies at the starting point of transport, range typically between 3 km and 6 km (Donner 1989). The 500 identified boulder fans in Finland have average half-distance values of only 1–5 km (Salonen 1987; Fig. 9).

However, on the margins of the Baltic shield transport of over 500 km has been documented (Fig. 10), and in North America erratics from Hudson Bay must have travelled between 1000 and 2500 km (Prest and Nielsen 1987). Donner (1989) notes that many of the far-travelled erratics on the margin of the Baltic shield are very large. Over 1900 erratic boulders with diameters over 3 m are known in Estonia, the largest being the rapakivi block 'Kabelikivi' near Tallinn with a diameter of 56.5 m, reported to be the largest Pleistocene erratic in NW Europe (Viiding 1976). Donner (1989) attributes the contrast in transport distances between the interior and margins of the shield to differences in the flow rates between the interior and marginal parts of the ice sheet (calculated from figures in Paterson 1981, 162; Fig. 11). There was simply not enough time available during the Weichselian glaciation to transport erratics from central Finland to the outer parts of the ice sheet, for instance to Estonia. A similar conclusion has been

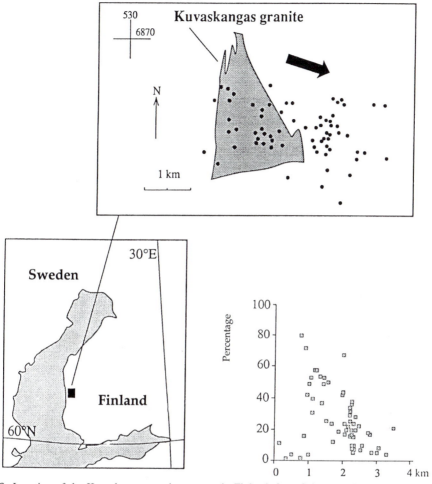

**Figure 9.** Location of the Kuvaskangas granite outcrop in Finland, from Salonen and Palmu (1989, adapted from figs 1 and 2). Boulder count sites shown as black dots. Graph shows percentage of boulders originating from the Kuvaskangas source in relation to the distance from the proximal contact of the rock. (Copyright: the Geological Survey of Finland.)

reached by Boulton *et al.* (1977) regarding the transport of erratics by the Late Devensian (Table 1) ice sheet covering the British Isles.

   Therefore, though the transport trajectories of subglacially transported boulders are often very short as a result of crushing and fracture beneath the ice, there are substantial data to support the existence of large far-travelled striated clasts of subglacial origin in ice-marginal areas. Such an interpretation would imply that the Wiltshire Downs represent the terminal zone of the glacier concerned. There is therefore no inconsistency between the presence of subglacially transported boulders at Stonehenge and glacial geological observations and theory.

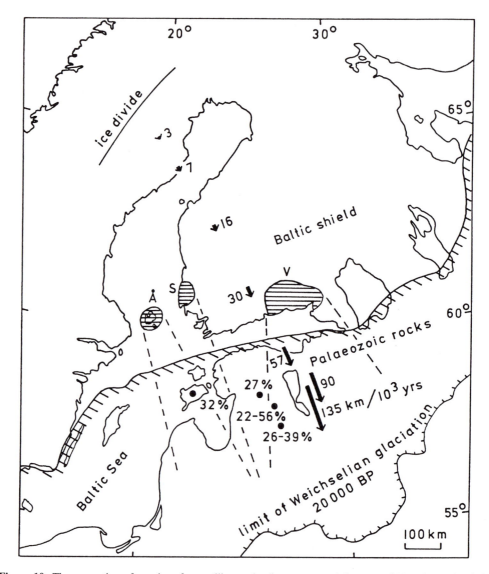

**Figure 10.** The proportion of erratics of crystalline rocks (in percentages) in parts of Estonia south of the boundary in the Gulf of Finland between the Baltic shield and the Palaeozoic sedimentary rocks, from Donner (1989, fig. 2). The outlines of indicator fans for the Åland rapakivi granite (Å), the Satakunta olivine diabase (S) and the Viipuri rapakivi granite (V) are shown, in addition to flow rates of the Weichselian ice sheet (after Paterson 1981) at various distances from the ice divide. The outer limit of the Weichselian ice sheet is also shown. (Copyright: the Geological Survey of Finland.)

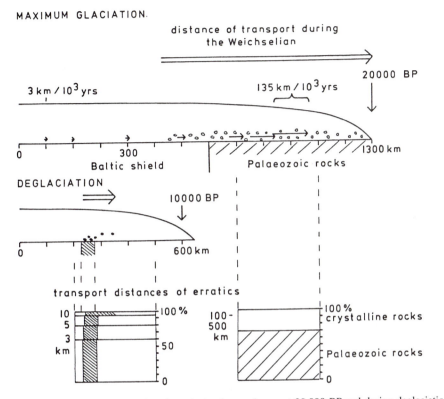

**Figure 11.** Profiles of the Weichselian ice sheet during its maximum at 20,000 BP and during deglaciation at 10,000 BP, from Donner (1989, fig. 3), showing typical transport distances of erratics of crystalline rocks from the Baltic shield in central Finland and the marginal area in Estonia. The flow rates used in Figure 10 are also shown. (Copyright: the Geological Survey of Finland.)

However, Kellaway (1991a) has suggested that the bluestones might have '. . . been carried for some distance downstream in floating ice' (op. cit., 228) and thus implies that they were not deposited directly from glacier ice. Depending on the lithology, striations on glacial clasts are rapidly removed in meltwater streams as a result of particle corrasion and this would therefore conflict with Kellaway's implication of extensive glaciofluvial outwash streams. On the other hand transport in river ice (Dionne 1972) can impart shallow striae to entrained clasts as they move across bedrock surfaces, so this mode of transport would not conflict with Kellaway's claim that some of the Stonehenge bluestones are striated.

*Pleistocene geology and geomorphology of southern Britain and adjacent shelves*

ERRATIC DISPERSAL

In response to criticism of his earlier papers (e.g. Kellaway 1971), Kellaway (1991b) has recently commented that '. . . the absence of a continuous chain of bluestone boulders heading all the way back from Stonehenge to the Preseli Mountains (thought by some to be the sole source of the bluestones) has been seriously urged as a valid reason for questioning their glacial origin!' (op. cit., 243). Despite Kellaway's apparent incredulity at such a suggestion, the examples cited above from Scandinavia and in North America provide convincing evidence that just such erratic 'trains' or 'fans' spreading from source to current location are typical of erratic dispersal by glacial transport. In recognition of this Thorpe *et al.* (1991) make considerable efforts to demonstrate continuity of the Preseli lithologies in a train from Pembrokeshire to Wiltshire. They review the evidence for presumed pre-Devensian transport of erratics from west to east in South Wales involving mainly Irish Sea sedimentary and igneous rocks, citing Bowen's (1970) compilation of Griffith's work (1937, 1939, 1940; Fig. 12) and additional recent evidence (Jenkins *et al.* 1985). They note from this that ice from the Irish Sea containing Pembrokeshire erratics did pass at least as far as Cardiff, with identical dolerites to the Stonehenge bluestones being transported as glacial erratics in south Dyfed (Strahan *et al.* 1914), and as isolated boulders as far as the island of Flatholm in the Bristol Channel.

This large dataset on erratic dispersal paths in South Wales is the result of decades of field research by many workers and is widely accepted as reliable. Whatever the age of the glaciation(s) concerned it is clear that the Irish Sea ice on crossing Pembrokeshire from north-west to south-east changed direction to west-east on entering the Bristol Channel area. The erratic transport paths clearly indicate movement of the Irish Sea ice in precisely the direction to be expected if it were to continue flowing towards Wiltshire; the consistency of the flow lines is striking.

In addition, the patterns of dispersal and concentrations of the Preseli dolerites as documented by Strahan *et al.* (1914) for Pembrokeshire itself (Fig. 13), and Thorpe *et al.* (1991) for the wider area, are entirely consistent with current theory on erratic dispersal (Figs 9 and 10; Donner 1989; Salonen and Palmu 1989). The spotted dolerite boulder train documented by Strahan *et al.* (1914) demonstrates the fan-shaped dispersal pattern with decreasing concentration away from source in a south-easterly direction, and the progressively isolated occurrence of spotted dolerite boulders further west in South Wales with increasing distance from source would be predicted by current theory (Pertunnen 1977; Salonen 1987). In fact, the distribution fits theory so well that it would be possible to locate the spotted dolerite source from the erratic dispersal path as in ore prospecting. This is what Thomas effectively did when mapping this area: 'The region immediately to the east and north of Narberth contained many examples [of boulders of spotted dolerite], and when an envelope was drawn around the occurrences it was found that the axis of the envelope pointed directly to the Prescelly Mountains' (Thomas 1923, 249; Fig. 13).

Despite this overall consistency between the erratic dispersal patterns in South Wales and the glacial hypothesis, the occurrence of a concentration of an assemblage of far-travelled boulders from Pembrokeshire in a small area of the Wiltshire Downs is not

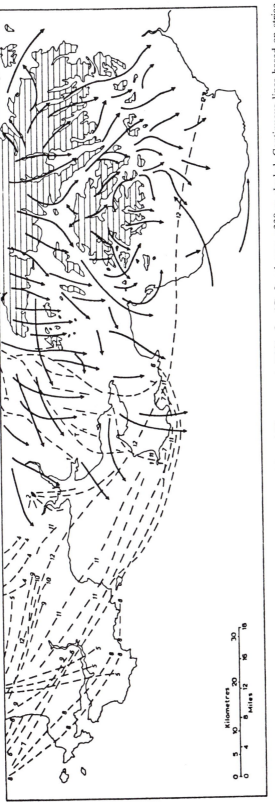

**Figure 12.** Ice movement in South Wales, from Bowen (1970, fig. 9.3) and Thorpe *et al.* (1991, fig. 15). Land over *c.*330 m shaded. Continuous lines based on striae and general erratics. Broken lines represent indicator fans after Griffiths (1940): (1) Llangynog rhyolite. (2) Llangynog rhyolite, agglomerate and diabase. (3) Builth Wells olivine dolerite. (4) Preseli 'diabase', rhyolite and 'spotted slate'. (5) Roch-Hayscastle andesite. (6) St. David's granite. (7) Ramsey Island quartz albite porphyry. (8) St. David's Head gabbro. (9) Clegyr agglomerate. (10) Llandeloy porphyrite. (11) Harlech (Barmouth) grit. (12) New Inn pyroxenic keratophyre. (T) Trilobites (*Asaphus* or *Ogygia*) from the Ffairfach Grit near Llandeilo. (Copyright: Longmans, London.)

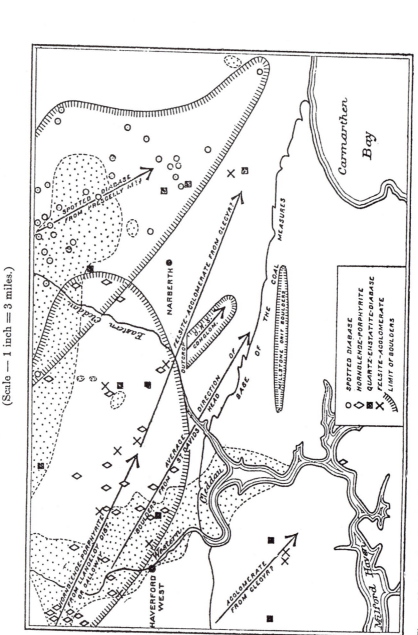
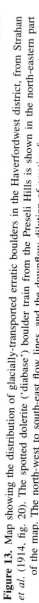

(Scale — 1 inch = 3 miles.)

**Figure 13.** Map showing the distribution of glacially-transported erratic boulders in the Haverfordwest district, from Strahan *et al.* (1914, fig. 20). The spotted dolerite ('diabase') boulder train from the Preseli Hills is shown in the north-eastern part of the map. The north-west to south-east flow lines, and the downflow dilution of erratics from source, are clear.

consistent with current data or theory on erratic dispersal in Scandinavia or North America. Such a pattern would require a marked downflow concentration in the Wiltshire area following dilution across South Wales. This is incompatible with dispersal theory and the empirical data from Scandinavia and North America. It might be compatible if one single large erratic had been quarried following deposition in Wiltshire, but the diversity of erratic types from a relatively small area of Pembrokeshire at Stonehenge argues against this. The reconstruction of erratic dispersal patterns across South Wales erected by Thorpe *et al.* (1991) is therefore supported by current glacial geological theory and observations; however, it fails with the proposed extension of ice across southern England.

## THE SOMERSET GLACIAL SEQUENCES

Thorpe *et al.* (1991) emphasise the significance of the discovery of glacigenic sediments in north Somerset during the 1970s (Hawkins and Kellaway 1971; Kellaway 1971). These were unknown to Thomas when he criticised the glacial hypothesis in the 1920s, and Thorpe *et al.* (1991) argue that these sequences demonstrate the ingress of Irish Sea ice from the Bristol Channel into the Somerset lowlands, and thus a little further along the route towards Stonehenge.

The sedimentology, stratigraphy and geomorphological relationships of the glacigenic sequences at Court Hill and Kenn (Fig. 1) have been described in detail by Gilbertson and Hawkins (1978a, 1978b) and related to other Pleistocene sequences in the area (Gilbertson and Hawkins 1974). The proglacial outwash and glaciolacustrine sediments and associated landforms described at Court Hill in particular (Gilbertson and Hawkins 1978a) are strongly indicative of an ice-marginal environment. Derivation from the west is clear from the abundance of Carboniferous Limestone and Rhaetic rocks, the presence of Greensand chert, Chalk-flints and Cretaceous microfossils and the absence of Coal Measures sandstone. However, no Pembrokeshire lithologies have been reported.

Though Kellaway (1971) attributed this sequence to a later glaciation than that responsible for the transport of the Stonehenge bluestones, it is clear that the data from these sites can only be interpreted as indicative of an ice-margin. This is not a subglacial landsystem (Eyles and Menzies 1983), nor is there any evidence of major glacio-tectonism of the Carboniferous Limestone ridge in this area. Both would be expected if the ice had continued flowing towards Wiltshire. Though providing unequivocal evidence for the presence of ice in north Somerset, the lack of erratic material from Pembrokeshire in these glacigenic sediments and the clearly ice-marginal style of sedimentation conflict with the scenario proposed by Thorpe *et al.* (1991). The only means of accommodating these data within their scenario is to attribute this sequence to a later glacial episode unrelated to the Stonehenge glaciation (see below).

## WIDER GLACIATION OF SOUTHERN ENGLAND AND ADJACENT SHELVES

In the twenty years or so since the appearance of Kellaway's views (Kellaway 1971; Kellaway *et al.* 1975) on the widespread glaciation of southern England and adjacent shelves, not a single piece of convincing evidence has been forthcoming to support this conviction. This is despite intensive mapping of the offshore region (Fannin 1989) and detailed site investigations of very many important Pleistocene localities across southern England. The original criticisms made by Green (1973) and Kidson and Bowen (1976) during the 1970s remain valid. To these may be added a whole series of others. The Burtle Beds have been shown to be marine, estuarine and freshwater beds (Kidson *et al*. 1978) of composite interglacial age (probably oxygen isotope stages 5e and 7; Bowen and Sykes 1988; Campbell *et al*. in press). There is no evidence for glaciation in the Somerset lowlands other than at Court Hill and Kenn (cf. Hunt *et al*. 1984). The erratics on the shore plat-form around Devon, Cornwall and along the Channel coast of both England and France are unlikely to have been emplaced by grounded ice and are much more convincingly explained both stratigraphically and sedimentologically as sea-ice or iceberg rafted (Van Vliet-Lanoë 1988; Hallégouët and Van Vliet-Lanoë 1989; Bowen 1994; Scourse 1996). Apart from the glacial sequence at Fremington (Croot *et al*. 1996), there is no evidence for any pre-Devensian glaciation of the Celtic Sea or of the English Channel. Glacigenic sediments do occur on the Isles of Scilly (Fig. 1) and in the Celtic Sea but these are localised in extent and relate to a Late Devensian surge of thin ice over deformable substrate beyond the stable margin of the ice in the St. George's Channel area (Scourse *et al*. 1990; Scourse 1991). This ice did not flow eastwards, but was instead topographically constrained south-westwards and had a glacimarine terminus. There is no evidence that Cornwall was ever glaciated (Scourse 1985a, 1985b, 1996). The current view is that the Fremington Till of north Devon (Fig. 1) is probably of glacigenic origin and may be Anglian in age; it is rich in derived Tertiary microfossils from the offshore Stanley Banks Basin immediately to the north (Croot *et al*. 1996; Fig. 5), but is very limited in extent.

The Axe Valley gravels in east Devon have been shown to be of periglacial fluvial origin (Green 1974, 1988; Shakesby and Stephens 1984), as have the gravels of the Hampshire Basin (Green 1973; Gibbard and Allen 1994; Fig. 1). The morainic evidence at Selsey is non-existent. The Slindon Sands (Fig. 1) are unequivocally of littoral inter-glacial origin; since the 1980s very detailed archaeological excavations in these and asso-ciated sediments have demonstrated the earliest hominid site in Britain with abundant associated artifact, macro- and microfossil evidence (Roberts 1986; Roberts *et al*. 1994). No evidence to support glaciation has been forthcoming. The palaeovalley system of the Channel relates to low-stand extension of periglacial fluvial networks during cold-stage lowstands (Hamblin *et al*. 1992; Bellamy 1995) and in part possibly to overflow of an ice-dammed lake in the southern North Sea through the Strait of Dover during the Anglian (Smith 1985, 1989; Gibbard 1988, 1995). The submerged clifflines are probably of littoral lowstand origin (Scourse *et al*. 1990). The concept of a large ice mass on the continental shelf west of the British Isles is not supported by any stratigraphic or geomorphological evidence, either on the shelf or down the continental slope; neither is there any obser-vational or modelling evidence for major glacio-isostatic rebound in this area which would accompany deglaciation of such a large ice mass.

The only possible and indirect support for the notion of the glaciation of the English Channel has been provided by Wingfield (1989) who suggested this on the basis of the occurrence of deep enclosed incisions attributed to jökulhlaup discharges. This view has, however, itself been heavily criticised (Hamblin 1990; Jeffery 1990).

In the light of this bank of evidence must be laid the charge that Kellaway (1971; Kellaway *et al.* 1975) did not sufficiently consider alternative hypotheses to explain features or sediments which he attributed to glaciation. That this is so is clear enough in the instances given above, but there are other examples. In interpreting the Slindon Sands as glaciofluvial Kellaway *et al.* (1975) emphasised the limited lateral extent of these deposits: '. . . one is struck by the severely limited extent of these deposits to coastal Hampshire and Sussex. No other fully authenticated marine deposits at this level are known from the shores and islands of the English Channel. This contrasts sharply with the widespread occurrence of raised beaches at a level 5–8m above present sea level in the same area, that are attributed to the high sea level of the Eemian interglacial. We consider it very curious that the supposed major interglacial stand of sea level at the Slindon level should have left such limited extent of its presence' (op. cit., 199). This was an astute observation but the wrong conclusions were drawn; this area has been tectonically uplifted since the Middle Pleistocene, unlike the areas to the west and east (Preece *et al.* 1990), so the limited spatial outcrop can be explained by regional uplift and has nothing to do with glaciofluvial sedimentation. The 'meltwater' channels in the Bristol district may indeed be partly of glacial origin, but many of the others can be explained alternatively in terms of drainage superposition, high-magnitide low-frequency flood events (cf. Hanwell and Newson 1970), periglacial fluvial channels or even exhumed Permo-Triassic wadi channels. These hypotheses require testing. The oversteepening and subsequent cambering of slopes in the Bath district can be more convincingly attributed to a combination of periglacial and fluvial processes than to glaciation (Hutchinson 1991; Parks 1991; Ballantyne and Harris 1994).

The only unequivocal evidence for the Pleistocene glaciation of southern England and adjacent shelves occurs in very localised areas of north Somerset, north Devon, the Isles of Scilly and more extensively in the Celtic Sea. The shore erratics are probably related to glacimarine rather than glacial processes. The remainder of southern England and adjacent shelves remained unglaciated during the Pleistocene. The scenario envisaged by Thorpe *et al.* (1991) is thus seriously weakened by their reliance on an hypothesis for which there is no supporting evidence.

THE NORTHERN AND MORETON DRIFTS AND THE SOLENT RIVER

Kellaway (1971) interpreted the Northern Drift (or 'Plateau Gravel') of the Cotswolds and north Oxfordshire (Fig. 1) as glacial in origin, and used this interpretation as supporting evidence for widespread glaciation during the 'Anglian' of central southern England. In his recent papers, Kellaway (1991a, 1991b) also interprets the Northern Drift as glacial in origin, and this forms a plank in his argument for the emplacement of the

Stonehenge erratics by ice and ice-related processes with glaciation from a northerly direction.

The Northern Drift Formation (Hey 1986) consists of scattered outcrops or patches of unstratified reddish sandy clay containing pebbles of Midlands (notably Bunter quartzite) origin. The Formation occurs both at high elevations on the Cotswolds and at lower elevations within the river valleys draining the Cotswold dip-slope, notably the Evenlode. In a recent re-examination of the Northern Drift Formation, Hey supports the conclusion of Shotton *et al.* (1980) that the lower elevation deposits are, for the most part, Anglian and pre-Anglian decalcified river gravels deposited by a river flowing down the present Evenlode Valley and tributary with the Thames system, and not glacial as suggested by Kellaway (1971; Kellaway *et al.* 1971) and earlier workers (Geikie 1877; Pocock 1908; Sandford 1926; Tomlinson 1929; Dines 1946; Arkell 1947a, 1947b). However, Hey also concurs with Shotton *et al.* (1980) in suggesting that the scattered pebbles on the Jurassic uplands might be of glacial origin '. . . these being the remnants of a till laid down by an ice-sheet advancing from the Midlands' (Hey 1986, 291). This conclusion has been supported by Worssam (1987) on the basis of stone-count data from a high-level exposure on the dip-slope of the Cotswolds. Worssam favours a glacial origin because the pebbles include ironstone from the Lias which outcrops at lower elevations. On the other hand, scattered pebble exposures on the southern Cotswolds are rich in flint, and glaciers introducing these from the south or east seem unlikely; these high-level exposures might therefore be explained alternatively as decalcified fluvial gravels of Tertiary age (R.W. Hey, pers. comm. 1996).

The glacigenic sequence of the Vale of Moreton (Fig. 1) has been described in detail (Bishop 1958) and is the nearest exposure to the north of Stonehenge of unequivocal glacial sediments. This supraglacial sequence contains proglacial outwash sediments and glaciolacustrine beds which clearly indicate ice-marginal conditions. As in the case of the Court Hill glacial sequence, there is no evidence here for dynamic subglacial sequences, landforms or tectonism which would be expected if this area had been overridden by a glacier flowing onwards towards the south. The Moreton Drift therefore represents an ice-marginal sequence, and there is some limited support for the interpretation of the high-level exposures of the Northern Drift Formation as glacial in origin which might support Kellaway's views (1971, 1991a, 1991b). However, the Midlands-derived pebble assemblages contained in both the Northern and Moreton drifts are entirely inconsistent with the Stonehenge bluestone assemblage and this weakens the significance of either the Northern or Moreton drifts to the Stonehenge problem.

Kellaway's recent (1991a, 1991b) scenario invokes river ice transport of the Stonehenge bluestones in the 'Southampton River' (= Solent river) fluvial or glaciofluvial gravels of which he identifies at Bathampton and Kingsdown (previously interpreted as glacial; Hawkins and Kellaway 1971; Fig. 5). This derives from an earlier idea of Varney (1921) who suggested that the Bathampton gravels might provide a link between the Avon and earlier headwaters in Wales. The continuous and thick fluvial gravels of the Solent river across east Dorset and Hampshire have recently been examined in detail by Gibbard and Allen (1994). This work supports the conclusion of Green (1973) that nowhere in this sequence is there evidence at any time for glacial input within the catchment (P.L. Gibbard, pers. comm. 1996). Not only is there is no geological evidence which supports Kellaway's view that the Solent river was an important conduit for the transport of the Stonehenge bluestones, but there is only very superficial evidence that the catchment of the Solent ever extended into the Bath-Wiltshire area, let alone Wales as he suggests.

GEOMORPHOLOGY OF THE CHALK ESCARPMENT

If the Wiltshire Downs had been glaciated by ice flowing from either the west (Kellaway 1971; Thorpe *et al.* 1991) or north (Kellaway 1991a, 1991b), the Chalk escarpment would at some point have been overridden by ice. Boulton *et al.* (1977) noted the striking change in the escarpment at the point where this crosses the accepted limit of Pleistocene glaciation in Hertfordshire. To the south, in the unglaciated area, the scarp has an altitude of some 250 m. To the north it is irregular and much lower, descending to only 90 m in northern East Anglia. They suggest that the scarp crest has been lowered by glacial erosion in excess of 100 m and set back by around 3 km. Bromley (1967) has also noted the southward and upward glacio-tectonic thrusting of huge masses of Chalk within the glaciated section of the scarp. Such geomorphological and glacio-tectonic structures are absent in the sections of the Chalk scarp expected to have been overridden if the Wiltshire Downs had been glaciated.

*Ice-flow directions and glaciology*

Thorpe *et al.* (1991) review evidence on the entrainment, transport and deposition of boulders by glaciers and claim this as support for the glacial hypothesis: 'In many areas erratic boulders are irregularly distributed on the surface of older till or bedrock, with no apparent matrix. These are termed "free boulders" (Flint, 1957, 129–130) and may reflect derivation from nunataks, removal of matrix by erosion, association with deflation, or deposition from clean glacier ice in a free condition' (op. cit., 148). In support of this latter concept they again cite Flint (1955) who interpreted the contrast between normal till ('boulder clay') to the east of the Missouri with bouldery till to the west, and attributed this to the Missouri river trench acting as a 'baffle' or 'cleat'. In this case '. . . the upper part of the ice unimpeded by the baffle flowed easily westward. The upper part of the ice mass, however, contains very little drift, and that little more is likely to be of distant origin' (op. cit., 148). The clear implication is that the limestone uplands of the Mendips, north Somerset and the chalk scarp of the Wiltshire Downs acted as such a baffle to strip supraglacial ice containing the large far-travelled unstriated erratics from Pembrokeshire from the basal ice rich in debris of more local origin. Such a concept of englacial shear caused by topographic highs, in which upper clean ice moves rapidly forwards over stationary or slow-moving debris-rich ice beneath, is very problematic indeed.

The Glen Flow Law (1) and the driving stress equation (2) indicate that the greatest flow deformation occurs in the basal ice, where the ice column is thickest, with a progressive reduction in deformation upwards through the glacier. Glaciers therefore flow by sliding over the bed or deforming predominantly in the basal region. Significant englacial shear of the kind required by Thorpe *et al.* (1991) is therefore difficult to reconcile with glacier physics.

However, there are both observational and modelling data to support the notion of limited englacial shear in particular situations. Drewry (1986) demonstrates how shearing can take place as a result of longitudinal compressive stress at specific temperature and bed roughness boundary conditions. The englacial shearing or thrusting can cause small steps in the glacier surface (Paterson 1981). In a tunnel in the icefall on Blue Glacier, Kamb and LaChappelle (1968) observed that the foliation near the bed was offset by many shallow thrust faults in a direction compatible with the direction of shear in the overall flow. In situations where glaciers move from a warm-based to a cold-based condition asymmetric folding can develop in the basal ice which may eventually develop into overturning or thrusting (Boulton 1972). Such shear thrusting is most common in glaciers in which the accumulation zone is warm-based and the ablation zone cold-based; in such cases the frozen subglacial layer represents an extension of the permafrost. Such polythermal glaciers are common in Svalbard (Schytt 1969; Boulton 1972) but similar situations have been observed in Antarctica (Drewry 1986). Where subglacial materials are frozen to the basal ice the adhesive strength between the glacier sole and the bed is greater than the shear stress across the contact so no basal sliding occurs, and failure instead takes place just above the bed within the ice (Boulton 1972).

Boulton (op. cit., 9) notes that where frozen bed is relatively thin then '. . . there exists the possibility of quarrying or plucking of very large erratics by the glacier'. In this case failure takes place not within the ice but within the bed. This situation is described in Figure 14. If the frozen mass is assumed to be rigid, the critical force is the shear stress at the bed. Fracture will occur if:

$$\tau l \geq F.AB + (N - u) \tan \phi \ BC \tag{3}$$

where $\tau$ is shear stress along the line ABC, $F$ is the shear strength of the frozen sediments and $(N - u) \tan \phi \ BC$ is the frictional resistance along BC, $N$ being the average normal load across BC in the absence of cohesion. Fracture is more likely if $l/AB$ is large because values of $F$ are likely to be greater than $\tau$. High pore-water pressure will reduce the strength of the sediments by reducing $F$. Boulton suggests that this mechanism could explain the plucking of large erratics such as the Chalk clasts embedded in the Anglian tills of the Norfolk coast. The mechanism is relevant to the Stonehenge problem because it provides a means of entraining large erratics in association with englacial shearing.

However, there are a number of attributes of this process inconsistent with the

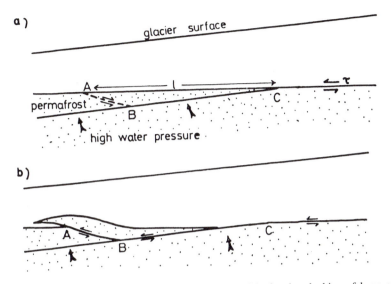

**Figure 14.** Schematic representation of the mechanism responsible for the plucking of large erratics where the glacier is cold-based but where the subglacial permafrost is thin (from Boulton 1972, fig. 4). (Copyright: the Institute of British Geographers.)

Stonehenge case. First, any failure within the ice will occur close to the bed because this is where $\tau$ is greatest; it will not occur high in the englacial zone. Second, the entrainment of large erratics can only occur in cold-based situations, and in particular where the ice moves onto permafrost. In the Stonehenge case this would be represented by the point where the ice moves over the 'baffle' or 'cleat' of the north Somerset and Wiltshire. The resultant sediments should therefore contain not erratics from Pembrokeshire but large clasts of the Carboniferous and Jurassic limestones and Chalk characteristic of this area. Third, Boulton (1970, 1972) notes that thrusting results in the movement of basal sediments upwards along shear planes, and in the movement of englacial material to a higher level. Deposition from such thermally complex glaciers is therefore characterised by ablation and flow tills associated with large quarried blocks and an absence of lodgement till; such an assemblage is absent from the Wiltshire Downs (see below). Finally, all the observed examples of such englacial or within-bed shear are at orders of magnitude smaller than the extent of shear required in the Stonehenge case.

Similar englacial shear propagated by frozen topographic highs has been invoked by Shaw (1979) to explain englacial fold complexes called 'Rogen moraines' which are common in glaciated shield areas. Such moraines form in areas of moderate bedrock relief with frozen zones on bed highs in situations where the local topography favours ice spreading and divergent flow. However, these features are characterised by the stacking of thick englacial debris sequences which are completely absent in the Stonehenge case (see below), and the topographic differentials required are much smaller than the 'baffle' posed by the Somerset-Wiltshire uplands.

These cases therefore provide no support for the 'baffle' concept suggested by Flint (1955) and adopted by Thorpe *et al.* (1991). In the absence of substrate thermal contrasts the observational and theoretical data indicate that englacial shear does not occur upflow of large bedrock highs and that ice slides and basally deforms around and over such obstacles (Fig. 7). Alternatively a downglacier transition from warm- to cold-based ice results in a sediment assemblage inconsistent with the regional geology.

There is another important sense in which the scenario envisaged by Thorpe *et al.* (1991) is implausible from a purely glaciological point of view. Drawing on the earlier views of Kellaway (1971) and Kellaway *et al.* (1975) they state that the Irish Sea glacier on exiting from the Irish Sea into the Bristol Channel was topographically constrained by Exmoor to the south and the South Wales Coalfield to the north before moving uphill towards Salisbury Plain. It has been noted that the driving stress equation (2) explains how glaciers are able to flow over topographic obstacles. If ice flow is topographically constrained, as Thorpe *et al.* (1991) have suggested, then this implies that the direction of the surface slope ($\alpha_s$) was consistent with the bed topography. This in turn implies that the ice thickness (h) was relatively small. This explains why glaciers tend to be more influenced by topography towards their margins as ice thickness decreases towards the terminal zone. It is clear that the Irish Sea ice stream during the Late Devensian (Scourse *et al.* 1990; Scourse 1991) behaved in just such a way, and the divergent fanning-out of pre-Devensian Irish Sea ice into the Celtic Sea and Bristol Channel area is clear from the erratic train evidence from South Wales (Bowen 1970; Fig. 12). From this it follows that if the ice surface gradient was consistent with the bed topography in the Bristol Channel it should remain consistent on exiting from the Bristol Channel. The proposal that the ice did not do this, but instead ascended the high ground of north Somerset, is not consistent with glacier physics. Ice flow discordant with bed topography can only be explained if the ice surface slope is similarly discordant. Therefore the only way in which the ice could have overcome this topographic obstacle is if the surface slope was orientated west-east from South Wales towards Wiltshire which would in turn imply relatively thick ice with an ice-dispersal centre on the western continental shelf, or in south-west England, or both. This requirement is also consistent with the earlier observation that the Preseli Hills were in the ablation area of the glacier. There is no evidence in either area for such a large ice mass.

### Lack of glacigenic sedimentary sequences on the Wiltshire Downs

Perhaps the strongest argument against the glacial hypothesis is the lack of convincing glacigenic sedimentary sequences anywhere close to the Wiltshire Downs east of the Clevedon district of Somerset and south of the Vale of Moreton. This was raised as a serious problem by Thomas (1923) and remains as serious in the light of recent data. Recognising this problem, Thorpe *et al.* (1991) attempt to explain the occurrence of isolated erratics as the product of sedimentation from clean, supraglacial, ice. That such ice should be sheared from debris-rich basal ice has been shown above to be glaciolog-ically implausible. It is also implausible in the light of glacial geological evidence. All the erratic dispersal evidence from Scandinavia and North America discussed above concern erratic boulders contained in, or on the surface of, thick glacial drift sequences. In lowland Estonia at the margin of the Baltic shield, for instance, the drift forms an almost continuous cover between 5 and 10 m thick. The same is true of the erratics dispersed by the Cordilleran ice sheet in North America. The only situation in which 'free erratics' occur on bedrock isolated from glacial sediments, which is the scenario envis-aged by Thorpe *et al.* (1991), is in the region of intense glacial erosion close to ice-dispersal centres such as the highlands of North Wales and Scotland (Fig. 15). Ice-marginal areas are typically characterised by complex landform-sediment assemblages associated with proglacial outwash and glaciolacustrine sequences (Eyles 1983). There are no such sequences anywhere near Stonehenge, even in *remanié* form.

## Problems with the glacial hypothesis: a summary

Though it has been demonstrated that bluestone-sized erratics can be transported many hundreds of kilometres as large unstriated blocks in supraglacial ice or as striated boul-ders in sub- and englacial routeways, the precise requirements for the transport of the Stonehenge bluestones are not consistent with either observational or modelling data in glaciology or glacial geology. The major problems are:

**1** The lack of glacigenic sediment sequences and depositional landforms close to Stonehenge on Salisbury Plain, or between Stonehenge and either the Vale of Moreton or north Somerset. Erosion and removal of such sediments is falsified by the absence of glacially-derived materials in the gravels of rivers draining Salisbury Plain, and of any *remanié* glacial materials on the Wiltshire Downs other than at Stonehenge itself.

**2** The lack of glacio-tectonic structures expected if the Chalk escarpment had been overridden by ice.

**3** The inconsistency between the driving stress equation (2) and the topographic characteristics of the proposed route between Preseli and Stonehenge.

**4** The inconsistency between the observational and theoretical data on englacial shear and associated sedimentary sequences, and the regional geological data.

## Additional evidence post-1991

*Clearance of erratic boulders from Salisbury Plain*

Thorpe *et al.* (1991), in support of the glacial hypothesis, emphasise some observations by de Luc (1811) made in the late eighteenth century (Bartenstein and Fletcher 1987). It is claimed that between 1780 and 1805 de Luc noted the removal of large boulders during field clearance on Salisbury Plain, and that whilst some of this material was local, much

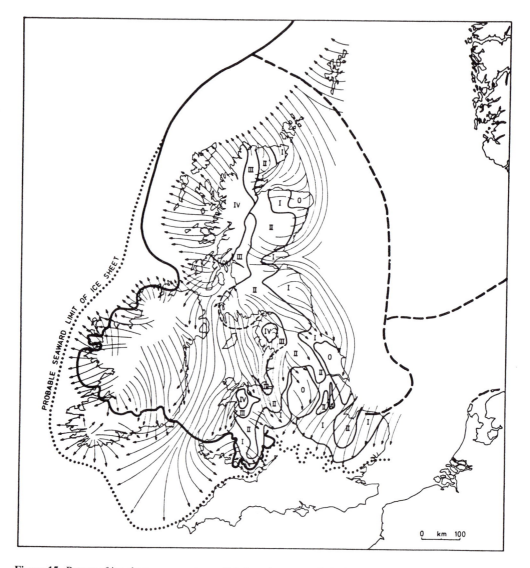

**Figure 15.** Pattern of ice-sheet movement over Britain and patterns of glacial erosion from Boulton *et al.* (1977, fig. 17.1). The dotted line shows the maximum extent of glaciation in Britain. The continuous line shows the assumed limit of the Late Devensian ice-sheet, dashed in the speculative North Sea area and omitted over central England. The arrows show generalised flow directions based on geological evidence. Zones of increasing erosional intensity, from 0 to IV are also shown. (Copyright by permission of Oxford University Press.)

of it was 'trap' (dolerite) and 'rhyolite' (granite). They therefore suggest this provides support for Judd's earlier contention that formerly '. . . Salisbury Plain was sprinkled over thickly with the great white masses of sarsen-stones ("greywethers") and much more sparingly with darker coloured boulders (the so-called "bluestones"), the last relics of the glacial drift, which had been nearly denuded away' (Judd 1902, 118), a view also shared by Briggs (1976a, 1976b, 1977).

Darrah (1993) has pointed out, however, that the nature of de Luc's observations have been misinterpreted. In fact de Luc was contrasting Salisbury Plain with other counties further north where he had observed boulder fields in that it was conspicuously devoid of far-travelled material. De Luc '. . . is certainly not saying there were boulders of igneous rock in Wiltshire; indeed the contrary could be inferred' (Darrah 1993, 78).

*Chlorine-36 date*

Bowen (1994) reports a chlorine-36 date of 14,000 years BP from a Stonehenge blue-stone and claims this as support against the glacial hypothesis. As this dating method provides an age for first exposure of a fresh rock surface, this result has therefore been interpreted to demonstrate that the bluestone concerned was '. . . still buried at its source outcrop during the Anglian (400ka), and did not become exposed by denudation to the atmosphere until the Late Devensian . . . after which it was presumably quarried by prehistoric people and taken to Stonehenge' (Bowen 1994, 211).

In order for this date to provide conclusive evidence on this important matter a number of points require clarification. First, technical details are required to enable independent assessment of the dating procedure, or of potential errors in the method, along with standard deviations or error bars. Second, the exact provenance of the sample needs to be established. It is reported that the measurement was undertaken on '. . . an igneous rock from the Stonehenge collection in Salisbury Museum' (op. cit., 211). Further detailed description of the petrology of the rock to demonstrate the reliability of the date is required. Third, details need to be provided of the presence or absence on the rock surface of either anthropogenic dressing or natural microwear. These data are prerequisites for interpretation of this method which is reliant on surface exposure.

The interpretation of this date involves an *a priori* assumption that the glaciation concerned is the Anglian (Bowen 1994). Even if the date is accepted as reliable, it would not be inconsistent with glacial derivation during the Late Devensian. The interpretation also involves an *a priori* assumption that the bluestone was quarried by man. Equally the boulder could have been collected for use from a Late Devensian glacial source; exposure could therefore have been natural rather than anthropogenic. Consequently further clarification of technical details is required if this promising dating technique is to have a conclusive bearing on the bluestone controversy.

# Age of glaciation

In the literature various ages are suggested for the glaciation responsible for the transport of the Stonehenge bluestones. An 'Anglian' age is preferred by Kellaway (1971),

Kellaway *et al.* (1975) and Thorpe *et al.* (1991), whilst Kellaway (1991a, 1991b) has recently suggested Pliocene glaciation at 2.47Ma. He derives this latter date from the presence of ice-rafted detritus in ODP552A in the Rockall Trough (Shackleton *et al.* 1984) and concludes that 'if, as seems likely, this ice developed primarily over Brittany, Ireland, Iceland and the western uplands of England, Wales and Scotland, then this would be the most likely time for movement of glacial erratics from Wales to Salisbury Plain to have taken place' (Kellaway 1991a, 215).

Aside from the fact that as there is no evidence for glaciation of Salisbury Plain at any time such age ascriptions are meaningless, this inference that the British Isles were glaciated in the Pliocene must be regarded as entirely speculative. To correlate deposits in the absence of any stratigraphical data whatsoever is to invite homotaxial errors of the most serious kind. It is most unsatisfactory that such correlations should appear in the literature because publication itself confers a reliability which is wholly unjustified. At least one other paper has appeared since this correlation which accepts the existence of glaciation in Britain at 2.47Ma (Donovan 1995). The earliest reliable evidence for Cenozoic glaciation in northern Europe is in the North Sea fan at 1.1Ma (Sejrup *et al.* 1995).

Recent data have been published concerning the age of the sequences at Court Hill/Kenn in north Somerset and in the Vale of Moreton, the nearest undoubted glacigenic sequences to Stonehenge. Current opinion places the Moreton Drift as part of the Wolston Formation on lithostratigraphic grounds, which is in turn correlated with the Lowestoft Formation of East Anglia and therefore Anglian in age (D. Maddy, pers. comm. 1996; Rose 1987, 1991).

In 1984 Andrews *et al.* (1984) published aminostratigraphic (AAR) data from the interglacial sediments overlying the glacigenic sequence at sites in and around Kenn. These fluvial, estuarine and marine sediments had previously been correlated with the Ipswichian temperate stage on pollen-stratigraphic grounds (Gilbertson and Hawkins 1978b; Hunt 1981), suggesting that the glacial sediments were pre-Ipswichian and probably Wolstonian in age. Though AAR data from *Macoma*, *Corbicula* and *Patella* from the Kenn Church and New Blind Yeo Drain sites supported correlation with oxygen isotope stage 5e (Ipswichian; Table 1), ratios on *Corbicula* from the Kenn Pier and Yew Tree Farm sites suggested that these riverine deposits are significantly older and correlated with 'Group IV' sites such as Purfleet in the Thames Estuary. Andrews *et al.* (1984) suggested a date of between 400 and 600k for these riverine deposits and concluded that the underlying glacial deposits must be older. This led Bowen and Sykes (1988) to infer that the glacial sediments were deposited in oxygen isotope stage 12 ('Anglian'; Table 1), but later Bowen *et al.* (1989) revised the correlation of the interglacial sediments to stage 15, confirmed in Bowen (1994): 'The aminostratigraphic method of Bowen *et al.* (1989) would correlate the Kenn Pier beds with ... oxygen isotope stage 15 (600ka). The underlying glacial deposits may, therefore, be time-equivalent to oxygen isotope stage 16 ... which the oxygen isotope signal shows was one of the largest ice-volume episodes of the Middle Pleistocene' (op. cit., 211).

There are a number of significant problems with these aminostratigraphic data and their interpretation. First, a number of methodological problems have emerged with respect to the AAR method as applied to molluscs. These have been described by Bowen *et al.* (1989) as 'diagenetic artefacts' and include analytical complications, sample contamination during diagenesis or analysis which lowers the D/L ratio, and leaching of free amino acids. To these may be added intra-shell diagenetic effects (Sejrup and Haugen 1994) which can cause D/L ratios to vary across an individual shell with amplitudes consistent with aminostratigraphic groups relating to different glacial-interglacial cycles. A second major problem is reworking causing mixing of samples of different ages during sedimentation. The known effects of reworking in generating mixed age populations (Bowen and Sykes 1988) should caution against correlation of sites on the basis of only a few shells, as in the Kenn case. These fundamental problems perhaps illuminate some specific inconsistencies with regard to the Kenn data. *Corbicula* remains unknown from any other well-established 'Cromerian Complex' (Table 1) site in the British Isles (R.C. Preece, pers. comm. 1996) suggesting that these age ascriptions are at least surprising. The correlation with Purfleet is a major problem because not only is it extremely well established that the Thames was not occupying this part of the valley during the pre-Anglian Pleistocene (Gibbard 1994; Bridgland 1994) but there is a wealth of independent biostratigraphic data to suggest that the interglacial beds here are much younger than the 'Cromerian Complex' (Bridgland *et al.* 1995). The age interpretation of the AAR data from Purfleet must therefore be incorrect.

The latitude with which AAR ratios can be interpreted in terms of age, as demonstrated in this instance, invites homotaxial error. Bowen (1994) has reinterpreted the correlation of the Kenn AAR data not on the basis of the data themselves but simply because the positive isotopic excursion of stage 16 is large and therefore suggests major glaciation. This procedure amounts to a simple pigeonholing of deposits into an external reference model. Its invalidity is demonstrated by the fact that whereas the oxygen isotope record is a measure of global ice volume, during the maximum of the Last Glacial Maximum (LGM; Table 1) the British ice sheet volume was equivalent to a lowering of glacio-eustatic sea-level by 0.91 m (Boulton *et al.* 1977), and therefore constituted 0.76% of the global ice mass difference between the LGM and the present day. Given the insignificance of this contribution of the British ice mass to the oxygen isotope record perhaps more attention should be paid to establishing the age of British glacial deposits by multiple and reliable methods rather than simply using the deep sea oxygen isotope stages as a convenient set of stratigraphic labels. This would assist in the analysis of hysteresis between the marine and terrestrial records, which may in turn demonstrate important causal feedback mechanisms in the climate system.

All that can therefore be stated with certainty about the age of the Kenn glacigenic sequence is that it is pre-interglacial and therefore pre-Ipswichian in age.

# Conclusion

The hypothesis that the Stonehenge bluestones were transported by ice to the Wiltshire Downs is not consistent with current glaciological or glacial geological theory or observational data. The bluestone lithological assemblage is, however, absolutely consistent with derivation from a glacial drift source in Pembrokeshire; this is supported by the limited evidence for striae on some of the undressed bluestone surfaces. If the $^{36}$Cl date is accepted, this might suggest that such a source was of Late Devensian age. Thomas' view (1923) that the boulders were '... taken from the boulder-strewn slopes on the immediate south and south-east of the Prescellys between Carn Meini and Cil-maen-llwyd where all the types have been collected together by glacial action' (op. cit., 251) remains unchallenged, as do his principal objections to the glacial transport hypothesis: apart from the ice-marginal sites in north Somerset, nowhere between South Wales and Stonehenge, is there '... evidence of glaciation of an intense character. There are no trains of far-travelled boulders, no ice-scratching and polishing of outstanding rocks, and no thick accumulations of boulder clay ... such a hypothetical ice-sheet, in order to account for the Foreign Stones of Stonehenge would have to gather from Pembrokeshire blocks all of about the same size and mainly of two rock-types. It would have to carry them all that distance without dropping any by the way. Further, it would have to pass over all kinds of rocky obstacles without gathering to itself any of the various materials over which it was forced to ride' (op. cit., 254).

The common element which unifies all advocates of the glacial hypothesis is incredulity that these stones could have been transported from Pembrokeshire to Wiltshire by prehistoric man. This centres around the copious bluestone fragments found on-site and was first expressed by Judd (1902): '... it is quite inconceivable that they [the bluestones] should have been hewed and chipped ... and reduced in some cases to half their dimensions, *after having been carried with enormous difficulty over land and water, and over hills and valleys*' (Judd's italics, p. 117). Kellaway expresses a similar view in 1971: '... the motives for conveying them ... to Stonehenge while ignoring local resources are incomprehensible' (op. cit., 34). In the light of this disbelief a mass of extremely circumstantial evidence has been marshalled into an hypothesis which in its totality has some apparent credibility but whose component parts are either capable of alternative explanation or equivocal or non-existent. As Sherlock Holmes said to Watson: 'How often have I told you that when you have eliminated the impossible, whatever remains, *however improbable*, must be the truth.'

*Acknowledgements*

For valued discussion of the Stonehenge bluestone problem I would like to thank Dr Stewart Campbell (Countryside Council for Wales), Dr David Croot (University of Plymouth), Professor Julian Dowdeswell (University of Wales, Aberystwyth), Dr Phil

Gibbard (University of Cambridge), Dr Richard Hey (formerly of the University of Cambridge), Dr Darrel Maddy (Cheltenham and Gloucester College of Higher Education), Dr Richard Preece (University of Cambridge) and Dr Helen Roe (University of Wales, Bangor). I would also like to acknowledge the inspirational teaching of Mr Jim Hanwell (formerly of the Blue School, Wells) who stimulated an early interest in the Stonehenge problem, and also Professor Geoffrey Boulton, FRS (University of Edinburgh) for encouraging me to undertake this review.

# References

ANDREWS, J.T., GILBERTSON, D.D. and HAWKINS, A.B. 1984: The Pleistocene succession of the Severn estuary: a revised model based upon amino acid racemisation studies. *J. Geol. Soc. London* 141, 967–74.

ARKELL, W.J. 1947a: *The geology of Oxford* (Oxford).

ARKELL, W.J. 1947b: The geology of the Evenlode gorge, Oxfordshire. *Proc. Geol. Assoc.* 58, 87–114.

ATKINSON, R.J.C. 1979: *Stonehenge* (London, Harmondsworth).

BALLANTYNE, C.K. and HARRIS, C. 1994: *The periglaciation of Great Britain* (Cambridge).

BARTENSTEIN, H. and FLETCHER, B.N. 1987: The stones of Stonehenge – an ancient observation on their geological and archaeological history. *Zeitschrift für deutsche geologische Gesellschaft* 138, 23–32.

BELLAMY, A.G. 1995: Extension of the British landmass: evidence from shelf sediment bodies in the English Channel. In Preece, R.C. (ed.), *Island Britain: a Quaternary perspective. Spec. Publ. Geol. Soc.* 96, 47–62.

BEVINS, R.E., LEES, G.J. and ROACH, R.A. 1989: Ordovician intrusions of the Strumble Head-Mynydd Preseli region, Wales: lateral extensions of the Fishguard Volcanic Complex. *J. Geol. Soc.* 146, 113–23.

BISHOP, W.W. 1958: The Pleistocene geology and geomorphology of three gaps in the Midland Jurassic escarpment. *Phil. Trans. Roy. Soc. London* B241, 255–306.

BOULTON, G.S. 1970: On the origin and transport of englacial debris in Svalbard glaciers. *J. Glaciology* 9, 231–45.

BOULTON, G.S. 1972: The role of thermal regime in glacial sedimentation. In Price, R.J. and Sugden, D.E. (eds), *Polar geomorphology. Inst. Brit. Geogr. Spec. Publ.* 4, 1–19.

BOULTON, G.S. 1978: Boulder shapes and grain-size distributions of debris as indicators of transport paths through a glacier and till genesis. *Sedimentology* 25, 773–99.

BOULTON, G.S., JONES, A.S., CLAYTON, K.M. and KENNING, M.J. 1977: A British ice-sheet model and patterns of glacial erosion and deposition in Britain. In Shotton, F.W. (ed.), *British Quaternary studies: recent advances* (Oxford), 231–46.

BOWEN, D.Q. 1970: South-west and central south Wales. In Lewis, C.A. (ed.), *The glaciations of Wales and adjoining regions* (London), 197–227.

BOWEN, D.Q. 1994: Late Cenozoic Wales and south-west England. *Proc. Ussher Soc.* 8, 209–13.

BOWEN, D.Q., HUGHES, S.A., SYKES, G.A. and MILLER, G.H. 1989: Land-sea correlations in the Pleistocene based on isoleucine epimerization in non-marine molluscs. *Nature* 340, 49–51.

BOWEN, D.Q. and SYKES, G.A. 1988: Correlation of marine events and glaciations on the NE Atlantic margin. *Phil. Trans. Roy. Soc. London* B318, 619–35.

BRIDGLAND, D.R. 1994: *Quaternary of the Thames* (London, GCR Rev. Ser. 7).

BRIDGLAND, D.R., ALLEN, P. and HAGGART, B.A. (eds) 1995: *Lower Thames. Field Guide* (London, Quaternary Research Association).

BRIGGS, C.S. 1976a: Notes on the distribution of some raw material in later prehistoric Britain. In Burgess, C. and Miket, R. (eds), *Settlement and economy in the third and second millennia BC* (Oxford, BAR 33), 267–82.

BRIGGS, C.S. 1976b: Cargoes and field clearance in the history of the English Channel. *Quat. Newslett.* 19, 10–16.

BRIGGS, C.S. 1977: Economy and erratics in stone age Britain. *Quat. Newslett.* 22, 3–6.

BROMLEY, R.G. 1967: Field meeting on the chalk of Cambridgeshire and Hertfordshire. *Proc. Geol. Assoc.* 77, 277–9.

BUDD, W.F., JENSSEN, D. and RADOK, U. 1971: Derived physical characteristics of the Antarctic Ice Sheet. *Univ. Melbourne Meteorology Department, Publ.* 18.

CAMPBELL, S., HUNT, C.O., SCOURSE, J.D., KEEN, D.H., CURRANT, A.P. and CROOT, D.G. in press: South West England. In Bowen, D.Q. (ed.), *A revised correlation of Quaternary deposits in the British Isles (Spec. Publ. Geol. Soc.).*

CHIPPINDALE, C. 1987: *Stonehenge complete* (London).

CROOT, D.G., GILBERT, A., GRIFFITHS, J. and VAN DER MEER, J.J. 1996. The character, age and depositional environments of the Fremington Clay Series, North Devon. In Charman, D.J., Newnham, R.M. and Croot, D.G. (eds), *Devon and East Cornwall. Field Guide* (London, Quaternary Research Association), 14–34.

CUNNINGTON, W. 1824: Stonehenge notes: the fragments. *Wiltshire Archaeol. Natur. Hist. Mag.* 21, 141–9.

DARRAH, J. 1993: The Bluestones of Stonehenge. *Curr. Archaeol.* 134, 78.

DINES, H.G. 1946: Pleistocene and recent deposits. In Richardson, L., Arkell, W.J. and Dines, H.G., *Geology of the country around Witney* (Memoir of the Geological Survey of Great Britain), 105–29.

DIONNE, J.-C. 1972: Caractéristiques des schorres des régions froides en particulier dans l'estuaire du Saint-Laurent. *Zeitschrift für Geomorphologie* 13, 131–62.

DONNER, J. 1989: Transport distances of Finnish crystalline erratics during the Weichselian glaciation. *Geol. Survey Finland, Spec. Pap.* 7, 7–13.

DONOVAN, D.T. 1995: High level drift deposits east of Bath. *Proc. Univ. Bristol Spelaeol. Soc.* 20, 109–26.

DOWDESWELL, J.A., HAMBREY, M.J. and WU, R. 1985: A comparison of clast fabric and shape in Late Precambrian and modern glaci-genic sediments. *J. Sedimentary Petrology* 55, 691–704.

DREWRY, D. 1986: *Glacial geologic processes* (London).

ENGLEHEART, G.H. 1921: Discussion after 'Stonehenge: interim report on the exploration by W.Hawley'. *Antiq. J.* 1, 40.

EVANS, W.D. 1945: The geology of the Prescelly Hills, north Pembrokeshire. *Q. J. Geol. Soc. London* 101, 89–110.

EYLES, N. 1983: The glaciated valley landsystem. In Eyles, N. (ed.), *Glacial geology: an introduction for engineers and earth scientists* (Oxford), 91–110.

EYLES, N. and MENZIES, J. 1983: The subglacial landsystem. In Eyles, N. (ed.), *Glacial geology: an introduction for engineers and earth scientists* (Oxford), 19–70.

FANNIN, N.G.T. 1989: Offshore investigations 1966–87. *Brit. Geol. Survey Technical Rep.* WB/89/102.

FLINT, R.F. 1955: Pleistocene geology of eastern South Dakota. *United States Geol. Survey Professional Pap.* 262.

FLINT, R.F. 1957: *Glacial and Pleistocene geology* (New York).

GEIKIE, J. 1877: *The great Ice Age* (London, 2nd ed.).

GIBBARD, P.L. 1988: The history of the great northwest European rivers during the past three million years. *Phil. Trans. Roy. Soc. London* B318, 559–602.

GIBBARD, P.L. 1994: *Pleistocene history of the Lower Thames Valley* (Cambridge).

GIBBARD, P.L. 1995: The formation of the Strait of Dover. In Preece, R.C. (ed.), *Island Britain: a Quaternary perspective. Spec. Publ. Geol. Soc.* 96, 15–26.

GIBBARD, P.L. and ALLEN, L.G. 1994: Drainage evolution in south and east England during the Pleistocene. *Terra Nova* 6, 444–52.

GILBERTSON, D.D. and HAWKINS, A.B. 1974: The Pleistocene deposits and landforms at Holly Lane, Clevedon, Somerset. *Proc. Univ. Bristol Spelaeol. Soc.* 13, 349–60.

GILBERTSON, D.D. and HAWKINS, A.B. 1978a: The col-gully and glacial deposits at Court Hill, Clevedon, nr. Bristol, England. *J. Glaciology* 20, 173–88.

GILBERTSON, D.D. and HAWKINS, A.B. 1978b: The Pleistocene succession at Kenn, Somerset. *Bull. Geol. Survey Great Britain* 66.

GLEN, J.W. 1955: The creep of polycrystalline ice. *Proc. Roy. Soc. London* A228, 519–38.

GREEN, C.P. 1973: Pleistocene river gravels and the Stonehenge problem. *Nature* 243, 214–16.

GREEN, C.P. 1974: Pleistocene gravels of the River Axe in south-western England, and their bearing on the southern limit of glaciation in Britain. *Geol. Mag.* 111, 213–20.

GREEN, C.P. 1988: The Palaeolithic site at Broom, Dorset, 1932–41: from the record of C.E. Bean, Esq. *Proc. Geol. Assoc.* 99, 173–80.

GRIFFITHS, J.C. 1937: *The glacial deposits between the River Tawe and the River Towy* (Unpublished Ph.D. thesis, University of Wales).

GRIFFITHS, J.C. 1939: The mineralogy of the glacial deposits of the region between the rivers Neath and Towy, South Wales. *Proc. Geol. Assoc.* 50, 433–62.

GRIFFITHS, J.C. 1940: *The glacial deposits west of the Taff* (Unpublished Ph.D. thesis, University of London).

HALLÉGOUËT, B. and VAN VLIET-LANOË, B. 1989: Les oscillations climatiques entre 125,000 ans et le maximum glaciaire, d'aprés l'étude des formations marines, dunaires et périglaciaires de la côte des Abers (Finistère). *Bulletin. Association Francaise pour l'Etude du Quaternaire* 23, 127–38.

HAMBLIN, R.J.O. 1990: Comment on 'Glacial incisions indicating Middle and Upper Pleistocene ice limits off Britain' by R.T.R. Wingfield. *Terra Nova* 2, 382–3.

HAMBLIN, R.J.O., CROSBY, A., BALSON, P.S., JONES, S.M., CHADWICK, R.A., PENN, I.E. and ARTHUR, M.J. 1992: *United Kingdom offshore regional report: the geology of the English Channel* (London, HMSO for the Geological Survey).

HANWELL, J.D. and NEWSON, M.D. 1970: The great storms and floods of July 1968 on Mendip. *The Wessex Cave Club, Spec. Publ. Ser. 1*, 2.

HAWKINS, A.B. and KELLAWAY, G.A. 1971: Field meeting at Bristol and Bath with special reference to new evidence of glaciation. *Proc. Geol. Assoc.* 82, 267–92.

HEY, R.W. 1986: A re-examination of the Northern Drift of Oxfordshire. *Proc. Geol. Assoc.* 97, 291–301.

HUNT, C.O. 1981: Pollen and organic-walled microfossils in interglacial deposits at Kenn, Avon. *Somerset Archaeol. Natur. Hist.* 125, 73–6.

HUNT, C.O., GILBERTSON, D.D. and THEW, N.M. 1984: The Pleistocene Chadbrick Gravels of the Cary Valley, Somerset: amino-acid racemisation and molluscan studies. *Proc. Ussher Soc.* 6, 129–35.

HUTCHINSON, J.N. 1991: Periglacial and slope processes. In Forster, A., Culshaw, M.G., Cripps, J.C., Little, J.A. and Moon, C.F. (eds), *Quaternary engineering geology. Geol. Soc. Engineering Geol. Spec. Publ.* 7, 283–331.

JEFFERY, D. 1990: Comment on 'Glacial incisions indicating Middle and Upper Pleistocene ice limits off Britain' by R.T.R. Wingfield. *Terra Nova* 2, 383–5.

JENKINS, D.G., BECKINSALE, R.D., BOWEN, D.Q., EVANS, J.A., GEORGE, G.T., HARRIS, N.B.W.

and MEIGHAN, I.G. 1985: The origins of granite erratics in the Pleistocene Patella beach, Gower, south Wales. *Geol. Mag.* 122, 297–302.

JOHN, B.S. 1984: *Pembrokeshire* (Newport).

JUDD, J.W. 1902: Note on the nature and origin of the rock-fragments found in the excavations made at Stonehenge by Mr Gowland in 1901. In Gowland, W., Recent excavations at Stonehenge. *Archaeologia* 58, 106–18.

KAMB, B. and LaCHAPPELLE, E.R. 1968: Flow dynamics and structure in a fast-moving icefall. *Trans. American Geophysical Union* 49, 318.

KELLAWAY, G.A. 1971: Glaciation and the stones of Stonehenge. *Nature* 232, 30–5.

KELLAWAY, G.A. 1991a: Structural and glacial control of thermal water emission in the Avon Basin at Bath. In Kellaway, G.A. (ed.), *Hot springs of Bath* (Bath), 205–41.

KELLAWAY, G.A. 1991b: The older Plio-Pleistocene glaciations of the region around Bath. In Kellaway, G.A. (ed.), *Hot springs of Bath* (Bath), 243–73.

KELLAWAY, G.A., HORTON, A. and POOLE, E.G. 1971: The development of some Pleistocene structures in the Cotswolds and Upper Thames Basin. *Bull. Geol. Survey Great Britain* 37, 1–28.

KELLAWAY, G.A., REDDING, J.H., SHEPHARD-THORN, E.R. and DESTOMBES, J.P. 1975: The Quaternary history of the English Channel. *Phil. Trans. Roy. Soc. London* A279, 189–218.

KIDSON, C. and BOWEN, D.Q. 1976: Some comments on the history of the English Channel. *Quat. Newslett.* 18, 8–10.

KIDSON, C., GILBERTSON, D.D., HAYNES, J.R., HEYWORTH, A., HUGHES, C.E. and WHATLEY, R.C. 1978: Interglacial marine deposits of the Somerset Levels, south west England. *Boreas* 7, 215–28.

LAITAKARI, I. 1989: How the glacial erratics were broken loose from the bedrock. *Geol. Survey Finland, Spec. Pap.* 7, 15–18.

LAWSON, D.E. 1979: Sedimentological analysis of the western terminus region of the Matanuska Glacier, Alaska. *Cold Regions Research and Engineering Laboratory Report 79–9*.

de LUC, J.A. 1811: *Geological travels. Volume III. Travels in England* (London).

MASKELYNE, N.S. 1878: Stonehenge: the petrology of its stones. *Wiltshire Archaeol. Natur. Hist. Mag.* 17, 147–60.

NEWALL, R.S. 1959: *Stonehenge* (London).

PARKS, C.D. 1991: A review of the possible mechanisms of cambering and valley bulging. In Forster, A., Culshaw, M.G., Cripps, J.C., Little, J.A. and Moon, C.F. (eds), *Quaternary engineering geology. Geol. Soc. Engineering Geol. Spec. Publ.* 7, 373–80.

PATERSON, W.S.B. 1981: *The physics of glaciers* (Oxford, 2nd ed.).

PERTUNNEN, M. 1977: The lithologic relation between till and bedrock in the region of Hämeenlinna, southern Finland. *Bull. Geol. Survey Finland* 291.

POCOCK, T.I. 1908: *The geology of the country around Oxford* (London, Memoir of the Geological Survey of Great Britain).

PREECE, R.C., SCOURSE, J.D., HOUGHTON, S.D., KNUDSEN, K.L. and PENNEY, D.N. 1990: The Pleistocene sea-level and neotectonic history of the eastern Solent, southern England. *Phil. Trans. Roy. Soc.* B328, 425–77.

PREST, V.K. and NIELSEN, E. 1987: The Laurentide ice sheet and long-distance transportation. *Geol. Survey Finland, Spec. Pap.* 3, 91–101.

RAMSEY, A.C., AVELINE, W.T. and HULL, E. 1858: *Geology of parts of Wiltshire and Gloucestershire* (London, Memoir of the Geological Survey of Great Britain).

REID, C. 1892: The Pleistocene deposits of the Sussex coast, and their equivalents in other districts. *Q. J. Geol. Soc. London* 48, 344–61.

ROBERTS, M.B. 1986: Excavation of the lower palaeolithic site at Amey's Eartham pit, Boxgrove, West Sussex: A preliminary report. *Proc. Prehist. Soc.* 52, 215–45.

ROBERTS, M.B., STRINGER, C.B. and PARFITT, S.A. 1994: A hominid tibia from Middle Pleistocene sediments at Boxgrove, UK. *Nature* 369, 311–13.

ROSE, J. 1987: Status of the Wolstonian glaciation in the British Quaternary. *Quat. Newslett.* 53, 1–9.

ROSE, J. 1991: Stratigraphic basis of the 'Wolstonian glaciation', and retention of the term 'Wolstonian' as a chronostratigraphic stage name – a discussion. In Lewis, S.G., Whiteman, C.A. and Bridgland, D.R. (eds), *Central East Anglia and the Fen Basin. Field Guide* (London, Quaternary Research Association), 15–20.

SALONEN, V.P. 1987: Observations on boulder transport in Finland. *Geol. Survey Finland, Spec. Pap.* 3, 103–10.

SALONEN, V.P. and PALMU, J.P. 1989: On measuring the length of glacial transport. *Geol. Survey Finland, Spec. Pap.* 7, 25–32.

SANDFORD, K.S. 1926: Pleistocene deposits. In Pringle, J. (ed.), *The geology of the country around Oxford* (London, Memoir of the Geological Survey of Great Britain), 104–72.

SCHYTT, V. 1969: Some comments on glacier surges in eastern Svalbard. *Canadian J. Earth Sciences* 6, 867–73.

SCOURSE, J.D. 1985a: The Trewornan 'Lake Flat': a reinterpretation. *Quat. Newslett.* 46, 11–18.

SCOURSE, J.D. 1985b: *Late Pleistocene stratigraphy of the Isles of Scilly and adjoining regions* (Unpublished Ph.D. thesis, University of Cambridge).

SCOURSE, J.D. 1991: Late Pleistocene stratigraphy and palaeobotany of the Isles of Scilly. *Phil. Trans. Roy. Soc. London* B334, 405–48.

SCOURSE, J.D. 1996: Late Pleistocene stratigraphy of north and west Cornwall. *Trans. Roy. Geol. Soc. Cornwall* 22, 2–56.

SCOURSE, J.D., AUSTIN, W.E.N., BATEMAN, R.M., CATT, J.A., EVANS, C.D.R., ROBINSON, J.E. and YOUNG, J.R. 1990: Sedimentology and micropalaeontology of glacimarine sediments from the Central and Southwestern Celtic Sea. In Dowdeswell, J.A. and Scourse, J.D. (eds), *Glacimarine environments: processes and sediments. Spec. Publ. Geol. Soc.* 53, 329–347.

SEJRUP, H.P., AARSETH, I., HAFLIDASON, H., LØVLIE, R., BRATTEN, A., TJOSTHEIM, G., FORSBERG, C.F. and ELLINGSEN, K.L. 1995: Quaternary of the Norwegian Channel: glaciation history and palaeoceanography. *Norsk Geologisk Tidsskrift* 75, 65–87.

SEJRUP, H.P. and HAUGEN, J.-E. 1994: Amino acid diagenesis in the marine bivalve Arctica islandica Linné from northwest European sites: only time and temperature? *J. Quat. Sci.* 9, 301–9.

SHACKLETON, N.J., BACKMAN, J., ZIMMERMAN, H., KENT, D.V., HALL, M.A., ROBERTS, D.G., SCHNITKER, D., BALDAUF, J.G., DESPRAIRIES, A., HOMRIGHAUSEN, R., HUDDLESTUN, P., KEENE, J.B., KALTENBACK, A.J., KRUMSIEK, K.A.O., MORTON, A.C., MURRAY, J.W. and WESTBERG-SMITH, J. 1984: Oxygen isotope calibration of the onset of glaciation in the North Atlantic region. *Nature* 307, 620–3.

SHAKESBY, R.A. and STEPHENS, N. 1984: The Pleistocene gravels of the Axe Valley, Devon. *Rep. Trans. Devonshire Assoc. for the Advancement of Science* 116, 319–22.

SHAW, J. 1979: Genesis of the Sveg tills and Rogen moraines of central Sweden: a model of basal melt out. *Boreas* 8, 409–26.

SHILTS, W.W. 1976: Glacial till and mineral exploration. *Roy. Soc. Canada, Spec. Publ.* 12, 205–44.

SHOTTON, F.W. 1976: The stone axe trade and Quaternary glaciation. *Quat. Newslett.* 20, 4–6.

SHOTTON, F.W., GOUDIE, A.S., BRIGGS, D.J. and OSMASTON, H.A. 1980: Cromerian interglacial deposits at Sugworth, near Oxford, England, and their relation to the Plateau Drift of the Cotswolds and the terrace sequence of the upper and middle Thames. *Phil. Trans. Roy. Soc. London* B289, 55–86.

SMITH, A.J. 1985: A catastrophic origin for the palaeovalley system of the eastern English Channel. *Marine Geol.* 64, 65–75.

SMITH, A.J. 1989: The English Channel – by geological design or catastrophic accident? *Proc. Geol. Assoc.* 100, 325–37.

STALKER, A.M. 1976: Megablocks or the enormous erratics of the Albertan Prairies. *Geol. Survey Canada Pap.* 76–1c, 185–8.

STRAHAN, A., CANTRILL, T.C., DIXON, E.E.L., THOMAS, H.H. and JONES, O.T. 1914: *The geology of the south Wales coalfield. Part XI. The country around Haverfordwest* (London, Memoir of the Geological Survey of Great Britain).

THOMAS, H.H. 1921: Discussion after 'Stonehenge: interim report on the exploration by W. Hawley'. *Antiq. J.* 1, 39–40.

THOMAS, H.H. 1923: The source of the stones of Stonehenge. *Antiq. J.* 3, 239–60.

THORPE, R.S., WILLIAMS-THORPE, O., JENKINS, D.G. and WATSON, J.S. 1991: The geological sources and transport of the bluestones of Stonehenge, Wiltshire, UK. *Proc. Prehist. Soc.* 57, 103–57.

TOMLINSON, M.E. 1929: The drifts of the Stour-Evenlode watershed and their extension into the valleys of the Warwickshire Stour and upper Evenlode. *Proc. Birmingham Natur. Hist. Phil. Soc.* 15, 157–96.

VAN VLIET-LANOË, B. 1988: *Le rôle de la glace de ségrégation dans la formations superficielles de l'Europe de l'Ouest. Processus et héritages* (Caen, Thèse de Doctorat d'Etat, Géographie, option Géomorphologie, Université de Paris I – Sorbonne, 1987).

VARNEY, W.D. 1921: The geological history of the Pewsey Vale. *Proc. Geol. Assoc.* 32, 189–205.

VIIDING, H. 1976: Andmete kogumisest Eesti suurte rändrahnude kohtra. In Viiding, H. (ed.), *Eesti NSV maapõne kaitsest* (Valgus, Tallinn), 148–61.

WINGFIELD, R.T.R. 1989: Glacial incisions indicating Middle and Upper Pleistocene ice limits off Britain. *Terra Nova* 1, 538–48.

WORSSAM, B.C. 1987: Constitution of Northern Drift at a Cotswold site. *Proc. Geol. Assoc.* 98, 269–70.

*Proceedings of the British Academy*, **92**, 315–318

# The Stonehenge Bluestones: Discussion

## O. WILLIAMS-THORPE, C. P. GREEN & J. D. SCOURSE

### Comments by Dr Williams-Thorpe following the papers by Drs Green and Scourse

THESE TWO PAPERS CONTAIN many interesting points—although no new evidence on the nature of the bluestones themselves was presented, rather, a different interpretation of the evidence.

I continue to find important inconsistencies in the human transport theory, and note the following in particular:

**1** There is a great variety of 'bluestone'. At least 13 'foreign' rock types are present at Stonehenge; the dolerites, rhyolites and sandstones alone originate at at least 12 different sources, some dispersed within south-west Wales and others not yet identified. There is also evidence for a limestone monolith once having existed at Stonehenge (noted in our paper). Even assuming that a glacial deposit in South Wales was exploited for at least some of the stones, this great variety does not speak of careful human selection. The existence of stones which do not match South Wales outcrops introduces another element at variance with selection in Preseli.

**2** A bluestone, by implication a boulder-sized piece not a small fragment, was certainly recorded at Bowls Barrow by William Cunnington. (The boulder now known as the Bowls Barrow boulder does indeed have an incomplete recorded history and we cannot be sure it is William Cunnington's bluestone. The name 'The Stonehenge Stone' could stem from its obvious similarity to the Stonehenge bluestones.)

**3** The monoliths include soft, easily-eroded stone types, astonishing choices for human transport. The probability that some monoliths were dressed on site at Stonehenge is also surprising if the stones were humanly carried.

**4** Bluestones found in a variety of archaeological contexts (including pre-dating their first erection at Stonehenge) are frequently recorded in barrow soil or fill, not in the grave: this positioning does not imply that they were valued or even noted.

On the specifically glaciological points, I am not a glaciologist so I am unable to judge whether that talk represents the definitive view or whether other views at variance with it might be allowed. However I would like to put three points to Dr Scourse:

**1**    The importance of recent and earlier human activity in the dilution of erratic dispersal (note, our reading of de Luc is supported in *Geology Today* May–June 1994, 95–96).

**2**    The potential of glaciers to remove rock selectively, accounting for the predominance of harder facies in the mixed bluestone monolith assemblage.

**3**    In the Thorpe *et al.* (1991) paper we cited the Wisconsin glacier till as a parallel for free boulders deposited on a large scale.

Proposals for glaciation of Salisbury Plain are bedevilled by a dearth of direct evidence because of the age and nature of the event. However the alternative of human bluestone transport raises significant inconsistencies in the available evidence.

## Response of Drs Green and Scourse to comments by Dr Williams-Thorpe

Before responding to the detailed comments made by Dr Williams-Thorpe, we would like to acknowledge the excellent and exhaustive mineralogical and geochemical investigation of the Stonehenge bluestones published by her with her late husband and their co-workers (Thorpe *et al.* 1991). Our criticism of their findings relates not to the work on bluestone petrology and provenance but to the proposed glacial transport mechanism, which draws on the work of Kellaway. We examine the points raised by Dr Williams-Thorpe in the order in which she presents them.

In highlighting the variety of bluestone lithologies, Dr Williams-Thorpe argues that this 'does not speak of careful human selection' and therefore, by implication, indicates glacial transport. We can look at this conclusion from two points of view.

Firstly, the fact that some bluestones have not yet been matched in Preseli does not mean that they do not come from south-west Wales; it means the case is unproven. Even if bluestone sources outside south-west Wales are eventually identified, this does not falsify the human transport hypothesis. Clasts in glacial deposits in Pembrokeshire represent a range of lithologies and as in all glacial deposits they are dominantly local, but a significant minority of far-travelled material is present. Drift sources in this area contain rocks from Scotland, Ireland, North Wales and from the floor of the Irish Sea. Unmatched bluestones may well come from this wider Irish Sea province.

Secondly, the significance of several of the points raised by Dr Williams-Thorpe, and this point in particular, rests on her perception of what motivated the builders of Stonehenge, or prehistoric people in general. It is unwise to suggest that the presence of several types of bluestone at Stonehenge, whether from south-west Wales or elsewhere, 'does not speak of careful human selection' when we know nothing about why the materials were chosen. The choice of stone may have been purely pragmatic or it may have had profound symbolic significance.

The same tendency to divine the thoughts of people long passed away is apparent in Dr Williams-Thorpe's comment on the name 'The Stonehenge Stone', given by the occupants of Heytesbury House in the nineteenth century to the so-called Bowls Barrow bluestone boulder. It can be argued with equal plausibility that it was called the Stonehenge Stone because these people thought it looked like the stones at Stonehenge, as Dr Williams-Thorpe asserts, or because they knew it came from Stonehenge. There is nothing in William Cunnington's very brief note on the discovery of bluestone in Bowls Barrow to indicate the size of the example that he found there. Exactly what his note means is a matter of opinion.

Dr Williams-Thorpe notes that the 'monoliths include soft, easily-eroded stone types'. She describes these as 'astonishing choices for human transport'. Surely an incautious verdict when we have no idea *why* particular rock types were chosen. And if it was astonishing to choose them in south-west Wales, would it not have been equally astonishing to choose them from a glacial assemblage on Salisbury Plain, had such an assemblage ever existed?

The dressing of the bluestones at Stonehenge rather than in their place of origin has to be seen in the context of their repeated rearrangement within the monument. Their original use in the structure is now thought to pre-date the erection of the sarsen circle and horseshoe in which dressed stone is extensively used. Nothing we know now conflicts with the conclusions reached by Thomas in 1923: 'It is my settled opinion that the facts and motives can only be explained by postulating the removal of a venerated stone circle from the eastern end of the Prescelly Mountains to Salisbury Plain.' He continues, '. . . it has been suggested that the transport of rough stones to Stonehenge, only to be dressed and reduced in bulk on their arrival, argued lack of intelligence on the part of the builders. But, surely, it does not follow that the two operations were carried out by the same people, or even the same generation . . . The drastic dressing these stones received at Stonehenge points, in my opinion, to their having been already erected on the site and that they were transformed by the builders of Stonehenge from their rough and inelegant state into monoliths more in harmony with the finished and elaborate structure at a somewhat later period.'

The discovery of bluestone fragments in barrow soil is a fascinating dimension of this story, but again we do not know that their apparently casual incorporation reflects the value attached to them. That these rock types had a special significance in the periods both before and after their use as building materials at Stonehenge is indicated in many ways—by the practices employed in quarrying them, by patterns of dispersal and by manufacture into ceremonial objects. It is not implausible to argue that even mere fragments of these rock types had talismanic significance. Once again we cannot enter the minds and souls of prehistoric people to know how they perceived their world.

We are sorry to see that Dr Williams-Thorpe is still claiming the support of De Luc (1811) for the assertion that blocks of far-travelled stone were present on Salisbury Plain in the eighteenth century. The De Luc text will *not* bear this interpretation, placed upon it by Bartenstein and Fletcher (1987) and subsequently adopted by Thorpe *et al.* (1991) and reiterated by Jenkins and Jenkins (1993) and Jenkins, Jenkins and Williams-Thorpe (1994). Quite apart from the issue of textual interpretation, the historical record and the field evidence provide absolutely no support at all for this misguided notion.

The reference to the 'potential of glaciers to remove rock selectively, accounting for the predominance of harder facies in the mixed bluestone monolith assemblage' adds little to the argument either way. Whether the rocks were selected by glaciers in south-west Wales and brought to Salisbury Plain by glacial ice, or selected from a glacial deposit in south-west Wales by the builders of Stonehenge and brought by them to Salisbury Plain, would make little difference to the ratio of durable to non-durable rock types. The presence of any non-durable rock types at Stonehenge argues, if anything, against the hypothesis of glacial transport, because such rocks would have had to survive for hundreds of thousands of years exposed to weathering on the surface of Salisbury Plain, only to be weathered away in the relatively short period since their incorporation into Stonehenge.

The Wisconsinan example cannot be used as an analogy for large-scale free boulder emplacement. It is a glaciological interpretation made in the 1950s and therefore predates the fundamental advances in glaciology that have been made since that time. In the light of recent glaciological work, based on principles of glacier physics and on observations of the behaviour of modern glaciers, this particular interpretation of possible glacier behaviour can no longer be regarded as a tenable explanation either for the Missouri case or for the occurrence of Welsh rock types at Stonehenge.

Finally, Dr Williams-Thorpe touches on the crucial evidence in this long-standing controversy—'the dearth of direct evidence' for glaciation on Salisbury Plain. Why has no single fragment of bluestone, large or small, ever been described from a natural context on Salisbury Plain, or, even more telling, in the river gravels that are the sweepings of this area, accumulated over the past two million years? The answer is simple. No natural agency has ever brought these rocks into Wessex. The glaciers of the Quaternary Ice Age, at their widest extent in Britain, never reached Salisbury Plain.

*Proceedings of the British Academy*, **92**, 319–334

# Stonehenge in its Wider Context

## GEORGE EOGAN

## Introduction

DUE TO MANY FACTORS such as a growing environmental awareness, a pride in the past, or commercial potential a new philosophy has been emerging in most countries regarding the archaeological inheritance. In view of its usefulness not only for academic study but for more general purposes also, the need to maintain it is a most relevant factor. People are, therefore, becoming more aware of the importance of the archaeological inheritance but also conscious of the fact that the remains cannot reproduce themselves; they are non-renewable and finite. But what value can we put on archaeological monuments almost at the dawn of the twenty-first century and how can we measure value in this current materialistic context? The term 'resource' is often applied to archaeology; I see nothing wrong with that term provided that it embraces all the different strands. Stonehenge and other monuments have many values, such as in the realms of general education and curiosity, but for me the primary one is that they constitute an unerring index to the achievements of past societies and provide documents for understanding them.

Stonehenge and its environment constitute a composite archaeological landscape. Therefore, dealing with such a site in its wider and comparative context is not an easy matter. This has of course been made easier—due to the recent magistral English Heritage publication we now know much more about Stonehenge than ever before. In the evaluation of any site many aspects have to be considered; these range from straightforward academic and cultural issues, to the role of scientific interpretation and preservation, and also making the monuments available for study by specialists but also for visiting by the general public.

As has been discussed on numerous occasions there are many problems associated with the preservation of Stonehenge. The major one is, of course, that it attracts so many visitors but in addition its location between two main roads presents difficulties. However, major work has been achieved over the years by the National Trust and English Heritage in acquiring land in the immediate vicinity and this has been an outstanding contribution to the re-creation of the rural setting for the monument and the other monuments that constitute the wider complex. This is an enormous achievement and one that should without delay be initiated elsewhere. The conservation programme would, of course, be helped by finding a solution to the problem of the roads and the location of the Visitors Centre. The latter could inform people about the richness of the archaeological environment of Stonehenge, and convey an understanding and appreciation of it. Despite its spectacular nature and its unique aspects there is more to Stonehenge than Stonehenge itself.

A thorough study of the wider setting of Stonehenge would involve an in-depth evaluation of a large segment of European prehistory and would have to be multi-faceted involving current land usage by farming communities, past usage as a ritual landscape as well as various technological aspects. Consequently one has to be selective and that is precisely what my approach is. My selection consists of four other areas—Orkney and Kilmartin in Scotland, the Boyne Valley (Brugh na Bóinne) in Ireland and Carnac-Locmariaquer in Brittany. As all of these areas constitute rich archaeological landscapes, they are well-known generally and scientifically, many publications have been devoted to them and they are sites that I have visited on more than one occasion. However despite that, I can claim to have a thorough knowledge of only one of the sites, the Boyne Valley; for the others it is superficial. As a result the Boyne will figure more prominently in my remarks that will follow, but even for that site I will not be offering detailed descriptions of its archaeological content, either from the point of view of its environmental setting or its monumental context. Neither will this paper attempt to provide an academic assessment or an interpretative review of the archaeology of any of the regions; that has already been done by more than one distinguished scholar. This paper is not the appropriate vehicle for a new review which would at least have to include an assessment of the then contemporary society in its regional setting. The main focus will be on the role of the monuments in each area in the context of modern society. I, of course, should say that while the areas that I am reviewing had a long archaeological life, nevertheless at least some aspects of all overlapped with the use of Stonehenge. Furthermore, all are rural sites and all have special characteristics. At least one type of monument is common to all, the open-air circle or henge, the precise form of which can vary from area to area. In addition each area contains significant monuments the construction of which involved large labour forces and, therefore, a social commitment well beyond the ordinary. This included control over labour but also control over resources. There must have been a population catchment of several hundred families over an area of say 16 square kilometres. In each area the leading monuments display sophistication in construction. All of the four areas contain notable monuments, the finest examples of their class, some even without exact parallels. This would have involved a skilled and trained work-force with different levels of accomplishment, scientific knowledge such as geology while some, as Stonehenge itself, have astronomical connotations. For instance, the Newgrange entrance faces the rising sun at the Winter solstice while at the same time Maes Howe faces the setting sun. Apart from the monuments themselves some splendid associated artifacts are a feature the manufacture of which involved precision, care and experience. But a main underlying comparison between all is that during the Neolithic and Chalcolithic/Early Bronze Age each constituted a major ceremonial centre and as a result of that the monuments then created have in modern times become foci for mass tourism. In addition all are in good agricultural land the utilisation of which can make monuments vulnerable and there are pressures such as the building of dwelling houses. Like Stonehenge all are noted for their long history of archaeological research: Newgrange was first described in 1699, accounts of Orkney mounds go back to 1772, Kilmartin from about the middle of the nineteenth century, and the Carnac area to around the middle of the seventeenth century. It is largely the fruits of that research, including publication, that have made the sites familiar, enriched our understanding and added to our appreciation of them.

Virtually from the beginning of human settlement the emergence of focal points has been a feature of the landscape in different parts of Europe. Back in the Upper Palaeolithic places such as the valley of the river Dordogne in France became ritual centres. In later prehistory, during Hallstatt D, sites such as Heuneburg/Hohmichele, southern Germany (Moscati *et al.* 1991, 114–15) fulfilled a similar role. Extending backwards into the Bronze Age we can cite the emergence of what has been termed 'wealth centres' in northern Europe (Thrane 1995). These include the Seddin complex in northern Germany with its spectacular *Königsgrab* underneath a circular mound 90 m in diameter and 11 m in height (Wüstermann 1974) and the equivalent site at Voldtofte in Funen also with its prominent burial mound, the Lusehoj, which measures 35 m in diameter and 7 m in height (Thrane 1984). Returning to the period equivalent to Stonehenge in its various stages (Cleal, Walker and Montague 1995) one can cite other comparative sites, not necessarily consisting of a single prominent site and associated structures, from other parts of Britain and Ireland.

## Orkney

In this connection an obvious place to mention is Orkney which was intensely occupied and where many of the monuments are spectacular to observe, not only the megalithic monuments but also the Early Bronze Age barrows. For an area of 970 sq km there are over 80 megalithic tombs (Davidson and Henshall 1989), 250 round barrows, the bulk of which may have been erected during the Bronze Age, and about 100 short cists, again probably of Bronze Age date (Renfrew 1985, 131). Even within the relatively small area of Mainland there are many favourite sites. Sometimes these occur in groups; probably the most notable clustering of all is to be found on the promontories between the Lochs of Stenness and Harray (Ritchie 1975–6), extending from Bookan to the Barnhouse stone (Fig. 1). This area, less than 4 km in length and 1 km in maximum width was a focus for ritual activities with its henge monuments at Stenness, Brodgar and Bookan and a number of standing stones some of which may have been connected with a ceremonial way between Stenness and Brodgar and its nearby passage tombs, including the

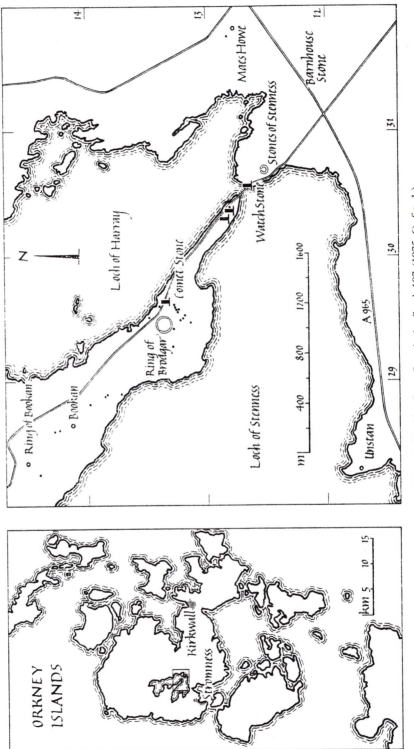

**Figure 1.** The Stenness (Orkney) archaeological area. (After G. Ritchie, *Proc. Soc. Antiq. Scotl.* 107 (1975–6), fig. 1.)

remarkable Maes Howe. Thom and Thom (1978) suggested that the Ring of Brodgar and its surrounding mounds could have served as a back-stage from which lunar observatories could be made. As was the case at Stonehenge, the Loch Stenness-Harray area was also a focus for burials in the early second millennium. There are a number of round barrows close by and not far away (but not part of the cluster) is the important group, the Knowes of Trotty, which consists of ten barrows. Investigations in 1858 in the larger of these, 18 m (60 ft) in diameter and 3 m (10 ft) in height revealed a cist containing human bones, part of a spacer plate, amber necklace and four decorated sheet-gold discs. As already noted all round barrows need not belong to the Bronze Age; nevertheless, it can be assumed that in addition to large-scale activity during the passage tomb and Grooved Ware stages the Early Bronze Age was also a significant stage with ritual still playing an important role.

Apart from scientific activities the monuments also constitute foci for tourists. All the well-known sites are easily accessible. There is already a small display at Skara Brae and currently plans are afoot to carry out a complete overhaul of access and visitor facilities including more comprehensive interpretation. In the Stenness-Maes Howe area due to the nature of the landscape care has to be taken not to intrude on it unnecessarily; landownership also presents some problems. At present large-scale tourist facilities are not called for but sensitive developments are and will take place when considered necessary.

## Kilmartin (Fig. 2)

Another circumscribed area occurs in the west of Scotland, in mid-Argyll (RCAHM (Scot) 1988). There, a valley in the parishes of Kilmartin and Kilmichael Glassary has a dense distribution of funerary and ritual monuments which indicate that settlement goes back to the beginning of the Neolithic. During the succeeding millennia the resources of the glen were extensively exploited; from the early sixth century AD the rock of Dunadd was the capital of the Gaelic kingdom of Dál Riata. As a result the area presents an array of monuments, some quite spectacular. For the prehistoric period there are about 80 barrows and cairns but also the densest and most elaborate concentration of rock art known from Scotland. Amongst the other monuments are long chambered cairns of the court-tomb (Clyde) family, henge monuments and stone circles, multiple cist cairns and the previously mentioned rock art.

Kilmartin Glen forms the core of an impressive archaeological landscape with a wide range of natural and managed habitats. Today this is farmed and afforested but archaeology also contributes an important element not only from the academic point of view but also from the tourist aspect. There are, therefore, different interests and parties involved so it is important to harmonise the various user needs. To meet this challenge interested parties have joined together to create a structure for the management and interpretation of the area. Several public bodies are actively interested in the area arising out of their

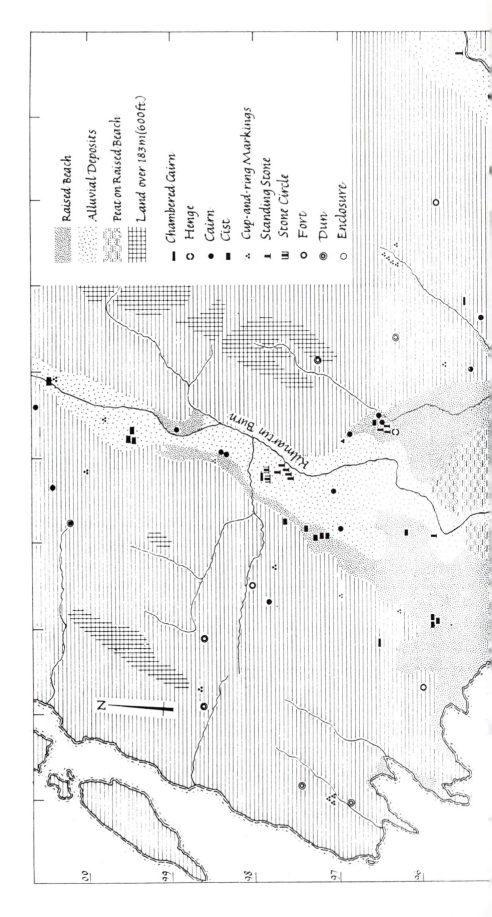

Raised Beach

Alluvial Deposits

Peat on Raised Beach

Land over 183m (600ft.)

| | Chambered Cairn |
|---|---|
| ○ | Henge |
| ● | Cairn |
| ■ | Cist |
| ∴ | Cup-and-ring Markings |
| ⌐ | Standing Stone |
| ⊞ | Stone Circle |
| ○ | Fort |
| ◎ | Dun |
| ○ | Enclosure |

Kilmartin Burn

N

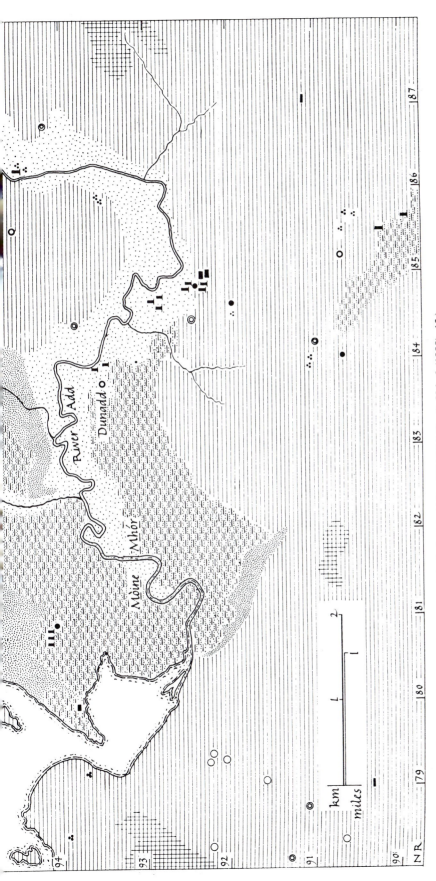

**Figure 2.** The Kilmartin-Kilmichael Glassary (Argyll) archaeological area. (After RCAHM (Scot), Vol. 6 (1988), 13.)

responsibilities for the natural and archaeological heritage, land-management, planning, tourism and recreation. At present an equilibrium exists but changes could have a major detrimental impact on the landscape. In order to prevent this and to harmonise the various user needs and interests a strategic framework for the management and interpretation of the landscape is currently being considered. A broadly-based working party was formed in December 1992. This led to an assessment of the problems and opportunities of the area and the consequent production of a detailed action plan. Basically this involves a co-ordinated approach by both the local communities and official bodies to the management of the countryside and visitors to it. A key principle in all of this is strict adherence to an environmentally sensitive approach and one that will include the conservation of the archaeological resources in their natural landscape. The achievement of this will involve the provision of long-term management, monitoring and maintenance regimes, part of which will be an integrated approach to interpretation, education management, the provision of facilities for research work and the generation of economic benefit for the area. The creation of an interpretative centre is central to the overall development.

## The Boyne (Fig. 3)

Ireland may be a rural country but nevertheless pressures on its monuments are just as intense as elsewhere. This is especially so in the east of the country with its rich farming land and population density. It is within this region that a particularly rich archaeological zone occurs. Large-scale archaeological excavations since 1960 have demonstrated the long sequence of human endeavour in the area, starting in Early Neolithic times and continuing through many subsequent archaeological stages down to modern times (O'Kelly 1982; Eogan 1986). In this connection it should be pointed out that in all areas where excavation has occurred additional monuments have come to light. Therefore, one cannot judge the extent of the archaeology from visible remains; to do so would underestimate the richness of the area both numerically and chronologically. Since the days of Sir William Wilde, 150 years ago, this portion of the Boyne Valley has been referred to as Brugh na Bóinne (Wilde 1849). But for a previous 150 years the area had been attracting sightseers and antiquarians. This is also an area of rich farming land; nearly 97% of the land is used for agricultural purposes, only 0.5% is in State ownership, and it is also close to centres of population. As a result, over the past 20 or so years it has become popular as a residential area. Within the overall area there is a population of about 1000 people, around 300 dwelling houses and three or so large farming complexes. Amongst its leading sites Newgrange was in a dilapidated state up to the early 1960s due to the growth of trees and scrub on the mound and animals trampling over it. The number of visitors was rapidly increasing and as a number of the passage orthostats, many of which were decorated, were leaning inwards they were being damaged by people rubbing against them. To ameliorate this situation it was decided in 1961 that greater care should be extended

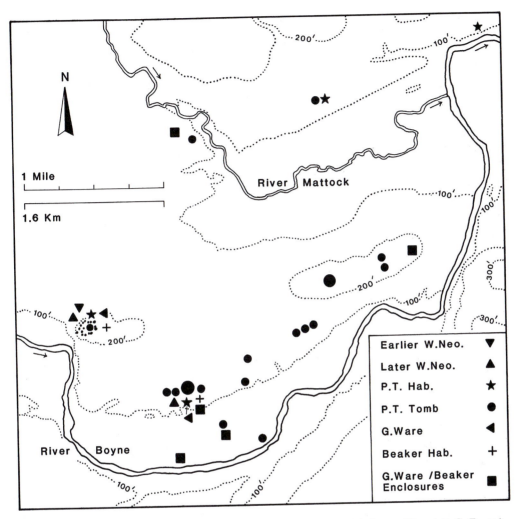

**Figure 3.** Prehistoric sites in the Brugh na Bóinne (Co. Meath) archaeological area. (Copyright G. Eogan.)

to the monument. This would involve conservation but before any work of that sort could be put in hand it was necessary to carry out excavations. Accordingly a programme of excavations commenced under the direction of Professor M.J. O'Kelly in 1962 and continued until 1975 (O'Kelly 1982). After subsequent conservation Newgrange was opened to the public. Today its chamber receives 150,000 visitors each year and the numbers are increasing. With hindsight it was an unwise move to allow unrestricted access to the tomb as it puts the site, and continues to put the site, under severe strain. Just as O'Kelly previously noted, passage orthostats, great works of art in their own right, are still being rubbed smooth by visitors' clothing. That, and the previously-mentioned agricultural and housing development, led to a review of the problem in the mid 1980s by a committee that was brought together under the auspices of the Royal Irish Academy and which included representations of the Office of Public Works, the National Museum of Ireland, the Meath County Council and the Department of Archaeology, University College, Dublin. Initially the Committee addressed a series of questions and set out plans for the future. For that the whole archaeological area was accepted as a monument. As a result planning and management issues should be addressed in an integrated fashion. In order to do that and to provide an overall evaluation of the various problems and issues a landscape architect and planner, Anthony M. O'Neill was commissioned (funded by Bord Fáilte) to draw up a study in archaeological resource management. The ensuing report, which was completed in January 1989, was all-embracing and dealt with physical resources, human activities, management, zoning analysis and proposals for future preservation, maintenance and availability including the provision of a visitors centre.

Arising out of this a first and important step that was adopted was to redefine the map of the area as a whole. This led to the identification of a core area with surrounding buffer zones. The core contains all the major visible sites and other monuments; it encompasses an area of 780 hectares and extends over an area that is 6 km in length and up to 2 km in maximum width. Of the two proposed buffer zones, that on the north contains about 700 hectares and that on the south is over 1000 hectares. These zones are intended to protect the environmental setting of the core area but in a portion of the northern buffer zone, at Monknewtown, there are also visible archaeological sites. Overall the total area is up to 3000 hectares. This provided a firm basis for devising management strategies (including planning controls), a new visitor access regime and the provision of an infrastructure. Equally important it acted as a focus for integration with regional socio-economic planning on a substantial basis and for the attraction of resources for conservation and management objectives. A key element in the overall management strategy was the provision of a visitors centre on the periphery of the archaeological area. This would act as a gateway to the overall complex, it would present and interpret the archaeological landscape as an entity and facilitate the management and distribution of visitors. A critical factor in all of this is to create conditions, such as the rights of way, which would allow visitors to comprehend the area as a whole but also to dissipate visitor pressure on Newgrange and other monuments. In this aspect of the development the acquisition of property by the State is a prerequisite necessary to the overall preservation plan.

The State has ownership of Knowth, Dowth and Newgrange as well as some other areas while all visible monuments have protection orders. In addition to the State the Local Authority, Meath County Council, can and is playing a significant role. In the County Development Plan the entire Boyne Valley is designated an area of High Amenity, Brugh na Bóinne as a special area of archaeological interest and the section between Navan and Drogheda as an area of High Natural Beauty. In that arrangement the core area has three orders of protection; the proposed buffer zones two orders.

The Boyne Valley monuments have, of course, a role to play in the wider theme of this conference—science and society. Their building implicated people with skills and knowledge and involved both construction and layout which included precise geometric shapes. Some of the monuments have features that characterize the concept of Neolithic science. In his recent study Andrew Powell (1994, 89) put forward the view that the distinctive heart shape of Newgrange can be attributed to the fact that it was built around a rigid frame comprising two 4:5:6 triangles and one 3:5:6 triangle. On the other hand Knowth was constructed around two 5:6:7 triangles. Jon Patrick (1974) argued that Newgrange was built to incorporate an astronomical alignment as is best demonstrated by the alignment of the passage on the rising sun at the Winter solstice, the shortest day of the year. The great Orcadian passage tomb of Maes Howe was aligned on the setting sun at the same time of the year. Knowth with its two tombs faces both the rising and setting sun twice a year, the Spring and Autumn equinox. Although Newgrange does not have a second chamber nevertheless the presence of Kerbstone 52 with its vertical central line directly opposite the entrance stone (K 1) indicates a front-back symmetry.

Stone selection, and therefore incipient geology, was also a feature of Brugh na Bóinne. This is most adequately demonstrated by the fact that nearly all the structural stones of the large sites and some in the smaller tombs had their origin in the Lower Palaeozoic geological zone the nearest part of the southern limits of which is about 3 km away (Eogan 1986, 112–13), but in order to acquire the most suitable stones the source could have been further away. This palaeozoic rock has distinctive qualities; it is hard and therefore will preserve better while its cleaved surfaces provide an ideal plane for the art. This demonstrates that the passage tomb builders had a knowledge of rock quality and accordingly selected building stones that were most advantageous from their point of view. But exotic stones, which were used for non-utilitarian purposes, were also acquired. For this category the varieties represented were quartz, granodiorite, granite, banded siltstones and gabbro (Mitchell 1992). Due to aspects of its composition the origin of the quartz can be attributed to the granite areas of the Wicklow mountains about 60 km to the south. The other four varieties could have been acquired in a limited region of north Louth-south Down, 50 km to the north. The primary geological source of granodiorite would have been the Newry igneous complex. The granite boulders would have been derived from the Mourne mountains while the banded siltstones may have originated in the Carlingford peninsula as did gabbro. Except for the quartz all the other exotic small stones could have originated in the adjoining geological complexes of the Carlingford, Newry, Mourne region. But the immediate source for these could have been on the sea shore, especially along the coasts of the Carlingford peninsula. Today all varieties occur, for instance, at Rathcor on the southern side of the peninsula (Mitchell 1992).

## Carnac-Locmariaquer (Fig. 4)

The main monuments are found in a limited coastal area between the Quiberon and Arzon peninsulas which is less than 20 km in length and about 6 km in maximum width. Here

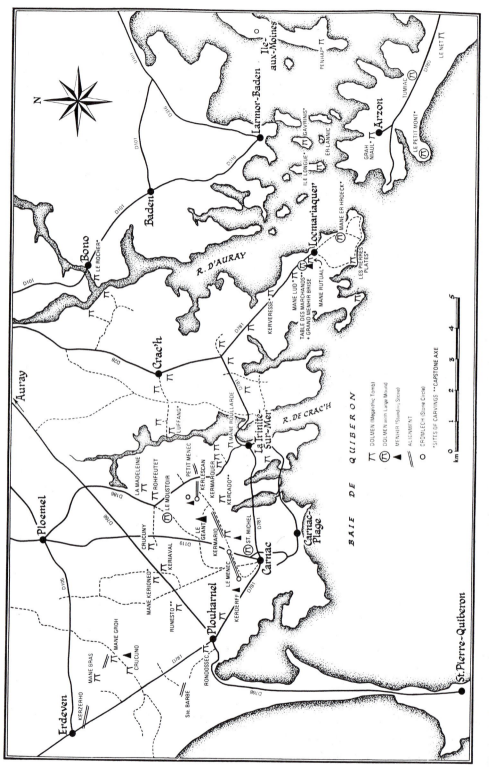

**Figure 4.** The Carnac-Locmariaquer archaeological area (Brittany). (After Pitkin Pictorials 1984.)

too, orientation is a feature of some monuments, such as the alignments at Kerlescan, Kermario and Le Menec (Bailloud *et al.* 1995, 48–68). This generally low-lying area is traversed by the rivers Crach and Auray and contains examples of impressive monuments —tombs, alignments, standing stones. Amongst these are some of Europe's classic and best known megalithic monuments—the massive long mound of Saint-Michael, the impressive passage tombs of Locmariaquer and Gavrinis, the stone alignments in the Carnac area and the massive Grand Menhir Brisé and its alignment at Locmariaquer. But this area is thickly inhabited, including towns and villages, agriculture is widely practised and it is a key tourist region. The latter is well-developed and established. Taking all these factors into account this renowned archaeological area is under threat and its landscape is endangered.

While the archaeological significance of the area has for long been known, recent excavations, especially in the Locmariaquer region by Jean L'Helgouac'h and Charles Le Roux, have added enormously to our understanding of the Neolithic inhabitants of the area. For the general public there is a most useful series of excellent guide books and associated with the excavations are programmes of large-scale conservation. In combination these have made, or are making, the sites accessible to the public both visually and in writing. Table des Marchands, Petit-Mont and Gavrinis have official and organised visitor arrangements and guide service from Easter to All Saints Day. These are the responsibility of the Société d'aménagement et de gestion du Morbihan (SAGEMOR) which is officially recognised and supported by the Département of Morbihan. There are certain problems in this area regarding access to a number of the monuments and their ownership. Gavrinis is the property of the Département of Morbihan but because it is situated on an island the Département has had to make arrangements with a boatman to provide an official link between the site and the mainland at Larmor-baden. The number of visitors is limited to 15–20 for each trip but there can be as many as two or three trips each hour. At the site there is a small visitors centre and a guide service is in place provided by SAGEMOR. Unaccompanied visits are not permitted. Petit Mont is the property of the town of Arzon. Large-scale excavations have taken place within recent years (Le Cornic 1994) and subsequently conservation work was completed. A guide service exists during the summer months (financed by SAGEMOR) but as yet no other facilities exist but there are plans to remedy this deficiency before too long.

The situation regarding monuments in the immediate area of Locmariaquer is more complex. Table des Marchands and the Grand Menhir are the property of the French State but ownership of Er Grah is divided between the town of Locmariaquer and the Morbihan Département. The complex nature of property ownership is clearly demonstrated by taking into account the situation that prevailed when the recent excavations were in progress. Er Grah and Table des Marchands were separated from each other by a pathway which is privately owned. Furthermore, all the land adjoining the megaliths was privately owned, several different owners being involved. Some years ago the State and the Département of Morbihan had plans to acquire more land and to provide access between the major sites by means of public pathways but due to local pressure this had to be largely abandoned. However the land around the megaliths has been acquired.

Carnac also presents problems. The alignments are the property of the State but nevertheless, due to an established practice of access, it may be difficult to organise a comprehensive programme of protection and conservation. It has been the custom that anybody could walk through the alignments and even interfere with them such as climbing on the stones. The area was being over-used, car-parks were too close to the monuments and this encouraged more and more people to walk through the rows; as a result soil erosion became a major problem. Fortunately this has now changed. The monuments are closed to the public and efforts are underway to reconstitute the surface and allow the growth of grass. A temporary visitors centre has been established near the western end of the Kermario alignment. It is the aim of the State to acquire additional lands around and in the neighbourhood of the alignments and to provide guided tours.

Obviously there is still a lot to be done in this area and this is difficult in view of the large permanent population and the presence of tourists in the environment of the monuments and on their fabric in some cases. In view of the importance of its megalithic art the continuation of allowing the practice of general access to the chamber at Gavrinis requires an evaluation.

# Conclusions

From what I have said it is clear that Stonehenge and the four complexes that I outlined have features in common. All consist of assemblages of monuments that in the main served non-utilitarian purposes such as tombs, temples and processional ways. In other words they constitute ceremonial or ritual landscapes, foci for ceremonies extending in time from the Neolithic into the Early Bronze Age. They reflect ritual centralisation but also a consolidation of society indirectly suggesting socio-political complexity, including people in authority, and a display of power. The building of these monuments reflects an abundance of labour as human energy was consumed on a grand scale, not only just 'casual' labour but people with skills, knowledge and training. In each area the quality and quantity of the monuments are high, some are exceptional and have today an international reputation. The monuments had a specialised function. Many are large and, therefore, highly visible and as a result had a better chance of survival. Their construction displays specialist building skills and organisational capabilities including the transportation from a distance of large stones used in building. Even though the type of building in use varied between the Neolithic, Grooved Ware, Beaker and Early Bronze Age stages, nevertheless a feature of all is the presence of monumental architecture (Trigger 1990).

Monumental architecture involved major efforts in building. In the areas that we are considering these were generally special purpose buildings of a lavish scale, they were non-utilitarian in nature and their construction demanded personnel with skills and specialist knowledge. Many are much more massive and enduring than their function would have required. The layout and orientation of some involved mathematical precision. The use of materials exotic to the area was in some cases a feature. Such materials demonstrate 'conspicuous consumption'.

Despite the significant role that the various complexes played in our understanding of past human endeavour and creativity and their added role within recent times as attractions for visitors, nevertheless, we should not lose sight of the equally important role that the apparently more mundane monuments play; these need not be visually inspiring or spectacular in form and may have no role in the time-table of the casual visitor or sightseer. In the overall scheme of preservation such monuments cannot be neglected, they are wide-ranging documentation of archaeology. In this connection we should never forget the philosophy of the first Inspector of Ancient Monuments, General Pitt Rivers who reminded us that in archaeology that which is important is that which is persistent—in other words it is the common things that matter (cf. Daniel 1950, 173). Those words are as true today as they were a century ago.

*Acknowledgements*

In the preparation of this paper I am most grateful for the assistance received from a number of people. In particular I would like to mention Dr Lesley MacInnes (Edinburgh), Mr Eugene Keane (Dublin) and Dr Jean L'Helgouac'h (Nantes). I also wish to thank my colleagues Niamh O'Broin and Carol Smith for all their help generously given.

# References

BAILLOUD, G., BOUJOT, C., CASSEN, S., LE ROUX, C-T. 1995: *Carnac* (Paris, CNRS Editions).

CLEAL, R.M.J., WALKER, K.E. and MONTAGUE, R. 1995: *Stonehenge in its landscape: Twentieth Century Excavations* (London, Engl. Heritage Archaeol. Rep. 10).

DANIEL, G.E. 1950: *A Hundred Years of Archaeology* (London).

DAVIDSON, J.L. and HENSHALL, A.S. 1989: *The Chambered Cairns of Orkney* (Edinburgh).

EOGAN, G. 1986: *Knowth and the Passage Tombs of Ireland* (London).

LECORNEC, J. 1994: *Le Petit Mont, Arzon–Morbihan* (Rennes, Documents Archéologiques de l'Ouest).

MITCHELL, F. 1992: Notes on some non-local cobbles at the entrances to the Passage-Graves at Newgrange and Knowth, Co. Meath. *J. Roy. Soc. Antiq. Ir.* 122, 128–45.

MOSCATI, S., FREY, O.H., KRUTA, V., RAFTERY, B. and SZABÓ, M. 1991: *The Celts* (Milan).

O'KELLY, M.J. 1982: *Newgrange* (London).

PATRICK, J. 1974: Midwinter Sunrise at Newgrange. *Nature* 249, 517–19.

POWELL, A.B. 1994: Newgrange—Science or Symbolism. *Proc. Prehist. Soc.* 60, 85–96.

RENFREW, C. (ed.) 1985: *The Prehistory of Orkney* (Edinburgh).

RITCHIE, J.N.G. 1975–6: The Stones of Stenness, Orkney. *Proc. Soc. Antiq. Scotl.* 107, 1–60.

ROYAL COMMISSION ON THE ANCIENT AND HISTORICAL MONUMENTS OF SCOTLAND 1988: *Mid Argyll and Cowal* Vol. 6 (Edinburgh).

THOM, A. and THOM, A.S. 1978: *Megalithic Remains in Britain and Brittany* (Oxford).

THRANE, H. 1984: *Lusehøj ved Voldtofte* (Odense).

THRANE, H. 1995: Centres of Wealth in northern Europe. In Kristiansen, K. and Jensen, J. (eds), *Europe in the First Millennium B.C.* (Sheffield).

TRIGGER, B.G. 1990: Monumental architecture: a thermodynamic explanation of symbolic behaviour. *World Archaeol.* 22, 119–32.

WILDE, W.R. 1849: *The Beauties of the Boyne and Blackwater* (Dublin).

WÜSTERMANN, H. 1974: Zur Socialstruktur im Seddiner Kulturgebiet. *Zeitschrift für Archäologie* 8, 67–107.

*Proceedings of the British Academy,* **92**, 335–341

# Future Directions for the Study of Stonehenge and its Landscape

## G. J. WAINWRIGHT

## Background

IN THE EARLY PART OF THE EIGHTEENTH CENTURY, William Stukeley recorded many of the monuments in the Stonehenge landscape and excavated a number of round barrows. Subsequently, in the first two decades of the nineteenth century, Sir Richard Colt Hoare and William Cunnington examined over 200 round barrows in the vicinity of Stonehenge—almost half the total number. Similar extensive campaigns of excavation were currently being carried out, not only within Wessex, but also in the Peak District and in Yorkshire. The sole object of these investigations was the collection of relics and to obtain these, a single trench or central pit was dug into the mound thus locating and removing the central burial but leaving the fabric of the mound intact. This is important for future research programmes because the surviving deposits contain much that is of value in terms of environment and dating which can be extracted with little damage to the monuments themselves.

Between 1980 and 1990, English Heritage commissioned Wessex Archaeology to undertake a study under the direction of Julian Richards which would 'identify the prehistoric settlements in the Stonehenge region and establish their state of preservation with a view to developing a management strategy for them'. The results of that study were published by English Heritage in 1990 and form the basis for our current understanding of the landscape. Finally in 1995, English Heritage published a volume—commissioned from Wessex Archaeology—which presents a detailed discussion of the structural history of Stonehenge derived from the primary records of the excavations carried out between 1901 and 1964 as well as more recent small-scale excavations. The volume is of fundamental importance to anyone who wishes to understand Stonehenge; wishes to advance a new theory about it, or wishes to improve its management. The research necessary to produce the volume has raised new questions about the monument and its setting and the purpose of this paper is to outline these issues which will be addressed in the context of a carefully designed research programme over the next five years.

# Aims and objectives

The effective management of the Stonehenge World Heritage Site depends on a clear understanding of its constituent parts—their history, structure, inter-relationships and condition. A research programme to create that understanding is essential, both for its future management and to inform the interpretative strategies for the public. English Heritage therefore intends to undertake a series of investigations at Stonehenge itself and in the surrounding landscape which will address the following themes.

## 1. *Who built Stonehenge?*

Where were the builders of Stonehenge living? What was the nature of their society and what were they doing in the landscape? Who were they? The potential for DNA analysis should be explored to determine family or other groupings within the human bone assemblage.

## 2. *Why build Stonehenge?*

Are there relationships in the content of the monuments and their spatial distribution in the landscape which shed light on why Stonehenge was built? The relationship of the monument with the natural and man-made environment should be explored in order to achieve a better understanding of the nature of the landscape and its interactions during the various phases of use at Stonehenge.

## 3. *What was the nature of society at the time of Stonehenge?*

Most of the investigations at Stonehenge and in the surrounding landscape pre-date the modern era when environmental data and samples for dating are systematically retrieved. A major theme of the research programme must therefore be to obtain good quality information on the environment, economy, chronology and relationships of the communities living around Stonehenge from the earliest times.

## 4. *Outreach and education*

The opportunity will be taken to undertake research into methods and techniques of investigation used in the archaeological process and to integrate this with the interpretative strategy for the public. Visitors will be able to observe the work at close quarters and interact with the archaeological process, both in the field and in processing areas within the visitor centre. The aim will be to develop an integrated programme of outreach and education designed to promote an understanding of the processes of archaeology as well as contributing to a wider understanding of Stonehenge and its landscape. This could include:

- the placement of the research team in the visitor centre;
- the use of excavations and fieldwork to act as a focus for the visitor;
- the production of guides, leaflets, posters, etc. describing the work in progress;
- talks, demonstrations, tours, etc.

## The study area

In 1810, Sir Richard Colt Hoare defined the environs of Stonehenge as extending from the valley of the river Till in the west to Amesbury and Durrington Walls in the east and from the Lesser Cursus in the north to the Wilsford Barrow Group in the south. For his purposes, Richards extended the study area to the north to include Robin Hood's Ball causewayed enclosure—which with its associated long barrows is considered to be a focal element of the early monumental landscape. This alignment has also been broadly followed by the boundary of the World Heritage Site as defined by UNESCO and confirmed—with some minor amendments—by studies undertaken on behalf of the Stonehenge Management and Conservation Project by the Central Archaeology Service of English Heritage.

The archaeological boundary has therefore been adopted as the study zone for the future programme and contains an unparalleled diversity and density of prehistoric monuments including:

7 ceremonial monuments
11 long barrows and related monuments
474 round barrows
6 hillforts and enclosures
462 hectares of field systems
22 km of linear earthworks

This diverse landscape is partly contemporary with the major phases of construction at Stonehenge and for the purpose of this research design, the monument and its landscape have been regarded as a single entity.

## The monument

There is scope for further research at the monument itself. Specific questions can be formulated on the basis of the 1995 volume which require only limited, carefully planned excavation at the site, and some which do not require any spade to be put to the earth. It is part of English Heritage's plan for the future of the monument that scientific research should continue at a level which is appropriate to the needs of academic inquiry but which is also compatible with the requirements of conservation and the long-term management of Stonehenge.

A number of key issues have therefore been identified which may be addressed by either non-intrusive or small-scale excavation at the monument but it did not and still does not stand in isolation and there are wider issues to consider than the individual relationships of one stone to another within the site itself. Any long-term research design for Stonehenge must look beyond the stones, both literally and metaphorically, and aim towards a much better understanding of the monument within its landscape and its relationship with other sites which form part of that landscape. The key issues are as follows.

## 1. *Understanding the archaeological record*

**1.1**   During Hawley's excavations at the monument from 1919 to 1926, only a sample of foreign stone from the site was retained, the rest was buried in a series of pits dug specifically for the purpose some distance to the south of the monument which became known as *Hawley's Graves*. Most of the cremated human bone recorded in his excavations was deposited in Aubrey Hole 7. One objective of a future field programme should be to re-excavate and analyse previously excavated materials re-interred by Hawley for comparison with the surviving assemblages.

**1.2**   The extent of pre-twentieth century excavations at the centre of the monument should be established. This will lead to an improved knowledge of the survival of deposits in that area and it will enable the stratigraphy to be recorded and central features to be planned.

## 2. *Recording the monument above ground*

**2.1**   A physical survey and description of Stonehenge is long overdue. The topographic data for the monument and its surrounding area has been collected. Further resources are needed to process all of this data and to produce the elevations and sections for all of the accessible stones.

**2.2**   A detailed study should be completed of all carvings, graffiti and stone-working techniques using photogrammetry, casts, and other appropriate high-resolution techniques. The face of each stone has been subjected to a photogrammetric survey and resources are required to process the data.

**2.3**   A detailed petrological description of each stone is desirable, together with the identification of its source—including examination of the collections of worked stone from the site. We now know that the igneous rock bluestones were brought from the Preseli Mountains in north Pembrokeshire and the remaining problems involve the sedimentary rocks at Stonehenge. The most prominent is the Altar Stone which has never been sampled and it is important to the story of Stonehenge that we find its true origin which is likely to be the Cosheston Beds near the shores of the Milford Haven estuary. Confirmation of this will be of great interest to those addressing the question of the route taken by the stones from north Pembrokeshire to Stonehenge.

3. *Investigating the monument*

**3.1** To refine our understanding of the structure and sequence of the Bank, Ditch and Counterscarp, more investigation is called for, not least because of the possibilities of associated post-holes.

**3.2** Investigate some undisturbed Aubrey Holes to re-evaluate the results of earlier work and attempt to resolve questions of date, function, internal sequence and relationship with the Bank.

**3.3** Examine the evidence for internal timber structures, particularly in the southern part of the interior of the enclosure.

**3.4** Currently, the pattern of excavations within the monument does not reflect its symmetry. In order to balance information from comparable areas of the monument, it is desirable to examine the area to the north or north-west of the centre to investigate the sequence of stone structures in that area and to explore anomalies revealed in the geophysical survey.

## The landscape

The main aim of this study will be to investigate the place of Stonehenge in its landscape, to establish the place of each monument within that landscape to the other, and to formulate management proposals to ensure their future well-being.

1. *The database*

A database to hold information relating to the World Heritage Site should be created. This will involve:

- a desk-based collation and assessment of the currently available data (archaeological information, soils, geology, hydrology, topography, etc.) assembled from existing sources (aerial photographs, satellite images, maps, SMRs, etc.);
- a carefully designed programme of targeted fieldwork will be undertaken to enhance specific elements of the topographic record (modern survey techniques offer us the opportunity to produce detailed records of the current state of monuments, not only important for their management but also their interpretation—inter-visibility, reconstruction, etc.);
- new survey techniques, such as multi-spectral imagery, will be explored to enhance specific aspects of the current record;
- the database will be regularly updated by monitoring new discoveries, monument condition and the modern use of the landscape.

## 2. Contemporary environments

**2.1**  A carefully designed programme of sampling within contexts disturbed by earlier excavations should record the environmental context of all phases of human activity within the Stonehenge landscape. The full range of scientific techniques now available to us and not available 30 or 40 years ago will vastly increase our understanding of chronology and contemporary environments through the re-excavation of nineteenth century trenches thus causing little or no damage to the archaeological deposits themselves.

## 3. Round barrows

Of the 500 monuments in the Stonehenge landscape, over 470 are round barrows and the main aim of their investigation will be to develop an interpretation of burial within an organised ritual landscape. This will involve:

**3.1**  A desk-based assessment of earlier excavations with particular reference to those undertaken by Colt Hoare and Cunnington.

**3.2**  A desk-based assessment to chart the topography and analyse the structure of the barrow cemeteries and their setting.

**3.3**  Limited excavations using the position of earlier investigations as much as possible in order to:

• obtain samples which will enhance our understanding of the contemporary environment and its date;

• investigate contemporary burial practice through the morphology of round barrows and its relationship to burial rite, gender and ritual diversity;

• investigate the occurrence of bluestone fragments within neighbouring round barrows and their relationship with the structural sequence at Stonehenge.

## 4. Durrington Walls and Woodhenge

**4.1**  A carefully focused programme of excavation and survey across the bank and ditch and in the interior of Durrington Walls is desirable in order to set the 1967 excavations in the context of improved techniques and knowledge.

## 5. The Avenue

**5.1**  A fresh investigation of the Avenue is required, to include geophysical and topographical surveys and limited excavation, to examine its structure, relationship with adjacent monuments, flint scatters and in particular, its junction with the river Avon.

6. *The Palisade Ditch*

**6.1**   An investigation of the Palisade Ditch north and west of Stonehenge is desirable, in particular on Stonehenge Down and close to the bend of the Avenue, which should include geophysical and topographical surveys and sampling by excavation. This should be seen against a background programme of investigating the other extensive linear ditches in the study area and an attempt to try to understand the development of land divisions.

7. *Extensive survey*

**7.1**   Within the Stonehenge landscape, there is considerable scope for mapping areas of prehistoric and Roman settlement suspected on the grounds of field-walking and aerial photography. Enclosed settlements and field systems seem to first appear in numbers in the landscape around Stonehenge in the later Bronze Age (1200 BC) and there is evidence that the landscape is changing in character from a mainly funerary emphasis to a more domestic use. The relationship of Stonehenge to this developing agricultural landscape in the later Bronze Age is one which needs further study. The evidence for this period could be explored further by targeting geophysical survey on areas containing scatters of later Bronze Age pottery located in previous surveys. Geophysical survey should assess the potential of sites defined by surface collection and aerial photography thus assisting the management of the archaeological resource in the Stonehenge landscape.

# Conclusion

Stonehenge and the cultural landscape within which it stands are uniquely important and form part of a UNESCO-approved World Heritage Site. The publication of the first comprehensive account of Stonehenge has enabled the conference to debate the themes which are not discussed at any length in that volume. The next step is the preparation of a research strategy for the next decade which will enhance our understanding of this unique resource and the undertaking of which will form part of a visitor experience which will stimulate their understanding and enjoyment of our heritage.

# Abstracts

COLIN RENFREW

## Setting the Scene: Stonehenge in the round

The special nature of Stonehenge as a complex monument constructed by mere barbarians is stressed, and long-standing traditions of diffusionist explanation reviewed. The alternative is to situate Stonehenge in the local constructional traditions of Neolithic stone monuments, of circular public enclosures, and of complex wooden ('megaxylic') structures. The role of such a monument as the focus for memory—for shared oral traditions of narrative—is emphasised.

Monuments orchestrate human movement, including dance. Drawing on the work of the contemporary sculptor Richard Long, linear and circular actions and physical markers are seen as indicators of human presence and activity, while Egyptian obelisks and Breton menhirs, through their striking verticality, are assertive of life and again of human action.

Stonehenge, the Avenue and the Stonehenge Cursus utilise all these general principles and derive much of their power from the masterly simplicity of their use.

ANDREW J. LAWSON

## The structural history of Stonehenge

A review of all available evidence from the twentieth-century excavations at Stonehenge, linked to a new suite of radiocarbon dates, has enabled the publication of a revised phasing of the monument. By placing the results of this research alongside the evidence from monuments and open areas in the surrounding landscape which have been examined previously, an understanding can be created of how Stonehenge articulated with its various neighbours through time. It is now certain that throughout its history, Stonehenge was only one element of a well-used landscape, the early use of which can be glimpsed from rare Mesolithic features or Early Neolithic monuments. Three phases in the structural history of Stonehenge can be discerned, each successive phase being more complex than its predecessor. During the Middle Neolithic, the major feature of the Phase 1 monument was earthen. In Phase 2, during the Late Neolithic, timber structures were set up, while Phase 3 encompassed a series of stone settings which have stood from the Early Bronze Age to the present day.

ALEX BAYLISS, CHRISTOPHER BRONK RAMSEY and F. GERRY McCORMAC

## Dating Stonehenge

As part of the recent research programme on the twentieth-century excavations at Stonehenge (Cleal *et al.* 1995), a series of nearly fifty new radiocarbon determinations was commissioned. A chronological model of the site has been developed which combines the evidence of the radiocarbon measurements with the stratigraphic sequences recovered during excavation. This has enabled much more precise estimates of dates of archaeological interest to be calculated.

A number of points of archaeological and scientific interest have been raised by this programme of work; in particular the importance and complexities of archaeological taphonomy are seen as crucial. Some of the choices which were encountered when building the model are also discussed. Above all this work is seen as both analytical and interpretative, and will inevitably be modified as more data become available, different questions are asked, and different interpretative frameworks adopted.

DAVE BATCHELOR

## Mapping the Stonehenge World Heritage Site

This paper describes the work of the Central Archaeology Service in creating an integrated and dynamic database that encompasses geographic and textual data from a number of disparate sources. It will concentrate on the physical and cultural landscape that surrounds Stonehenge rather than the monument itself.

A. DAVID and A. PAYNE

## Geophysical surveys within the Stonehenge landscape: a review of past endeavour and future potential

The techniques of archaeological geophysics now have a very widespread currency in British archaeology. Those most commonly in use, magnetometry and resistivity surveying, can be particularly effective for the mapping of the buried outlines of domestic, industrial and funerary sites from later prehistory until the present day. Given the pre-eminent reputation of Stonehenge and its surroundings it is perhaps surprising that such techniques have not been used more exhaustively to explore the area for hidden detail. However, in recent years, fuelled both by research initiatives and the modern pressures now affecting this World Heritage Site, geophysical survey has indeed been applied with increasing determination. This paper provides an overview of this recent work, both at Stonehenge itself and at neighbouring sites, and will confront both its present limitations as well as its future potential.

MICHAEL J. ALLEN

## Environment and land-use; the economic development of the communities who built Stonehenge (an economy to support the stones)

Quaternary scientists and archaeologists employ palaeo-ecological evidence to investigate the development of past landscapes. Unlike their earth science colleagues, however, archaeologists use the interpretation of these data to illustrate and explain *human* action.

Stonehenge was constructed and reconstructed over a period of 1500 years. The communities providing work-forces for this enormous labour must have been large, structured and have operated under strong political control. Most importantly they had to be locally resident and capable of sustaining both the labour-force and residential population. But how was this possible for simple prehistoric farming communities 5000 years ago?

The secure economic base underpinning these communities required long-term investment. By employing palaeo-environmental analyses to examine the development of the prehistoric landscape and land-use in the Stonehenge region, we can provide an explanation of how that landscape was used to support a highly organised society and enabled the diversion of human resources for the construction of Stonehenge.

ALASDAIR WHITTLE

## Remembered and imagined belongings: Stonehenge in its traditions and structures of meaning

Meanings can be ascribed to Stonehenge, especially in its main phase of lithic monumentality in the Later Neolithic, by considering: its contemporary setting; the tradition of sacred monuments, circular and other, to which it belonged; the layouts of successive phases; the materials from which it was formed; and the patterns of approach and experience which the monument may have engendered.

TIMOTHY DARVILL

## Ever increasing circles: the sacred geographies of Stonehenge and its landscape

Using perspectives from sociology and social archaeology, this paper explores the changing meaning and use of Stonehenge and its immediate environment from *c*.4000–1000 BC. Distinctions are drawn between 'space' and 'place' to understand the development of certain sites, while the principle of structuration is used to show how ideas find expression in material culture, monuments, and landscape organization. Although Stonehenge had special significance for more than 2000 years, the successive structures reflect ever-changing relationships between people, their beliefs, and the cosmological systems of meaning that underpinned those beliefs. Physical and celestial 'markers' were used at different periods to articulate meanings relative to the use and social significance of space, both within the monument and in the surrounding landscape. Four phases to these changes are proposed, each identified with a series of structuring principles: linear binary, linear quadruple, radial concentric, and linear concentric. All four phases are marked archaeologically by a re-design of Stonehenge and the restructuring of space around about.

CLIVE RUGGLES

**Astronomy and Stonehenge**

This paper begins by making some general observations about the perception and use of celestial phenomena in prehistoric times, what exactly is meant by 'astronomy', and why the prehistorian might be interested in it. We then proceed to establish a conceptual framework for studying prehistoric astronomy, identifying possible horizon 'targets' for symbolic alignments (which are less precise, fewer, and different in nature from those very often assumed), and explaining the significance of declination. This is followed by a critique of recent ideas about astronomy in and around Stonehenge, in the light of the newly published reports of twentieth-century excavations. The paper concludes with a summary of what we can begin to say with reasonable confidence about the nature and meaning of astronomy at Stonehenge, and presents some suggestions for the future research agenda at and around the site.

JULIAN RICHARDS and MARK WHITBY

**The engineering of Stonehenge**

A series of practical experiments, carried out at the instigation of the BBC, involved the transport and erection of the individual components of a full-scale replica of the Great Trilithon at Stonehenge. The use of a simple sledge running on a greased timber track demonstrated that a 40 tonne stone, representing one of the uprights, could be moved up a 1 in 20 slope using the motive power of 130 individuals. The raising of this stone to vertical was accomplished by rotating the stone over a solid pivot point with the assistance of a composite 6 tonne weight running along its length. An angle of 70 degrees to the horizontal was achieved by this method and the stone was hauled to vertical using a timber 'A' frame as a lever. The lintel was raised on a sledge running on rails up a ramp although a comparative experiment demonstrated that the orthodox timber 'crib' or platform provided a viable alternative method. For the purposes of all experiments a degree of proficiency in both woodworking and the manufacture of rope was assumed.

The overall labour requirements for the building of the sarsen structures at Stonehenge are recalculated from the newly available data. In addition, alternative interpretations of some elements of the physical record of Stonehenge are offered and suggestions are made for the future direction of experimentation.

C. P. GREEN

**The provenance of rocks used in the construction of Stonehenge**

The geological evidence in Wiltshire gives no support to the view that the stones forming Stonehenge were found by its builders close to the site of construction. The presence of suitable sarsen stones near Stonehenge in the Early Bronze Age is indicated neither by the geological history of the area nor by the present-day distribution of sarsens. The absence of glacial or glacially-derived material on Salisbury Plain makes it unlikely that glacial ice carried the bluestones of Stonehenge from the Preseli Hills to Wessex. The history of the bluestone supposedly found in Bowls Barrow is reviewed.

J. D. SCOURSE

**Transport of the Stonehenge bluestones: testing the glacial hypothesis**

Two principal mechanisms have been invoked to explain the transport of the far-travelled bluestones used in the Stonehenge monument from their source region in Pembrokeshire: by glacier or by man. Glaciers have been thought to represent the only natural agency capable of transporting boulders of the size of the bluestones over the distances required, and this mechanism has periodically received serious attention since it was first proposed by Judd in 1902. There are two current propositions invoking transport of the bluestones by ice; Thorpe *et al.* (1991) envisage Anglian ice flowing eastwards from Pembrokeshire across South Wales and into central southern England, whilst Kellaway (1991a, 1991b) suggests deposition from the north in association with a Pliocene glaciation at 2.47Ma. The glacial hypothesis is critically tested by addressing four issues: the physical principles underlying the entrainment and transport of large boulders by glaciers; the occurrence/absence and implications of diagnostic surface microwear and particle shape characteristics of the bluestones; the Pleistocene stratigraphy and geomorphology of southern England and adjacent shelves; and the glaciological plausibility of a source trajectory from Pembrokeshire. It is demonstrated that though glaciers are capable of transporting erratic boulders many thousands of kilometres irrespective of bed topography, the particular case posed by the Stonehenge problem is not compatible either with the mechanics of ice flow or with the geological evidence. The weight of the current available evidence strongly indicates that the Stonehenge bluestones were not transported by ice from Preseli to Salisbury Plain.

GEORGE EOGAN

## Stonehenge in its wider context

A feature of Europe during prehistory is the emergence of core areas. Stonehenge and its environs is of course one of the most notable but in different parts of Europe the clustering of monuments or artifacts or both is a feature. As at Stonehenge the other sites that I will mention include spectacular monuments; one variety that is characteristic of all is an open-air ceremonial enclosure. Apart from its scientific importance Stonehenge and also the other four complexes are significant tourist attractions and this has led to the development of visitor facilities, management regimes and programmes of monument and landscape conservation.

In Britain an obvious analogy to the Stonehenge area is to be found in the Orkneys, especially on Mainland, particularly in the general area of Stenness with its great passage tomb of Maes Howe, its henge monuments, standing stones and the significant settlement of Grooved Ware date at Barnhouse.

Another significant area, again in Scotland, is the Kilmartin area of Argyll which is a naturally defined archaeological region. Plans are afoot with the development of a major conservation programme and also to make the area more readily available for both scientific activities and general visitor needs.

In Ireland a most relevant area is in the valley of the river Boyne, known as Brugh na Bóinne. There, at different times during prehistoric and historic times a succession of cultural complexes arose. At the time of building and use of the passage tombs the area must have constituted a ritual landscape but the tombs also inform us about the scientific accomplishments of their builders.

One of the most celebrated archaeological areas of continental Europe is in the Carnac-Locmariaquer region of Brittany. In particular this area is renowned for its passage tombs and stone alignments including such spectacular sites as Gavrinis. This is an area with a considerable resident population but also an area that attracts large numbers of tourists.

GEOFFREY WAINWRIGHT

## Future directions for the study of Stonehenge and its landscape

Many campaigns of excavation and fieldwork have been carried out at Stonehenge and in the surrounding landscape over the past 150 years. The work at the monument this century has recently been published by English Heritage and the proposal to create a Millennium Park around Stonehenge has been seen as the opportunity to undertake a programme of research which will address fundamental questions and integrate the work with the presentation of that landscape to the public.

# Index

NOTE: references in *italics* denote illustrations.